Private Lives and Public Affairs

Studies on the History of Society and Culture
Victoria E. Bonnell and Lynn Hunt, Editors

Private Lives and
Public Affairs

The Causes Célèbres of
Prerevolutionary France

Sarah Maza

UNIVERSITY OF CALIFORNIA PRESS

Berkeley / Los Angeles / London

University of California Press
Berkeley and Los Angeles, California

University of California Press, Ltd.
London, England

© 1993 by
The Regents of the University of California

Library of Congress Cataloging-in-Publication Data

Maza, Sarah C., 1953–
    Private lives and public affairs: the causes célèbres of prerevolution-
ary France / Sarah Maza.
        p.   cm.—(Studies on the history of society and culture; 18)
    Includes bibliographical references and index.
    ISBN 0-520-08144-7 (alk. paper)
    1. France—History—Louis XVI, 1774–1793. 2. France—His-
tory—Louis XV, 1715–1774. 3. Political corruption—France—History—18th century. 4. Trials—France—History—18th century.
I. Title. II. Series.
DC136.9.M39   1993
944'.034—dc20   93-4518
                                                       CIP

Printed in the United States of America

9 8 7 6 5 4 3 2 1

Material from chapters 1, 2, 4, and 6, respectively, has appeared in the
following: "The Véron-Morangiès Affair (1772–1773): The Social Imagery of a Political Crisis," *Historical Reflections/Réflexions Historiques*
18, no. 2 (Summer 1993): 101–35; "The Rose-Girl of Salency: Representations of Virtue in Prerevolutionary France," *Eighteenth-Century
Studies* 22, no. 3 (1989): 395–412; "The Diamond Necklace Affair
Revisited (1785–1786): The Case of the Missing Queen," in *Eroticism
and the Body Politic,* ed. Lynn Hunt (Baltimore: Johns Hopkins University Press, 1991): 63–89; and "Domestic Melodrama as Political
Ideology: The Case of the Count of Sanois," *American Historical Review* 94, no. 5 (1989):1249–64.

For Jonathan and Brigitte,
Suzy and Sam,
and in memory of Hannah

Contents

Illustrations

Acknowledgments

The only debts that are pleasant to acknowledge are those accumulated with colleagues and friends over the course of a long-term project such as this one. In some cases, the debt is specific and memorable—Jeremy Popkin unwittingly touched off the whole enterprise in the Newberry Library eight years ago by pushing across my desk the trial briefs of the Kornmann case, and Christian Jouhaud physically led me to Alexandre Corda's great printed catalog of judicial *mémoires* in the Bibliothèque Nationale. In most cases, however, help has come in the more nebulous form of support and stimulation over the long haul.

There is nothing nebulous, however, about the material support I have received from a number of institutions, without which this book would never have been written. The bulk of the research was carried out in 1984–85 thanks to a fellowship from the National Endowment for the Humanities, and I was able to take care of unfinished business thanks to two summer grants from Northwestern University. The National Humanities Center in North Carolina, where I was in residence in 1988–89, was an ideal place to sort out my ideas and begin writing. I deeply appreciate the help and good spirits provided by the Center's director that year, Kent Mullikin, by the Center's terrific staff, and by my fellow fellows; and I look back with nostalgia on the Sunday-night meetings of the Triangle area's lively and congenial group of French historians. I also thank the librarians of the Bibliothèque Nationale, the

Bibliothèque Historique de la Ville de Paris, the Newberry Library in Chicago, and the Northwestern University Library.

The ideas in this book were shaped by many conversations and much manuscript swapping with scholars in the field. I thank especially a number of colleagues in French history whom I am fortunate to count as friends, for their intellectual companionship and constant encouragement: Ray Birn, Jack Censer, Carolyn Dean, Dena Goodman, Lynn Hunt, Lloyd Kramer, Patricia O'Brien, Jeremy Popkin, Debora Silverman, and Dale Van Kley. I am also grateful to those who allowed me to read and cite their unpublished work: David Bell, Robert Darnton, Michel Guillot, Elaine Kruse, Albert Poirot, Barry Shapiro, and Shanti Singham. I have learned a great deal from friends in other disciplines, especially Mary Sheriff in Art History and Susan Herbst in Communications Studies. In Paris, the friendship and help of all sorts extended to me by Roger Chartier, Christian Jouhaud, and Jacques Revel have made my annual trips more productive and a lot more fun.

I have gotten moral support over the years from Sheila Levine of the University of California Press, who believed in this book when it was still a gleam in its author's eye; my thanks also extend to Rose Vekony, who at the other end of the process gave the manuscript the benefit of her fine editorial skills. I am deeply indebted to four scholars working on concerns close to my own, who gave the penultimate draft of the book the benefit of especially thorough and helpful critiques: David Bell, Jack Censer, Dena Goodman, and Dale Van Kley made me rethink some of the book's central arguments and saved me from a large number of embarrassing mistakes. On a daily basis I get stimulation (sometimes too much of it!) from my colleagues in the Northwestern history department, an outstanding group of scholars whom I wish to thank collectively. And also locally, I owe particular debts to Joel Mokyr, who kept his sense of humor while coaxing me into the computer age, and to Bernadette Fort, who over many years has shared with me her extensive knowledge of eighteenth-century culture.

I could not have written this book without the love of my family and close friends; this goes without saying, but it is worth saying from time to time.

Introduction

> *Man is nothing but a mythical animal. He becomes*
> *human—he acquires a human being's sexuality and heart*
> *and imagination—only by virtue of the murmur of stories*
> *and the kaleidoscope of images that surround him in the*
> *cradle and accompany him all the way to the grave.*
>
> Michel Tournier, *The Wind Spirit*

This is a book about stories, about the public impact of
tales of private life. The stories in question are those of the parties to a
series of highly publicized court cases, or causes célèbres, which gripped
the attention of the French—and especially the Parisian—reading public in the two decades preceding the Revolution of 1789. Gossip and
scandal have always been with us and have always sold well; but the literature of judicial scandal was consumed in unusual quantities and with
unusual avidity in prerevolutionary France. This work explores the
meaning of a body of sensational courtroom literature and seeks to explain the nature of its impact on social and political life in France at the
end of the old regime.

The causes célèbres of the 1770s and 1780s first caught my attention
as I was perusing the chronicles, gazettes, and underground newsletters
of the period. Like all other students of Old Regime France, I knew of
the impact of a few great trials on the prerevolutionary public: starting
in the 1760s, Voltaire had campaigned against religious bigotry by pub-

1

licizing such miscarriages of justice as the Calas case; the playwright Beaumarchais had made a name for himself at about the same time in well-publicized judicial duels against powerful enemies; four years before the Revolution, Queen Marie-Antoinette's reputation had been sullied when a sordid scandal known as the Diamond Necklace Affair was brought to light in court. Little did I expect, however, the sheer number of sensational trials I encountered in contemporary sources, or the excitement with which they were reported to the public. At times, hardly a week—sometimes hardly a day—went by without a contemporary chronicler informing his readers that this or that *affaire* had broken, or that another was about to be judged.

Thus I became acquainted with the great, but now mostly forgotten, court cases of late-eighteenth-century France: the dispute between the unsavory count of Morangiès and a family of crooked commoners; the charges of forgery levied against Mme de Saint-Vincent, a highborn lady of questionable morals; the penniless serving-girls and laborers rescued from torture and execution, with much fanfare, by zealous young barristers. I learned more about these cases in exactly the same way as eighteenth-century French men and women did, by reading the briefs known as *factums* or *mémoires judiciaires* penned by the parties' lawyers. Indeed, the publication of a mémoire relating to a highly publicized case was considered an event in itself; newsletters and gazettes usually reported on the appearance of a major cause célèbre brief, evaluated its qualities and shortcomings, and described the reading public's reaction to it. Combing through the pages of an eighteenth-century bookseller's journal, I discovered that these published trial briefs were issued in quantities that outstripped those of most other kinds of printed matter at the time—press runs of six to ten thousand in the 1770s, up to twenty thousand in the 1780s. I stumbled across anecdotal evidence indicating that any given copy of a hot mémoire in a sensational case was read by several people; and, most strikingly, I ran across several texts describing mob scenes around bookseller's shops and lawyers' houses when an eagerly awaited trial brief was finally made available to the public.

For reasons having to do with their peculiar legal status, their literary and polemical qualities, and especially their extraordinary popularity, the *mémoires judiciaires* became the central source and object of this study. This is less a book about the court cases themselves—what happened and who did it—than about the publicity surrounding them. The central argument of this work concerns the ways in which the writing and reading of sensational courtroom literature contributed to the birth of public opinion and of a new public sphere in the decades just before the French Revolution. I hope that the analyses and arguments in the following chapters will say something significant both about the history of this period and, more generally, about ways of writing history; or, to use the jargon of the academic historian's trade, that they will have significant historiographical and methodological implications.

The broader issue that frames this study is the vexed and ever-intriguing question of the ideological and cultural origins of the French Revolution. For nearly two centuries after the Revolution, it was widely believed that the single most important ideological cause of the French Revolution was the movement of ideas known as the French Enlightenment, which included both the "mainstream" Enlightenment symbolized by Diderot's massive *Encyclopédie,* and the intellectually iconoclastic, but hugely influential, works of Jean-Jacques Rousseau.[1] It was probably the rise of the "new social history" in the 1960s that led an American scholar, Robert Darnton, to challenge the assumption of a direct link between the ideas of the canonical philosophes and the radical ideologies of the revolutionary years.[2]

In one of his earliest and most famous articles on the subject, Darnton argued that both the problem and its solution could be found in the dynamics of the literary world.[3] Since the nineteenth century, historians, and most conspicuously Marxist historians, had argued that the Enlightenment was an ideology that reflected the class interests, and hence the aspirations, of a rising but frustrated bourgeoisie, and that *les lumières* were therefore revolutionary. But many well-known facts, Darnton pointed out, contradicted such assumptions. Quite a few of the philosophes were blue-blooded noblemen, and those who were not, like Voltaire, aspired mightily to noble status; most of these writers, including the misanthropic and egalitarian Rousseau, were entertained,

1. The most notable and comprehensive recent statement of this position in English is Peter Gay, *The Enlightenment: An Interpretation,* 2 vols. (New York: Vintage, 1966 and 1969; new ed. New York: Norton, 1977).

2. See Robert Darnton's critique of Peter Gay and his call for a new approach to the subject, "In Search of Enlightenment: Recent Attempts to Create a Social History of Ideas," *Journal of Modern History* 43 (March 1971): 113–132.

3. Robert Darnton, "The High Enlightenment and the Low-Life of Literature in Pre-revolutionary France," *Past and Present* 51 (May, 1971): 81–115; reprinted in Robert Darnton, *The Literary Underground of the Old Regime* (Cambridge, Mass.: Harvard University Press, 1982), pp. 1–40.

patronized, fussed over, and read by the cream of high society; none of them, ever, explicitly called for social or political revolution. Given these facts, how "revolutionary," as opposed to simply innovative, could their ideas really have been?

Darnton suggested that we go looking elsewhere for the polemical sparks that ignited the flames of revolution. He himself argued that the more extreme ideologies of the Revolution reflected the experiences of frustrated young writers, the embittered denizens of Grub Street. After mid-century, ambitious young men, lured to Paris by the example of the philosophes but excluded from the staid and overpopulated literary establishment, found both catharsis and a source of income in the writing of violent or pornographic pamphlets attacking the social and political elites.[4]

In the twenty years since Darnton first articulated his "Grub Street" thesis, it has not, of course, gone unchallenged.[5] Its enduring merit, however, has been to direct the attention of scholars away from the canonical Enlightenment and toward the sorts of texts and writers that had never before found their way into the standard literary histories of the period. Nobody would deny, of course, that the well-known writers and works of the "High Enlightenment" contributed greatly to the undermining of established certainties and to the development in the reading public of a taste for critical thinking. But many different moles, it turns out, were burrowing away under the manicured gardens of the Old Regime. Thanks to the recent work of specialists in the history of

---

4. Ibid., pp. 17–40.

5. It is a tribute to the power of Darnton's thesis that scholars dealing with the social history of the French Enlightenment routinely use it as a framework against which to articulate their own arguments. Dena Goodman, for instance, in "Governing the Republic of Letters: The Politics of Culture in the French Enlightenment" (*History of European Ideas* 13, no. 3 (1991): 183–199), sees in the radical writings of the prerevolutionary period a sign of generalized anarchy in the Republic of Letters, following the decline of the great female-governed salons (see esp. pp. 195–196); Roger Chartier, in an important recent synthesis, suggests that "Grub Street" pamphleteering and pornography was probably not taken as seriously, and did not have as deep and lasting an impact, as Darnton believed: *The Cultural Origins of the French Revolution*, trans. Lydia Cochrane (Durham, N.C.: Duke University Press, 1991), pp. 81–83. To my knowledge, the most comprehensive challenge to the "Darnton thesis" is that advanced by Jeremy Popkin, who argues on the basis of substantial evidence that, even on the eve of the Revolution, muckraking pamphleteers of the sort studied by Darnton either were themselves fairly prosperous and established or were in the pay of wealthy patrons: Jeremy Popkin, "Pamphlet Journalism at the End of the Old Regime," *Eighteenth-Century Studies* 22 (Spring 1989): 351–367.

publishing we now know a great deal about the censored pamphlets and books, handwritten newssheets, and foreign-based newspapers from which French readers also learned to criticize established institutions and to scoff at the high and mighty.[6]

It would be a mistake, however, to assume that all of the literature that challenged the status quo of the Old Regime was illicit—or, for that matter, that all clandestine material was genuinely subversive. There was nothing illegal, for instance, about the provincial academies where local elites gathered to cultivate their minds and assign prizes to essays on controversial topics; Rousseau was only one of the many progressive thinkers who wrote important works as entries in such contests.[7] To take another example, the "remonstrances" of the *parlements* (courts of high justice) were also a perfectly legal part of the judicial process whereby the courts could express reservations with respect to a royal decree; but by the eighteenth century the parlements' magistrates had taken to publishing remonstrances, which were in theory a private communication from the courts to the monarch.[8] To be sure, the increasingly incendiary *remontrances* of the eighteenth-century courts were often banned and published illegally. But, as Dale Van Kley has convincingly demonstrated, the rhetoric emanating from this central institution of the French royal administration did as much as any amount of muckraking underground literature to challenge the institutional and ideological status quo.[9]

6. Robert Darnton remains the leading specialist in the English-speaking world on the prerevolutionary book and pamphlet trade; besides *The Literary Underground*, see *The Business of Enlightenment: A Publishing History of the Encyclopédie* (Cambridge, Mass.: Harvard University Press, 1979), and *Edition et sédition: L'univers de la littérature clandestine au XVIIIe siècle* (Paris: Gallimard, 1991). On the periodical press, especially of the illicit variety, see the works listed in the bibliography by Jack Censer, Nina Gelbart, and Jeremy Popkin. The literature on these subjects produced by French scholars is even more abundant; for a convenient compilation of pieces by many of the leading French specialists, see Roger Chartier and Henri-Jean Martin, eds., *Histoire de l'édition française*, vol. 2, *Le Livre triomphant, 1660–1830* (Paris: Promodis, 1984; new ed. Paris: Fayard, 1991).

7. On the history, membership, and activities of the provincial academies in the eighteenth century, see Daniel Roche, *Le Siècle des lumières en province: Académies et académiciens provinciaux, 1680–1789*, 2 vols. (Paris: Mouton, 1978).

8. The voluminous historical literature on the eighteenth-century French *parlements* is surveyed in William Doyle, "The Parlements," in Keith Baker, ed., *The Political Culture of the Old Regime* (Oxford, Pergamon Press, 1987), pp. 157–167.

9. See Dale Van Kley, *The Jansenists and the Expulsion of the Jesuits, 1757–1765* (New Haven: Yale University Press, 1975) and *The Damiens Affair and the Unraveling of the*

Finally, recent work in the field increasingly reveals the extent to which the social and political "establishment" of late-eighteenth-century France was directly responsible—albeit usually under a veil of secrecy—for the production and dissemination of subversive political propaganda. Starting at least as far back as the so-called Maupeou crisis of 1771–1774, when Louis XV's chief minister forcibly disbanded the parlements, and continuing until the very eve of the Revolution, factions of courtiers and ministers hired their own pamphleteers to rebut the arguments of their adversaries.[10] By the mid-1780s, writes Jeremy Popkin, "a broad spectrum of France's traditional elites had come to accept the desirability of permitting the publication of specific comments on ongoing issues."[11] As the following chapters will also show, new forms and increasing amounts of printed propaganda gave ever-widening resonance not only to conflicts between the monarchy and its critics in the country at large, but also to traditional internecine disputes among the governing elites.

In sum, recent work in the field suggests, first, that the ideological turmoil that prepared the way for the Revolution had many more sources than just "the Enlightenment" as traditionally defined, and second, that the pattern of attacks upon the sociopolitical status quo was a great deal more complex than can be suggested by any simple dichotomy between "insiders" and "outsiders." In a recent synthesis on the subject, Roger Chartier makes the point that, *pace* Tocqueville, it is impossible to reduce the ideological tensions of the end of the Old Regime to an opposition between utopian abstractions, on the one hand, and pragmatic politics, on the other, to a clash between *pensée philosophique*

Ancien Régime, 1750–1770 (Princeton: Princeton University Press, 1984); "The Jansenist Constitutional Legacy in the French Prerevolution," in Baker, ed., *Political Culture*, pp. 169–201. Among older works concerning *parlementaire* opposition to the monarchy, see especially Jules Flammermont, *Le Chancelier Maupeou et les parlements* (Paris: Picard, 1883); Elie Carcassonne, *Montesquieu et le problème de la Constitution française au XVIIIe siècle* (Paris, 1927; reprint, Geneva: Slatkine, 1970); Franklin Ford, *Robe and Sword: The Regrouping of the French Aristocracy after Louis XIV* (Cambridge: Harvard University Press, 1953); and Jean Egret, *Louis XV et l'opposition parlementaire, 1715–1774* (Paris: Armand Colin, 1970).

10. David Hudson, "In Defense of Reform: French Government Propaganda during the Maupeou Crisis," *French Historical Studies* 8 (1973): 51–76; Durand Echeverria, *The Maupeou Revolution: A Study in the History of Libertarianism, France, 1770–1774* (Baton Rouge: Louisiana State University Press, 1985), esp. chaps. 2–4; Vivian Gruder, "The Bourbon Monarchy: Reforms and Propaganda at the End of the Old Regime," in Baker, ed., *Political Culture*, pp. 347–374.

11. Popkin, "Pamphlet Journalism," p. 356.

and *autorité d'Etat,* given the demonstrable overlap between these two "fields of discourse."[12] Chartier argues against attempting to establish patterns of linear causality (a text is published and read, causing a person or group to think, write, or act in a certain way); instead, he suggests that we adopt a structural approach to the question by way of replacing the concept of "ideology" with that of "culture": "In this sense, attributing 'cultural origins' to the French Revolution does not by any means establish the Revolution's causes; rather, it pinpoints certain of the conditions that made it possible because it was conceivable."[13]

The recent work of Keith Baker on the ideological origins of the Revolution is the most successful and currently influential example of the type of approach advocated by Chartier.[14] Baker's work represents a reaction against the "sociology of literature" or "social history of ideas" practiced in the 1930s by Daniel Mornet and more recently in *Annales*-inspired, often quantified, studies by French and American scholars of the diffusion of books and other printed matter.[15] Books are more than commodities to be counted, Baker has argued, and ideas cannot be apprehended in isolation: "Texts, if read, are understood and hence reinterpreted by their readers in con-*texts* that may transform their significance; ideas, if received, take on meaning only in relation to others in the set of ideas into which they are incorporated."[16] The work of Baker and others in the same vein might seem to return to the classic methods of textual analysis practiced by traditional intellectual historians. But its purpose is in fact to *resist* the teleological biases of a more conventional history of ideas by choosing either to concentrate on nontraditional texts or to reread canonical texts by replacing them within the "discursive context" of their times.[17]

12. Chartier, *Cultural Origins,* pp. 15–16.

13. Ibid., p. 2.

14. Baker's important essays on the subject, published in the last decade, have been gathered as *Inventing the French Revolution* (Cambridge: Cambridge University Press, 1990).

15. The most venerable model for a quantified approach to the history of ideas in this field is Daniel Mornet's classic *Les Origines intellectuelles de la Révolution Française* (Paris: Armand Colin, 1933; reprint, 1967), although Mornet also used a wide range of non-quantitative approaches. The heyday of quantified approaches to Old Regime literary culture took place in the 1960s and 1970s and is best represented by Furet and Bollème's *Livre et société* volumes. The works of Robert Darnton cited in note 6 follow in Mornet's tradition of making significant, but far from exclusive, use of quantification.

16. Baker, *Inventing,* p. 19.

17. Baker's methodology is drawn from what he tags the "Cambridge" school of the history of political discourse, an approach that is simultaneously linguistic and contextu-

One of the implications of Baker's approach is that we need not dispense with the reading of Montesquieu, Diderot, and Rousseau, providing we relate their writings to other, often less celebrated, contemporary texts; we need not necessarily throw out the baby of Great Works along with the bathwater of teleological distortion. But only if we trace the connections between canonical texts and lesser-known works will we be able to reconstitute the linguistic, and broader cultural, contexts within which the Revolution became "thinkable." It is to this end that Baker and other practitioners of this "linguistic" approach are now highlighting the works of authors outside of the traditional literary canon but whose insights or demonstrable impact on contemporaries, or both, can help us to understand the manifold ideological currents at work at the end of the Old Regime. The authors recently resurrected to this end include radical political theorists associated with the Parlement of Paris, such as Adrien le Paige, Claude Mey, and Nicolas Maultrot; highly popular writers of fiction and social criticism like Louis-Sébastien Mercier; skillful propagandists for the monarchy like Jacob-Nicolas Moreau; forgotten but influential followers of Rousseau, such as Guillaume-Joseph Saige; and rabble-rousing journalists and pamphleteers like Charles Théveneau de Morande and Simon-Nicolas Linguet.[18]

The trial briefs and other courtroom literature examined in this book also belong in the category of works that, though now forgotten, were immensely popular and influential in their time—published in the tens of thousands, eagerly awaited, devoured by readers, and dissected by critics. The argument I make in this book about their appeal to, and influence on, readers relies heavily on internal textual analyses of the most successful *mémoires judiciaires* of the prerevolutionary period. I will stress, for instance, the heavily fictionalized quality of the most pop-

---

alist in that it seeks to anchor the terms and categories used by salient political thinkers firmly within their historical contexts (Baker, *Inventing*, pp. 4–6, 307–308). Prominent examples of such an approach include J. G. A. Pocock, *The Machiavellian Moment: Florentine Political Thought and the Atlantic Republican Tradition* (Princeton: Princeton University Press, 1975) and *Virtue, Commerce and History* (Cambridge: Cambridge University Press, 1985); Quentin Skinner, *The Foundations of Modern Political Thought*, 2 vols. (Cambridge: Cambridge University Press, 1985). There are important similarities between this approach and Michel Foucault's focus on the discourse rather than the text as the basic unit of intellectual history.

18. See Baker, *Inventing*, passim but esp. chaps. 3–6; Van Kley, "The Jansenist Constitutional Legacy"; Jeremy Popkin, "The Prerevolutionary Origins of Political Journalism," in Baker, ed., *Political Culture*, pp. 203–224; Darline Gay Levy, *The Ideas and Careers of Simon-Nicolas-Henri Linguet: A Study in Eighteenth-Century French Politics* (Urbana: University of Illinois Press, 1980).

ular mémoires, whose barrister-authors borrowed from contemporary literature such genres as the Rousseauean sentimental autobiography or the theatrical melodrama. The texts of the mémoires also have much to tell us about the relationship between author and readers—about how the former appealed with increasing openness to the latter to serve as judges and witnesses to the truth and righteousness of a given case, a textual strategy that had significant and even concrete implications in the context of Old Regime judicial practice.

Nonetheless, what follows is not only a textual, or linguistic, analysis of the courtroom literature of the end of the Old Regime. It also seeks to explore and explain the social and political dynamics behind the publication and resonance of these texts. The extraordinary success of these publications was symptomatic, I argue, of the growing ambitions and visibility of the legal profession at the end of the Old Regime; the ultimate relevance of this trend has to do, of course, with the fact that legal practitioners, and especially *avocats,* made up the single largest occupational group in all of the governing assemblies of the Revolution.[19] The extent to which these lawyers operated on their own in any given case, driven by some combination of conviction and ambition, and the extent to which they were acting on behalf of groups or individuals with an interest in publicizing this or that *affaire,* are matters that will receive careful consideration in the chapters that follow. My textual analyses of the mémoires, my retelling of the stories that so fascinated contemporary readers, are framed by arguments that concern the broader social and political trends of the 1770s and 1780s.

My aim here is not only, however, to add another item to the checklist of writers and texts that left their imprint on the culture of prerevolutionary France and whose influence helps to explain the dramatic events of the 1790s. My broader purpose in this book is to say something significant about what texts are read and how they are read, when we seek to analyze a political ideology in the making. The arguments in this

19. The local committees that drew up *cahiers de doléances* in 1789 were made up of 70 to 90 percent lawyers; about half of the deputies to the Third Estate were barristers, while many others were other sorts of "men of law"; 444 of the 648 members of the Constituent Assembly came out of legal careers: Edmond Seligman, *La Justice en France pendant la Révolution,* 2 vols. (Paris: Plon, 1901–1913), vol. 1, chap. 3; Alfred Cobban, *Aspects of the French Revolution* (New York: George Braziller, 1968), chap. 5; André Damien, *Les Avocats du temps passé* (Paris: Henri Lefebvre, 1973), p. 163; Michael Fitzsimmons, *The Parisian Order of Barristers and the French Revolution* (Cambridge, Mass.: Harvard University Press, 1987), pp. 35–40; David Bell, "Lawyers and Politics in Eighteenth-Century Paris, 1700–1790" (Ph.D. diss., Princeton University, 1991), p. 5.

book are designed to raise the sorts of questions that are only beginning to receive attention in contemporary historiography. These questions have to do with the interrelation of public and private issues in the genesis of political ideologies; with the relationship between narrative and ideology; and, more broadly, with the status of fiction in historical analysis.

What drew me to the mémoires in the first place was exactly what had led other historians to neglect them: the fact that these texts, although a precious source of information on any given judicial case, seemed to have little relevance to the "big issues" faced by the French nation in the decades before the Revolution. (Even when they had an obvious connection to political developments, as in the case of the Diamond Necklace Affair, their import was considered to be purely anecdotal.) Perhaps previous historians had not read these texts closely enough to realize that the "big issues" *did* often make an appearance in the trial briefs—albeit sometimes implicitly and usually in their final pages—in texts that seemed to concern only private, particular, or trivial issues; that a dispute over a rural festival could become an allegory of political regeneration; that the defense of a falsely accused female servant in a provincial town could be a vehicle for indicting the whole judicial system of the realm; that adultery cases could be made to stand, metaphorically, for the breaking of the social contract. These texts are rich precisely because of their hybrid nature, because of their unexpected coupling of private and public matters.

As with much of the current work in the area of French prerevolutionary culture, this study makes use of insights drawn from Jürgen Habermas's influential *The Structural Transformation of the Public Sphere*;[20] it focuses, however, on an element in Habermas's theory that is usually overlooked, namely, the role of intimate experience in the construction of the bourgeois, or modern, public sphere. To summarize briefly, Habermas's project is the discovery of the origins of attitudes and institutions that were eventually to develop, in opposition to monarchical absolutism, into the foundations of a modern, democratic "public sphere." Although this evolution was a plurisecular one, Habermas locates a crucial turning point at the end of the seventeenth century, in the tensions

20. Jürgen Habermas, *The Structural Transformation of the Public Sphere: An Inquiry into a Category of Bourgeois Society*, trans. Thomas Burger and Frederick Lawrence (Cambridge, Mass.: MIT Press, 1989); the original German text was first published in 1962.

and frictions between the developing commercial classes, on the one hand, and the fiscal and regulatory needs of the absolutist state, on the other. Thus, he writes, "that zone of continuous administrative contact became 'critical' also in the sense that it provoked the critical judgment of a public making use of its reason." [21] (For better or worse, most recent studies derived from Habermas's work choose simply to ignore his staunchly Marxian approach to what he often terms the *bourgeois* public sphere.)

By the eighteenth century, this nascent public sphere made up of private individuals using their critical faculties had acquired institutional form, most concretely in salons, coffeehouses, literary academies, and the like, and more diffusely in networks of correspondents and of readers of newspapers and other printed matter; the Enlightenment's "Republic of Letters," in sum, developed as a blueprint for a democratic public sphere, challenging and competing with the absolutist state. "The public sphere in the political realm," writes Habermas, "evolved from the public sphere in the realm of letters." [22] The characteristics of this burgeoning public sphere derived from its origins in the commercial classes and from its identity as a site of criticism of the sociopolitical status quo. Its members adhered to formal principles of equality and inclusiveness (although in practice they were all members of the wealthy and educated elite), and its defining occupation was the critical appraisal of the increasingly commodified products of culture—works of art, literature, and philosophy. [23] A crucial segment of civil society, in short, moved away from its assigned role as an *audience* for the displays of power and exhibitions of art staged by the monarchy; it became a judging, debating, criticizing entity—a *public*.

Habermas's theses have already significantly affected our understanding of the intellectual and cultural history of late-eighteenth-century France, by validating structural approaches to "the Enlightenment" both as a set of protodemocratic institutions (academies, Masonic lodges, and the like) and as a set of concepts that challenged or negated absolutist "discourse." Both Keith Baker and Mona Ozouf, for instance, have written important articles exploring the appearance, at about midcentury, of the concept of "public opinion," not only in the writings of

21. Ibid., p. 24.
22. Ibid., pp. 30–31.
23. Ibid., pp. 36–37.

critics of the monarchy, but even within official administrative language.[24] In different ways, they argue that political commentators and administrators increasingly claimed to enjoy the sanction of "public opinion," although no actual social group, of course, had been consulted. "Public opinion," writes Baker, was "an abstract category of authority, invoked by actors in a new kind of politics to secure the legitimacy of claims that could no longer be made binding in the terms . . . of an absolutist political order."[25] Usually equated with a transcendent concept of Reason, it served increasingly as a substitute for the desacralized, morally and politically bankrupt monarchy, although, ironically, it often took on the unitary and infallible characteristics of monarchical absolutism.

As the following chapters will show, the concept of "public opinion," and indeed that of a "public," were central to the language of *mémoires judiciaires*, reflecting the ambiguous status and purpose of these pamphlets. (Indeed, even in texts other than the mémoires the "public" was frequently portrayed as a court of law, in such phrases as *le tribunal de la nation*.) The mémoires as documents belonged to a closed judicial system in which members of "the public" played no role, either in selecting judges or in judging cases themselves. Officially, these trial briefs were destined solely for the magistrates judging cases, but there really was a public of thousands of readers ready to get into street brawls to acquire a sensational and highly publicized mémoire. Was the public addressed in trial briefs a mere rhetorical category invoked by self-aggrandizing lawyers? Or did these documents help bring into being, through debates around the cases they presented, a *real* public, Habermas's "public sphere" of flesh-and-blood "bourgeois"?

Whatever its status, the "public" of trial briefs was both seduced and instructed by stories revolving around private scandals—bankruptcy, financial fraud, swindling, forgery, abuse of authority, and all manner of sexual misconduct. Why should the lofty authority of "the public" be brought to bear upon such seemingly trivial, or at least particular, matters? To put it another way: how is it possible to argue for the "political" importance of matters that seem to amount to mere gossip? The answer,

24. Baker, *Inventing,* chap. 8 (originally published in Jack Censer and Jeremy Popkin, eds., *Press and Politics in Pre-Revolutionary France* (Berkeley: University of California Press, 1987), pp. 204–246; Mona Ozouf, "L'Opinion publique," in Baker, ed., *Political Culture,* pp. 419–434, and "Public Opinion at the End of the Old Regime," *Journal of Modern History* 60 (Supplement, September 1988):S1–S21.

25. Baker, *Inventing,* p. 172.

if we follow Habermas's argument, lies in the identity of the new "public" and the very style and themes of the trial briefs themselves.

In Habermas's scheme the "private realm"—that is, the domain of social life outside of the state and the court—is made up of two concentric circles: the realm that he calls "civil society," which is that of "commodity exchange and social labor," and embedded within it, but increasingly separate from it, the "intimate sphere" of conjugal and familial life.[26] It was not the former but the latter, Habermas argues, that provided the "bourgeois public sphere" with the first elements of its identity. Because the bourgeoisie was slow to acquire an understanding of its identity as commodity trader and property owner and to articulate these interests into a critique of existing public institutions, it derived its first identity from the common experiences of human beings within the intimate sphere of marriage and the family: "Even before the control over the public sphere by public authority was contested and finally wrested away by the critical reasoning of private persons on political issues, there evolved under its cover a public sphere in apolitical form— the literary precursor of the public sphere operative in the political domain."[27]

It therefore follows that the first expressions of this prepolitical, literary public sphere pertained more often to individual psychology and intimate relations than to political economy. As Benjamin Nathans puts it, the central activity of this "literary" public sphere "is not criticism of the state but self-enlightenment; its principal subject is itself."[28] A central feature of this "public sphere" was then, paradoxically, a preoccupation with matters common to the scattered "subjectivities" of its inhabitants and which we would call "private"—communication, criticism, and debate about intimate matters such as love, marriage, child-rearing, and family life. This was precisely the subject matter that drew readers to the causes célèbres and to the seemingly apolitical mémoires.

The appeal of Habermas's thesis is that it allows one to explain the popularity, and the ideological import, of certain works of fiction in the eighteenth century without resorting to the sort of reductionist Marxism that makes fictional characters such as Robinson Crusoe, Clarissa

26. My reading of this element of Habermas's thesis has been much helped by Dena Goodman, "Public Sphere and Private Life: Toward a Synthesis of Current Historiographical Approaches to the Old Regime," *History and Theory* 31 (1992): 1–20.

27. Habermas, *Public Sphere*, p. 29.

28. Benjamin Nathans, "Habermas's 'Public Sphere' in the Era of the French Revolution," *French Historical Studies* 16 (Spring 1990): 623.

Harlowe, or Figaro into simple literary transpositions of *homo economicus* or of the struggling bourgeoisie.[29] The argument that a modern "public sphere" first took shape in a "literary," "prepolitical" form, through the common concern of "private" persons with matters of intimate experience, helps us to understand, for instance, why the prerevolutionary reading public responded so passionately to Rousseau's *Emile* and *La Nouvelle Héloïse* (both of which concern love, marriage, and child-rearing) and to his intimate *Confessions,* while neglecting his more abstract, more obviously "political," works on government.

In the following chapters, I argue along these very lines, that the "intimate" or "particular" stories recounted in the causes célèbres briefs brought French readers together in a common concern with issues pertaining to private life. In the 1770s, the broader public implications of the private crises dealt with in the mémoires were usually left implicit; by the 1780s, they were often spelled out.

Forensic rhetoric leans by nature toward the Manichaean, since its purpose is most often to contrast the innocence of one party with the guilt of another. What the *mémoires judiciaires* offered their readers were melodramatic narratives and heavily typed characters. Their stories were "fictionalized" in the etymological sense of the term, as used recently by Natalie Zemon Davis—not so much invented as formed, shaped, molded.[30] Their characters were closer to social archetypes than to complex literary creations: the debauched grandee, the virginal heroine, the man of feeling hounded by his enemies. These were the characters that peopled the collective imagination of French men and women at the end of the Old Regime, the stock characters of what French scholars call *l'imaginaire social.*[31] Most of the social stereotyping that goes on in the mémoires could have been easily pressed, a generation ago, into the service of the dominant interpretation of the Revolution as the outcome of a class struggle between rising bourgeoisie and decaying nobility. But the current revisionist trend away from social explanations of eighteenth-century French history, and toward matters of "political culture" as broadly defined, makes the meaning of such archetypes in

29. The classic statement of this thesis is Ian Watt, *The Rise of the Novel* (Berkeley: University of California Press, 1957).

30. Natalie Zemon Davis, *Fiction in the Archives: Pardon Tales and Their Tellers in Sixteenth-Century France* (Stanford: Stanford University Press, 1987), p. 3.

31. See Bronislaw Baczko, *Les Imaginaires sociaux: Mémoires et espoirs collectifs* (Paris: Payot, 1984). For a successful use of this concept, see Georges Duby, *Les Trois Ordres ou l'imaginaire du féodalisme* (Paris: Gallimard, 1978).

these and other "fictions" both more problematic and potentially more interesting. Where, we will ask, did these images come from? Why did they prove so popular? What role did this social imagery play in public life at the end of the Old Regime? Seeking answers to these questions is important if we are to understand why and how the demonization of certain groups—nobles, clerics, prominent women— came to prove such a potent theme in different strands of revolutionary ideology.[32]

It is difficult to draw a hard and fast line between character and plot in examining the content of the mémoires, so closely did the latter follow from the former in the heavily stereotyped stories they told: a wealthy nobleman will always be in debt, always lie, always act with arrogance; a royal mistress will always have a lurid past and always be prone to intrigue. But the meaning and importance of the mémoires lie precisely in the stereotyping of plot and character, in the *lack* of nuance and shading in these stories that gives them the starkly predictable quality of myth.

The contemporary meaning of these stories must be teased out, not only of the texts themselves, but also of the ways in which they echo other leitmotifs in contemporary fiction, drama, and pamphlet literature. (For this reason the protean figure of Beaumarchais, prominent dramatist and publicist but also celebrated author of mémoires, inevitably weaves its way in and out of several of the chapters.) Noticeable changes in the themes of the causes célèbres are interpreted here as symptomatic of shifts in the major objects of public concern. In the 1770s, for instance, several cases revolving around conflicts between powerful or titled men, on the one hand, and downtrodden commoners, on the other, served as parables for the central political issue of those years, the tyrannical misuse of authority; in the 1780s, familial and matrimonial cases served as the means for addressing the nature of the social contract by pointing to analogies with the marriage contract; throughout the period, cases that involved prominent women raised the volatile and increasingly problematic issue of the role of femininity within the public sphere.

---

32. On antinoble sentiment, see Patrice Higonnet, *Class, Ideology, and the Rights of Nobles during the French Revolution* (Oxford: Oxford University Press, 1981). On revolutionary hostility to prominent women, especially Marie-Antoinette, see Lynn Hunt, "The Many Bodies of Marie-Antoinette," in Lynn Hunt, ed., *Eroticism and the Body Politic* (Baltimore: Johns Hopkins University Press, 1991), pp. 108–130; and Jacques Revel, "Marie-Antoinette and Her Fictions: The Staging of Hatred," in Bernadette Fort, ed.,

The stories that unfolded in the mémoires were more than just commentary on contemporary matters of ideology and power. The very function of storytelling within these documents carried within it the seeds of institutional, and even sociopolitical, change. The courtroom is, of course, one of the prime locations within many cultures, including our own, for the telling of stories. The fascination that the genre of courtroom drama exercises upon readers, and especially upon viewers of film and television, has everything to do with the thrill of watching conflicting versions of the same story unfold, as lawyers vie with one another to wrest snippets of "truth" from the witnesses and press these into the service of their own emplotting of the past.

As Lance Bennett and Martha Feldman have argued, forensic storytelling is central to the jury trial, in that it allows lawyers to order the facts of their cases in a way that will make them graspable and memorable to the lay participants. Since actions alone can only be ambiguous, the case narrative serves to endow isolated events with a meaning intelligible within the sociocultural context in which the jurors operate.[33] A crucial form of communication between specialists and laypersons, courtroom storytelling reflects a democratic ideal of the dispensing of justice. The judicial system of Old Regime France was anything but democratic, however, since the judging of cases was almost entirely within the hands of magistrates who operated privately, behind closed doors. While lawyers' briefs were in use throughout the Old Regime, their role was in theory just advisory and entirely private. The printing of mémoires in large quantities, their growing popularity as a form of pamphlet literature, their increasingly open appeals to lay readers to judge the cases for themselves, became a powerful tool in propagating the need to reform France's system of justice. And inasmuch as judicial power was the foundation of monarchical power in France, the political impact of mémoires that called upon "public opinion" to perform a function once invested in the king alone could be, and was, greater still.

This book describes a critical turning point in French political, or

---

Fictions of the French Revolution (Evanston, Ill.: Northwestern University Press, 1991), pp. 111–129.

33. Lance Bennett, "Storytelling in Criminal Trials: A Model of Social Judgment," *Quarterly Journal of Speech* 64 (1978): 1–22, and "Rhetorical Transformation of Evidence in Criminal Trials: Creating Grounds for Legal Judgment," *Quarterly Journal of Speech* 65 (1979): 311–312; Lance Bennett and Martha Feldman, *Reconstructing Reality in the Courtroom: Justice and Judgment in American Culture* (New Brunswick: Rutgers University Press, 1981), pp. 3–10.

public, culture as, to put it broadly, the metaphor used to describe the public sphere shifted from that of the theater to that of the courtroom. Earlier in the eighteenth century the concept of "the public" was most closely associated with the theater and with the highly theatricalized world of high society. In order to understand how "the public" became something different and much broader, this book examines the interplay between the themes and techniques of the theater and those of the courtroom at the end of the Old Regime. But on a broader methodological level, I also plead for greater attention to the social role of fiction, in the widest sense of the term, in our approach to the past. It is hardly necessary to emphasize the powerful role played by narrative in shaping our understanding of ourselves and of our world, whether in the media, in the courtroom, or on the analyst's couch.[34] As Peter Brooks has put it, "We define and construct our sense of self through our fictions, within the constraints of a transindividual symbolic order."[35] Stories give us both an individual and a collective sense of identity and purpose; they can undermine our world just as easily as they order and confirm it. For these reasons there is much to learn about a nation's sense of itself and of its future in the stories that held sway over its reading public some two hundred years ago.

34. My reading of the stories in the *mémoires judiciaires* has been aided by the prolific scholarly literature on narrative, especially that produced by literary critics, psychologists, and anthropologists: see, for instance, Michael Riffaterre, *Fictional Truth* (Baltimore: Johns Hopkins University Press, 1990); Wayne Booth, *The Rhetoric of Fiction* (Chicago: University of Chicago Press, 1983); Thomas M. Leitch, *What Stories Are: Narrative Theory and Interpretation* (University Park: Pennsylvania University Press, 1986); Theodore Srabin, ed., *Narrative Psychology: The Storied Nature of Human Conduct* (New York: Praeger, 1986); Bruce Britton and Anthony Pellegrini, *Narrative Thought and Narrative Language* (Hillsdale, N.J.: Lawrence Erlbaum, 1990); Victor Turner and Edward Bruner, eds., *The Anthropology of Experience* (Urbana, Ill.: University of Illinois Press, 1986). The historical work whose approach most closely resembles that adopted here is Davis, *Fiction in the Archives*.

35. Peter Brooks, *Reading for the Plot: Design and Intention in Narrative* (New York: Knopf, 1984), p. 36.

1

The Social Imagery
of Political Crisis, 1771–1773

In the early 1770s, large numbers of Parisians followed the unfolding of a particularly complex and riveting court case. A nobleman named Jean-François de Molette, count of Morangiès, field marshal in the royal army, had decided in the fall of 1771 to borrow a large amount of money, ostensibly for the purpose of investing it in the improvement of some land he owned in southern France. An intermediary directed him to a young man named François Liégard-Dujonquay, who along with his mother, Geneviève Gaillard-Romain, and his grandmother, the widow Véron, worked as a "banker," that is, a money broker. The parties met in September of 1771 and agreed that the Vérons (as they were later to become known) would procure for the count the impressive sum of 300,000 livres.[1]

A few days after the deal had been struck, however, Morangiès and the Vérons were hurling bitter accusations and counteraccusations at one another. The count asserted that only 1,200 livres out of the total sum had been delivered to him by young Dujonquay; the latter, brandishing four *billets à ordre*, which he claimed were receipts, maintained that the count had indeed received the whole 300,000 livres. The stakes

---

1. This general account of the case is based on chapter 1 of John Renwick, "Voltaire et Morangiès 1772–1773 ou les lumières l'ont échappé belle," *Studies on Voltaire and the Eighteenth Century* 202 (1982): 9–149; see also the day-to-day account of the case in the highly partisan anti-Maupeou [Pidansat de Mairobert], *Journal Historique de la révolution opérée dans la constitution de la monarchie françoise par M. de Maupeou, Chancelier de France*, 7 vols. (London, 1776–1777), vol. 4.

were high, and the parties took their dispute before the police lieutenant of Paris, Sartine, who promptly had Dujonquay and his mother held in custody and cross-examined. Under the pressure of relentless questioning and, it seems, some physical violence, mother and son broke down and confessed that the *billets* had been given to them only for the purposes of negotiating the brokerage.

This unremarkable, if sordid, affair might have ended there, with Mme Romain and her son awaiting judgment in the prison of Fort-L'Evêque. These two, however, immediately reneged on their confession, claiming that it was extorted from them under pressure, and took the case before the judges of the lower court of Paris, the *bailliage*. Twenty months later, in May of 1773, the Paris *bailli* ruled against Morangiès, condemning him to pay back the staggering sum, plus the interest accrued, and to remit several thousand livres in damages to his opponents and their associates. The case was immediately appealed to the higher jurisdiction of the Parlement of Paris, which after three months of feverish activity overturned the *bailliage*'s judgment and found for Morangiès. On 4 September 1773 the count was cleared of charges of swindling and bribery and was awarded 1,000 livres in damages; his opponents, however, received surprisingly light sentences: Dujonquay was banished from Paris for three years, his mother was given a warning and a small fine, and most of the witnesses who testified for them were discharged.[2] For a case that had lasted two years, mobilized eight lawyers, fourteen witnesses, and several famous writers, and had generated an unending stream of publications, oratory, and passionate public debate, this was a disappointingly ambiguous conclusion.[3] The Parlement's final verdict, if unpopular at the time, was apparently the correct one; this at least is what John Renwick has argued in the only careful analysis of the affair to date. Morangiès was widely known to be a chronic spendthrift and debtor, a man who had often lied and prevaricated in order to keep his creditors at bay. It was poetic justice, no doubt, that he met his match in the unscrupulous Véron family: they had only to convince him to enter an agreement with them, and then trust that, given the count's reputation, the scales of justice would tip in their favor once they sounded the alert. Although it is hard to feel much sympathy

2. The two judgments and the sentences are recorded in [Pidansat], *Journal Historique* 4:182–184, 297–299.

3. Ibid., 299–300; Renwick, "Voltaire et Morangiès," pp. 13–20.

for Morangiès, it is probable that he was the victim of an extremely audacious frame-up.[4]

To a cultural historian, however, the question as to which of the parties was guilty of deceit on a grand scale is not the most interesting issue raised by the case. The real mystery is why this squabble over money between a debt-ridden officer and a family of obscure financial operators, a case that involved no sensational bloodshed and implicated nobody famous, so quickly attained the status of a cause célèbre. As early as August of 1772, Melchior Grimm announced in his *Correspondance littéraire:* "I will not weary you with the details of this sordid affair, which one can learn enough about in the trial briefs published by both parties, and which all of Paris has followed with extraordinary excitement"; he could not resist, however, expounding his own views of the case on the very same page.[5]

The affair was certainly worthy of interest, as Grimm pointed out, if only because of the "boldness of the deceit and lying that was necessarily involved on either part."[6] It is significant, however, that in Grimm's view the key to the matter could most likely be found in the obvious disparity in social rank between the parties. The presumption was in favor of Morangiès, he sanctimoniously went on, because "one must suppose that a man of his estate and rank is not capable of repudiating a debt, still less of endangering, by means of a fraudulent denial, a whole family that had helped him out in a time of trouble."[7] Although many a contemporary might have snickered in response to the argument that a nobleman would never repudiate a debt, there is plenty of other testimony to corroborate Grimm's suggestion that issues of social rank were widely perceived as central to the case. In April of 1772, the bookseller Siméon-Prosper Hardy noted in his journal that the case that was riveting the attention of "the Public" had already escalated into a confrontation between "the party of the Nobility and that of the Commoners."[8]

---

4. Renwick's conclusion is confirmed by his discovery that the witnesses who testified for the Vérons all had significant criminal records; the main witness for the prosecution, Pierre Gilbert, was condemned to the galleys in 1776 for theft and forgery. See Renwick, "Voltaire et Morangiès," pp. 14–15, 73–75.

5. Melchior Grimm et al., *Correspondance littéraire, philosophique, et critique,* 16 vols. (Paris: Garnier, 1877–1882), 10:40.

6. Ibid., 10:39.

7. Ibid., 10:40.

8. Manuscript journal attributed to the bookseller Siméon-Prosper Hardy, Bibliothèque Nationale (hereafter B.N.) Ms. Fr. 6680-6685; quote in Ms. Fr. 6681, 11 April 1772.

It was perhaps inevitable, given the bare facts of the affair, that the parties' lawyers should seize on its social dimensions to make their clients' case. Contrary to what Grimm asserted, public sentiment originally ran in favor of the Véron family, whose lawyers, as we shall see, played heavily upon pro-*peuple* and antinoble sentiment among the public at large.[9] On one side were a young man, his mother, and an eighty-eight-year-old grandmother (she conveniently died "of grief" in the midst of the proceedings) living in mediocre but respectable circumstances; on the other was a haughty and grasping nobleman whose proclivity to indebtedness was well known. Who could doubt where innocence lay, and where guilt? The count's defenders were quick to expose and denounce this tactic: Morangiès was being persecuted on account of his rank, they claimed; he was being tried for what he was, not for anything he had done.[10]

To a scholar examining the case a generation ago, the meaning of such rhetoric would have been abundantly clear. It was widely assumed until recently that the French Revolution was a crisis that grew out of (and resolved) the growing tension between an increasingly wealthy and ambitious middle class, or "bourgeoisie," and a declining aristocracy desperately clinging to the tattered remnants of its bygone economic and social power. This classic view of eighteenth-century history, once espoused by Marxists and non-Marxists alike, would lead one easily to argue, as did Henri Carré some seventy years ago, that the Véron-Morangiès case and others like it were emblematic of the deep social antagonisms that led directly to the Revolution.[11]

Such an interpretation, of course, persuasive as it might seem at first sight, is no longer tenable, or at least would have to be significantly modified in light of the last twenty years of scholarship in the field. In the 1960s and 1970s the "orthodox" class-based view of the causes of the Revolution came under attack from all directions. The eighteenth century in France may have been an age of growing prosperity, revisionists argued, but it witnessed neither an agrarian nor an industrial revolution; such commoners as managed to amass fortunes in financial or

9. Renwick, "Voltaire et Morangiès," pp. 18–20.
10. See Simon-Nicolas-Henri Linguet, *Plaidoyer pour le comte de Morangiès* (Paris: Louis Cellot, 1772), p. 27.
11. Henri Carré, *La Noblesse de France et l'opinion publique au XVIIIe siècle* (Paris: Honoré Champion, 1920), pp. 280–283. Carré's excellent synthesis, which has never really been superseded, is the only work I know of to offer an overall discussion of the causes célèbres of the 1770s and 1780s: see his chap. 6.

commercial ventures were far more prone to convert their gains into land and titles than to reinvest them; fiscal and social "privilege" were not an aristocratic preserve, but were shared widely by nobles and non-nobles alike; far from being a "bourgeois ideology," the Enlightenment appealed mostly to the traditional social elites and was generally ignored by the commercial and manufacturing classes.[12]

In short, it now seems extremely difficult to locate a protocapitalist bourgeoisie in eighteenth-century France, and such groups as might fit the definition (merchants and financiers, for instance) showed no signs of a separate class consciousness or of class-bound political aspirations.[13] Social tensions of different sorts were certainly manifest, as one might expect in a society undergoing rapid population growth but where access to wealth and opportunity were still limited to a small elite;[14] but such tensions can no longer be reduced to a clear-cut antagonism between nobles and bourgeois.

Nor, for the most part, do the facts of the Véron-Morangiès case support a simplistic view of class antagonism. It was perhaps the case—although we have only the most general comments to corroborate this—that nobles and commoners tended to take sides along class lines, and it is certainly true that none of the Vérons' most conspicuous defenders were aristocrats. But the identities of Morangiès's two most prominent champions may come as a surprise: the great Voltaire, who had so eloquently denounced aristocratic pretensions in his writings, entered the fray in defense of the count, as did Simon-Nicolas Linguet,

12. Some of the most significant contributions arguing these points are Alfred Cobban, *The Social Interpretation of the French Revolution* (Cambridge: Cambridge University Press, 1964); George Taylor, "Types of Capitalism in Eighteenth-Century France," *Economic History Review* 76 (1964): 478–497, and "Noncapitalist Wealth and the Origins of the French Revolution," *American Historical Review* 72 (1967): 469–496; Betty Behrens, "Nobles, Privileges, and Taxes in France at the End of the Ancien Régime," *Economic History Review* 15 (1962\3): 451–475; William Doyle, "Was There an Aristocratic Reaction in Pre-Revolutionary France?" *Past and Present* 57 (1972): 97–122; Robert Darnton, "The High Enlightenment and the Low-Life of Literature in Pre-Revolutionary France," *Past and Present* 51 (May 1971): 81–115; Daniel Roche, "Milieux académiques provinciaux et société des lumières," in François Furet, ed., *Livre et société dans la France du XVIIIe siècle*, 2 vols. (Paris: Mouton, 1965), 1:73–92.

13. For an excellent overview of the state of the field, see William Doyle, *Origins of the French Revolution* (Oxford: Oxford University Press, 1980), especially Part 1. See also the essays in Colin Lucas, ed., *Rewriting the French Revolution* (Oxford: Oxford University Press, 1991).

14. See Colin Lucas, "Nobles, Bourgeois, and the Origins of the French Revolution," *Past and Present* 60 (1973): 84–126.

a middle-class lawyer famous for his eccentric, vaguely Rousseauean, radicalism.[15]

The Véron-Morangiès case is interesting precisely because it is opaque, because the stark images of social antagonism around which it revolved are not simple transpositions of a broad social reality. The meaning of the case, and the nature of its impact on public opinion, should be interpreted, it is argued here, in relation to a more specific context—or rather, three different, overlapping contexts. First, the resonance of the case must be related to the growth of public interest in the judicial arena, as epitomized by Voltaire's successful involvement in the Calas affair; second, the early 1770s in Paris were a time of great political tension and intense public debate, the nature of which shaped both the presentation and the reception of the Morangiès affair; and finally, the narrative style and imagery typical of the most successful accounts of the case grew out of new modes of dramatic presentation pioneered on stage and in writings about the stage. The convergence of these three developments, and the way in which they came to bear upon this judicial drama, have implications that go beyond the Morangiès case: taken together, they begin to suggest some of the ways in which such concepts as "the public" or "public opinion," and the very idea of a public sphere, were being defined or redefined in the waning years of the Old Regime.

Public interest in court cases long antedated the later eighteenth century. The judge Jean de Coras's *Arrest Mémorable du Parlement de Tolose* of 1561, his account of the famous trial of the man who impersonated Martin Guerre, was successful enough to enjoy several editions and sufficiently "memorable" to be mentioned in Montaigne's *Essays* many years later.[16] In the seventeenth century, François de Rosset's compilation of famous court cases under the title *Histoires tragiques de notre temps* was reprinted thirty-five times between 1614 and 1721.[17] The

15. Renwick, "Voltaire et Morangiès," passim; Darline Gay Levy, *The Ideas and Careers of Simon-Nicolas-Henri Linguet: A Study in Eighteenth-Century French Politics* (Urbana: University of Illinois Press, 1980), pp. 148–150; in her analysis of one of Linguet's most important works, the *Nécessité d'une réforme dans l'administration de la justice*, Levy concludes that he showed "real but qualified commitment to the common cause of king and propertied commoners against an economically, politically, and socially resurgent aristocracy" (p. 28).

16. Natalie Zemon Davis, *The Return of Martin Guerre* (Cambridge, Mass.: Harvard University Press, 1983), pp. 118–122; Natalie Zemon Davis, "On the Lame," *American Historical Review* 93 (1988): 574, nn. 9, 10; 591, n. 74; 595–599.

17. Hans-Jürgen Lüsebrink, "Les Représentations sociales de la criminalité en France au XVIIIe siècle" (Ph.D. diss., University of Paris-I, 1983), p. 129.

heyday of courtroom literature in France, however, began in 1734, when a lawyer from Lyon named François Gayot de Pitaval began to publish a twenty-volume compendium entitled *Causes célèbres et intéressantes;* the first edition went through nine printings in fifteen years and was still a standard bookseller's item by the end of the century.[18] The success of Gayot de Pitaval's venture spawned several sequels and imitations in the second half of the century, most notably the massive *Journal des causes célèbres* of Nicolas Le Moyne Des Essarts, which by 1789 attained a total of 179 volumes.[19]

The success of these collections of tales from the courtroom is symptomatic both of the growing proliferation of printed matter in eighteenth-century France,[20] and of a steady level of interest in matters of jurisprudence among educated laypersons as well as members of the legal profession. The social impact of these publications, however, may not have been very wide. Gayot de Pitaval wrote in the prefaces to his collections that these volumes were designed not just to satisfy the curiosity of readers, but also to "instruct their minds in the rules of Jurisprudence"; he identified his potential readers, presumably in order of decreasing likelihood, as "members of the Bar, members of society (*les gens du monde*), and even the ladies."[21] Indeed, at a time when a skilled artisan earned one livre for a full day's work, only professional jurists or members of the social elite would think of parting with the forty livres (for a full set) or thirty livres (for a half-set) that the Gayot de Pitaval collection was fetching in the 1760s and 1770s.[22]

While they point to a growing interest among laypersons in courtroom proceedings, then, the *Causes célèbres* collections remained for the most part costly items. Their contents were made up primarily of long-winded accounts of civil cases (marital separations, breaches of contract,

18. Ibid., pp. 130–137.

19. Ibid., p. 130.

20. On the growth of the eighteenth-century book and newspaper trades, see Henri-Jean Martin, "Une Croissance séculaire," and Jean Sgard, "La Multiplication des périodiques," in Roger Chartier and Henri-Jean Martin, eds., *Histoire de l'édition française,* vol. 2, *Le Livre triomphant* (Paris: Fayard, 1990), pp. 113–127, 247–255.

21. Ibid., pp. 132, 136.

22. Prices from booksellers' catalogs in B.N. Le Senne collection: Prault n.d. (probably early 1760s); Moutard, 1775; Cellot 1772, 1773, and 1774. It should be noted that less-expensive editions did exist: the 1772 Cellot catalog includes a 2-volume *Abrégé des Causes célèbres* for six livres. Lüsebrink suggests that readers might have belonged to the *moyenne bourgeoisie* of lawyers, merchants, rentiers, and so forth, whose income averaged 1,500 to 2,000 livres a year: "Représentations sociales," p. 180.

guardianships), aimed at demonstrating a point of law, and read like a curious conflation of generic gossip-sheet—names are usually omitted—with legal casebook. Curiously, these collections for the most part ignore the great judicial cases of the 1770s and 1780s with which this study is concerned; beginning in 1775, however, a specialized periodical, the *Gazette des tribunaux,* offered its readers synopses of famous contemporary cases along with reviews of books and journals pertaining to legal affairs.[23] The Morangiès trial and many of the great cases that followed it were no more intrinsically interesting or sensational than dozens of the affairs chronicled in the *Causes célèbres et intéressantes;* they simply acquired a greater resonance, as we shall see, because they were more effectively pressed into service by publicists in a rapidly changing political and cultural environment.

While the *Causes célèbres* recounted the judicial embroilments of private, mostly anonymous, individuals, political trials involving public figures also took place throughout the century. In 1757 the trial of the would-be regicide François Damiens was followed by much of the country with predictably rapt attention, especially after it became clear that the "monster" Damiens had somehow been inspired to "touch" Louis XV with his dagger as a result of escalating tensions between the monarch and his parlements over religious matters involving dissenting Jansenists.[24] The same overlapping religious and political animosities fueled, a few years later, the trial of the French Jesuit order, which resulted in their wholesale expulsion from the realm in 1764: magistrates, lawyers, and pamphleteers, many of them harboring Jansenist sympathies, had relentlessly denounced the order's "despotic" structure and principles, its obeisance to foreign powers, its alleged involvement in regicidal plots.[25]

By the late 1760s, judicial proceedings moved closer still to the center of power. The duc d'Aiguillon, the king's military commandant in

23. Lüsebrink, "Représentations sociales," p. 163. The *Gazette des tribunaux* was published by an *avocat au parlement* named Mars from 1775 to 1789; it was successfully revived in the early nineteenth century.

24. Dale Van Kley, *The Damiens Affair and the Unraveling of the Ancien Régime, 1750–1770* (Princeton: Princeton University Press, 1983); Pierre Rétat et al., *L'Attentat de Damiens: Discours sur l'évènement au XVIIIe siècle* (Lyon: Presses Universitaires de Lyon, 1979).

25. Dale Van Kley, *The Jansenists and the Expulsion of the Jesuits from France, 1757–1765* (New Haven: Yale University Press, 1975), pp. 29–36; Joachim Gaudry, *Histoire du Barreau de Paris* (Paris: Auguste Durand, 1864; reprint, Geneva: Slatkine, 1977), pp. 256–260.

the province of Brittany, had gone toe-to-toe with the parlement of Brittany over the levying of forced labor for the construction of a new system of roads; the province's traditional governing body, the estates, backed by the magistrates, claimed that the levy infringed on long-standing provincial rights. There ensued a protracted and complex struggle between the local and royal administrations, which resulted, quite sensationally, in d'Aiguillon's being put on trial by the parlements of Brittany and Paris; before the case could escalate into a vast political embarrassment, however—d'Aiguillon was shortly to be appointed secretary of state for foreign affairs—Louis XV quashed the proceedings by a show of force in September of 1770.[26]

Before the 1770s, then, court cases fell into two clearly distinct categories: there were, on the one hand, the private affairs of individuals, the marital and familial squabbles that provided fodder for the publishers of *Causes célèbres* anthologies, and, on the other, the great *causes d'Etat* like the trials of the Jesuit order and of the duc d'Aiguillon, which mobilized the efforts of monarchs, ministers, and magistrates, and had begun to serve as a vehicle for the public hammering-out of political and ideological principles. Nobody imagined that the judicial tribulations of obscure individuals or families could have broad social or political implications, could serve as illustrations of a moral principle rather than a point of law. Nobody did, that is, until 1762, when the most famous writer in Europe heard of the grueling ordeals suffered by Jean Calas and his family.

The story of the Calas case, for all of its familiarity, remains one of the most shocking examples of the miscarriage of justice.[27] The Calas family were Protestant shopkeepers in Toulouse, a town where tensions ran high between Catholics and Huguenots. There was nothing very remarkable about the family, father, mother, and six children, not even its problems: one of the Calas sons, Louis, was estranged from his parents, having converted to Catholicism, and another, Marc-Antoine, was subject to fits of severe depression. Real tragedy first struck the family on the evening of 13 October 1761 while they were dining in the apart-

26. John Rothney, *The Brittany Affair and the Crisis of the Ancien Régime* (New York: Oxford University Press, 1969); Levy, *Linguet*, pp. 137–143.

27. Significant accounts of the Calas case include Marc Chassaigne, *L'Affaire Calas* (Paris: Perrin, 1929); David Bien, *The Calas Affair: Persecution, Toleration and Heresy in Eighteenth-Century Toulouse* (Princeton: Princeton University Press, 1960); and Edna Nixon, *Voltaire and the Calas Case* (New York: Vanguard, 1961).

ment above their shop. Marc-Antoine had brooded throughout the meal and left the room abruptly. The family claimed that they had discovered his strangled body downstairs some time later, stretched out on the shop floor. A rope and thick wooden rod were lying nearby under the counter.

Modern historians of the case believe either that the family found Marc-Antoine's body hanging from the shop doors and lied in order to save themselves and the deceased from the taint of suicide or that an unknown person—a common thief or one of the young man's many drinking and gambling associates—committed the murder and fled unobserved. In the weeks after the event, however, the family's awkward lies and self-contradictions, the fact of Louis's recent conversion, and most of all the pressure of popular anti-Protestant prejudice, led several of the judges in the Toulouse parlement to give credence to the rumor that was flying around the streets of the city: that Jean Calas had killed his own son to prevent him from following his brother into the Catholic faith.

Some of the judges remained unconvinced: the case against Calas and his family rested on the wildly implausible assumptions either that the entire family, including their Catholic servant and a guest, had committed the deed together after enjoying a good dinner or that the sixty-two-year-old Jean Calas had singlehandedly choked to death his vigorous young son. Nonetheless, Jean Calas, who steadfastly protested his innocence under torture, was found guilty by eight votes against five and broken on the wheel in Toulouse on 10 March 1762. As if in recognition of their own doubts about the matter, the judges then proceeded merely to banish one of Calas's sons and to acquit the other family members.

Voltaire heard of the case shortly after Jean Calas's execution. His lifelong commitment to the struggle against confessional fanaticism, the deep horror he felt at the thought of torture or mutilation (to which most of *Candide* bears witness), and an encounter in Switzerland with the youngest Calas son, Donat, all spurred him into action on behalf of the Calas family.[28] "It can plausibly be maintained," writes Voltaire's foremost modern biographer, "that by his activity in the Calas case Voltaire created public opinion as a new and increasingly weighty factor in

28. Nixon, *Voltaire and the Calas Case*, pp. 131–140.

1. Voltaire promising his support to the Calas family. (Phot. Bibl. Nat. Paris)

the life of a civilized community."[29] This assessment of Voltaire's role, shared by most students of the case, reflects the sage of Ferney's own view of the power he shared with his philosophical brethren: "Opinion governs the world," he wrote in the wake of the affair, "and in the end the philosophes govern men's opinions."[30]

Neither Voltaire nor his most celebrated literary colleagues were prone to underestimate the influence that they wielded, but most of their educated contemporaries would have agreed that by the later eighteenth century, success in the world of letters made for unequaled fame and moral authority.[31] Louis XVI's minister Malesherbes, a friend of the

29. Theodore Besterman, *Voltaire* (Oxford: Basil Blackwell, 1969; 3d ed., 1976), p. 466.

30. Cited in ibid.

31. The most famous—although no doubt extreme—assessment of the influence of men of letters in eighteenth-century France is in Alexis de Tocqueville, *The Old Regime and the French Revolution*, trans. Stuart Gilbert (New York: Doubleday, 1955), pp. 138–147. Some modern studies offer evidence corroborating Tocqueville's claim about the cultural hegemony of the philosophes, most notably Robert Darnton, "The High Enlightenment and the Low-Life of Literature in Prerevolutionary France" and "The

philosophes, echoed much contemporary sentiment when he wrote in 1775: "In an enlightened century, in a century in which each citizen can speak to the entire nation by means of print, those who have the talent for instructing men and the gift for moving them—men of letters, in a word—are, among the dispersed public, what orators were in the midst of the public assembly."[32]

Some thirteen years earlier, Voltaire had been the first, perhaps, to grasp and to act upon what Malesherbes so eloquently stated: that the combination of literary brilliance, powerful conviction, and the printed word (and in this case, it must be admitted, some very high-placed connections), made for a force "independent of all powers, and which all powers respect."[33] The printed word in this instance took the form of trial briefs, or mémoires, and letters attributed to members of the Calas family but written by Voltaire, which were published and then disseminated in Paris, Toulouse, and other European cities.[34] Voltaire's writings for the widow Calas and her children are the first widely circulated instance of a particularly effective rhetorical strategy: Voltaire involved his readers in the affair by promoting close identification with the protagonists of the case while constantly reminding them of its general, indeed universal, meaning.

Voltaire's writings adopted the "techniques of illusion" that were standard fare in eighteenth-century French fiction.[35] Although most readers must have known or suspected the author's identity, the three letters, one mémoire, and one déclaration took the form of first-person narratives allegedly written by the widow and her two sons, Pierre and Donat; their status as "truthful" documents was asserted, and readers' response to them presumed, by strategically placed passages in which the family members (and others) react emotionally to each other's writings. The first piece, *Extrait d'une lettre de la Dame Veuve Calas,* is followed by a response from Donat to his mother, which begins: "My dear, unfortunate and respected mother, I saw your letter of June 15 in the

---

Facts of Literary Life in Eighteenth-Century France," in Keith Baker, ed., *The Political Culture of the Old Regime* (Oxford: Pergamon Press, 1987), pp. 261–291.

32. Guillaume-Chrétien Lamoignon de Malesherbes, *Discours prononcé dans l'Académie française* (1775), cited in Mona Ozouf, "'Public Opinion' at the End of the Old Regime," *Journal of Modern History* 60 (Supplement, September 1988): S9.

33. Ibid.

34. Nixon, *Voltaire and the Calas Case,* p. 152.

35. Vivienne Mylne, *The Eighteenth-Century French Novel: Techniques of Illusion* (Manchester: Manchester University Press, 1965).

hands of a friend who wept as he read it; I wet it with my tears. I fell to my knees."[36] Donat's mémoire is similarly "framed" by Pierre's *déclaration,* which opens: "As I arrived to weep with my brother Donat, I found him holding this mémoire for the justification of our unhappy family, which he had just finished writing."[37]

The choice of the fifteen-year-old Donat—who was away from Toulouse at the time of the affair—as the narrator in two of the main pieces was particularly apt, since the boy's guileless faith in the obviousness of his family's innocence could be set up as a foil for the increasing horror of the news he received: Donat may not have believed that he was living in "the best of all possible worlds," but his faith in humanity, like Candide's, turned into despair in the face of atrocities he could not have imagined and could barely comprehend.[38] Some typically Voltairean *elevatio ad absurdum* does make its way into the young boy's prose: "Above all people were convinced," he writes of the rumors in Toulouse, "that all Protestants make it a rule to strangle their son as soon as they have the slightest suspicion that their son wants to be a Catholic."[39] For the most part, however, Voltaire refrained from injecting such shots of sarcasm into his writings for the Calas family: the reader was to experience their horror and grief undiluted while being constantly reminded of the broader meaning of their tragic fate. Voltaire's writings made the Calas case intensely personal, and at the same time universal.

As soon as he heard of the Calas case, Voltaire likened it to the Damiens affair, with the comment that "both of these trials concern the human race"; he used the word *parricide* in reference to both cases, thereby implying that the judicial murder of a father, even one as obscure as Jean Calas, should be treated as seriously as the attempt on the life of the king-father, Louis XV.[40] His subsequent writings for the Calas family are punctuated with similar reminders of the case's universal meaning, as when he has Donat Calas write: "Our suit is that of every family; it is that of nature: it is of interest to the state, to religion, and to our neighboring nations."[41] While defining the "public" at which his

36. Voltaire, *Oeuvres complètes* (Paris: Garnier, 1877–1885) 25:369.

37. Ibid., 24:392.

38. Ibid., "Lettre de Donat Calas Fils à la Dame Veuve Calas sa mère" and "Mémoire de Donat Calas pour son père, sa mère, et son frère," 24:369–376, 383–397.

39. Ibid., 24:388.

40. Letter to Mademoiselle ***, 15 April 1762, in Van den Heuvel, ed., *L'Affaire Calas,* p. 36.

41. Voltaire, *Oeuvres complètes* 24:385.

writings were aimed in these broad rhetorical terms, Voltaire simultaneously invoked that public's sanction as a legitimation for his crusade. *Le cri du public,* he wrote early on, was supporting his endeavors; the "public," of course, had made no such outcry as yet.[42] As "Pierre Calas" he later wrote: "The public, the judge of honor and shame, is rehabilitating my father's memory; the [Royal] Council will confirm the verdict of the public, if it deigns to examine the documents."[43] This rhetorical trick was hardly unprecedented: throughout the 1750s, both the monarchy and its *parlementaire* opponents had vied with each other in print by appealing in this fashion to "the public" while claiming to enjoy its sanction.[44] Voltaire's innovation consisted in adapting this newly minted convention of political language to a very particular, highly personalized case of judicial error and religious bigotry.

Voltaire's efforts on behalf of the Calas family ultimately proved successful. On 7 March 1763, almost one year exactly after Jean Calas died on the wheel, the Royal Council (the king's private court of justice, which served as the realm's ultimate court of appeals) authorized the appeal of the parlement of Toulouse's verdict, and two years later it officially cleared the memory of Jean Calas and the reputation of his family.[45] The Patriarch of Ferney did not achieve this victory singlehandedly: the efforts of the lawyers he enlisted, Sudre, Mariette, Loyseau de Mauleon, Elie de Beaumont—we will hear more about some of these subsequently—and the help extended to him by such eminences as the powerful duc de Choiseul and Mme de Pompadour played a significant role in the case's being overturned. Voltaire did not "create public opinion," nor can it be proven that this amorphous entity had a decisive impact on the outcome of the case. What Voltaire did do, however, was to invoke rhetorically the support of the large reading public whose attention he commanded, in defense of an obscure family. By assuming a "public" for matters outside of high politics while mobilizing the communication networks he already commanded, Voltaire considerably expanded the range and power of "public opinion" both as a concept and as a real force.

At the same time, Voltaire's political and social stances, as revealed by

42. Letter to Pierre Mariette, 11 June 1762, in Van den Heuvel, ed., *L'Affaire Calas,* p. 37.

43. Voltaire, *Oeuvres complètes* 24:397.

44. Keith Baker, *Inventing the French Revolution* (Cambridge: Cambridge University Press, 1990), pp. 168–172.

45. Nixon, *Voltaire and the Calas Case,* chaps. 4 and 5.

the case, proved predictably hierarchical and elitist. His appeal to the higher authority of the Royal Council against the judges in Toulouse may have been the logical course to take, but it also reflected his confidence in the beneficent power of enlightened government to counteract the "subaltern tyranny" of the parlement and other courts.[46] The language and very arguments of Voltaire's letters, appeals, and briefs for the Calas family are permeated with and shaped by his contempt for the ignorant multitude (and implicitly for the pernicious Church that misled them). He was indicting, not the judges of Toulouse, he claimed over and over again, but the popular ignorance and prejudice, the "cries of a senseless multitude," that misguided them.[47] Some of Voltaire's most effective passages show the increasingly absurd rumors, fueled by religious hatred, originating even as the body was discovered ("Already the populace was thronging around our house"), and then swelling as they are whispered and then shouted from house to house in Toulouse.[48]

Voltaire's entire argument, in fact, is structured around an explicit opposition between popular prejudice and enlightened reason, a rallying of the forces of the educated *public* against the ignorant *populace:* "Blind prejudice caused our ruin," writes "Pierre Calas," "enlightened reason takes pity on us today."[49] Voltaire's defense of the Calas family, and his subsequent efforts on behalf of other victims of judicial error and religious bigotry, rhetorically extended the purview of "the public" beyond affairs of state to the victimization of private persons by the judicial system.[50] But the landlord of Ferney was not prepared, nor would he ever be, to extend the definition of that public beyond his own restricted world of enlightened wealth and privilege. He used his "public" as a weapon, not so much against arbitrary power as against the misguided and threatening "multitude."

Long before the 1760s and 1770s, the history of the ancien régime was punctuated by sensational court cases: the previous century had wit-

---

46. Van den Heuvel, *L'Affaire Calas,* p. 19; see also Peter Gay, *Voltaire's Politics* (New York: Random House, 1965), chap. 2.

47. Voltaire, *Oeuvres complètes* 24:374.

48. Ibid., 24:370, 385–389.

49. Ibid., 24:397.

50. On Voltaire's subsequent use of the concept in another famous case, see Eric Walter, "L'Affaire La Barre et le concept d'opinion publique," in Pierre Rétat et al., *Le Journalisme d'Ancien Régime* (Lyon: Presses Universitaires de Lyon, 1982), pp. 361–388.

nessed, among other judicial events, the political trials of the marquis de Cinq-Mars, who conspired against Richelieu, and of the powerful Nicolas Fouquet, whom Louis XIV was bent on destroying, the indictment of the notorious Urbain Grandier for his alleged bewitching of the nuns of Loudun, and the exposure of the sinister marquise de Brinvilliers, beheaded in 1676 for administering fatal doses of arsenic to several members of her immediate family.[51] These cases were every bit as lurid, if not more so, as anything the late eighteenth century produced. What distinguished the great—and lesser—court cases of the late ancien régime from their predecessors was the fact that after 1750 such events were systematically publicized, at increasingly shorter intervals, for the benefit of the reading public. The main vehicle for this publicity was a curious type of document called a *factum* or *mémoire judiciaire*— the trial brief or memorandum, whose function can only be grasped within the context of contemporary judicial procedure.

The criminal procedure of the Old Regime, based until the seventeenth century on a combination of customary law and discrete royal ordinances, was given systematic expression in the great *Ordonnance Criminelle* of 1670.[52] Investigation into a case was carried out by the judges themselves or delegated to clerks, bailiffs, or police sergeants. Witnesses either came forward following the publication of a *monitoire* concerning the case, which was posted and read from church pulpits, or were assigned by decree to appear before the judge. They were then questioned separately behind closed doors in the presence of the investigating judge, as were the defendant and other parties to the case; this preliminary stage was called the *instruction préparatoire*. In the second stage of proceedings, the *instruction définitive*, witnesses were required to repeat their testimony (*récolement*) and then confronted the accused one by one and, as the case demanded, one another. The voluminous paperwork thus generated was assembled, along with petitions (*requêtes*) by the plaintiff, the defendant, and the public prosecutor, in a bundle known as the *sac du procès*, which served as the basis for the decision by the assembled court.

To the modern reader, two features of this procedure, which applied

51. Jean Imbert, ed., *Quelques procès criminels des XVIIe et XVIIIe siècles* (Paris: Presses Universitaires de France, 1964), chaps. 4–7.

52. The following summary of the main dispositions of the *Ordonnance Criminelle* of 1670 is based on André Laingui and Arlette Lebigre, *Histoire du droit pénal*, vol. 2, *La Procédure Criminelle* (Paris: Cujas, 1979), pp. 81–103, and Imbert, *Quelques procès criminels*, pp. 2–7.

in both lower courts and courts of appeal, will seem especially remarkable: first, the process took place entirely in private, behind closed doors; and second, although plaintiff and defendant could seek aid from lawyers, they usually faced the judges alone, in the absence of their counsel. (Oral pleading by barristers was permitted in civil cases but not in criminal ones.) The lawyers' role took place essentially outside of the courtroom and consisted mainly in the drafting of yet another set of documents, which they presented to the judges on their clients' behalf. A lawyer's brief, which could range in length from a few pages to several hundred, traditionally comprised first a narration of the case from his client's point of view (*les faits*) and then a technical discussion, *les moyens*. These documents were called *factums,* or more commonly *mémoires*—a term that means memorandum but that had suggestive historical or autobiographical connotations.[53] Mémoires often made up the bulk of the legal paperwork in civil cases; and although in theory defendants had no access to counsel in criminal cases, mémoires were routinely filed as amicus briefs in connection with criminal trials—especially, as we shall see, as the printing of trial briefs became increasingly attractive to barristers as a public forum and a source of income.[54]

Mémoires were originally handwritten and were theoretically destined solely for use within the courtroom, where they were read aloud to or consulted by the judges before the final verdict was handed down.[55] Over the course of the seventeenth century, however, the custom had developed of printing such documents in multiple copies so that friends, relatives, and other interested parties could be apprised of the lines along which the case was being argued, and of its progress.[56] For well-to-do French families of the Old Regime, litigation over wills, guardianships, and the like was not a sensational onetime occurrence, but an ongoing fact of family life; such was the case, for instance, for the descendants of the baron d'Esclans in Besançon, whose forty-year-

53. Claude-Joseph Ferrière, *Dictionnaire de droit et de pratique,* 2 vols. (Paris: Brunet, 1749), 1:888. The *Encyclopédie méthodique* explained in its article "Factum" that the Latin term had been dropped as discordant with the long-established practice of composing such documents in French: see vol. 4 of the volumes on Jurisprudence (Paris: Pancoucke, 1784), p. 457.

54. On the use of mémoires in civil and criminal cases, see David Bell, "Lawyers and Politics in Eighteenth-Century Paris (1700–1790)" (Ph.D. diss., Princeton University, 1991), pp. 29–30.

55. Ferrière, *Dictionnaire* 1:888; *Encyclopédie méthodique* 4:457.

56. Maurice Daumas, *L'Affaire d'Esclans: Les conflits familiaux au XVIIIe siècle* (Paris: Le Seuil, 1988), pp. 11–14.

long squabbles over the baron's fortune have recently been chronicled on the basis of the mémoires written and published for the feuding family members.[57] Nor was the printing of mémoires limited to the affairs of the upper classes: thousands of legal briefs were published in the eighteenth century in connection with cases within and between artisanal *corporations*.[58] In a society obsessed by litigation, trial briefs represented the only substantial link between the courtroom and the outside world, the only access for laypersons to a hermetic judicial system.

The fact that trial briefs were produced and consumed in increasingly large quantities as the eighteenth century progressed must of course be related to the spread of literacy and the general proliferation of printed matter, whether in the form of books or of ephemera such as newspapers and pamphlets. The production of books in France tripled between 1701 and 1770, the newspaper press went from three titles to several hundred, and the volume of pamphlet literature grew by leaps and bounds after mid-century.[59] Compared with other forms of printed matter, however, mémoires enjoyed a particular status. The only law that regulated their production was the Parlement's decree of 11 August 1708, which stated that a printed legal document, such as a *factum* or *requête*, could not be published unless it bore the names of both the lawyer who wrote it and the printer who produced it.[60] A 1727 gloss on the decree explained that the "license" with which such documents were produced threatened to make them into vehicles for the most scandalous exchanges of abuse between warring parties, so that unsigned mémoires could be considered the equivalent of defamatory *libelles;* finally, in 1774, a new decree reiterated the earlier provisions and added a volley of new restrictions.[61]

---

57. Ibid., passim.

58. Michael Sonenscher, *Work and Wages: Natural Law, Politics and the Eighteenth-Century French Trades* (Cambridge: Cambridge University Press, 1989).

59. Roger Estivals, *La Statistique bibliographique de la France sous la monarchie au XVIIIe siècle* (Paris: Mouton, 1965); François Furet et al., *Livre et société dans la France du XVIIIe siècle*, 2 vols. (Paris: Mouton, 1965 and 1970); Henri-Jean Martin and Roger Chartier, eds., *Histoire de l'édition française*, vol. 2, *Le Livre triomphant, 1660–1830* (Paris: Promodis, 1984); Jack Censer and Jeremy Popkin, *Press and Politics in Pre-Revolutionary France* (Berkeley: University of California Press, 1987).

60. B.N. Anisson Collection, Ms. Fr. 22062, no. 5. Ferrière, *Dictionnaire* 1:888.

61. François Isambert et al., *Recueil général des anciennes lois françaises depuis 420 jusqu'à la Révolution*, 29 vols. (Paris, 1821–1833), 21:305 and 22:561–562; on the definition of *libelles*, which were actionable, see Ferrière, *Dictionnaire* 2:214–215.

The decree of 1708, which seems generally to have been respected, is in fact more revealing for what it fails to point out (because everyone knew it) than for what it actually states: if it was *necessary* for a mémoire to bear the names of both author and printer, this was also *sufficient* for the brief to appear in print. Since the legal fiction survived that these were documents internal to the courtroom, and since it was assumed that those who signed them would take responsibility for their contents, they escaped formal censorship altogether.[62] It could be argued, of course, that the requirement of a signature constituted a form of censorship, since those responsible for producing mémoires would take care not to jeopardize their case by giving offense to the authorities; this was generally true, at least until late in the century, and those lawyers like Simon-Nicolas Linguet who repeatedly failed to apply such self-censorship saw their mémoires regularly "suppressed"—albeit after the fact. The point, however, is not only that such ex post facto control operated less effectively than the preventive censorship to which other pamphlets were subjected, but, more important perhaps, that trial briefs could be produced more rapidly than anything else: no other form of licit ephemeral literature, in eighteenth-century France, could be written and then published within hours, and this must account in no small measure for the increasing success of trial memoranda as a form of "current events" literature.

The use and abuse of *mémoires judiciaires* for purposes of publicity was common throughout much of the ancien régime. Appeals to "public opinion" in documents of this sort went as far back as the 1720s and 1730s, when barristers attached to the Paris Parlement used widely circulating mémoires to defend Jansenist priests and prelates who refused to submit to the *Unigenitus* bull.[63] Jansenist causes célèbres, such as the case of Bishop Soanen who defied his superiors by refusing to accept the *Unigenitus* bull in 1727, or of the three Augustinian priests from the Orléans district who refused to submit to their orthodox bishop in 1730, served as fodder for briefs written by Parisian barristers, thousands of copies of which circulated throughout the realm.[64] The

---

62. On the complexities of censorship under the Old Regime, see François Furet, "La 'Librairie' du royaume de France au XVIIIe siècle," in *Livre et société* 1:4–10, and Daniel Roche, "La Censure," in *Histoire de l'édition* 2:78–83.

63. Bell, "Lawyers and Politics," chap. 3.

64. Ibid., pp. 150–189.

confessional struggles of the early eighteenth century even spawned a particularly scandalous court case, that of a Jesuit priest of Toulon, Jean-Baptiste Girard, tried by the parlement of Aix in 1731 for allegedly bewitching and raping his young charge Catherine Cadière; the Girard-Cadière case served as a vehicle for the continuing altercation between Jesuits and Jansenists (the latter claiming that Father Girard had used Molinist arguments to get his way with the young woman), and it too brought forth a rush of mémoires.[65]

For all of these precedents, there is considerable evidence suggesting that the early 1770s, and the Véron-Morangiès trial in particular, represent a dramatic turning point in the growth of public attention to the courtroom. One of the most erudite older histories of the French bar asserts that, and that "it was then [in the early 1770s] that the custom was introduced of flooding the capital and the provinces with mémoires that carried afar interest and scandal," and goes on to surmise that this development in effect undermined the pristine authority of the courts, since "the judges were judged everywhere where there were readers."[66] The new ruling concerning mémoires issued by the Parlement in March of 1774 is also telling: it was now prohibited to publish briefs outside of the context of an ongoing case; booksellers were forbidden to sell them before the case they addressed was closed; both publishers and authors of mémoires were threatened with heavy fines if the pieces they produced failed to observe "moderation and decency," and lawyers with disbarment if they insulted their colleagues in print.[67]

The Morangiès case certainly produced a proliferation of printed matter, at least forty-seven different items, some of which went through more than one edition.[68] Three thousand copies were printed, Hardy tells us, of one of the first mémoires in the case, which was "extremely well received by the Public"; at about the same time, one of the lawyers in the case wrote that the three thousand copies of a brief he had just completed "could not satisfy the public's burning curiosity"; and by 1774 one of Dujonquay's petitions to the courts, which was anticipated

65. Gaston Delayen, *La Sainte de Monsieur de Toulon: Le Procès de la Cadière et du Père Girard et la grande querelle du Parlement de Provence* (Paris: Justitia, 1928). At least 66 items relating to the case were published, and some of them were several times reprinted.

66. Gaudry, *Histoire du Barreau*, p. 276.

67. Isambert et al., *Recueil général* 22:561–562.

68. Augustin Corda, *Catalogue des factums et autres documents judiciaires antérieurs à 1790*, 7 vols. (Paris: Plon, 1890–1905), 3:682–685.

to "produce the greatest sensation," had a printing of ten thousand.[69] This was true, it must be remembered, at a time when moderately successful books enjoyed printings of five hundred to three thousand copies, which were sold, of course, over time.[70] What was it, then, that readers apparently found so engrossing about the trial briefs for Morangiès and his adversaries?

The fact that the case became almost overnight a cause célèbre was due mainly to the efforts of the lawyers who took on the Vérons' defense, François Vermeil, Ambroise Falconnet, and Jacques-Vincent Delacroix. The eldest of the three, Vermeil, was in his early forties and already had an established reputation as a skillful defense lawyer.[71] Delacroix and Falconnet were aged twenty-nine and thirty, respectively, in 1772, and the case propelled them from relative obscurity into the national limelight. Although they were trained as lawyers—Delacroix had in 1768 been received into the select Parisian Ordre des Avocats—both young men, prior to the 1770s, had most conspicuously devoted themselves to literary pursuits: Falconnet had in 1770 published two novels, whose titles evoke the traditions of eighteenth-century salon literature, Le Début and Mémoires du chevalier de Saint-Vincent, while Delacroix had revived and edited a literary journal, Le Spectateur Français, before trying his hand at fashionably Rousseauean pieces with titles like Lettres d'un philosophe sensible (1769) and Mémoires d'un Américain (1770).[72]

Inspired, no doubt, by Voltaire's example, these men put their youthful ambitions as budding literati and barristers in the service of the rather unsavory Véron-Dujonquay clan; the result was that the case quickly shifted from the realm of the ordinary to that of the sensational. The Vérons enjoyed a legal advantage over their adversary from the start, in that they were in possession of the four billets à ordre that could

69. Hardy, B.N. Ms. Fr. 6681, 11 April 1772 and 20 April 1774; Jacques-Vincent Delacroix, Mémoire pour le Sieur Dujonquay et la Dame Romain contre le comte de Morangiès (Paris: P. G. Simon, 1772), p. 34.

70. Wallace Kirsop, "Les Mécanismes éditoriaux," in Histoire de l'édition française 2:29–30.

71. Albert Poirot, "Le Milieu socio-professionnel des avocats au Parlement de Paris à la veille de la révolution (1760–1790)," 2 vols. (Ecole des Chartes thesis, 1977), 1:193.

72. On Delacroix, see the articles in Louis Michaud, Biographie universelle ancienne et moderne (Paris: Desplace and Michaud, 1877) 10:238–242; Ferdinand Hoefer, Nouvelle biographie universelle (Paris: Firmin Didot, 1852–1866), 13:387–389; Alphonse Rabbe, Biographie universelle et portative des contemporains (Paris: Levrault, 1854), 3:35; on Falconnet, Michaud, 22:349; Hoefer, 17:38, and Roman D'Amat, Dictionnaire de biographie française (Paris: 1923), 13.

be used as proof of the loan. Rather than organizing their defense around this technicality, however, their lawyers immediately seized upon and exploited the dramatic possibilities of the story. Two of its features became central to the presentation of the Vérons' case because of their narrative, indeed theatrical, potential: the disparity in rank and style between the feuding parties, and the brutal treatment allegedly meted out to Dujonquay and his mother by the judicial authorities.

The mémoire that first, and with resounding success, brought the case to the attention of readers, was Vermeil's *Mémoire pour la Demoiselle Geneviève Gaillard,* which began not like a legal document but like a tale: "The Dame Véron died at the age of eighty-eight during the course of this sad case, and no doubt the hardships that had been eating away at her for six months accelerated the term of her long existence."[73] The account goes on to chronicle the fate of this allegedly peaceful and prosperous middle-class family: the small fortune amassed by grandfather Véron, a parsimonious and quietly successful banker; the happy marriage of the daughter Geneviève to one Dujonquay, by whom she had two children before his death, and her remarriage to the fickle Nicolas Romain, a sergeant who abandoned her; the widow Véron's love for her grandchildren and especially for young François, who was working as a clerk in preparation for a legal career.[74] "The young man was the only male child among her grandchildren," wrote Vermeil; "he was the eldest; he had become the most precious thing in the world to her."[75]

Although the Véron family was in fact much fragmented by death and separation—the variety of patronymics it sported is bewildering— the lawyers worked hard at portraying it as a tight-knit cluster of generations clutching one another like the characters in a Greuze painting. The purpose of this was obviously to dramatize the contrast between the familial warmth of the Vérons and the haughty isolation of the count. Vermeil's narration of the first encounter between these utterly asymmetrical parties is an especially skillful piece of writing. Young Dujonquay, who has decided that his grandmother's fortune should be invested, is put in touch with a shady woman named Charmet. The latter directs him to the count, whom she describes as a man of such charm

73. François Vermeil, *Mémoire pour la demoiselle Geneviève Gaillard, femme séparée quant aux biens du sieur Nicolas Romain* . . . (Paris: P. G. Simon, 1772), p. 1.

74. Ibid., pp. 5–10.

75. Ibid., p. 11.

and probity that "if the blood in my veins were gold I would immediately go and offer it to him."[76] She leads the young man to the count's residence and leaves him waiting while she steals up the back staircase to confer with Morangiès about the role he is to play. As the action pauses, so does the narrative; while Morangiès is being primed for his role, the reader is prepared for his appearance.

"We must stop for a moment here to consider the scene which is about to take place between the count of Morangiès and the sieur Dujonquay. . . . One must imagine on the one hand a man born to the highest circles, accustomed to constantly cutting a figure there [*figurer*], gifted with an appearance that is both charming and commanding, [adept at] that tone of intimacy, those ingratiating words, those facile promises which can so easily flatter one's inferiors, give them a high opinion of themselves, and make them the dupes of their own self-esteem at the expense of their very fortune."[77] Opposite the count, there stood a young man "without experience, equipped only with the naive and trusting spirit he had acquired in the bosom of his family."[78] Dujonquay is soon manipulated into handing over his family's entire fortune to Morangiès, for such, we are told, was the object of the count's *profonde politique*.[79]

The message reiterated in this and other mémoires for the Véron family was effective if not especially subtle. While protesting somewhat lamely their respect for Morangiès's class as a whole ("there exist within the French nobility truly great and generous souls"),[80] Vermeil and his colleagues were trafficking in fairly crude, one-dimensional social imagery. The nobility that Morangiès so obviously represents is a world of factitiousness, of mere appearances: the count's splendid dwelling, his doorman and swarms of lackeys, his coach and his fine manners, all of this, wrote Falconnet, would easily impress "a woman of the bourgeoisie [Dujonquay's mother] unaccustomed to the lavish appearances that serve in Paris to mask true poverty."[81] Morangiès described the property

76. Ibid., p. 17.
77. Ibid.
78. Ibid., p. 18.
79. Ibid., p. 34.
80. Ibid.
81. Ambroise Falconnet, *Réplique aux derniers écrits du comte de Morangiès et de ses adhérens* (Paris: P. G. Simon, 1773), p. 23, and *Preuves démonstratives en fait de justice dans l'affaire des héritiers de la dame Véron* (Paris: P. G. Simon, 1773), p. 9.

he was planning to exploit with the borrowed money as a superb forest of full-grown trees, whereas, according to Falconnet, it amounted to "a sort of rock covered with snow and moss and a few clusters of shriveled beech trees."[82]

While the count's showy expenditures concealed an abyss of debt, the Vérons' parsimonious style, by utter contrast, belied their true, and substantial, wealth. Although the widow Véron had moved her family to a modest third-floor apartment in the socially mixed Saint-Antoine district, they had inherited the wealth of her late husband, who at one point had owned a twelve-bedroom country house where meals were served "in flat dishes."[83] It was the lawyers' defense strategy, of course, that dictated the setting up of this contrast. While it was easy to claim that Morangiès was living beyond his means, since this was in fact the case, it was also necessary to convince readers and judges that the seemingly impoverished Véron family had a large sum of money to place— without bringing up their unsavory connections to the underworld of Parisian usurers and money brokers. The circumstantial "evidence" of the Vérons' wealth gained plausibility, however, from being embedded within broad social stereotypes. Men of law and philosophes, wrote Vermeil in his opening pages, must "explore the mores of their age"; they know that "if honor is the first motive of the ancient nobility, it is within the middling conditions, where one lives free of ambition and need, that modest virtue often seeks an asylum."[84] This seemingly innocuous dichotomy was in fact anything but innocent: the aristocratic "honor" that Vermeil alludes to with such seeming deference would be exposed in his writings and those of his colleagues as a shallow and destructive cult of appearances.

Under the pens of the Vérons' lawyers the case ultimately became a parable about social authority, an implicit indictment—albeit one laced with deferential disclaimers—of a world where social style and the habit of command could so easily overpower and exploit the middle-class embodiments of moral and financial substance. When he is confronted (in yet another mémoire) with the witness Pierre Gilbert who testified for Dujonquay, the count's *politesse* and *séduction* give way to the authoritarian habits of his class: "Beware that you are insulting me, said the count of Morangiès, interrupting him, and that if you persist in in-

82. Falconnet, *Réplique*, p. 6.
83. Vermeil, *Mémoire pour Geneviève Gaillard*, pp. 6–10; Falconnet, *Réplique*, p. 8.
84. Vermeil, *Mémoire pour Geneviève Gaillard*, p. 3.

terceding I'll have them hanged."[85] And Delacroix imagines the count responding to his judges in the imperious tones of a Louis XV bringing his rebellious parlements to heel: "Sirs, I wrote receipts for one hundred thousand *écus,* which I will not pay because I do not owe them; I do not owe them because I say so; and you must believe me because I am noble, and therefore incapable of lying and of forswearing a legitimate debt."[86]

The count's displays of wealth, his charm and polished manners, are a veneer that conceals the reality of a power based on intimidation and the threat of violence. In eighteenth-century French towns, the social elites did indeed often maintain their power by flaunting their wealth in public while having their servants and subalterns engage in the dirty work of harassing and roughing up potential opponents.[87] Morangiès's behavior, as portrayed in the mémoires, conforms to this pattern, except that the violence carried out on his behalf is taken over by the judicial authorities. The sections of the trial briefs in which such scenes were reported were those that initially most gripped the attention of readers: according to Hardy, Vermeil's first mémoire caused a sensation "because of the touching and pathetic way in which the mistreatments exercised upon the widow Véron and her family were detailed."[88] These, indeed, were scenes of high melodrama, replete with action, dramatic dialogue, and carefully construed changes of scene, the likes of which had probably never been seen in a document of this sort.

After their arrest, Dujonquay and his mother, Romain, are hauled before the police inspector Dupuis; there they fall into the clutches of a clerk named Desbrunières who has been won over by Morangiès and, "a true Proteus in the hands of the count," will do anything to get them to confess that they are lying.[89] Mother and son are separated, and Desbrunières sets to work on young François: "You wretch, you and your family are done for; we will drag you off to your cells, I will take your grandmother and your sisters there by the hair. . . . Ah, scoundrel, you are lost, your mother has confessed to everything." The odious clerk

85. Jacques de Vergès, *Mémoire pour Pierre Gilbert appellant et demandeur contre le Comte de Morangiès intimé et défendeur* (Paris: P. G. Simon, 1772), pp. 5–6.

86. Jacques-Vincent Delacroix, *Réponse à l'imprimé du Comte de Morangiès pour les héritiers de la dame Véron* (Paris: P. G. Simon, 1772), p. 9.

87. Sarah Maza, *Servants and Masters in Eighteenth-Century France: The Uses of Loyalty* (Princeton: Princeton University Press, 1983), chap. 5.

88. B.N. Ms. Fr. 6681, 11 April 1772.

89. Vermeil, *Mémoire pour Geneviève Gaillard,* pp. 37, 41.

pauses to ask his helpers whether they have the shackles ready, to which the thugs respond with ominous rattling sounds.[90] Dujonquay is questioned and, protesting his innocence, is rewarded with a violent punch in the stomach, which sends him reeling over a nearby desk. The questions and blows continue, punctuated by dialogue. Would he swear before God to tell the truth? "Yes," answered the young man, "I swear that everything I say is true, and that you are all monsters."[91] In the intervals between these interrogations, Desbrunières visits the woman Romain, whom he subjects to similar verbal (if not physical) intimidation: "You damned hussy, I will teach you to tell such bold lies. . . . You miserable wretch, if you scream I will have you swallow my cane."[92] Eventually the mother, in terror for her son's life, confesses that they never delivered the money to the count, and her son, scared and exhausted, follows suit.

It is easy to imagine, reading these pages, the effect that their heightened theatricality must have had on readers. The dialogue is vivid, if heavily stereotyped. To Morangiès, who has come to survey the scene, Desbrunières says: "You are too good, my lord, neither one of them is worth anything"; and then to Romain, switching from *vous* to *tu:* "Do you have the bills? . . . You are lying, you shrew, I will have to search you."[93] The props are there, ominously tangible: the cane, the shackles, the armchair on which the young man collapses after a beating, the desk to which he is dragged by the collar to sign his confession. Expressions and gestures are recorded as well, from Desbrunières's raised fist to Dujonquay's disdainful smile when his persecutors try to trick him, to the count's stammering confusion when he realizes what cruelties are being inflicted on the family he has ruined.

Vermeil's initial account of the case—elements of which were borrowed in nearly all of the subsequent briefs for the Vérons—is a narrative punctuated by changes of scene, which take the reader from one distinctive locale to the next, from the Vérons' middle-class home to the count's townhouse, to the dark rooms where innocents are victimized. In the wake of the interrogation scenes, an episode occurs in the Luxembourg gardens, where the increasingly satanic Desbrunières tracks down Dunjonquay's younger sisters and successfully persuades them

90. Ibid., p. 40.
91. Ibid., p. 44.
92. Ibid., p. 41.
93. Ibid., p. 43.

that they can save their family by writing an incriminating statement.[94] "But," writes the author, "in following Desbrunières, we have strayed away from the interest most dear to us; let us return to the prison where we are called back by the groans of an innocent."[95] And indeed we follow Dunjonquay to a cell on the highest floor of the Châtelet prison, a room with arched ceilings and a small skylight that reveals the iron rings set into the walls; the young man's blood goes cold when he is informed that this is where the bandit Cartouche was roped to the wall to prevent his escaping before his execution.[96]

Although the Vérons' lawyers did also appeal to reason and legal technicality, they based their clients' case primarily on the power and coherence of a heavily fictionalized narrative. The possession of four *billets à ordre* suggested the family's innocence, although it did not prove it; but melodramatic accounts of the encounter between a manipulative grandee and a wide-eyed youngster, or of innocents tormented by sadistic police agents, promoted the identification of readers with the Vérons' point of view in a way that no dryly factual reasoning could match. Vermeil and his colleagues proved successful in seizing the initiative and imposing on the narrative of the case a dramatic coherence that their opponents never quite managed to puncture. And those opponents were far from being nonentities, since Morangiès was defended by the celebrated Simon-Nicolas Linguet and, paradoxically perhaps, by Voltaire himself.

Although today only specialists know of Linguet, the name of this gifted and idiosyncratic polemicist (in turn a political theorist, a lawyer, and a journalist) was a household word to anyone interested in current events in France in the third quarter of the eighteenth century. Whenever there was a political crisis or a cause célèbre, Linguet was not long in being heard from, usually espousing the unexpected or unpopular position and lashing out with especial gusto at the liberal pieties of his day. Simon-Nicolas-Henri Linguet, in his mid-thirties at the time of the Morangiès affair, had opted for a legal career after a prolonged stint in Grub Street, where he had mostly associated with the anti-philosophe coterie around Voltaire's enemy, Elie Fréron.[97] In the 1760s Linguet annoyed his right-thinking philosophical and legal colleagues by de-

94. Ibid., pp. 51–54.
95. Ibid., p. 54
96. Ibid., pp. 61–62.
97. Levy, *Linguet,* chap. 1.

fending both the Jesuit order and the duc d'Aiguillon against the magistrates of the Parlement, while publishing treatises, such as his *Théorie des loix civiles* (1767), that advanced provocative defenses of paternalistic monarchy and of "Asian despotism."[98] Nor did Linguet's writings hold much appeal for conservative monarchists, shot through as they were with Rousseauean rhetoric, strident denunciations of the moneyed elites, and admiring references to such unattractive authorities as Nero, Caligula, and Hobbes. Linguet's actions and publications did, however, keep him where he wanted to be, namely, very much in the limelight.

In the early 1770s, Linguet had shifted his energies from political confrontations, such as the d'Aiguillon case, to the defense of more obscure individuals, such as the viscountess de Bombelles. Posing as Demosthenes, as Cicero, or, when pitted against the highly respected Jean-Baptiste Gerbier, as David facing Goliath, the flamboyant advocate managed to turn the most mundane cases into highly publicized causes célèbres.[99] The Morangiès affair no doubt owed its initial celebrity to Linguet's decision to defend the count. As for Voltaire, he became involved in the case by accident rather than design, after one of Linguet's early writings for the count caught his attention in the spring of 1772 and a friend of Morangiès's father asked him to intervene. Voltaire felt little personal sympathy for the count, nor did he view the case, as he did the Calas and La Barre affairs, as a matter of high principle; he did, however, believe that Morangiès was innocent, and that conviction along with his commendable loyalty and doggedness embroiled him further and further in what ultimately proved to be a disappointingly unpopular crusade.[100]

There were ironies to Linguet's and Voltaire's involvement in the case that went beyond the fact that these two sons of the Parisian bourgeoisie found themselves championing the interests of an arrogant grandee against a middle-class family. Voltaire, as we have seen, had broken new ground in his mémoires for the Calas family by resting his case on appeals to the heart and professions of ideological principle as much as on legal technicality; his was, if not perhaps the first, then certainly the most

---

98. Ibid., pp. 63–66.

99. Ibid., pp. 145–155. See also Simon-Nicolas-Henri Linguet, *Mémoire à consulter et consultation sur la validité d'un mariage contracté en France selon les usages des Protestans* (Paris: Louis Cellot, 1771).

100. Renwick, "Voltaire et Morangiès," chap. 2.

famous use in his day of sentimental narrative as a form of forensic argument. Ten years later, Linguet had followed suit: in defending Mme de Bombelles, whose husband sought to annul their marriage on the grounds that she was a Protestant, he appealed over the heads of judges and lawyers to "the Public" in the streets and cafés, and countered his opponents' (solid) arguments from statute law with expressions of commiseration and outrage on behalf of the abandoned wife. The public admitted to hear him plead in the Palais de Justice "roared their support" for the viscountess and her lawyer.[101] Voltaire and Linguet were the foremost initiators of a trend, which in the Morangiès case turned against them, since their opponents in effect stole their thunder; although they won the case in the end, theirs was a Pyrrhic victory, widely greeted with skepticism and discontent.

Despite the aggressive tone that was his trademark, Linguet remained, in his writings in the case, very much on the defensive. He devoted himself to denouncing his opponents' narrative as fanciful, demagogic, and self-serving, without managing effectively to substitute for it his own version of the facts. In his first major speech for Morangiès, which was subsequently printed, he attempted to expose the motivations of his adversaries who, as he put it, " are mostly working at stirring up in people's hearts the secret maliciousness that takes pleasure in the humiliation of persons of high rank."[102] Hoping, no doubt, to rally to his client's side the social elites of the capital, he accused the opposing counsel, not without reason, of basing their case against Morangiès mainly on his rank, and thereby "putting on trial the entire nobility of the realm."[103]

Linguet's counterattack, however, simply reversed the terms of the argument by favorably contrasting Morangiès, with his ancient lineage and high-ranking connections, to "the grandson of a speculator, son of a lowly female usurer, a broker himself, and the agent of his mother's transactions."[104] He repeatedly denounced his fellow lawyers Falconnet and Delacroix as obscure *libellistes* devoured by ambition, who thought nothing of ruining a gentleman's reputation for the sake of their own

101. Levy, *Linguet,* pp. 145–147.

102. Simon-Nicolas-Henri Linguet, *Plaidoyer pour le Comte de Morangiès* (Paris: Louis Cellot, 1772), p. 5.

103. Ibid., p. 27.

104. Simon-Nicolas-Henri Linguet, *Observations pour le Comte de Morangiès* (Paris: Quillau, 1773), p. 5.

careers.[105] Over the course of a year, Linguet's "defense" of his client degenerated into a public brawl between himself and his colleagues; his ire had reached such a pitch that when, on the day after the verdict, a fellow jurist complimented Linguet in tones dripping with irony, the latter responded by whacking the man across the face with a *sac de procédures*.[106] Aggrieved by his obnoxious behavior during the case, members of the Order of Barristers began procedures that culminated in Linguet's disbarment in 1775.[107]

Whereas Linguet undermined his case through excessive passion and *ad hominem* outbursts, Voltaire's contributions suffered from an excess of dryness. Faced with the stalemate resulting from the two contradictory versions of the facts, and influenced by the *Encyclopédie*'s article on juridical "Probabilities," Voltaire produced as his first contribution to the case a pamphlet that attempted a mathematical evaluation of relative plausibilities: Dujonquay's claim that he made thirteen trips to deliver the gold was highly implausible, hence minus fifty points on a scale of one hundred against the family; one hundred points to the Vérons, for the possession of the receipts, one point for the likelihood that the grandmother wanted her money placed, minus the fifty points for the trips left the family with fifty-one; and so on.[108] Needless to say, the count came out ahead by a very large margin.

The problem, as John Renwick points out, was that Voltaire's use of this mathematical gimmick concealed neither his bias in Morangiès's favor nor his more general social prejudices.[109] It was hardly plausible in the first place, Voltaire concluded, to suspect a blue-blooded officer, more "natural" to be wary of a young man whose associates were a coachman, a carpet-maker, and a syphilitic.[110] Voltaire's elitism, less apparent during the Calas case because of the modest standing of the people he was defending, came out here in full force. During the second stage of the proceedings, when the case was being appealed before the

105. Ibid., p. 50; see also *Réplique pour le Comte de Morangiès* (Paris: Prault, 1773), pp. 31–32; *Supplément aux observations pour le Comte de Morangiès* (Paris: Louis Cellot, 1773), pp. 68–69.

106. B.N. Ms. Fr. 6681, 4 September 1773.

107. Levy, *Linguet*, pp. 149–155; Henri Carré, *Le Barreau de Paris et la radiation de Linguet* (Poitiers: Millet et Pain, 1892).

108. Renwick, "Voltaire et Morangiès," pp. 29–31; Voltaire, *Essai sur les probabilités en fait de justice. Seconde édition très augmentée* (n.p., n.d.), p. 12. The first edition of Voltaire's *Probabilités* was published in May 1772; see Renwick, p. 90.

109. Renwick, "Voltaire et Morangiès," p. 33.

110. Voltaire, *Essai sur les Probabilités*, p. 27.

Parlement, Linguet appended to one of his briefs a letter written by the noblemen of Morangiès's native province, the Gévaudan, a testimony to the count's character and to the reputation of his family.[111] This document spurred a new offensive on Voltaire's part in the form of two open letters to the nobility of Gevaudan; the gist of these pieces was that the case could only be resolved through a correct assessment of the count's *honor* (the word recurs repeatedly), a matter on which the judgment of fellow noblemen should cancel out the testimony of "usurers, coachmen, and syphilitics."[112] Linguet's writings in the case similarly dripped with contempt for the lower classes, whose support, he claimed, had been courted by the Vérons' lawyers: the *vile populace* was being recruited, he wrote, free pamphlets were being distributed, and "the *peuple*, understanding nothing, examining nothing, furiously applauds these insulting shafts aimed at the nobility."[113]

Voltaire and Linguet committed a huge tactical mistake in advertising so openly their contempt for a "public" that, ironically, they had both helped bring into being. What reader of Vermeil's or Falconnet's writings would fail to be offended by Linguet's claim that these were aimed "not at educated people . . . but at the infinitely more numerous and active class of superficial minds"?[114] The Vérons' "numerous and active" supporters evidently responded in kind, since contemporary accounts of the case suggest that reactions to the writings of Linguet and Voltaire, as to the final verdict, were mostly negative. Grimm's *Correspondance,* initially favorable to Voltaire and Morangiès, by October 1772 was dismissing Voltaire's second *Probabilités* pamphlet as "no better reasoned than the first" and adding that "the patriarch has the misfortune of having the public go against him in this affair."[115] The bookseller Hardy, who commented favorably on the trial briefs for the Vérons, described Linguet as a consummate spinner of lies, and his writings as insults to the judges.[116] Mathieu Pidansat de Mairobert, the author of an underground newsletter, reported in February 1773 that Fal-

111. Renwick, "Voltaire et Morangiès," pp. 57–59.
112. Voltaire, *Lettre de Monsieur de Voltaire à MM. de la noblesse de Gévaudan* (n.p., Geneva, 10 August 1773) and *Seconde lettre de Monsieur de Voltaire à Messieurs de la noblesse du Gévaudan* (n.p., Geneva, 16 August 1773).
113. Linguet, *Plaidoyer,* pp. 5–6; *Observations,* p. 10; *Résumé général pour le comte de Morangiès* (Paris: Louis Cellot, 1773), p. 12.
114. Linguet, *Observations,* pp. 9–10.
115. Grimm, *Correspondance,* 10:84.
116. B.N. Ms. Fr. 6681, 11 April 1772 and 1 July 1773.

connet had bested the patriarch of Ferney: "This young orator utterly crushes him."[117] Later entries record rumors that Voltaire had been bought off by the Morangiès camp and characterize his style as "artful" and "bitter" persiflage. As for Linguet, the public booed his speech for Morangiès and found his writings "devoid of the eloquent warmth that might appeal to a reader."[118] According to Mairobert (admittedly, as we shall see, a biased observer), the final verdict in favor of Morangiès was highly unpopular and left "sensible people" in a state of shock; a full month after the *inique arrêt*, a drawing of Morangiès hanging from a gallows was found nailed to the prosecutor's door.[119]

What were Voltaire and Linguet up to, and why did it arouse such antipathy? What was really at issue in this case, that it should provoke such passionate and widespread concern? The most obvious answer seems to be the one suggested by contemporaries who described the antagonisms to which the case gave rise as a conflict between nobles and commoners. The efforts of Morangiès's supporters were reportedly perceived as "a conspiracy against the Third Estate," and people took sides, wrote Linguet, "according to their rank."[120] No doubt some such social polarization did take place, although there seems to exist no solid evidence as to which social groups actually did support either side.[121] Furthermore, the social categories alluded to in the trial briefs were elastic and extremely vague. Who or what were the Vérons meant to represent? A plebeian underclass (as their opponents insisted), the industrious middle class, or all commoners, even the wealthy ones, of the "third estate"? And what exactly did Morangiès stand for? All of the nobility, the corrupt *petits-maîtres* of the capital, or the wealthy and powerful in general? And what was one to make, symbolically, of his alliance with sadistic thugs like Desbrunières?

In most societies there exist strong latent tensions between haves and have-nots, and between privileged social or intellectual elites and indi-

117. [Mathieu-François Pidansat de Mairobert], *Journal historique de la révolution opérée dans la constitution de la monarchie françoise par M. de Maupeou, Chancelier de France,* 7 vols. (London, 1774–1776), 4:54.

118. Ibid., 4:77, 101, 122, 279.

119. Ibid., 4:297–300, 332.

120. *Précis du Procès de M. le comte de Morangiès contre la famille Véron* (n.d., n.p.), p. 14; Linguet, *Plaidoyer,* p. 5.

121. Darline Gay Levy, for instance, identifies the Vérons' supporters as "non-titled entrepreneurs, merchants, shopkeepers—all those who had invested important sums of money in dealings with profligate spenders," and the *Morangistes* as "aristocrats and some philosophes," but she cites no source for this information: *Linguet,* p. 148.

viduals or groups struggling for recognition, and late-eighteenth-century France was certainly no exception.[122] The fact that such perennial tensions can be capitalized on by polemicists in search of supporters was as obvious, no doubt, to lawyers and writers in the early 1770s as it would be to politicians and publicists in 1789 and beyond. Paris in the years after 1771 was indeed a society riddled with tensions and open conflicts that were ready to be exploited; however, the evidence from chronicles, newspapers, pamphlets, and the like overwhelmingly suggests that the most conspicuous tensions in those years were political rather than social.

The so-called Maupeou Revolution, the protracted crisis that followed the disbanding of the parlements in January of 1771 by Chancellor René de Maupeou, was a political convulsion that both revealed and accentuated the growing ideological conflicts among the governing elites of late-eighteenth-century France. Although the crisis triggered by Maupeou's coup d'état abated somewhat over the course of the following three years, it did not end until after the death of Louis XV, when his successor courted popularity among his subjects by reinstating the high courts in the fall of 1774.

The crisis that came to a head in 1771 had its origins in several decades of struggles between, on the one hand, the monarchy and its ministers and, on the other, the realm's thirteen courts of high justice, headed by the Parlement of Paris, which in the eighteenth century increasingly laid claims to constitutional powers beyond their traditional right of *remontrance,* or legislative veto. These conflicts, which occurred throughout the period between 1715 and 1770, mostly centered on religious and fiscal matters.[123] The Parlement of Paris, which traditionally upheld a Gallican position in religious matters, had harbored within its ranks since the seventeenth century a vocal and influential Jansenist

122. See, for instance, Colin Lucas, "Nobles, Bourgeois, and the Origins of the French Revolution," *Past and Present* 60 (1973): 84–126, and Darnton, "The High Enlightenment."

123. Echeverria, *The Maupeou Revolution,* introduction; Van Kley, *The Jansenists and the Expulsion of the Jesuits;* see also Jules Flammermont, *Le Chancelier Maupeou et les Parlements* (Paris: Alphonse Picard, 1883); Jean Egret, *Louis XV et l'opposition Parlementaire* (Paris: Armand Colin, 1970); Lucien Laugier, *Un Ministère réformateur sous Louis XV: Le triumvirat (1770–1774)* (Paris: La Pensée Universelle, 1975); and especially Shanti Singham, "'A Conspiracy of Twenty Million Frenchmen': Public Opinion, Patriotism, and the Assault on Absolutism During the Maupeou Years, 1770–1775" (Ph.D. diss., Princeton University, 1991).

minority; in the eighteenth century it became the institutional center for resistance to the papacy's attempts to force French Jansenism into submission. The widespread support the Parlement garnered as a result of its championing of religious dissidents was reinforced by its repeated opposition to the levying of new taxes, to the liberalization of the grain trade, or to the lowering of interest rates on government *rentes*.

Throughout the 1750s and 1760s, the Parlement of Paris capitalized on—and no doubt contributed to—the increasing unpopularity of Louis XV's government. The phenomenon that some historians have termed the "desacralization" of the French monarchy under Louis XV had its roots in many causes, including, besides the controversy over Jansenism, the debilitating effects of the Seven Years' War on national morale, the recurrent grain shortages of the 1750s and 1760s, and the personal unpopularity of a monarch whose sexual profligacy was widely known and commented on.[124] As Dale Van Kley has suggested, these issues may have overlapped in the minds of many of the king's subjects, so that hostility to the authorities for their denial of the bread of sacrament to dying Jansenists, for instance, merged with accusations that the government was involved in a "famine pact" that robbed the poor of their daily bread.[125] Although tensions over religious matters abated after the Parlement successfully engineered the expulsion of the Jesuit order from the realm in 1764, other issues came in to take their place. By the late 1760s the Parlement and the monarchy were once again headed on a collision course after the trial of the duc d'Aiguillon had become the new arena in which the Parlement and the monarchy staked out their competing claims.[126] Starting in November of 1770, Maupeou launched a series of escalating attacks on the Parlement. When the court struck back by suspending its judicial operations, the chancellor responded in January by issuing *lettres de cachet* against those who refused to resume their functions. The showdown resulted, over the course of the next few months, in the wholesale drastic purging of the parlements and the restructuring of the entire judicial system.[127]

The nature and meaning of Maupeou's onslaught on the Parlement have been the matter of some debate among historians. The traditional

124. Van Kley, *The Damiens Affair;* Arlette Farge and Jacques Revel, *Logiques de la Foule: L'affaire des enlèvements d'enfants, Paris, 1750* (Paris: Hachette, 1988).

125. Van Kley, *The Damiens Affair,* p. 48.

126. Echeverria, *The Maupeou Revolution,* pp. 13–14.

127. Ibid., pp. 14–19.

view of this episode has been that Maupeou was a clear-sighted, if ruthless, reformer who deliberately planned and carried out the destruction of the main institution to stand in the way of progressive reform, and that the recall of the parlements in 1774 was a fatal mistake on the part of Louis XVI.[128] By contrast, William Doyle has argued that Maupeou was above all an ambitious court politician whose attack on the Parlement was the mostly unintended side effect of the struggle that pitted him against his political foe Choiseul. In Doyle's view, neither the abolition of the parlements in 1771 nor their restoration in 1774 made very much difference; few substantial reforms were in fact undertaken after 1771, but neither did the restored parlements throw their weight around very much or stand in the way of government policy after 1774.[129]

While the impact of the Maupeou "coup" on the actual course of government policy has been questioned, nobody to date has disputed its importance as a turning point in the development of national political consciousness. The drastic action undertaken by Maupeou touched off a propaganda war between the ministry and its opponents, the likes of which had rarely, if ever, been witnessed before. Between 1771 and 1774, the capital was flooded with printed propaganda. Various courts in Paris and the provinces immediately issued polemical petitions to the king (*arrêts* and *remontrances*), which were intended for wide circulation; pamphleteers sympathetic to the magistrates jumped into the fray and started to produce a stream of pieces ranging from high-minded protest to libelous satire, and Maupeou in turn recruited his own team of hack writers to rebut the arguments of his opponents.[130]

Although it is difficult to assess the tenor of public sentiment at the time with any degree of certainty, hostility to the chancellor and his reforms seems to have predominated by far: Maupeou had become, for the literate public, the embodiment of the principle of *despotisme*, which philosophes and magistrates had been warning against for many years. Opposition to Maupeou was widespread in many quarters; it was espe-

128. The classic formulation of this case can be found in Alfred Cobban, "The Parlements of France in the Eighteenth Century," *History* 35 (1950): 64–80, reprinted in *Aspects of the French Revolution* (New York: George Braziller, 1968), pp. 68–82.

129. William Doyle, "The Parlements of France and the Breakdown of the Old Regime, 1771–1788," *French Historical Studies* 6 (1970): 415–458.

130. Singham, "'A Conspiracy,'" chaps. 2–4; Echeverria, *The Maupeou Revolution*, pp. 22–24; David Hudson, "In Defense of Reform: French Government Propaganda during the Maupeou Crisis," *French Historical Studies* 8 (1973): 51–76.

cially strong among most of the 544 members of the Parisian Ordre des Avocats, the largest and most prestigious group of barristers in the realm, made up of those, known as *avocats au Parlement,* who worked for the Parlement of Paris.[131] In December of 1770 the barristers went on strike in support of the magistrates, even though none of Maupeou's actions affected them directly, and for several months they refused to resume their functions before the new courts set up by the chancellor.

In November of 1771, however, a large majority of the Ordre's members capitulated to Maupeou and, apparently out of fear of financial ruin, resumed their functions.[132] The turmoil of the Maupeou years did more than create within the legal profession a legacy of personal bitterness between those barristers, known as the *rentrants,* who caved in and returned to work and those who stood their ground. During those three fateful years, the powerful and independent Ordre des Avocats, which had tightly controlled the professional behavior of its members, went into abeyance. (It was restored in 1774, but never regained its former power.) The order's temporary collapse cleared the way for the emergence of a new breed of lawyers and new style of legal practice. The "Maupeou years" saw the rise to prominence, David Bell has argued, of a new generation of barristers. These were younger men with literary as well as judicial ambitions, hungering after success and fame. Most of them returned to work for Maupeou's new courts—either willingly or because as rank beginners they could not afford to jeopardize their incomes and careers. These men were ready to break the old Ordre's unspoken rules of decorum and hierarchy and to promote themselves by taking on sensational cases and publicizing them by means of crowd-pleasing mémoires.[133] These were the sorts of barristers who found themselves on both sides of the Véron-Morangiès case.

The political crisis of the early seventies divided the nation just as it split the Order of Barristers. The broad cross section of the Parisian population who opposed Maupeou and favored the return of the old courts were known as *patriotes.* Lawyers, especially the striking *avocats au Parlement,* were conspicuous among the authors who, in scores of

131. Michael Fitzsimmons, *The Parisian Order of Barristers and the French Revolution* (Cambridge, Mass.: Harvard University Press, 1987), pp. 24–25; Gaudry, *Histoire du Barreau,* pp. 122–152.

132. Singham, "'A Conspiracy,'" pp. 44–47.

133. Bell, "Lawyers and Politics," chap. 5, and "Lawyers into Demagogues: Chancellor Maupeou and the Transformation of Legal Practice in France, 1771–1789," *Past and Present* 130 (February 1991): 107–141.

pamphlets, books, and periodical newsletters, articulated *patriote* ideas and grievances: André Blonde, Jean-Baptiste Elie de Beaumont, Jean-Baptiste Target, Jacques Martin de Mariveaux, and Guillaume Saige, the authors of some of the most articulate and hard-hitting anti-Maupeou tracts and treatises were all men of law associated with the former Parlement.[134]

Despite the centrality of the Paris Parlement in the political crisis of the early 1770s, *patriote* ideology was much more than just a reiteration of *parlementaire* constitutionalism (as formulated most famously by Montesquieu), with its invocation of an ancient French "Constitution," its claim that the magistrates should share power with the king, and its blistering denunciations of "ministerial despotism." Those elements remained central to anti-Maupeou pamphleteering but, as Shanti Singham has persuasively argued, *patriote* ideology also picked up on other oppositional traditions—Jansenist religious dissent, the "High Enlightenment" of the philosophes, and the radical Enlightenment represented by thinkers like Rousseau and Mably. Out of these different materials *patriote* thinkers and pamphleteers fashioned a new, more radical synthesis—one that vested power squarely in the will of the people, elevated the public good over private concerns, and outflanked traditional magisterial claims by demanding the convocation of the Estates-General of the realm as the only solution to the political crisis.[135]

The widespread ideological effervescence that accompanied the Maupeou crisis best explains the meaning and impact of the Véron-Morangiès case. In those years, the political issues of the day were the main topic of every conversation; even elegant dinner parties, according to the baron de Bésenval, had become "miniature estates-general where women, transformed into legislators, spouted maxims of public law."[136] Although it is impossible to document precisely the size and social composition of the categories of the population that resisted the coup, historians familiar with the sources estimate that a majority of the literate and politically conscious portion of the Parisian population opposed the chancellor's show of force. While supporters of the ministry were mostly confined to the conservative clergy, some sections of the court, a minor-

---

134. Echeverria, *The Maupeou Revolution*, pp. 40–41.

135. Singham, "'A Conspiracy,'" chap. 2.

136. Pierre Victor, baron de Bésenval, *Mémoires,* as quoted in Elie Carcassonne, *Montesquieu et le problème de la constitution française au XVIIIe siècle* (Paris: Presses Universitaires de France, 1927).

ity of the nobility, and a few intellectuals, opposition to Maupeou spanned a broad range of social groups, including peers and royal princes, magistrates, lawyers, Jansenist clergymen, a majority of the intelligentsia, and large segments of the educated middle and lower-middle classes of the capital; much of the strength of the *patriote* movement came from its cross-class appeal.[137]

But while *patriote* leanings could be found in a wide range of social groups, from princes to artisans, there can be no doubt that lawyers played a pivotal role in the formulation and dissemination of anti-Maupeou sentiment. They appear prominently, for instance, in the records of the Bastille as one of the groups (along with Jansenists) most closely watched and frequently arrested by the police in the early seventies for the possession and dissemination of subversive reading matter. Not only was the legal profession in the eye of the political storm because of its association with the old Parlement, but lawyers themselves were a heterogeneous group with contacts spanning the range of the social order. For every legal eminence like Adrien Le Paige or Jean-Baptiste Target involved in *patriote* activity, there were many struggling barristers like Jean-François Levasseur, with his lower-class drinking mates, pamphlet-peddling girlfriend, and lodgings full of forbidden tracts, including some written by himself. During the "Maupeou years" the Palais de Justice became the city's liveliest center for meetings, gossip, gawking, and all manner of oppositional activity—it was the seat of the controversial new court, the setting of important trials, and the workplace of the largest segment of the legal profession.[138] Given the intense political ferment surrounding the old and new parlements, and the lawyers' role in the political and ideological turmoil of the early seventies, a sensational case like the Véron-Morangiès affair could hardly escape being politicized—indeed, the case probably *became* sensational because of its political subtext.

Near the beginning of the Véron-Morangiès case, Delacroix wrote in one of his briefs that "all of Paris seemed to have forgotten the great [political] events and become only preoccupied by this particular case."[139] But could those political concerns really be far from people's minds? The extraordinary resonance of the Véron-Morangiès case for

137. Singham, "'A Conspiracy,'" chap. 3 and passim; Echeverria, *The Maupeou Revolution*, pp. 25, 38–40.
138. Singham, "'A Conspiracy,'" pp. 168–172, 184–187, 289–296.
139. Delacroix, *Mémoire pour Dujonquay*, p. 33.

the reading public of the early 1770s seems on the contrary to have been intimately connected to the sudden opening up of the public sphere that resulted from the Maupeou crisis. In these years of intense public debate, the burning issues of the day were political ones concerning the use and abuse of absolute power and the legitimacy of despotic government. Under the pens of men like Falconnet, Delacroix, Voltaire, and Linguet, the dispute between a nobleman and a family of commoners was inevitably construed as a parable for such concerns.

The evidence that most convincingly suggests the political undertones of the case is the fact that Morangiès's two most celebrated partisans were also the most famous, or notorious, advocates of Maupeou's reforms: Voltaire and Linguet. Although Voltaire was generally a political pragmatist who shied away from a priori systems, his position with regard to French politics and the Maupeou crisis in particular was unambiguous: this son of the middle class, protégé of kings and ministers, and crusader against judicial corruption and bigotry had no patience for the social and political pretensions of the parlementary aristocracy. Firmly convinced that in France only royal authority was strong enough to counteract selfishness and obscurantism, he applauded Maupeou's show of force while lampooning the parlements' protests and remonstrances.[140] Linguet's beliefs rested on abstract principles rather than pragmatic observations, on the Hobbesian premises that liberty and government are antithetical and that only absolute power can guarantee peace and property; from this he derived an eccentric and deliberately provocative defense of "oriental despotism" as the ideal form of government, a stance calculated to infuriate right-thinking *patriotes*. Linguet, who had never made a secret of his contempt for the magistrates of the old Parlement, was one of the few lawyers to sign up enthusiastically with the new courts—before he alienated these too and was disbarred.[141]

Patriote sentiment, on the other hand, seems to have weighed in on the side of the Véron family. Among those who reported on the case, for instance, the congruence between pro-*patriote* sentiment and support for the Vérons is quite striking. The bookseller Hardy, for instance,

140. Gay, *Voltaire's Politics,* chap. 2; Echeverria, *The Maupeou Revolution,* pp. 148–160; Hudson, "In Defense of Reform," pp. 67–68.
141. Echeverria, *The Maupeou Revolution,* chap. 6; Levy, *Linguet,* chap. 4; Carré, *Le Barreau de Paris.*

systematically described the mémoires for the Vérons as "touching" or "pathetic" while he dryly attributed Morangiès's successes to the "great credit" the count enjoyed; as anyone who has perused his journal will know, the bookseller was a staunch supporter of the exiled parlements and scathingly contemptuous of the Maupeou courts.[142] Mathieu Pidansat de Mairobert, editor of the underground *Journal historique* during the Maupeou years, was one of the leading proponents of *patriote* thought.[143] Mairobert's newsletter, relentless in its attacks on Maupeou, was also highly partisan in its reporting of the Véron-Morangiès case: the Vérons' lawyers always argued with "honesty and moderation," Falconnet's briefs were remarkable for their "force and logic," whereas Voltaire wielded an "artful pen," and the count always appeared surrounded by "captains of intrigue and rogues from the court."[144]

It would be rash to conclude, however, that the lawyers who wrote briefs for the Vérons were simply pressing the case into the service of anti-Maupeou sentiment. Some evidence does suggest that Delacroix and Falconnet, at least, harbored oppositional sympathies. Delacroix was the editor of a journal, *Le Spectateur français,* which came under suspicion and was banned by the Maupeou government in 1773; and Falconnet served as counsel to Beaumarchais during the Goezman affair, a case that helped to make the playwright into the most popular foe of the new Maupeou courts (Vermeil's political allegiances remain unclear).[145] But the fact that these men were *avocats rentrants* working for the Maupeou courts put them, along with many of their colleagues, in a situation that was, to say the least, ambiguous.[146] There is much to

142. B.N. Ms. Fr. 6681; see entries for 11 April 1772, 1 July 1773, 20 April 1774. On Hardy's politics, see Carcassonne, *Montesquieu,* p. 455.

143. Echeverria, *The Maupeou Revolution,* pp. 41, 54–55; Jeremy Popkin, "The Prerevolutionary Origins of Political Journalism," in Baker, ed., *Political Culture,* pp. 212–216.

144. [Pidansat de Mairobert], *Journal historique,* passim between February and September 1773.

145. Nina Gelbart, "The *Journal des dames:* Politics, Censorship, and Feminism in the Old Regime Press," in Censer and Popkin, eds., *Press and Politics,* pp. 64–65. Louis de Loménie, *Beaumarchais et son temps: Etudes sur la société en France au XVIIIe siècle,* 2 vols. (Paris: Michel Levy, 1856), 1:351. On Beaumarchais's role in the Goezman case, see below, chap. 3.

146. There is currently some lively disagreement among students of this period as to the motivations of the barristers who, like Falconnet and Delacroix and indeed a vast majority of the Order of Barristers, returned to work for the Maupeou courts. David Bell

suggest that the portrayal of Morangiès by the lawyers who argued against him reflected, in the most general terms, the major preoccupation of those years—questions about the nature and source of political authority, its use and abuse. But the image of Morangiès in the briefs written against him appears to have brought together two important themes in contemporary political writing: the denunciation of "despotism" and the attack on "aristocracy."

The portrayal of the count of Morangiès by his adversaries is symptomatic of the convergence of social and political themes that was increasingly to characterize the most sensational of the causes célèbres. The count, as we have seen, was portrayed as man whose entire universe was one of shallow appearances: the wealth he displayed to the world was a sham, as were the fine manners and elegant *jargon* that concealed his *profonde politique*. Morangiès, as depicted by his enemies, belonged to a world in which authority derived from the illusion of wealth, the ability to seduce and manipulate, and the power to delegate the more brutal forms of authority to fawning *créatures* like the clerk Desbrunières. His character was a compound of social *and* political villainy, since he was both a self-serving nobleman able to seduce *and* a petty tyrant with the power to coerce.

It is possible to interpret the portrayal of Morangiès as a pure reflection of *patriote* ideology—the count's shallowness and manipulativeness, and his recourse to brutal coercion, can be read as the behavior of the consummate courtier, his character an indictment of the abusive authority that came from Versailles. As Shanti Singham suggests, the case may have been perceived as the expression of the growing rift between Versailles and Paris.[147] But the ambiguous situation of the barristers pleading for the Véron family suggests yet another explanation: that the case drew upon and brought together the two major (and compet-

---

believes that many of them harbored some sort of "royalist" proclivities, or at least saw something positive in Maupeou's attempt at thorough administrative reform (Bell, "Lawyers and Politics," pp. 272–276, 299–302). Shanti Singham maintains, on the contrary, that financial need must have played the greater role in impelling the barristers to return to work, since, unlike the wealthier magistrates, they lacked the financial resources to sustain exile and the loss of their incomes for very long (Singham, "'A Conspiracy,'" pp. 142–145). Because of Delacroix and Falconnet's youthfulness and ambition, and the evidence discussed above that both may have harbored oppositional sympathies, I am inclined to agree with Singham that their return to work was a strategic decision rather than an indication that they were favorably disposed toward the Maupeou ministry.

147. Singham, "'A Conspiracy,'" pp. 295–296.

ing) ideological currents of the age, "magisterial" opposition to "despotism," and "ministerial" attacks on "aristocracy."

While anti-Maupeou writers excoriated despotic authority in the name of the exiled Parlement, the writers hired by the chancellor counterattacked by denouncing the magistrates as self-serving "aristocrats" whose interest were opposed to those of the "nation." It seems likely that the barristers, whose own situation was extremely ambiguous, borrowed from both of those registers in order to launch their rhetorical attack on Morangiès—the concern with arbitrary and brutal authority that infused the *patriote* literature, and the denunciation of aristocratic selfishness common in the ministerial pamphlets.[148] The count's antagonists, the Véron family, for whom the likes of Voltaire and Linguet so cavalierly advertised their contempt, became in turn the emblems of the ill-defined *peuple* or *public* that was victimized by ministerial tyranny (in the *patriote* literature) or magisterial selfishness (in the pro-Maupeou pamphlets). The Véron-Morangiès case, then, offers us a first striking example of the process whereby political concerns (with "despotism" *and* "aristocracy") came to be transformed into social imagery.

The Véron-Morangiès case can be read therefore as analogous to, or a surrogate for, the political controversy that had erupted with the Maupeou crisis: as the protests of the exiled parlements waned after 1771 and the lawyers knuckled under and rejoined the new courts set up by Maupeou, public debate gradually migrated from the realm of the political to that of the judicial. But the fact that the issue of political authority was a burning concern at this time does not entirely explain why authority came to be embodied in precisely those images of a haughty seigneur victimizing a pathetic family of virtuous commoners. The most persuasive answer to this question is to be found in the theory and practice of the drama, which were being redefined at this very time by a generation of writers and critics.

At the end of 1773, the critic Jean-François de La Harpe complained that the season had offered little of great interest on stage, but he added that "by way of compensation the bar has become a great arena, which draws the attention of all of France. . . . The scenes that take place and

---

148. For sustained discussions of these two traditions, see Dale Van Kley, "New Wine in Old Wineskins: Continuity and Rupture in the Pamphlet Debate of the French Prerevolution," *French Historical Studies* 17 (Fall 1991): 448–465; Dale Van Kley and Jeremy Popkin, "The Pre-Revolutionary Debate," section 5 of *The French Revolution Research Collection,* ed. Colin Lucas (Oxford: Pergamon Press, 1990), pp. 1–22.

the actors who gain distinction there are equally worthy of curiosity." [149]
La Harpe's suggestion of an increasing convergence between the theater
and the bar—indeed that the latter was threatening to displace the former—was a comment echoed by many of his contemporaries. Such sen-
timents reflected in part the crises that, beginning in the late 1750s, had
led to an attempt to redefine the nature and very purpose of French
drama.

The two most famous expressions of this crisis and rebirth of the
French theater were published within a year of each other: Denis Diderot's call for a new genre of "serious" or "bourgeois" drama, the *Entretiens sur le Fils naturel* appeared in 1757, and Jean-Jacques Rousseau's
blistering attack on contemporary theatrical form and function, his
Lettre à M. d'Alembert sur le théâtre, in 1758. Rousseau's arguments
against the theater of his day are well known: that most plays, far from
teaching virtue, prompted audiences to identify with corruption; that
actors and especially actresses were models of hypocrisy and debauched
living; and that theatrical institutions sapped the moral fiber of the communities into which they were introduced. [150] But while Rousseau envisioned as the only alternative to the corrupting effects of the theater the
institution of nontheatrical "republican" ceremonies, Diderot believed
that the theater could become an agent of moral education if the reper-
toire were rewritten. Although a few plays in the sentimental and moralizing mode were written and performed before mid-century, it was Diderot's *Le Fils naturel* and especially his exegesis on that play which most
contributed to the attempt to recast stage productions into dramatic
exercises in moral instruction, and the theater into a form of lay
preaching.

Diderot argued for a new type of drama, which he called the *genre
sérieux,* in opposition to traditional tragedy or comedy. (The term
drame, which was also applied to such plays, was first coined by the
playwright Desfontaines in 1741.) The essence of the *genre sérieux* was
its didactic conveying of a moral lesson that would impress upon spectators "the love of virtue and the horror of vice." [151] Diderot's premise—

149. Jean François de La Harpe, *Cours de littérature,* as cited in Renwick, "Voltaire
et Morangiès," p. 11.

150. Jean-Jacques Rousseau, *Lettre à M. d'Alembert sur le théâtre;* English translation
by Allan Bloom, *Politics and the Arts: Letter to M. d'Alembert on the Theatre* (Ithaca: Cornell University Press, 1960).

151. Denis Diderot, *Paradoxe sur le comédien précédé des Entretiens sur "Le Fils Naturel"* (Paris: Garnier-Flammarion, 1967), p. 97.

no doubt derived from his Lockean beliefs—was that moral truths were not inscribed in the unchanging reality of a person's "character," but rather derived from the dynamic relationships between members of a family or different groups in society; these were what needed to be dramatized if a lesson in morality was to be spelled out:

Dorval: So you would wish to put on stage the man of letters, the philosopher, the tradesman, the judge, the lawyer, the politician, the citizen, the magistrate, the financier, the great nobleman, the steward.

Moi: Add to that every sort of relationship, the father, the husband, the sister, the brothers. . . . Just think that every day new conditions are taking shape. Think that nothing is more unknown to us than those conditions, and that nothing ought to interest us more. We each have our own station in society, but we have truck with men of every other estate. Conditions! What a multiplicity of important details! of public and domestic actions! of unknown truths![152]

A decade later another prominent playwright, Beaumarchais, reiterated the message that the moral truth of drama was to be found in the free play of social and familial relations rather than the blind workings of destiny, for "any belief in fate degrades man by depriving him of the freedom without which there is no morality to his actions." [153]

Accordingly, most of the hundreds of plays of the later eighteenth century that can be classified as *drames* revolve around familial crises, social tensions, or both. Many playwrights, taking their cue from Diderot and Beaumarchais, included the words *époux, épouse, fils, mère, père,* and so on in their titles, while others alluded to occupations or social stations: *Le Fabricant de Londres, Les Gens de lettres, La Brouette du vinaigrier, Le Bon Seigneur, L'Indigent, Les Trois Fermiers.*[154] Predictably, the action in many of these (forgettable) plays was often fueled by the contrast between the moral decadence of the upper classes, whose conjugal and familial life was characterized by alienation and indifference, and the close and loving bonds that allegedly united husbands and wives, parents and children, among those of middling and lower social condition.[155] In his treatise *Du Théâtre,* published in 1773, Louis-Sébastien Mercier exhorted the playwright to consort with the *honnête*

152. Ibid., pp. 97–98.

153. Pierre Augustin Caron de Beaumarchais, "Essai sur le genre dramatique sérieux," in *Théâtre complet* (Paris: Gallimard, 1957), p. 9.

154. See the listing of plays in what remains the major study of the genre, Félix Gaiffe, *Le Drame en France au XVIIIe siècle* (Paris: Armand Colin, 1910), pp. 557–577.

155. Ibid., pp. 263–269, 341–371.

bourgeois: "There you will see mores that are frank, gentle, open, diverse; there you will see the picture of daily life as Richardson and Fielding observed it; there you will see those worms of the morning [grandees], polished crooks, appear to deceive the good man and seduce his daughter." [156]

There can be little doubt that such plays served as the principal model and source of inspiration for Vermeil, Falconnet, and Delacroix when they set about writing their trial briefs for the Véron family; the opposition between crooked grandees and worthy commoners was one of the standard themes of the *genre sérieux*. In fact, one of the foremost authors of *drames*, Louis-Sébastien Mercier, produced in 1772 a play whose plot bore many resemblances to the Morangiès case: in Mercier's *L'Indigent*, a wealthy nobleman, de Lys, tries to swindle a family of poor workers out of their inheritance with the help of a corrupt attorney, pointedly named Du Noir.[157] In Mercier's plays of the early seventies the rich and corrupt always stand alone while the poor but virtuous usually arrive onstage in clumps. In *Le Juge* (1774), the laborer Girau, persecuted by a local count, first appears, according to the stage directions, "with his wife and five or six children"; the rapacious aristocrat, whose designs on Girau's land are foiled by the eponymous magistrate, is single and childless.[158] Both of these plays conclude with the solipsistic villain both gaining a family and undergoing a change of heart: de Lys realizes that the penniless but pure Charlotte, whom he had tried both to bilk and to seduce, is his long-lost sister, and the count in *Le Juge* reveals, amidst much weeping and exclaiming, that the magistrate, who has a wife and child, is his previously unrecognized son.

The new genre of trial briefs that appeared with the Morangiès case drew on the subject matter of the *drame*. It also adopted some of the *drame*'s style and technique, its use and abuse of hyperbole, exclamation, faltering speech, and the awkward emphasis on identity and state of mind that served as signposts to a theater audience: "O mère vertueuse!" "Epoux infortuné!" [159] Finally, the authors of *mémoires* adapted to their own purposes Diderot's recommendation that the playwright

---

156. Louis-Sébastien Mercier, *Du Théâtre ou nouvel essai sur l'art dramatique* (Amsterdam, 1773; reprint, Geneva: Slatkine, 1970), p. 84.

157. Louis-Sébastien Mercier, *L'Indigent* (Paris: Le Jai, 1778). The play was written in 1772 but not performed until 1782.

158. Louis-Sébastien Mercier, *Le Juge* (n.p., n.d.); the first performance date, 1774, is given by Gaiffe in *Le Drame en France*, pp. 391–392.

159. Gaiffe, *Le Drame en France*, pp. 514–516.

concentrate on the creation of static painterly *tableaux* rather than contrived *coups de théâtre,* or dramatic surprises.[160] Vermeil's depiction of the encounter between Dujonquay and the count, or of the young boy groaning in his cell in the Châtelet prison, are particularly successful examples of the adaptation of such theatrical form to forensic literature.

If trial briefs successfully drew their inspiration from the stage, conversely the new dramatic style pioneered by the likes of Diderot, Mercier, and Beaumarchais went looking for its subject matter in the judicial arena. In his treatise on the theater, Mercier insisted that the stage would only acquire its true function as a forum for public debate and moral education when its subject matter and style came to approximate those of the courtroom. He suggested that great court cases be reenacted on stage so that the public could witness them and then "confirm by cheering . . . the triumph of the law."[161] In his futuristic fantasy *L'An 2440* Mercier imagined waking up, Rip Van Winkle style, in the future, when the theater had indeed become "a public school for morality and taste," and going to see a play about the Calas affair.[162] When he wrote those lines in 1770, he must have known that this was not entirely a figment of his imagination, since several playwrights had already used the Calas case as a subject for theatrical melodrama, although none of those plays were allowed on stage in France before the Revolution.[163]

Mercier's theories about the theater were, like Rousseau's, explicitly and provocatively political. The moral purpose of the stage, as he saw it, was above all to endow the nation, including its most humble citizens, with a true public arena: we have no real spectacle in France, he thundered, only private assemblies where a few of the wealthy cultivate their taste for obscurely refined productions. "Governed by monarchs, excluded from participating in public affairs, how far we are from a national tragedy!"[164] Mercier dreamed of a true *drame politique* that would reveal to the public the secrets of ministerial cabinets and royal councils; better still, he exhorted the playwright, go to the cottages and farms of the poor, where the truths about nature and politics are re-

160. Diderot, *Entretiens,* pp. 36–37.

161. Mercier, *Du Théâtre,* p. 153; see also p. 62: "Le théâtre seroit une cour souveraine où l'ennemi de la patrie seroit cité et livré à l'infamie: le bruit des applaudissements seroit à ses oreilles le tonnerre de la postérité."

162. W. D. Howarth, "Tragedy into Melodrama: The Fortunes of the Calas Affair on the Stage," *Studies on Voltaire and the Eighteenth Century* 174 (1978): 125–126.

163. Ibid.; Gaiffe, *Le Drame en France,* p. 378.

164. Mercier, *Du Théâtre,* pp. 3, 27–28.

vealed in the gestures of everyday life: "There, if the poet is skilled, he will be able to write of the national interest with more force and success than if he depicted the inside of a palace. . . . There is no man, however obscure, who can be regarded as a stranger to the public concern."[165]

A decade after the Calas affair, Mercier's prescriptions for the stage echoed Voltaire's path-breaking demonstration that the ordeals of an obscure family could become a matter for public concern and educate those unused to thinking of public matters as a concern to each and every citizen of the nation. But where Voltaire's everyman was a well-heeled, educated philosophe, Mercier wrote with deliberate provocation of opening up the theater to the "rabble" so feared by the patriarch: "Enlarge that puny hall, double the benches, throw open the doors; let the multitude enter in throngs and fill up those boxes: the immense assembly of the people will inflame the languishing actor and give new warmth to the drama."[166] The most lucid—and extreme—advocate of the *drame,* Mercier fully realized its potential as a democratic form, one that ideally could be used as a tool to pry open the hermetic universe of traditional upper-class theater. Lawyers in turn were increasingly resorting to the sharp moral and social dichotomies of the *drame,* and its expressive, hyperbolic language, to cast a bridge between the courtroom and the street.

The Véron-Morangiès case was the first in the series of sensational courtroom dramas whose unfolding spanned the last years of the reign of Louis XV and continued until the outbreak of the Revolution. Voltaire can be credited with initiating this development through his propagandistic efforts in the 1760s on behalf of the Calas family, and in the subsequent La Barre and Sirven cases. Although Voltaire continued to be lionized as "le défenseur des Calas," the impact of his judicial crusades waned, inevitably, with the passing of time. The expulsion of the Jesuits, the end of the struggles over Jansenism, the general liberalization of social attitudes which was soon to result in the granting of civil rights to Protestants—all of these were making the struggle against *l'infâme* seem somewhat superannuated. The Calas affair was the culmination of an ideological crusade, not a new departure; and by the 1770s the patriarch's smug intellectual and social elitism was coming to seem distasteful to a new generation of writers and readers.

165. Ibid., pp. 157–159.
166. Ibid., pp. 214–215.

It was not until the early 1770s, then, that the courtroom emerged as an important arena for public persuasion and debate. This happened, it has been suggested, as the result of two developments: first, the qualitative leap in the volume and the nature of public debate that resulted from the political crisis of 1771, and second, the transformation that was affecting both the form and the function of theatrical writing. What resulted from these combined developments was a whole new rhetoric and imagery aimed at an expanding "public." Starting in the 1770s, trial briefs conspicuously adopted the idiom of the new *drame* as the theater, in turn, began to borrow its subjects from the courtroom: in both arenas the favored style was melodramatic, the genre that Peter Brooks has called the "mode of excess."[167]

The characteristics of melodrama, those of the *drame,* and increasingly of the mémoire, are instantly recognizable: extreme moral polarities, hyperbolic expressions and gestures, sketchy characterization, complicated plotting, and emphatic moral didacticism—some, if not all, of these are usually included in that which we term "melodramatic." The melodramatic impulse, as Brooks has argued, is that which seeks to heighten and make explicit the moral meaning of everyday life: the *genre sérieux,* as pioneered by Diderot, is a "drama of the ordinary."[168] In broad historical terms, the emergence of melodramatic writing—in eighteenth-century novels, in the *drame,* even in the Manichaean rhetoric of the French Revolution—coincides with the waning of the traditional sacral authorities of the European Old Regime. In the later eighteenth century and early nineteenth, at a time when established religions and divine-right political authorities were gradually losing their accepted role as arbiters of right and wrong, melodramatic aesthetics sought, in compensation, to "resacralize" the world by dramatizing "the cosmic moral sense of everyday gestures."[169] Brooks rightly draws attention to the implicitly political dimension of melodrama, a genre that, by spelling out moral lessons, seeks to assign a clear and unambiguously legible meaning to the events it portrays: "While [melodrama's]

---

167. Peter Brooks, *The Melodramatic Imagination: Balzac, Henry James, Melodrama and the Mode of Excess* (New Haven: Yale University Press, 1976; reprint, New York: Columbia University Press, 1985), especially chap. 1. See also Julia Przybos, *L'Entreprise Mélodramatique* (Paris: José Corti, 1987), and Scott Bryson, *The Chastised Stage: Bourgeois Drama and the Exercise of Power* (Stanford French and Italian Studies, vol. 70, Stanford: Anima Libri, 1991).

168. Brooks, *Melodramatic Imagination,* p. 13.

169. Ibid., pp. 15–16.

social implications may be variously revolutionary or conservative, it is in all cases radically democratic, striving to make its representations clear and legible to everyone." [170] The melodramatic mode thus represents the urge to resacralize a postsacral world, and to do so in terms that are both intensely personal and universally intelligible; in later-eighteenth-century France, the adoption of this new style by playwrights and lawyers testifies to their impulse to reach out to, and shape, an emergent "public sphere."

The publicity that surrounded the Véron-Morangiès case is thus symptomatic of the complicated process whereby a protodemocratic public sphere came into being in the decades preceding the French Revolution. In order to understand that process, one must bring to bear upon one another developments in areas that historians have traditionally kept separate: the private or "literary," on the one hand, the public or "political," on the other. The symbiosis of political concerns (about "despotism") and new literary forms effected in lawyers' briefs had one very important, if probably unintended, consequence: that of translating political tensions into social imagery, for instance by pitting the count of Morangiès, an embodiment of arbitrary authority, against his exact social opposites, the powerless but pure middle-class Vérons.

To argue this is not to deny the reality of social antagonisms in late-eighteenth-century France; historians have long since documented the existence of deep and widespread tensions in Old Regime society, between rich and poor, between country and town, between political "insiders" and "outsiders," and so on. This argument does, however, imply a reciprocity between social "structures" and "ideologies," or between "reality" and its "representations," a belief that the one cannot exist without the other. It suggests that the primary dynamic that was eventually to result in a revolutionary upheaval had to do with culture and politics in the broadest sense of those two terms. It implies that, paradoxically, the consciousness of real social grievances was a by-product of the struggle to define and control a wider, and more open, political arena.

170. Ibid., p. 15.

2

The Rose-Girl of Salency

From Theatricality to Rhetoric

In late-eighteenth-century France, notions of "the public" and of a "public space" were connected to two competing metaphors: that of the stage, the traditional arena for public "representation," and the emerging idea of the courtroom as a forum for public debate. As we saw in the preceding chapter, the rhetoric and themes of the stage and the courtroom could overlap and feed upon one another: in the 1760s and 1770s ambitious barristers began to adopt the language and imagery of the new *drame*, while socially conscious critics and playwrights dreamed of putting real courtroom dramas on stage. To suggest simply that ideas of a modern "public sphere" and of "public opinion" resulted from a neat convergence of the theater with the courtroom would, however, be inaccurate. In the late eighteenth century, dominant forms of theatrical entertainment—and indeed of "theatricality" in the broader sense of the term—remained closely bound to the needs and tastes of a very small social and political elite.

While the Diderotian *drame*, with its high-minded moralism and emotionally charged rhetoric, could be pressed into the service of courtroom argument, many other forms of theatrical writing remained utterly antithetical to the increasingly "open," melodramatic language of the bar. The story that forms the core of this chapter, that of the discovery and uses of a picturesque rural ceremony, illustrates the profound divergence between, on the one hand, the form and function of courtly and aristocratic theatricality and, on the other, the increasingly subversive use of forensic rhetoric by politically minded barristers. The case of the *rosière*, or rose-girl, of Salency was far from being the most sensational of the prerevolutionary causes célèbres. Yet it reveals much about the culture and ambitions of the most progressive among Parisian lawyers, and the increasing contrast between their ideology and that of the more traditional social and intellectual elites. It also begins to suggest the importance of metaphors of gender and sexuality in the new discourse of French public life.

Salency is a hamlet located near Noyon in Picardy, whose inhabitants, the Salenciens, became for a brief period in the early 1770s the most famous villagers in France. Their celebrity derived from a festival allegedly founded in the sixth century by a bishop of Noyon, Saint Médard. Whatever the original form of this ancient *fête de la rose*, any literate French man or woman of the 1770s could have described it in its late-eighteenth-century version.

Early in May, the villagers assembled to designate three young women, all of them natives of the village, marriageable and certifiably chaste. The nominations went to the seigneur of Salency, who then chose among the three the girl who was to be honored as rosière, or queen of virtue, on the day of the festival, 8 June. On that day, the lord presented himself at the rosière's dwelling and led her to the chateau, where he bestowed on her a dowry of twenty-five livres. In the afternoon, the rosière was led through the village, escorted by a local fanfare of musicians and a procession of twelve young girls dressed like her in white with blue ribbons, their long hair tumbling free about their shoulders. The entire village assembled in the church to hear vespers, with the rosière prominently placed on a prie-dieu in the middle of the choir. The procession then made its way to the Chapel of Saint Médard, where the priest crowned the fortunate girl with a wreath of roses, the symbol of her virtue and her good fortune. The day ended with a rustic banquet and the bestowing of more symbolic gifts, and the rosière was normally married off within the year.[1]

This is the standard account of the *fête de la rose*, printed versions of which began to circulate all over France in the late 1760s, after the festival was "discovered" in 1766 by an enterprising young woman of letters, the countess de Genlis, whose country estate was located not far from Salency. In the seventies and early eighties the festival became a fashionable theme for amateur and professional playwrights, spawning

1. This is the account found in works such as Edmé-Louis Billardon de Sauvigny, *La Rose ou la feste de Salency* (Paris: Gauguery, 1770), and Jean-Baptiste Nougaret, *Les Rosières* (Paris: Le Fuel, n.d.), pp. 7–13.

at least a dozen different plays and operatic pastorales. Meanwhile, imitations of the festival sprang up all over northern France, promoted by landlords and other members of the local elites. Rosières were crowned mainly in Normandy and Picardy and in villages in the countryside outside of Paris.[2] The village of Canon in Normandy did its competitors one better, with a "festival of the good people," which rewarded a "good girl," a "good mother," a "good old man," and a "good householder."[3]

The renown and appeal of the original festival did not derive solely, however, from the sometimes dubious literary efforts of Mme de Genlis and her successors. In 1773, the seigneur of Salency, a young man named Charles-Laurent-Antoine Danré, clashed with his villagers over the details of the fête. For reasons that remain obscure, Danré decreed for himself the right to choose the girl entirely on his own, insisted that she hear vespers not in the middle of the church but seated beside him in the seigneurial pew, and tried to cut costs by chiseling the money for the wreath and other ceremonial gifts out of the twenty-five-livre dowry. The squabble developed into a lawsuit that the villagers brought before the local judicial authorities of the *bailliage* of Chaulny, who ruled against Danré. Undaunted, the latter appealed to the Parlement of Paris and once again lost his case. On 20 December 1774, the Parlement issued a regulation that ordered the election and ceremony according to the wishes of the Salenciens and their priest.[4] Danré's obstinacy in bringing his suit before the highest judicial body in the realm suggests, at least in retrospect, rank stupidity on his part: even before the case reached Paris, some of the most celebrated lawyers in the capital were sharpening their pens in preparation for rhetorical eulogies of rural virtue and filling their inkstands to blacken Danré's name. The trial drew crowds, and the published legal briefs that appeared in connection with the case proved immensely successful, giving new life to the craze for real and fictional rosières.

2. William Everdell, "The *Rosières* Movement, 1766–1789: A Clerical Precursor of the Revolutionary Cults," *French Historical Studies* 9 (Spring 1975): 28; Michel Guillot, "La Rosière de Suresnes et le mouvement des rosières en Ile-de-France, 1772–1830," unpublished manuscript, pp. 4–5. I thank M. Guillot for allowing me to quote from his fine study of the rosières movement.

3. Abbé Le Monnier, *Fêtes des bonnes gens de Canon et des rosières de Briquebec* (Paris: Prault, 1777), pp. 17–24.

4. Emile Collas, "Le Procès de la Rosière," *Revue de France* 5 (1924): 193–200. The only record of the trial I have been able to locate in the archives of the Paris Parlement is the manuscript copy of the final regulation: Archives Nationales, Paris, X1B 8453.

Rose festivals derived from that of Salency survived into the nine-teenth century, when perhaps a thousand such ceremonies took place throughout the nation, in towns as well as villages; in some places, in-deed, the custom has lasted well into the twentieth century.[5] Ethnolo-gists explain the enduring popularity of rosière ceremonies by pointing to their origins in rural folklore. These festivals appear to derive from spring fertility rites, from the *reinages,* or crowning of May queens, that can be traced back to the late Middle Ages; the custom can also be understood as an atavistic survival of vassalic rites, the rosière's mock "premarriage" to her lord echoing across the centuries some dimly re-membered droit du seigneur.[6]

What will concern us here, however, is not the long-term social and ethnographic meaning of this festival, but its discovery and fictionaliza-tion in different forms by the educated elites of prerevolutionary France. Beginning in the late 1760s, this ancient ceremony attained, under the pens of its promoters, the status of a singularly rich and malleable myth. The crowning of a rustic and virginal female could conjure up visions of rural arcadia, serve as an allegory of seigneurial or communal power, or promote female virginity as an emblem of national cohesion. Al-though these different meanings often overlapped, in general terms, it will be argued here, the meaning of the rosière ceremony evolved in the 1770s from a theatrical exercise in self-legitimation by the aristocracy to a symbol of political regeneration. The trial between Danré and his villagers, which happened to coincide with the demise of the hated tri-umvirate of Maupeou, Terray, and d'Aiguillon and the beginning of the reign of Louis XVI, played a crucial role in recasting the meaning of the ceremony: it provided some of the most skillful and ambitious members of the legal profession with yet another parable of the clash between arbitrary authority and the national interest.

Stéphanie-Félicité, the newlywed wife of the count de Genlis, was barely twenty years old in the spring of 1766. Mme de Genlis was no stranger to the stage, having been raised by her pleasure-loving mother in the household of the financier Guillaume Le Normant d'Etiolles, in a

---

5. Martine Segalen and Josselyne Chamarat, "La Rosière et la 'Miss': Les 'reines' des fêtes populaires," *L'Histoire* 53 (February 1983): 47–54. Segalen and Chamarat argue persuasively that the rosières' functional replacements in the twentieth century were American-style beauty queens.

6. Ibid., pp. 45–46; Guillot, "La Rosière de Suresnes," pp. 2–3.

wealthy milieu addicted to amateur playwriting and acting.[7] That spring, she indulged in her favorite pastime by staging plays by Molière and Gresset on her husband's estate at Genlis. "We had as spectators our neighbors and our peasants, who laughed immoderately," she wrote in her memoirs.[8] It was the local *intendant,* Le Pelletier de Morfontaine, who one day apprised her of the forthcoming festival in nearby Salency. On the day of the crowning, the Genlis household took off for the village, where Le Pelletier had organized for their benefit a rustic ball held in a barn decorated with garlands and colored lanterns. Before the ball Mme de Genlis played her harp for the villagers, which, as she herself put it, "caused inexpressible enthusiasm among the good Salenciens and the musicians from Noyon."[9] Having brought the village into the estate as an audience for their theatricals, Mme de Genlis and her friends had simply reversed the process by moving their performance out to the village. Along the way they had all developed a passion for the crowning of rustic maidens, and there ensued a rash of elegant verses on the subject, which they dedicated to one another and sent to Paris.[10]

We will probably never know what the Salency festival was like before its discovery by Mme de Genlis and her friends. But we may surmise that some degree of poetic license must have shaped their accounts of the event, since an almost exact description of such a ceremony had been penned some years earlier by an author well known to Mme de Genlis, Jean-Jacques Rousseau. Rousseau's *Letter to M. d'Alembert on the Theatre* concludes with a description of "republican" entertainments for virtuous people.[11] Such festivities should be public, held out of doors, he wrote; they might include balls that would bring together in innocent pleasure the youth of both sexes: "I wish that every year, at the last ball, the young girl who during the preceding one has comported herself most decently, most modestly, and has most pleased everyone in the judgment of members of the box, be honored with a crown from the hand of the Lord Commissioner and with the title of Queen of the Ball, which she will bear throughout the year. I wish that at the close of this gathering she be

7. Violet Wyndham, *Madame de Genlis* (London: A. Deutsch, 1958), pp. 23–26.
8. Stéphanie-Félicité de Genlis, *Mémoires,* 8 vols. (Paris: Ladvocat, 1825), 1:274.
9. Ibid., 1:275–277.
10. Everdell, "The Rosières Movement," pp. 25–26.
11. Jean-Jacques Rousseau, *Politics and the Arts: Letter to M. d'Alembert on the Theatre,* trans. Allan Bloom (Ithaca: Cornell University Press, 1960), pp. 125–131.

brought back home by a cortege, and that her father and mother be congratulated and thanked for having a daughter of so good a nature, and raising her so well." [12] This was written in 1758, some eight years before Mme de Genlis set foot in Salency. Whether or not she or her friends had read this page, the idea was clearly in the air: if the festival of Salency had not existed, it would have had to be invented.

It is no small irony, of course, that this early description of a rosière should have appeared in the midst of Rousseau's hard-hitting tract against aristocratic theatricality, for it was members of the highest social circles who most conspicuously frequented such festivals and made them into occasions for playacting. Thus, the rose festival of 1776 in Salency was patronized by the count and countess de La Tour du Pin, Mme de Richemond, and a long string of their aristocratic friends. [13] The following year it drew marshal de Broglie and his family and the countess de Lameth; most of these people were members of the highest court aristocracy, some of them intimate friends or members of the royal family. [14] In the late 1770s, the count and countess Du Roure invited the king's brother, the count of Provence, to their festival at Louville in the Beauce, while the king's other brother, the count of Artois, founded his own *fête de la rose* in the town of Nantes. [15] Some of these festivals even became occasions for the French aristocracy to display their *bienfaisance* before foreign counterparts: the audience of six thousand that attended the marquis de Tourny's fête in 1778 included a smattering of dignitaries from abroad, the duke of Braganza, Count Strogonoff, Prince Toubieski, and the marquis of Spinola. [16]

The most lavish of these festivals were engineered as extensions into the countryside of traditional court festivities that centered on a theatrical performance. Aristocratic grandees tended to ignore the village procession to and from the church, favoring instead elaborate static tableaux that emphasized the hierarchical message of the event. At Canon, a theater was set up and decorated with columns, royal insignias, and background paintings showing members of the royal family alleviating the sufferings of the rural poor. The little daughters of a visiting mar-

12. Ibid., p. 130.

13. *Histoire de la Rosière de Salancy, ou recueil de pièces tant en prose qu'en vers sur la Rosière* (Paris: Mérigot, 1777), p. 90.

14. Nougaret, *Les Rosières,* p. 19.

15. Ibid., pp. 157–159.

16. Ibid., p. 131.

quise, got up as peasant girls, presented wreaths and medals, and the day ended with fireworks and illuminations.[17] The engraving by Moreau Le Jeune that serves as a frontispiece to the abbé Le Monnier's account of the Canon festival shows a table at the top of a flight of stairs, surmounted by an elaborate canopy decorated with garlands of flowers and greenery. Behind the table, which is covered by a white tablecloth and set for a meal, are seated the two designated "bonnes filles," wearing bridelike veils and wreaths, the daughters of an aged paralytic who sits between them. At either end of the table, framing the girls and their father, are an elegantly clad lady and a cleric wearing robes and a skullcap. At the foot of the stairs the assembled villagers gaze and point up at the scene.[18]

Even in much simpler settings, visiting noblemen and women engaged in self-conscious role-playing, acutely aware of the presence and reactions of their audience. After the crowning at Salency in 1776, a few noblewomen emerged from the crowd, embraced the rosière, offered her a large gift, and "disappeared immediately, as if they had come only to grace virtue with this offering. The timid rosière was abashed, onlookers were filled with wonder."[19] And when the court and the salon could not transport itself to the village, villagers were commandeered to reenact such scenes in town. One of the two girls crowned one year at Briquebec was moved to Paris for the benefit of two ladies "of the first rank" who had not been able to attend the ceremony. The rosière was honored in their drawing room by daughters of the household who sang verses and offered bouquets.[20]

The object of all this playacting was probably not to demonstrate to the villagers of Salency, Briquebec, or Canon the all-too-obvious social preeminence of the aristocratic grandees who descended upon them each spring. The rose festivals should be interpreted, not as a simple exercise in the assertion of social hegemony, but rather as a more complex extension into the countryside of stylized social games that normally took place within the confines of rococo salons or of boxes at the Comédie-Française. The ultimate meaning of such behavior is perhaps best illustrated, albeit in the mode of extreme cynicism, by a famous

17. Le Monnier, *Fêtes de Canon*, pp. 38–49.
18. Ibid., frontispiece.
19. *Histoire de la Rosière*, p. 19.
20. Nougaret, *Les Rosières*, pp. 116–117.

episode in Choderlos de Laclos's great libertine novel, *Les Liaisons dangereuses*.

The scene takes place on a country estate, where the diabolical vicomte de Valmont, a consummate actor and manipulator, seeks to break down the resistance of the virtuous Mme de Tourvel. Upon learning that Mme de Tourvel is having him followed on his hunting expeditions, Valmont arranges a "fortuitous" scene in a nearby village; there, he encounters a destitute family of laborers whom the tax collector is threatening to evict. Under the gaze of Mme de Tourvel's spy, Valmont produces the money for their taxes, and the entire family falls to their knees about him, weeping with gratitude. "In the midst of these voluble benedictions I appeared not unlike the hero in the last act of a drama," observes Valmont, with his customary clinical detachment.[21] The spy's report convinces Mme de Tourvel of the rake's innate goodness, and soon after she takes the first step on the path that will lead her to ruin. Such, mutatis mutandis, was the meaning of the behavior of noble men and women who sought to impress one another by means of theatrical ventures into the world of rural poverty.

This is not meant to suggest that the involvement of upper-class women and men in the rosière movement sprang from cynical calculation. More damningly, perhaps, it can be attributed to the sort of narcissistically sensual cult of emotion that is captured in the preface to the abbé Le Monnier's account of the Canon festivities: "The manuscript of this work, read in society, deeply touched several persons, and especially one respectable lady. She asked me with tears in her eyes to allow her to witness a crowning: it is a celebration she wishes to give herself [*c'est une fête qu'elle veut se donner*]";[22] or in a description of the reactions of wealthy patrons to the Salency festival: "Eyes teared up, one lacked the strength to applaud. . . . Such pleasant occasions are indeed worthy of respect. O you who are wealthy, how easy it would be for you to feel ecstasy! [*qu'il vous seroit aisé de jouir!*]."[23]

In more general terms, this aristocratic infatuation with a certain vision of the countryside had probably much to do with a crisis of self-definition affecting the more progressive segments of the nobility after

21. Pierre-Ambroise Choderlos de Laclos, *Les Liaisons dangereuses* (1782), letters 21–22, trans. P. W. K. Stone (London: Penguin Books, 1961), pp. 56–60.

22. Le Monnier, *Fêtes de Canon*, pp. v-vi.

23. *Histoire de la Rosière de Salancy*, p. 90.

a first generation of enlightened thinkers had successfully challenged the prerogative of birth as a criterion for social supremacy. Beginning in the 1760s, educated members of the aristocracy sought to redefine the claims of their class to leadership of the nation by grounding them in utilitarian categories such as merit, virtue, and *bienfaisance*.[24] Much was made, in accounts of the festival, of the fact that the rosière had not only to be virtuous herself, but also to be descended from four generations of morally irreproachable ancestors: hers was a "new nobility," that of virtue.[25] The rose festival symbolized the displacement of a genealogy of inherited privilege by one of personal merit. The promotion of such festivals by the upper classes had probably less to do with a desire to offer moral instruction to the peasantry than with an urge to appropriate for themselves this new, and more ideologically persuasive, form of lineage. The virtue and destitution of the rural world thus became mediating categories, through which noble men and women sought to persuade one another—and other segments of the educated elites—of their collective moral stature and social utility.

The adoption of the rose festival of Salency by the upper classes must be linked to the habit of studied theatricality which for at least a century had characterized French aristocratic culture. The development of court society at Versailles had promoted a cultural system in which power, or indeed mere survival, depended upon one's ability to behave with elegant decorousness while concealing one's feelings and controlling one's emotions. This code of behavior first cultivated at court soon extended to *la ville*, so that by the eighteenth century, society life had come to resemble a performance endlessly played out before a small "public" of social equals, in Peter Brooks's words "a theater closed to the outside world but utterly public to its members who [were] both actors and spectators."[26] The term *le public*, which occurs so frequently in

24. Guy Chaussinand-Nogaret, *La Noblesse au XVIIIe siècle: De la féodalité aux lumières* (Paris: Hachette, 1976), chaps. 1 and 2; David Bien, "La Réaction aristocratique avant 1789: L'Exemple de l'armée," *Annales: Économies, Sociétés, Civilisations* 29 (1974): 23–48, 505–548.

25. Billardon de Sauvigny, *La Rose ou la feste de Salency,* p. ix. This theme was echoed and amplified in the legal briefs written on the occasion of the trial: see, for instance, Jacques-Vincent Delacroix, *Second Mémoire en faveur de la rosière pour les syndic et habitans de Salancy contre le sieur Danré, seigneur de Salancy* (Paris: P. G. Simon, 1774), pp. 4–5.

26. Norbert Elias, *The Court Society,* trans. Edmund Jephcott (New York: Pantheon Books, 1983); Laurent Versini, *Laclos et la tradition: Essai sur les sources et la technique*

eighteenth-century French novels of manners—for instance in such phrases as *le jugement du public*—designates the members of a small social elite that scrutinized the behavior of each one of its members.[27]

But eighteenth-century high society was also theatrical in a more concrete and literal sense. In the waning decades of Louis XIV's reign, as the old king fell under the sway of his devout second wife, many forms of artistic and literary life shifted away from the court and from official academic institutions, to fall increasingly under the patronage of private individuals. Under the Regency (1715–1723), for instance, much of the capital's artistic life was centered around the household of the opulent financier Pierre Crozat, whose taste for elegantly countrified entertainment is reflected in the paintings of his protégé Antoine Watteau.[28] The late seventeenth and early eighteenth centuries also witnessed the flowering of a fashion for private theatrical entertainment, which was to last until the eve of the Revolution. The trend originated on the estates of court grandees such as the duchesse du Maine, whose *grandes nuits,* lavish theatrical entertainments at her chateau at Sceaux, drew crowds between 1700 and 1726, effectively replacing the festivities of the increasingly deserted court.[29]

The fashion soon spread to households of lesser pedigree, such as that of the powerful financier Charles Le Normand de Tournehem. In the early 1740s, the elder Le Normand had the most elaborate private theater in France built on the estate of his nephew Guillaume Le Normand d'Etiolles, who had just been wed to a dazzling young woman named, somewhat inelegantly, Jeanne Poisson. The theater was meant to showcase the talents of the young Mme d'Etiolles, who may well have been the elder Le Normand's illegitimate daughter. It did not serve this purpose for long, however, since in 1744 the young woman was introduced to the king, and, after a hasty separation from her husband had been arranged, was installed at court as Louis XV's official favorite

des *"Liaisons dangereuses"* (Paris: Klincksieck, 1968), chap. 4; Peter Brooks, *The Novel of Worldliness: Crébillon, Marivaux, Laclos, Stendhal* (Princeton: Princeton University Press, 1969), introduction and chap. 1, quote on p. 18.

27. Ibid.; see also Bernadette Fort, *Le Langage de l'ambiguïté dans l'oeuvre de Crébillon fils* (Paris: Klincksieck, 1978), pp. 18–22.

28. Thomas Crow, *Painters and Public Life in Eighteenth-Century Paris* (New Haven: Yale University Press, 1985), introduction and chaps. 1 and 2.

29. Adolphe Jullien, *La Comédie à la cour: Les Théâtres de société royale pendant le siècle dernier* (Paris: Firmin Didot, 1885), pp. 3–137; Victor Fournel, *Curiosités théâtrales anciennes et modernes françaises et étrangères* (Paris: Garnier, 1878), chap. 5.

under the title Marquise de Pompadour. Etiolles remained an important center for private theatrical entertainment: it was there, as we have seen, that Mme de Genlis was raised and got her first lessons in acting and play writing. Celebrated playwrights like Voltaire and Crébillon the elder were frequent visitors at Etiolles, and it was there that the young Beaumarchais wrote his very first plays, the bawdy, pseudo-popular farces known as *parades.*[30]

Meanwhile the former Mme d'Etiolles, now ensconced in Versailles, proved reluctant to relinquish the theatrical pastimes to which she was accustomed. In 1747, she had a small theater set up in one of the galleries of Versailles, where she and her friends could perform for one another. For several years, the elite of princes and courtiers vied with one another for even the smallest roles in the productions of Molière, Dufresny, Voltaire, or Gresset staged in what had become known as the *théâtre des petits cabinets.*[31] The social trajectory and artistic influence of Mme de Pompadour might be seen as emblematic of the complicated cultural interchanges that took place in the eighteenth century between *la cour* and *la ville*, between the older aristocracy of birth, the urban nobility, and the moneyed elite of financiers and tax-farmers. It was the former Jeanne Poisson, daughter of a wholesale merchant, protégée of a tax-farmer, groomed in the salons and country estates of the aristocracy, who reintroduced the theater to the court; but where theatrical entertainment under Louis XIV had taken the form of lavish public festivities, under his successor court theater reappeared as a select and privatized pastime.

Given the widespread taste among the aristocracy for both drama and self-dramatization, it is not surprising that the rose festivals quickly metamorphosed into plays and operettas for elite consumption. Such productions in the 1770s and 1780s seem to have been mostly produced and consumed by the social elites. The *Mémoires Secrets* scathingly described the marquis de Masson de Pezay, author of one of the most successful "rosière" plays, as a foppish wit (*bel esprit petit-maître*) who sported red heels and a fake title and fawned before the aristocracy.[32] Indeed, Masson de Pezay was a consummate courtier, the *arri-*

---

30. Jullien, *Le Théâtre à la cour*, pp. 142–145; Crow, *Painters and Public Life*, pp. 110–113; Pierre Augustin Caron de Beaumarchais, *Parades*, introduction by Pierre Larthomas (Paris: S.E.D.E.S., 1977), pp. 11–14.

31. Jullien, *La Comédie à la cour*, part 2, chaps. 1–7.

32. *Mémoires secrets pour servir à l'histoire de la république des lettres en France*, 36 vols. (London: J. Adamson, 1777–1789), 7:180.

viste son of an iron manufacturer who had wheedled his way into the position of military instructor to the future Louis XVI.[33] Pezay's *La Rosière de Salenci*, a pastoral in three acts, was performed before the elites of court and town, twice at Fontainebleau and nine times in Paris. The audience for the opening night at the Comédie-Italienne included the daughter-in-law, brother, and sister-in-law of the monarch.[34]

Not surprisingly, most of these plays culminated in an unabashed glorification of the social and political status quo. Sometimes the point was driven home explicitly, as for instance in the 1778 divertissement composed in Nantes to commemorate the count of Artois's establishment of a rosière festival in the town the previous year. The threadbare "plot" of *La Rosière d'Artois ou la vertueuse nantaise* has the beautiful shepherdess Rosine demonstrate her virtue by refusing to give in to her lover, Bastien. The amorous but chaste exchange between these rustic sweethearts serves mostly as a prelude to a lengthy panegyric to the count d'Artois, identified under the suitably antique pseudonym Daphnis.[35] Most of the other plays on this theme, whether written by amateurs or by professionals, revolve around a slightly more elaborate, if predictable, plot. An impeccably chaste young woman is to be honored as rosière and to wed the boy she loves, who is usually named Lucas, Colin, or Basile. On the eve of the ceremony, a crisis breaks out either in the form of a quid pro quo casting doubt on the young woman's virtue, or as the result of the predatory attentions of one of the seigneur's underlings; the confusion is resolved in extremis by the arrival of the lord, who crowns the rosière to the accompaniment of choral singing in which *seigneur* invariably rhymes with *bonheur.*

For the most part, these plays were aimed, not at delivering a social or moral message, but at providing light and pleasant entertainment. Most of them fall into the category known at the time as *opéra-comique,* a genre that grew out of the fusion of popular fair vaudeville with light opera.[36] Such productions usually took the form of short comedies written in prose, punctuated by singing and dancing interludes; they were

33. Robert D. Harris, *Necker: Reform Statesman of the Ancien Régime* (Berkeley: University of California Press, 1979), p. 100.

34. *Nouvelles extraordinaires de divers endroits (Gazette de Leyde),* 11 March 1774; Masson de Pezay, *La Rosière de Salenci* (Paris: Delalain, 1775), pp. vii, xviii-xix.

35. *La Rosière d'Artois ou la vertueuse nantaise* (Nantes: Despilly, and Paris: Veuve Duchêne, 1778).

36. Pierre Larthomas, *Le Théâtre en France au XVIIIe siècle* (Paris: Presses Universitaires de France, 1980), pp. 63–65.

usually set in some prettified village, and their plot revolved around the love, quarrels, and reconciliation of a pair of country lovers, as in Favart's *Annette et Lubin* (1762) or Sedaine's *Rose et Colas* (1764).[37] The rosière theme proved an ideal vehicle for the standard trappings of the opéra-comique: cottages, shepherds, cleverly engineered storms, and choirs of beribboned villagers.

Charles Favart, a playwright noted for his successes in the genre, penned one of the first plays about the virginal village queen. His *La Rosière de Salenci,* first performed at court in October of 1769, revolves around two young couples.[38] Hélène, the rosière-to-be, loves Colin; her friend Thérèse loves Thomas; Thomas imprudently tries to send Thérèse a letter and a ribbon, which are intercepted by Hélène's suspicious mother. Hélène quarrels with Colin and throws the ribbon at him, causing Thomas to conclude that *his* girl gave it to Colin. The seigneur's steward steps in and tries to claim Hélène as his bride, whereupon Colin collapses in a faint; and so on. Plays such as Favart's, with their flirtatious exchanges, stolen letters and pins, and pointlessly busy plots, remained very much within the conventions of eighteenth-century light comedy, sometimes set to music—as was Masson de Pezay's effort—by fashionable composers like Grétry. Although dutifully punctuated by appeals to virtue and seigneurial goodness, they culminated in implicitly sensual celebrations of love: "The festival of the rose is the festival of love" runs the refrain in Masson de Pezay's operetta.[39]

After 1771, however, in the wake of the trial, themes of power and social tension did make their way into the rosière plays. Later plays, which unambiguously cast the seigneur's bailiff as a scheming villain, inch away from the complexity of light comedy toward the Manichaean structure of the *drame.* Here and there the language of the courtroom echoes on stage, in tirades that refer to laws and rights. The wicked bailiff in *La Rosière de Rosny* has had the young girl's lover imprisoned for poaching. "Monseigneur," he protests to his lord, "I was only following the law." To which the seigneur retorts: "[The law] only exists

37. Charles Lenient, *La Comédie en France au XVIIIe siècle,* 2 vols. (Paris: Hachette, 1888), chaps. 21–23.

38. Charles Favart, *La Rosière de Salenci* (Paris: Veuve Duchesne, 1770); according to one contemporary this play, first performed in 1769, was the one on the theme of the rosière "dont le succès fut le moins contesté": Nougaret, *Les Rosières,* p. 28.

39. Masson de Pezay, *La Rosière de Salenci* (1773), in *Recueil de festes et spectacles donnés devant sa majesté à Versailles et à Choisy et Fontainebleau en 1773,* 2 vols. (Paris, 1773), 1:83–84.

to punish culprits; he who dispenses justice must know how to distinguish the criminal from the destitute, whose only crime is to seek subsistence."[40] In Masson de Pezay's play, the seigneur pointedly declares to the village elders upon arrival: "Old men, I do not come to usurp your rights / I know that in giving the crown / I must always confirm your choice."[41] What is remarkable, however, about the plays written after 1773 is the way in which they appropriate the fashionably progressive issues raised by the court case—village rights and the rule of law—and at the same time explicitly negate the central theme of the trial, namely, seigneurial usurpation. This sleight of hand is carried out by means of the ideological reflex common to most absolutist societies, which consists in affixing the blame for social or political dysfunction to the ruler's emissaries or underlings. The more villainous the steward or bailiff, the better the demonstration, in the final scene, of the enlightened seigneur's benevolence and justice.

Had a Diderot or a Mercier tried his hand at making the rose festival into a *drame*, something quite different might have resulted. Without the *ariettes*, the benevolent squires, and the conventions that made female virginity into an excuse for mild titillation, the story could have been rewritten as a parable of social inequality and sexual exploitation. But this did not happen. In its theatrical incarnation, the rosière story remained wedded to the form of the opéra-comique, a type of entertainment that carried distinctly upper-class connotations. Both the style and the content of the rosière plays ultimately became so vacuously repetitive that the theme eventually spawned its own parodies. Such is the case in Fonpré de Fracansalle's *La Rosière à la mode*, in which the rose-girl Colette is so far from being a virgin that she has long before the crowning given birth to a fat and healthy baby boy. The easygoing seigneur accepts the situation, philosophically observing: "What can we expect from the weakness of youth? Let us reward her merit, and her talent at dissembling."[42]

Only one play on the theme, penned by the radical playwright and art critic Louis de Carmontelle, can be considered an authentically subversive effort. A biting satire of aristocratic self-promotion, Carmon-

40. "La Rosière de Rosny, comédie en trois actes par un amateur" (1783), Bibliothèque Nationale Ms. Fr. 9264, Act II, sc. 2.

41. Masson de Pezay, *La Rosière de Salenci*, p. 30.

42. Fonpré de Fracansalle, "La Rosière à la mode," n.d., Bibliothèque Nationale Ms. Fr. 9270.

telle's *La Rosière* is set not in some prettified village but in the salon of Mme de Bréville.[43] The latter has decided to found a rosière festival on her estate, but her main concern is with the looks and attire of her rosière, for, as she explains to her friend Mme de Favières, "I would like my peasant boys and girls to look like the ones at the opera."[44] The village curé, who has been dispatched to locate a queen of virtue in the village, announces that he has found several candidates, prompting Mme de Bréville to query suspiciously: "They are ugly, are they not, little priest?" "That is to say, they are graced with the charms of virtue," stammers the curé. "I knew it, they are horrible!" exclaims the lady. The curé goes on to suggest that Mme de Bréville cannot have free rein in choosing the rosière, who must be selected by the assembly of villagers, "the voice of the people." "Oh, the people," sneers Mme de Bréville, "they will do what I want!"[45] The end of the play has Mme de Bréville mercifully giving up her plans—which involved giving out straw bonnets with ribbons to the village boys and girls "to protect their complexions"—and taking off for the theater with her friends.[46] Carmontelle's exposure of selfish upper-class frivolity is in its own way quite effective. But by using the theater to satirize theatrical posturing, he simply sends up the whole process from within instead of challenging it from without. Understandably perhaps, neither he nor any other playwright was willing or able to recast the meaning of the rose festival, to redefine it in Rousseauean terms as a negation of the very essence of aristocratic theatricality.

Any attempt to link the rosières movement to a specific ideological faction or movement within the educated upper-class world of prerevolutionary France is likely to run up against difficulties arising from the social and ideological fluidity of that very world. William Everdell, for instance, has argued that the Salency festival grew out of the efforts of a group associated with the writer Elie Fréron's anti-*philosophe* journal,

43. Very little is known of the life of the playwright Carmontelle (1717–1806), by his real name Louis Carrogis, son of a Parisian shoemaker. He published most of his plays between 1768 and 1781, although it is not known when exactly he wrote them. *La Rosière* seems to fall within the genre that one critic has called *comédie dénigrante*—a sort of dramatization of nasty gossip: Jean-Hervé Donnard, *Le Théâtre de Carmontelle* (Paris: Armand Colin, 1967), pp. 8–9, 16–19.

44. Louis de Carmontelle, *Proverbes et comédies posthumes*, 3 vols. (Paris: Ladvocat, 1825), 2:324.

45. Ibid., 2:325–326.

46. Ibid., 2:327, 351–352.

L'Année littéraire, and that the movement's strong religious underpinnings can be viewed as a clerical response to Voltairean skepticism.[47] As further evidence of the movement's conservatism, Everdell points to the prominent role played by the lawyer Elie de Beaumont, treasurer of the comte d'Artois, in founding rosière festivals in Normandy.[48] Artois, of course, was to become one of the most vociferous defenders of aristocratic privilege in 1789, soon fleeing the country to organize the counterrevolution from abroad. Elie de Beaumont, however, was mostly famous in the 1770s for having lent his assistance to Voltaire during the Calas affair.[49] And what are we to make of the alleged conservatism of the Genlis circle, when we learn that a few years later Mme de Genlis served as governess to the children of the duc d'Orléans, the same duke who subsidized radical pamphleteers in 1789, later took the name Philippe-Egalité, and voted for the death of his cousin, the former king?[50] Orléans himself had close connections with the rosières movement: the foundation at Romainville, which flourished between 1775 and 1788, was headed by a society of noblemen and administrators associated with the Compagnie des Indes, a group that may have included the duke himself.[51]

The inescapable conclusion seems to be that the rosière festivals were directly or indirectly headed by a broad cross section of the French elites; that although molded by the cultural style of the aristocracy, these celebrations of virtue brought together individuals quite disparate in their social origins, occupations, and precise ideological leanings. They included members of the royal family, such as Artois and Orléans; fa-

47. Everdell, "The Rosières Movement," passim. The main thrust of Everdell's argument is that the rosières movement represented a prerevolutionary attempt at creating a civic religion based on virtue, in response to the anticlericalism of the philosophes. The suggestion is not at all implausible, since there is plenty of evidence for reading the festivals in this way, but it fails to take into account the many other possible meanings of this phenomenon. The rosière, it is argued here, was a malleable symbol, which could accommodate a range of overlapping or indeed contradictory ideological messages; its trappings, for instance, were incorporated into the antireligious Festival of Reason of 1793. Everdell's argument, in short, does not so much misrepresent the meaning of these festivals as oversimplify it.

48. Ibid., p. 28.

49. A contemporary, Nougaret, identified Elie de Beaumont as a "célèbre avocat au barreau de Paris, principalement illustre par son mémoire pour les Calas": *Les Rosières,* p. 43. See also David Bien, *The Calas Affair: Persecution, Toleration, and Heresy in Eighteenth-Century Toulouse* (Princeton: Princeton University Press, 1960), p. 135.

50. Wyndham, *Madame de Genlis,* chap. 4–8.

51. Guillot, "La Rosière de Suresnes," p. 18.

mous lawyers like Elie de Beaumont and Jean-Baptiste Target; enlightened members of the clergy who later sided with the Third Estate, such as Henri Grégoire and Claude Fauchet; and members of interest groups like the Compagnie des Indes, or of voluntary associations like the Freemasonry.[52] A roll call of all those involved in the movement over a decade would read like a who's who of well-heeled, well-educated, and enlightened France.

Nor would it do to set up simple equations between social class, on the one hand, and aesthetic or moral "style," on the other. The traditional view, for instance, which saw in the flouncy hedonism of rococo art a quintessential expression of "aristocratic" taste, as opposed to the "bourgeois" moralism of a Chardin, a Greuze, or a Diderot, is hard to sustain upon closer examination. No doubt François Boucher, the foremost painter of the French rococo, owed much of his fame and fortune to the tight-knit clan of wealthy parvenus around Mme de Pompadour—an "aristocracy" of money and taste, if not of lineage. But Pompadour's brother, the marquis de Marigny, as Directeur général des bâtiments, also personally sponsored the young Jean-Baptiste Greuze, whose dark-hued, lachrymose family scenes were promoted by this moneyed upper crust as replacements for traditional history painting.[53] It would not be too farfetched to see in the swooning fiancée in Greuze's *Village Bride* (1761), with her white dress, pink rose, and chastely lowered eyes, one of the many prototypes for the rosière: both fictions originated within exactly the same milieu of wealthy and self-dramatizing elites.

Sentimental moralizing, then, was far from being a characteristically "bourgeois" stance; nor can one draw a sharp distinction between libertine sensuality, on the one hand, and the cult of emotion, on the other, given the ease with which, in this post-Lockean cultural universe, the one shaded into the other. As anyone acquainted with the writings of Diderot, Laclos, and Rousseau will know, the line between pure sexual pleasure and the higher delights of moral sentiment was one that became easily blurred. (In the episode of Laclos's novel discussed above, Valmont admits, with cheerful cynicism, to getting sensual pleasure out of his act of charity, phoney as it was: "I felt within me an unwonted but delicious emotion. I was astonished at the pleasure to be derived from doing good, and I am now tempted to think that what we call

52. Ibid., pp.18–19.
53. Crow, *Painters and Public Life*, pp. 104–113, 134–147.

virtuous people have less claim to merit than we are led to believe.")[54] At once erotic and virtuous, the rosière, like Greuze's pulpous virgins, was an ideal object of desire for those unable or unwilling to draw the line between sensuality and *sensibilité*.

In the course of the trial, however, the rosière became something quite different. From the visual—indeed, almost palpable—center of a highly theatricalized ritual, she was transformed into a political abstraction whose essence could only be conveyed through words, rather than images; and one cannot make sense of this transformation by appealing to classic distinctions between "libertinism" and "moralism," or between "aristocratic" and "bourgeois" culture. The shift in the meaning of the Salency festival precipitated by the trial is more intelligible within the terms suggested by Marie-Hélène Huet, who argues that under the Revolution the administration of justice shifted "from the order of figuration to the order of representation," that is, from image to sign, or from icon to abstract representation.[55] It has been suggested, in other words, that in the later eighteenth century the traditional symbolism of power, which centered on the visible, theatricalized body of the father-king, was displaced by a competing semiotic system, which vested social authority in such linguistic abstractions as "public opinion" or "the Law."[56]

If it is easy enough to point to signs that such a change took place over the long run—the Salency case, as we shall see, provides one striking example—it is much harder to discover and describe the social dimensions of this profound cultural mutation. Although few historians would feel comfortable today in ascribing this transformation, as Jürgen Habermas did a generation ago, to the rise of something labeled "the

54. Laclos, *Liaisons Dangereuses,* p. 58.

55. Marie-Hélène Huet, *Rehearsing the Revolution: The Staging of Marat's Death, 1793–1797,* trans. Robert Hurley (Berkeley: University of California Press, 1982), pp. 49–58; for a fuller discussion along these lines, see Joan Landes, *Women and the Public Sphere in the Age of the French Revolution* (Ithaca: Cornell University Press, 1988), chap. 2.

56. This argument owes a great deal to the arguments of Jürgen Habermas's analysis in *The Structural Transformation of the Public Sphere,* trans. Thomas Burger and Frederick Lawrence (Cambridge, Mass: MIT Press, 1989); independently of Habermas, similar ideas were formulated by Furet over a decade ago in his influential *Penser la révolution française* (Paris: Gallimard, 1978); Furet's ideas are both developed and challenged in Lynn Hunt's *Politics, Culture and Class in the French Revolution* (Berkeley: University of California Press, 1984); Hunt does not explicitly address one outstanding problem, that of the tension between the predominance of rhetoric in revolutionary culture and the visual, iconic nature of revolutionary festivals.

bourgeois public sphere," it does not follow that we should jettison the attempt to write a social history of the changing eighteenth-century public sphere. Where the story of the Salency festival is concerned, one social group does appear to have played a determining role in recasting the meaning of the festival: the transformation of the rosière from a visual to a textual symbol seems to have been intimately linked to the presence and activity of members of the legal profession both in the course of the trial and in the festivals themselves.

One of the first festivals of the rosière type set up in the wake of the trial was the "Fête of the good people" founded by a wealthy lawyer, Elie de Beaumont, on his estate at Canon. Guests of honor at the first banquet included, besides the designated good-girl and good-old-man, a collection of local seigneurs and the man who was at the time probably the most famous trial lawyer in France, Jean-Baptiste Target.[57] Target, as we shall see, had just buttressed his growing reputation by taking on the defense of the rosière and villagers of Salency against their seigneur. Other men of law, albeit much lesser luminaries than Target, were often important figures on the committees that set up rosière festivals after the mid-1770s. The first founders in Romainville in 1774 were local magistrates: an *avocat au parlement*, a judge, and a fiscal attorney; the foundations at La Falaise and Suresnes were set up by members of the nobility of the robe, families of ennobled lawyers and judges at the Paris Parlement.[58]

In the wake of the trial that took place in 1774, men of law emerged as prominent among the many groups—including rural and urban nobles, clergymen, and men and women of letters—that had a stake in the rose festivals. Members of the legal profession, it seems, used the occasion of the trial to appropriate the rural maiden as a symbol of its own, a symbol that was later to have considerable political repercussions. In order to understand how this came about, and the role played by lawyers in this case as in others, we must explore in some detail the social backgrounds, culture, ambitions, and ideologies of the men of law whose writings were shaping this and other causes célèbres.

The fact that many historians have been interested in the eighteenth-century legal profession is not surprising, given the extremely conspicu-

---

57. Nougaret, *Les Rosières,* pp. 43–60.
58. Guillot, "La Rosière de Suresnes," pp. 14, 25, 30.

ous role played by some of its members from the very beginning of the Revolution. No matter where one looks, beginning in 1789, lawyers seem to be everywhere: in the provinces they often made up between 70 and 90 percent of the members of the local committees that drafted the *cahiers de doléances;* in Paris 68 of the 407 electors who chose deputies for the Third Estate were *avocats au parlement,* as were 23 of the 120 members of the new municipal government set up in July.[59] Within the Estates-General the prominence of lawyers was even more striking, since at least half of the deputies of the Third Estate, it has been estimated, were legal practitioners, and this carried over into the Constituent Assembly, 444 of whose 648 members were lawyers or legally trained officers.[60]

If lawyers played such an important role, both individually and collectively, in the political effervescence of 1789, does this mean that they somehow contributed to bringing about the Revolution, that they formed the core of the ever-elusive "revolutionary bourgeoisie"? This question has been at the heart of several fine studies of the legal profession in eighteenth-century France, and the answer to it has almost invariably been negative.[61] The typical eighteenth-century French lawyer was not an overeducated, frustrated, ambitious young barrister, eager for leadership and chomping at the bit, but a rather prosperous, sedate, and well-integrated member of the urban establishment.

The social origins of lawyers, for instance, were not such as to suggest rapid or disruptive upward or downward mobility. Whether in Paris or

---

59. Roger Chartier, *The Cultural Uses of Print in Early Modern France,* translated by Lydia Cochrane (Princeton: Princeton University Press, 1987), p. 112; Michael Fitzsimmons, *The Parisian Order of Barristers and the French Revolution* (Cambridge, Mass.: Harvard University Press, 1987), pp. 35–40.

60. André Damien, *Les Avocats du temps passé* (Paris: Henri Lefebvre, 1973), p. 163; Alfred Cobban, *Aspects of the French Revolution* (New York: George Braziller, 1968), pp. 90–111.

61. The most notable of these recent studies are Lenard Berlanstein, *The Barristers of Toulouse in the Eighteenth Century (1740–1793)* (Baltimore: Johns Hopkins University Press, 1975); Maurice Gresset, *Gens de justice à Besançon,* 2 vols. (Paris: Bibliothèque Nationale, 1978); Albert Poirot, "Le Milieu socio-professionnel des Avocats du Parlement de Paris à la veille de la Révolution (1760–1790)," 2 vols., thesis, Ecole Nationale des Chartes, Paris, 1977; Richard Kagan, "Law Students and Legal Careers in Eighteenth-Century France," *Past and Present* 68 (August 1975): 38–72; Fitzsimmons, *The Parisian Order of Barristers.* For a recent synthesis, see Lenard Berlanstein, "Lawyers in Pre-Revolutionary France," in Wilfred Prest, ed., *Lawyers in Early Modern Europe and America* (New York: Holmes and Meier, 1981), pp. 164–180. The most recent contribution to this literature is David Bell's important dissertation, "Lawyers and Politics in Eighteenth-Century France" (Ph.D. diss., Princeton University, 1991).

the provinces, lawyers were usually the sons of other lawyers, or of members of similarly middling urban groups such as office-holding administrators or petty rentiers, more rarely the offspring of wealthy merchants; only a tenth of them on average came from noble families (in Paris 20 percent of the barristers' order claimed nobility) while almost none were the children of peasants or laborers.[62]

The middle-class youth who was to pursue a legal career in the eighteenth century would enroll in a law faculty in his late teens or early twenties. Although the legal curriculum had been overhauled in 1679 by Colbert in an effort to improve the quality of the education dispensed to future lawyers, many law schools remained poorly managed and attended. In theory the three-year curriculum marched students through a rigorous program of Roman, canon, and French law, but in practice many students did little more than enroll every semester. Most budding lawyers seem to have learned the rudiments either from their families or by working as clerks, and there were plenty of indulgent or corrupt faculties willing to confer degrees on absentee students. The lawyer's real education was acquired on the job, especially in the three to seven years after graduation when he worked under another lawyer as a so-called *avocat écoutant*.[63]

A young lawyer prepared in this way to enter a life of comfortable respectability similar, in many cases, to that led by his father and grandfather. In most towns he would be permitted to join the local corporate body, the "order" or "community" of lawyers. In Paris, he would most likely hope for admission among the five to six hundred members of the prestigious Ordre des Avocats attached to the Parlement; entry into that body required the recommendation of six senior lawyers, the payment of a thirty-livre fee, and an elaborate oath-swearing ceremony.[64] In the capital, a few sought-after trial lawyers could edge their way into the upper classes and live like seigneurs: Jean-Baptiste Gerbier, the star of the Paris bar in the 1750s and 1760s, was a regular guest at Mme Geoffrin's salon, entertained artists, writers, and musicians in his

---

62. Kagan, "Law Students and Legal Careers," pp. 53–61; Poirot, "Avocats au Parlement" 2:118–125; Berlanstein, *Barristers of Toulouse,* pp. 34–35; "Lawyers in Prerevolutionary France," p. 167; Bell, "Lawyers and Politics," pp. 37–48.

63. Kagan, "Law Students and Legal Careers," pp. 40–42; Berlanstein, "Lawyers in Pre-Revolutionary France," pp. 167–168; Poirot, "Avocats au Parlement" 2:7–13.

64. Berlanstein, "Lawyers in Pre-revolutionary France," pp. 170–171; Poirot, "Avocats au Parlement" 1:14–31.

home, and married his daughter off to a count.[65] The small number of barristers who worked on retainer for important clients or for institutions, such as churches, towns, or universities, could also enjoy large and steady incomes—Linguet, for instance, was reputed to have raked in 23,000 livres in the late 1760s for his defense of the duc d'Aiguillon.[66]

If such incomes were highly unusual, so, it seems, was dire poverty. In provincial towns like Toulouse, Besançon, and Lyon, lawyers made on average a comfortable five to six thousand livres a year from their practices (in Toulouse the usual fee for a case ranged from twenty-five to eighty livres), often enjoyed additional income from bonds or rents, and left fortunes at death averaging between thirty and forty thousand livres.[67] In Paris the range of incomes and fortunes was, as might be expected, much more spread out: about one-quarter of the Paris barristers lived in or close to poverty, while another quarter were very wealthy men whose fortunes exceeded a hundred thousand livres.[68]

In general, however, whether in Besançon, Toulouse, or Paris, the picture that emerges is one of a group of men comfortably well off, fiercely attached to their corporate traditions and prerogatives, and acutely aware of their position within the rigid pecking order of the broader legal milieu. Barristers felt distinctly superior to the more specialized practitioners like attorneys and clerks (procureurs and gréffiers or clercs), who did most of the routine paper shuffling in preparation for a case; but they were also keenly aware of the considerable distance that separated them from the wealthy and aristocratic magistrates of the parlements, to whom they were regularly enjoined to demonstrate "respect and submission." Although lawyers shared in the common social ideal of ennoblement through landownership, office holding, and marriage, they never openly challenged the rigid caste division between the bar and the aristocratic magistracy, and social contacts or mobility be-

65. Poirot, "Avocats au Parlement" 2:167–168; Francis Delbèke, L'Action politique et sociale des avocats au XVIIIe siècle: Leur part dans la préparation de la Révolution française (Paris: Sirey, 1927), pp. 106–107, 119–120.

66. Fitzsimmons, The Order of Barristers, p. 20; Damien, Avocats du temps passé, pp. 135–141; Poirot, "Avocats au Parlement" 2:94–100.

67. Berlanstein, Barristers of Toulouse, pp. 27–49, and "Lawyers in Pre-revolutionary France," p. 168; Gresset, Gens de Justice à Besançon 1:323–442; see table, p. 442.

68. Poirot, "Avocats au Parlement" 2:128–140.

tween the two groups remained, up to the end of the Old Regime, highly unusual.[69]

Finally, most barristers appear in the end to have been as attached to the political as to the social status quo. Most of the lawyers of Toulouse, for instance, although initially sympathetic to revolutionary change, soon began actively or passively to resist the social and political upheavals of the 1790s: only 54 of the town's 276 barristers remained active in support of the Revolution in the early 1790s, while some went over to the counterrevolution.[70] In Paris, similarly, a majority of barristers eventually turned against the Revolution, especially after their order was abolished in 1790. Shaped by and devoted to the corporate ethos of the Old Regime, most lawyers were disoriented and antagonized by the revolutionary and Napoleonic regimes' subordination of the legal profession to the state.[71]

It seems difficult, then, to view the legal profession as a whole as the embryo of a "revolutionary bourgeoisie," or even as a social "stress zone" whose ambitious but underprivileged members longed to overhaul the status quo. But to deny that the legal profession, or at least certain segments of it, had a significant impact on the changing political culture of late-eighteenth-century France would be falling victim to teleological reasoning or to the tyranny of numbers. The fact that so many barristers eventually resisted the revolutionary process does not necessarily mean that they did not contribute to its beginnings: like other groups, such as parlementary magistrates or liberal nobles, lawyers contributed in significant ways to the onset of a dynamic that eventually proved more radical than they had wished or anticipated. Furthermore, the social and political attitudes of the mass of lawyers may matter less, in certain respects, than the beliefs and behavior of an active and visible minority of their number.

Whatever the attitudes of its individual members, the legal profession was more conspicuously present in social and cultural life after 1750 than it had ever been before. For one thing, the number of lawyers in the realm increased significantly after 1750, even more rapidly than the rising population. In Besançon the number of names on the Tableau

<hr/>

69. Berlanstein, *The Barristers of Toulouse,* pp. 5–6, and "Lawyers in Pre-revolutionary France," pp. 165–167; Fitzsimmons, *The Order of Barristers,* pp. 2–3; Delbèke, *L'Action politique et sociale,* chap. 4; Poirot, "Avocats au Parlement" 2:19, 121–125.

70. Berlanstein, *The Barristers of Toulouse,* chap. 6.

71. Fitzsimmons, *The Parisian Order of Barristers.*

des Avocats jumped from 82 in 1735 to 134 in 1783; in Toulouse there were 87 barristers attached to the parlement in 1740, 215 on the eve of the Revolution.[72] Nationally, both matriculations in and graduations from law schools increased rapidly after 1750, reaching a peak in the 1770s and 1780s, and outstripping the overall rise in the population. As Richard Kagan suggests, this rise in numbers, which seems also to have affected rural areas, probably both reflected and contributed to an increase in the recourse to litigation, especially in the countryside, since "just as litigation breeds lawyers, so do lawyers breed litigation."[73]

Evidence from Burgundy, for instance, shows that starting in the mid-eighteenth century, peasant communities more and more frequently took to contesting seigneurial prerogatives and authority in court, and that many lawyers acquired expertise and a whole new vocabulary by serving as counsel in such disputes.[74] When the villagers of Salency brought their conflict with their lord before the authorities of the local *bailliage*, their action was hardly unique in the mid-1770s, whereas it would have been highly unusual just a few decades earlier. The Salency case was exceptional, however, in that it was appealed to the Parlement of Paris and thus fell into the hands of lawyers associated with the institution that stood in the eye of the political storms of the mid-1770s; this, more than anything, explains the politicization of what had begun as an unremarkable dispute between a rural squire and his villagers.

Lawyers made up one of the most highly educated groups in eighteenth-century society, and many of them were cautiously open to new ideas. In the provinces as well as in Paris, leading barristers owned sizable collections of books, ranging from theology and jurisprudence to literature and history; many of them read and appreciated the philosophes—Voltaire was especially popular—championed religious tolerance, and believed in enlightened reform.[75] On the whole, however, the ideological leanings of the majority of barristers remained as timid as their social and political stances: they were progressive enough to see the need for reform, but most would have been horrified at the thought

72. Gresset, *Gens de justice à Besançon* 1:93; Berlanstein, *The Barristers of Toulouse*, p. 12.

73. Kagan, "Law Students and Legal Careers," pp. 62–68.

74. Hilton Root, *Peasants and King in Burgundy: Agrarian Foundations of French Absolutism* (Berkeley: University of California Press, 1987), pp. 155–169, 183–192.

75. Berlanstein, *Barristers of Toulouse*, pp. 99–122; Poirot, "Avocats au Parlement" 2:187–200.

of an overhaul of the judicial system, or indeed of the social order in which they were so comfortably ensconced.[76]

Given their social situation, however, many lawyers could hardly escape political involvement, and this was especially true of members of the Parisian Ordre des Avocats, whose work associated them closely with the Parlement of Paris. As soon as the Parlement regained its right of remonstrance, following the death of Louis XIV, it resumed its pattern of political obstructionism; and in every one of the many collisions between the high courts and the royal government that took place from the 1720s to the 1770s, the *avocats au parlement* demonstrated in word and deed their loyalty to the magistrates. From July to December of 1720, for instance, the Paris lawyers suspended their work after the Regent exiled the Parlement to Pontoise for refusing to register a series of financial edicts.[77] From the 1730s through the 1750s, the *avocats* remained steadfast supporters of the *parlementaires* through the increasingly bitter disputes that opposed crown and law courts over the rights of Jansenists—all the more so since many of the leading barristers, like some of the most prominent magistrates, were Jansenists or Jansenist sympathizers themselves.[78]

As we have seen, it was within the context of the decades-long struggle over the papal bull Unigenitus that the Paris bar began to emerge as a forceful political ally to the dissenting magistrates. In 1730, for instance, a famous brief in defense of three Jansenist priests of the diocese of Orléans, signed by forty Parisian barristers, argued its parliamentary-constitutional case in incendiary terms: "It is therefore because the parlements, composed of both ecclesiastical and secular orders, are by nature representative of public authority, that they may reform acts of both lay and ecclesiastical jurisdiction that impinge upon the laws of the State."[79] Despite a volley of royal and ecclesiastical edicts sup-

---

76. Berlanstein, "Lawyers in Pre-revolutionary France," pp. 172–174.

77. Joachim Gaudry, *Histoire du Barreau de Paris* (Paris: Auguste Durand, 1864; reprint Geneva: Slatkine, 1977), pp. 122–126.

78. See Dale Van Kley, *The Jansenists and the Expulsion of the Jesuits from France, 1757–1765* (New Haven: Yale University Press, 1975), chap. 2.

79. *Mémoire pour les sieurs Samson, curé d'Olivet . . . et autres ecclésiastiques contre Monsieur l'évêque d'Orléans, et autres archevêques et évêques de différens diocèses . . .* (Paris: Lottin, 1730), in Bibliothèque Nationale, Collection Anisson, vol. 22090, item 49, vol. 2. On the background of the *affaire des quarante avocats,* see Van Kley, *The Jansenists,* p. 57; Gaudry, *Histoire du barreau,* pp. 138–139; and esp. Bell, "Lawyers and Politics," pp. 166–179.

pressing it, the heretical brief nonetheless circulated widely, as a near-contemporary, Jean-François Fournel, reported, albeit no doubt with some exaggeration: "The brief of the forty lawyers had become the object of universal curiosity; it could be found in every house and was avidly read, even by women. . . . Horsemen of the *maréchaussée* scoured the highways, the countryside, and the farmhouses to remove copies that might be found there."[80]

The political radicalization of a certain number of barristers, in Paris especially, in connection with such religious controversies must be connected to the "Jansenization" of the bar itself, which by the middle of the century, according to Dale Van Kley, "was beginning to replace the Parisian magistracy itself as the lay stronghold of Jansenism."[81] Robert de Saint-Vincent, a leading Jansenist magistrate, surmised that educated young men with Augustinian leanings, unable to enter the priesthood, which now required that they swear obeisance to the Unigenitus Bull, turned instead to the bar, which demanded no such oath of them.[82] This may have been true of the most influential Jansenist lawyer of the century, Adrien Le Paige, whose two uncles and one great-uncle were clerics who resisted the Bull. Le Paige followed in his father's footsteps to become a lawyer in the Parlement of Paris, secured the protection of a powerful grandee, the prince de Conti, and emerged as one of the leading theoreticians of the political resistance to the Maupeou coup.[83] David Bell's careful examination of the Parisian Ordre des Avocats in the first half of the century concludes that although the number of avowed Jansenists among the barristers was in fact very small (fifteen or so at any given time), their influence was far in excess of their numbers.[84]

Both vertical loyalties within the judicial world and a common allegiance to, or sympathy with, the dissident Augustinian faith thus cemented the political solidarity between magistrates and barristers in Paris and elsewhere. This solidarity was expressed, of course, in opposition to the will of the monarchy and its ministers, and it manifested itself most dramatically, as we saw in the preceding chapter, during the Maupeou crisis of the early 1770s, when the Parisian lawyers and some

80. Jean François Fournel, *Histoire des avocats au Parlement et du Barreau de Paris depuis Saint Louis jusqu'au 15 octobre 1790*, 2 vols. (Paris: Maradem, 1813), 2:463–464.

81. Van Kley, *The Jansenists*, p. 58.

82. Ibid.

83. Ibid., pp. 60–61.

84. Bell, "Lawyers and Politics," pp. 129–139.

of their provincial colleagues suspended their functions in solidarity with the disbanded magistrates.[85] But while the Maupeou crisis saw a continuation, indeed a culmination, of the established political solidarity between the bar and the magistracy, it also can be viewed as the turning point that marked the end of that alliance: after midcentury, and especially after 1771, many signs point to growing tensions, both between magistrates and lawyers and among the barristers themselves.

The Calas affair of 1762 brought some of these incipient tensions to light, as Voltaire recruited talented young lawyers, Sudre in Toulouse and Elie de Beaumont in Paris, to assist him in his crusade against the obscurantism of the Toulousan magistrates. The subsequent unfolding of the case, as the alliance between philosophes and lawyers triumphed over the incompetence and prejudice of the judges, publicly dramatized what the patriarch had expressed privately in a letter of 1762: "A learned and respected barrister is certainly superior to those who have acquired for a bit of money the right to be unjust; such a lawyer would make an excellent magistrate; but where is the magistrate who would make a good lawyer?"[86] By the late 1760s, a famous trial lawyer like Jean-Baptiste Gerbier had acquired such personal renown that court grandees came to his house to beg him to defend them, and that the king of Denmark, on a state visit, insisted on meeting him and on hearing him plead.[87]

From the 1760s to the eve of the Revolution, there were unmistakable signs of the growing status and influence of certain barristers, and of the animosity that the most talented and ambitious among them felt toward the parliamentary aristocracy from which they were excluded. Tradition had it that the bar was a stepping-stone toward the magistracy, which indeed was originally true. A venerable handbook for lawyers, *Règles pour former un avocat*, devoted a lengthy chapter to detailing the many claims to nobility enjoyed by lawyers, beginning with the fact that the legal profession was "a necessary degree for acceding to all of the

85. In provincial parlementary towns as well as in Paris, barristers mostly acted in support of the local magistrates against the government's decisions; see Gresset, *Gens de justice à Besançon* 2:704–715; in Toulouse the magistracy was divided and indecisive, and the lawyers' resistance as a result was more timid.

86. Cited in Delbèke, *L'Action politique et sociale des avocats,* p. 103. See also Poirot, "Avocats au Parlement" 2:216–217.

87. Poirot, "Avocats au Parlement" 2:219–220.

positions within the magistracy."[88] In the eighteenth century, there were still some lawyers who believed that this sort of social promotion was possible. In the early nineteenth century Pierre-Nicolas Berryer remembered toiling over his cases as a young man: "I was stimulated by the stories that were told to us daily of the great fortunes to which lawyers in every epoch had acceded, by the sole power of their talents. In every age of the monarchy, the bar had been the seedbed of the magistracy: the most illustrious families of the parlement had no other origin."[89]

Many other lawyers, however, believed that the venality of offices introduced by the Bourbon kings had driven a wedge between two groups whose social origins and professional functions were in fact very similar, so that industrious talent found itself in effect subordinated to hereditary incompetence. Ambroise Falconnet, the Vérons' defender, wrote in 1773 of the frustration experienced by lawyers who saw young men without talent or experience succeed their fathers to prestigious positions within the parlements.[90] In 1777, François Chavray de Boissy pointedly explained that "the lawyer acts alone, without outside help, owing nothing to such fleeting shadows as birth, heredity, credit, venality, or blind fate. All of his glory is personal, all of it drawn from his own resources."[91]

Despite ostentatious displays of political solidarity in the face of ministerial or royal "despotism," the relationship between magistrates and lawyers in the eighteenth century was often one of latent tension or even open conflict. In Paris, strains between the two groups became manifest as early as the 1730s. There were tensions over the "convulsionaries," illuminated Augustinians who went into trances and practiced self-mutilation (barristers, Le Paige prominently, supported them, while magistrates kept a prudent distance), and tussles over honorific

88. Antoine-Gaspard Boucher d'Argis, *Règles pour former un avocat tirées des plus célèbres auteurs anciens et modernes* (Paris: Durand, 1778), chap. 19; quote p. 189. Boucher d'Argis was not in fact the main author of this volume, which was written in 1711 by Biarnoy de Merville; as the preface explains, Boucher merely added a prefatory "Histoire abrégée de l'ordre des avocats" to the older text.

89. Pierre Nicolas Berryer, *Souvenirs de M. Berryer, doyen des avocats de Paris de 1774 à 1848*, 2 vols (Paris: Ambroise Dupont, 1839), 1:87–88.

90. Ambroise Falconnet, *Essai sur le barreau grec, romain, et français* (1773), cited in Poirot, "Avocats au Parlement" 2:218.

91. François René Chavray de Boissy, *L'Avocat ou réflexions sur l'exercice du barreau* (Paris: Louis Cellot, 1777), pp. 204–205.

matters.[92] The same was true in Besançon, where in the 1730s the town's lawyers lodged an official protest at having to address the magistrates as "Nosseigneurs" rather than simply "Messieurs," explaining in a written brief that "the magistrate is no more useful [to society] than is the lawyer."[93] In eighteenth-century Besançon, more and more barristers came from outside the town—over half of them in 1783, in contrast to one-quarter a century earlier—while only well-established native families, if not exclusively nobles, could hope to join the ranks of the parlement.[94] The widening social gap between lawyers and magistrates in Besançon became particularly conspicuous in about 1780, when the parlement refused to register the royal decree abolishing the *mainmorte,* a particularly onerous feudal right from which many of the magistrates, as substantial landowners, drew profits. It had become increasingly common even before that date for barristers to take on the defense of village communities against landlords who sought to revive or increase their seigneurial rights, and in the 1780s many of them continued to uphold the interests of communities against the *mainmorte.* The squabble over the *mainmorte* thus reinforced, in this local context, the perception that the parliamentary magistrates had the same interests as the landowning nobility, while the barristers were the champions of an oppressed peasantry.[95]

Nor was the situation in Franche-Comté atypical of developments in the rest of the realm, as the near-contemporary case of the Salency rosière, and the examples from Burgundy cited earlier, also suggest. In many places, lawyers were asserting their social and ideological independence from the magistracy by posing as defenders of an idealized rural *peuple.* Chavray de Boissy, again, expressed this with hyperbolic eloquence in the late 1770s when he exhorted his fellow lawyers: "Let us courageously take the defense of this people eternally crushed with burdens, of laborers, of these country-folk always prostrate, collapsing to the ground, yes, to this ground soaked with their tears or their sweat, but which serves to fatten the indolent proprietor; of all those, in sum, whose arduous labors are the subsistence and the support of the state."[96]

It would not do, of course, to conclude on a simplistic scenario of

92. Bell, "Lawyers and Politics," pp. 194–206.
93. Gresset, *Gens de justice à Besançon* 2:718–720.
94. Ibid., 2:722–724.
95. Ibid., 2:727–742.
96. Chavray de Boissy, *L'Avocat,* p. 178.

social conflict pitting the peasantry and its barrister champions against an alliance of seigneurs and magistrates, for reality was in fact a good deal more complex. In the mid-1770s, as we have seen, one prominent Parisian lawyer, Elie de Beaumont, was entertaining court grandees on his seigneurial estate at Canon, while his friend Target was defending the villagers of Salency. Rather, the involvement of lawyers with village communities reflects the growing size and social "presence" of the legal profession as a whole; at the same time, the high-minded rhetoric of social justice that accompanied such disputes was symptomatic of the barristers' increasing social and ideological independence from the magistracy. The fact that many, perhaps most, barristers eventually turned against the Revolution should not blind us to the crucial role played by members of the legal profession in shaping the public discourse of prerevolutionary France.

This detour through the social history of the legal profession is aimed at providing a context for understanding why lawyers, especially *avocats au parlement*, sometimes used even minor cases like that of the rosière as vehicles for the articulation of social and political grievances or ideals. The social and political consciousness of barristers associated with the high courts, especially that of Paris, grew out of their ambiguous and increasingly volatile relationship with the magistrates. On the one hand, lawyers had acquired radical political ideas through their alliance with *parlementaires* in struggles over taxation, Jansenism, and against ministerial "despotism"; on the other hand, their growing resentment of and independence from those very same magistrates may well have played an important part in the barristers' espousal of an antielitist social rhetoric. The combination was eventually to prove quite explosive. In the summer and fall of 1774, however, the recent death of Louis XV, the dismissal of his hated ministers, and the recall of the old Paris Parlement kept political issues very much in the forefront of people's concerns. It was these issues—about iniquitous authority and national regeneration—rather than the more obvious social themes of the story, that ultimately shaped the lawyers' account of the Salency case.

   That the Salency trial offered excellent material for displays of rhetorical skill and touching sentiment must have been immediately obvious to ambitious members of the legal profession. "How many powerful protectors, how many zealous defenders the rosière was offered!" intoned the author of a speech delivered in 1776; "it was the cause of honor; the pleasure of collaborating in her defense was avidly sought after and competed for. People snatched from one another those writings, full of *sensibilité,* in which the festival of the rose was depicted and her rights reclaimed."[97] The unhappy seigneur of Salency, Danré, complained that a full six months before the trial a brief composed against him by the lawyer Delacroix was already being disseminated in a popular in-duodecimo edition.[98] Delacroix, of course, we have already met as the young lawyer (he was now thirty-one) who had coasted to fame on his defense of the middle-class Véron family against the count of Morangiès in the early 1770s.

Although Delacroix wrote two mémoires for the rosière of Salency, which met, as we shall see, with considerable success, he was overshadowed in the case by his even more famous senior colleague, Guy-Jean-Baptiste Target. Born in 1733, Target was the son of an *avocat au parlement* whose forebears were prosperous provincial bourgeois.[99] A precocious student, the younger Target entered law school before his sixteenth birthday and by the age of eighteen was collaborating in his father's cases. Shortly before he was admitted to the Paris bar in 1752, he won a case that had for generations pitted his own family against the seigneurs of Belleville over the juridical status of lands whose ownership was in dispute. Instead of approaching the case from within the premises of feudal law, as his training and tradition dictated, Target challenged those very premises by arguing that ancient vassalic usages had been supplanted by the principles of natural and Roman law.[100]

Cases like this predisposed Target—like many lawyers of his generation—to the sort of antiseigneurial rhetoric that was to come to the fore in the Salency case. But more important, perhaps, was his exposure to the political storms of the day, as he was asked in 1759 to take a prominent role in the case against Father La Valette, the head of the Jesuit order in the West Indies, in the trial that led to the expulsion of the order from the realm.[101] In the course of that affair, Target began to compete with Jean-Baptiste Gerbier, a barrister eight years his senior,

97. *La Rosière . . . ou recueil de pieces,* p. 84.
98. Charles Danré de Salency, *Mémoire pour Messire Charles-François-Laurent Danré* (Paris: Claude Simon, 1774), p. 2.
99. For biographical details on Target, see Paul Boulloche, *Un Avocat du XVIIIe siècle* (Paris: Calmann-Levy, 1893); Sylvain Dumon, "Notice sur Target," in *Annales du barreau français: Barreau ancien* (Paris: Waree, 1826) 3:3–13; Joseph Hudault, "Guy-Jean-Baptiste Target et sa contribution à la préparation de l'Édit de novembre 1787 sur l'état-civil des protestants" (Law thesis, University of Paris, 1866).
100. Hudault, "Target," pp. 38–41.
101. Boulloche, *Un Avocat du XVIIIe siècle,* pp. 11–12.

who also pleaded against the Jesuits and was considered the premier trial lawyer in the realm.[102]

The rivalry between Gerbier and Target remained civil and respectful as it was played out over the course of the following decade, only to turn bitter in the aftermath of the Maupeou crisis. In the course of the lawyers' strike, Gerbier forever tarnished his reputation in the eyes of many people by caving in to Maupeou's threats and entreaties and leading a group of barristers to rejoin the new courts. Meanwhile Target, steadfast in his opposition to the chancellor, became one of the leaders of the anti-Maupeou *parti patriote,* especially after he wrote a diatribe against the chancellor cryptically entitled *Lettres d'un homme à un autre homme.*[103] The rift among the Parisian lawyers that resulted from this crisis thus crystallized around the persons of the two lawyers, with Gerbier identified with the so-called *avocats souillés* who had given in to Maupeou, while Target emerged as the pristine leader of the *avocats vierges.* The Salency case came before the newly restored Parlement in December of 1774 as Target was basking in the glory of his untarnished resistance to "despotism."

Target's fame, which rested on the conspicuous *engagement* as well as his legal skills, was buttressed by his reputation as a stylist—a reputation that was to be crowned in 1785 by his election to the Académie Française. Not only did he argue well, he often did so in a style that was unabashedly fiery and *pathétique,* punctuating his speeches and briefs with novelistic descriptions and appeals to the heart. In 1770, for instance, he took on the defense of a young man named Alliot, whose father wanted him to take orders, but who instead fell in love with the daughter of a surgeon, with whom he had several illegitimate children.[104] The opening pages of Target's mémoire for young Alliot offer the reader a tantalizing summary of what lies ahead: "Indigence, flight, vagrancy, terror, exile, imprisonment, prison cells, the perils of the sea, deportation to savage climates, shackles, yes, even the shackles with which his feet and his hands have been burdened."[105]

And indeed, the mémoire does live up to the promise of its opening, delivering a narrative that reads like a combination of Diderot's *La Reli-*

---

102. Ibid., pp. 22–24.

103. Gaudry, *Histoire du barreau,* chaps. 17 and 21; Echeverria, *The Maupeou Revolution,* chap. 1.

104. Boulloche, *Un Avocat du XVIIIe siècle,* pp. 28–30.

105. Guy-Jean-Baptiste Target, *Mémoire pour le Sieur Alliot, fils* (Paris: Louis Cellot, 1770), p. 4.

2. Guy-Jean-Baptiste Target (1733–1807): Lawyer, political activist, and pamphleteer. This portrait was done in 1790, when Target was president of the National Assembly. (Phot. Bibl. Nat. Paris)

gieuse with Prévost's *Manon Lescaut*. The story takes the lovers, fleeing Alliot's father, throughout northern and eastern France, then to Koblenz, Basel, and Paris; they escape by night through hedges and over rooftops; she miscarries twice, he is shipped off to Guadeloupe; through it all they retain their passion for each other and their respect for Alliot senior. The narrative is punctuated with well-crafted theatrical scenes, like the one near the end in which young Alliot seeks out his father in a desperate—and unsuccessful—attempt at reconciliation: "He enters; [the older] Alliot is preparing to go out; he sees his son and draws back in surprise. O terrible moment, O moment so dear to nature, Oh, let this moment not pass in vain! Young Alliot falls to his knees and embraces those of his father, grasps his hand, covers it with kisses, wets it with his tears. His voice extinguished, choked, he cannot pronounce a word. What words could have equaled this silence? . . . The tremor of nature overpowers him. He utters a cry, succumbs, and falls in a faint. Had his father deigned to remain with him . . . but he leaves. The son comes to his senses, looks around for him, and sees that the moment is lost." [106] In Delacroix and Target, then, the villagers of Salency had been given for their defense two of the ablest practitioners of the new melodramatic style of forensic argument, and two political *patriotes,* to boot.

It was Target, as the senior of the two, who was charged with the oral pleading in the case (oral argument, as we have seen, was permissible in civil cases). He delivered no less than four different orations, whose success was matched only by that of his printed briefs for the inhabitants of Salency. Monsieur Target, wrote a contemporary, "wished to distribute some of his mémoires himself. The public assembled in the great hall of the Palais [de Justice] surrounded [the publisher] Knapen's stall, where the distribution was going on. The mémoires were so snatched about that they only reached the assembled crowd sheet by sheet. There was a rush on the stall, which was looted. Upon returning home, M. Target discovered that the copies he had left there had been treated with no more respect. Never was a cause so worthy of interest that it could make one forgive such displays of enthusiasm." [107] The objects of this paper-ripping enthusiasm were of course *mémoires judiciaires,* or trial briefs, and it was the function of these texts and the conventions of forensic writing that contributed most to recasting the meaning of the rosière ceremony in the course of the trial.

As we have seen, it had become common, at least since the Calas case, for lawyers to address their briefs, in cases they considered significant enough to warrant it, over the heads of the judges to "the Public" or "the Nation." Accordingly, Target organized his defense of the inhabitants of Salency by identifying their interests with those of "the Nation." Any festival that promotes virtue, he began, "is a public and national good, which belongs to all of France and not to the seigneur of Salency. . . . The Rose of Salency has become as famous as she deserves to be, and our case is today that of the Public." In his concluding pages,

106. Ibid., pp. 44–45.
107. *La Rosière . . . ou recueil de pièces,* p. 85, n. 2.

he hammered away at the same idea: the rose festival belongs not just to the Salenciens, he wrote, "but to all who are listening to me, to the Public, to the Nation."[108]

One of the most popular handbooks for lawyers, Pierre-Louis Gin's *L'Eloquence du barreau,* explained that the fundamental rule for producing a good *plaidoyer* was unity; in order for a speech to culminate in a single point, as it should ideally, the lawyer needed to isolate "a fundamental principle of which his conclusions should be the consequence."[109] Target's *Plaidoyer pour la rosière,* considered at the time a model of the genre, followed the rule: "All is simple, all must be simple in this case," it began.[110] Target found his unitary principle in one of the central conventions of classical rhetoric, that of opposition or antithesis.[111]

For the rosière to be erected into a symbol of civic spirit, a representative of "the Nation," what she stood for had to be pitted against the selfishly centrifugal machinations of the seigneur. The radiant publicity of the festival and its heroine found its antithesis to Danré's pursuit of occlusion, secrecy, and silence. The lord's insistence that the girl remain in his pew during the service fit nicely into this pattern. According to Target, the seigneur wanted "to take her away from the Public to whom she belongs . . . by hiding her in the remotest place."[112] Delacroix echoed this, explaining in his first mémoire in the case that what Danré most hated about the ceremony was its publicity and "fame"; hence he forbade nominations from the pulpit and tried to exclude the village fanfare from the procession: "What a man, this seigneur of Salency!" the lawyer ironized; "how he loves silence!"[113]

Danré's attempts at hiding and muting the ceremony were carried out, according to the trial briefs, by means of violence. On the day of the ceremony, wrote Delacroix, he surrounded the chapel with officers of the local police, the *maréchaussée,* "who forbade its access to the vil-

108. Guy-Jean-Baptiste Target, *Plaidoyer en faveur de la rosière pour les syndic et habitans du village de Salency* (Paris: Knapen, 1774), pp. 18–19.

109. Pierre-Louis Gin, *De l'Eloquence du barreau* (Paris: Herisant, 1767), pp. 32–34.

110. Target, *Plaidoyer,* p. 4.

111. Peter France, *Rhetoric and Truth in France: Descartes to Diderot* (Oxford: Clarendon Press, 1972), pp. 12, 105–106.

112. Ibid.

113. Jacques-Vincent Delacroix, *Mémoire pour les syndic et habitans de Salancy contre le sieur Danré* (Paris: P. G. Simon, 1774), p. 18–19.

lagers and pushed them back with brutality, as if to take away from them even the spectacle of the crowning." The lord's bailiff, intent on aping his master, even appeared in church wearing boots and spurs and carrying a whip.[114] The central villain in the case, then, as in the Morangiès affair of a few years earlier, was a corrupt grandee whose wishes were carried out by brutal underlings. (It should be noted that in this respect the emplotment of the mémoires diverges completely from the plots of the rosière plays and operas, in which the wicked steward or bailiff acts, not in collusion with the lord, but always behind his back and against his wishes.)

The story of the Salency case, then, represents another version of the parable of arbitrary and violent authority, which had also been at the heart of the Morangiès affair and which can plausibly be related to the explosion of "antidespotic" polemical literature that accompanied the Maupeou crisis. The Salency story, however, also pointed to a theme that was not present in the earlier case, that of sexual aggression and appropriation. Target did not dwell on this aspect of the case, although he did use the loaded term *droit du seigneur* in his brief; Delacroix, by contrast, imagined a whole scene to dramatize the point that in the hands of a capricious seigneur the choice of a nubile young woman could turn into a form of sexual blackmail: "Lise, if you want to be rose-girl, it is up to you; to have one hundred and forty-five livres this year, to see the blue ribbons of which your friends are so proud floating about your head; to march, as they did, preceded by fanfares and followed by young boys who will admire your beauty and want you as their wife; Lise, love your seigneur a little, and you will be crowned."[115]

This young woman cajoled by her lord is much more than just another village maiden, another Mozartean Zerlina; she derives her title, her certificate of virginity, from the universal suffrage of the assembled villagers.[116] The rosière's lawyers, steeped in classical and historical learning, resurrected for the occasion the ancient symbolic meaning of female virginity as civic power, integrity, and impregnability. The helmeted Minerva, the Lady and the Unicorn circled by walls and closed

114. Target, *Plaidoyer*, p. 14.

115. Jacques-Vincent Delacroix, *Second Mémoire en faveur de la rosière pour les syndic et habitans de Salancy* (Paris: P. G. Simon, 1774), p. 8.

116. Ibid., p. 6.

gates, the Maid of Orléans encased in her suit of armor—all these were possible points of reference.[117] And the man who ravished this virginal symbol of the *res publica* became, like Tarquin raping Lucretia, the embodiment of violent political villainy.[118]

The dispute over the rosière festival thus gained political meaning from the suggestion that its central themes—authority and sexuality—acquired more general meaning once it was established that the virgin's fate was of concern to "the Nation." In general this followed from the trend established since the Calas case, which sought to posit an equation between private and particular matters, on the one hand, and affairs of state, on the other. One of the most powerful tools for setting up this equivalence was legal rhetoric: Pierre-Louis Gin explained that the sublime, the mode deemed appropriate for *grands sujets,* and the pathetic, more suited to lesser cases, were equally effective and admirable modes of eloquence; they should no more be judged according to a hierarchy than "painting, which excites our admiration as much in the naive subjects of a Tenniers or a Greuze as in the magnificent paintings of a Le Brun or a Le Sueur."[119]

The new fashion in rhetoric—as indeed in painting and drama—insisted on the equivalence between mundane and "great" subjects, implicitly perhaps on the superiority of the former over the latter. Target and Delacroix acted upon this assumption, pressing into service for this purpose one of the classic rhetorical tropes, the syllogism. The structure of the argument in all three main mémoires in the case could be expressed as follows: the rosière stood for Salency, Salency stood for France—therefore, the rosière was a national emblem. For between the virgin and the nation for which she stood lay the microcosm described in every account of the festival: the arcadian community of Salency. Delacroix's presentation of the village is typical: "Half a league from Noyon there lies a little town named Salency. Its inhabitants, unlike our other coarse villagers, have preserved to this day the touching simplicity of country life. These are no mercenaries, no slaves to a rich farmer, no

117. Segalen and Chamarat, "La Rosière et la 'Miss,'" pp. 44–45; see Marina Warner, *Alone of All her Sex: The Myth and Cult of the Virgin Mary* (New York: Random House, 1976), and *Joan of Arc: The Image of Female Heroism* (New York: Knopf, 1981).

118. See Ian Donaldson, *The Rapes of Lucretia: A Myth and Its Transformation* (Oxford: Clarendon Press, 1982), and Tony Tanner, *Adultery in the Novel: Contract and Transgression* (Baltimore: Johns Hopkins University Press, 1979), introduction.

119. Gin, *L'Eloquence du barreau,* pp. 7–8.

souls depraved by indigence. All of them enjoy the sweet rewards of property: each one is devoted to the plot of land he owns, and which he cultivates in peace." [120]

We are a long way here from the heartrending misery or pastel-colored prettiness of the aristocratic vision of Salency. Under the pens of lawyers, the Picard village became a republic of small proprietors deftly handling the plow, a country located somewhere between Montesquieu's allegorical nation of Troglodytes and the social ideals of the sans-culottes—a utopian vision, in sum, of what the realm of France could become under the benevolent rule of young Louis XVI. No wonder Danré failed to recognize his own village in these descriptions, as he pointed out with some exasperation in his own, extraordinarily clumsy, trial brief: "I see nothing in my village of what they see there. . . . I cannot doubt that it contains more vices than virtues, many poor people and a few rich ones, mercenaries, day-laborers, in a word, men, country folk just as coarse as everywhere else." [121]

The fictional Salency was not just a physiocratic dream of agrarian prosperity but a political blueprint as well. The choice of the rosière, explained Delacroix, derived from a "felicitous combination of two powers," popular will and sovereign prerogative. [122] While the village community represented the people or the nation, the seigneur normally stood for monarchical authority: it was well known that Louis XIII had originally patronized the festival by sending the rosière the blue ribbon and silver ring that had become part of the traditional ceremony. In the best of enlightened traditions these two powers, sovereign and people, collaborated in the abolition of social rank: "In the presence of the Rosière," wrote Target, "there is no distinction for any person, all disappears before virtue." [123] Causing all participants, including the seigneur, to "disappear" or "efface themselves" in her presence, the queen of virtue created for a day the egalitarian, unmediated "transparency" of hearts that was Rousseau's political dream. [124] By obstinately asserting his prerogatives, Danré remained opaque, refusing to fade into this communion of civic spirit. In his selfish obtuseness, he threatened to

120. Delacroix, *Mémoire*, p. 2.
121. Danré, *Mémoire*, p. 14.
122. Delacroix, *Mémoire*, p. 2.
123. Target, *Plaidoyer*, p. 9.
124. Ibid., pp. 16–17; on Rousseauean "transparency," see Jean Starobinski, *Jean-Jacques Rousseau: La transparence et l'obstacle* (Paris: Gallimard, 1971), esp. pp. 116–121.

turn the festival into semiotic chaos by "confusing the distinctions of the civil order with the triumph of virtue, which has nothing to do with them."[125]

Danré, it is true, had made himself into an easy mark for his opponents by flatly stating that the village council had no claim, because such local institutions did not exist under King Clovis, when the festival was founded "and our peasants were serfs."[126] Target retorted that the founder, Saint Médard, was "owner rather than seigneur of Salency, for back then there were no fiefdoms"; he derided the pretensions of this benighted lordling who insisted "that the homage of his vassals be paid to him alone."[127] This sort of antiseigneurial rhetoric was not at all unusual for a lawyer of Target's generation. As we have seen, Target, like many of his contemporaries in the profession, had been involved in court cases that led him to challenge seigneurial rights on the grounds of natural law. But the denunciation of "feudal" pretensions had also by the 1760s and 1770s become common in the works of a whole spectrum of writers ranging from monarchist historians like the abbé Dubos to physiocrats who believed that seigneurial rights stood in the way of agricultural improvement.[128] Although Target drew upon the "antifeudal" ideology that many lawyers shared with enlightened intellectuals, he subordinated such ideas, in the end, to the political message he drew from the case. The leveling of social distinctions, as symbolized by the triumph of the rosière's virtue, whould allow for a healthy political order based on direct, unmediated contact between an enlightened state and its citizens.

The meaning of the Salency case, as presented to the public in the lawyers' briefs, was determined above all by the precise political context in which it occurred. The death of Louis XV in May of 1774 effectively put an end to the protracted crisis that had begun with Maupeou's attack on the parlements. The hated chancellor and his two colleagues were dismissed that very summer, and it was the newly recalled Parlement of Paris that judged the case in December of 1774. The official reconvening of the Parlement took place on 28 November 1774, and Target, as a leading barrister and anti-Maupeou activist, was chosen

---

125. Target, *Plaidoyer,* p. 4.
126. Danré, *Mémoire,* p. 7.
127. Target, *Plaidoyer,* pp. 5, 14.
128. J. Q. C. Mackrell, *The Attack on "Feudalism" in Eighteenth-Century France* (Toronto: University of Toronto Press, 1973).

to give one of the speeches that marked the occasion. The message that Target delivered on this momentous occasion was one of political rebirth and regeneration. The crisis through which the nation had just lived, he proclaimed, should no longer be lamented, as it had in the end taught citizens to love and revere the rule of law and of the public good: "It will increase for all citizens the conviction that nothing is greater than the public interest; that in the presence of this noble object any particular object must fade away." [129] At this moment of transition and rebirth, he enjoined the magistrates to act as faithful servants of "that double interest which, under a happy reign, becomes fused as one, that of the Prince and that of the People." [130]

Target's speech before the reassembled Parlement touched on some of the main themes of the *patriote* political thinking that the Maupeou crisis had brought into being. In response to the chancellor's authoritarian actions, writers like André Blonde, Adrien Le Paige, Claude Mey, and Target himself—significantly, these were all *avocats au parlement*—had formulated a constitutional ideology whose origins were diverse but whose main themes were clear and, by 1774, widely known. As we saw in the previous chapter, *patriote* thinkers drew upon *parlementaire* tradition, northern European natural-law philosophy from Grotius to Locke, French legal thought, and the oppositional language of embattled Jansenism. They argued that the basis of all government in France lay in the written and unwritten "fundamental laws" of the nation, that these laws made up the French "constitution," and that the purpose of this "constitution" (as formulated and upheld by the parlements and their lawyers) was to serve and protect the "public interest" of the nation.[131] In short, *patriote* thinkers articulated, some twenty years before the Revolution, a clear and coherent thesis of national sovereignty that was also explicitly a repudiation of the principles of absolute monarchy.

The elements of such a theory had been in existence for decades, in

---

129. Guy-Jean-Baptiste Target, *Discours prononcé en la Grand'Chambre par M. Target, avocat, le 28 novembre 1774, à la rentrée du Parlement* (Paris, n.d.), p. 2.

130. Ibid., p. 3.

131. Echeverria, *The Maupeou Revolution,* chaps. 1–3; Dale Van Kley, "The Jansenist Constitutional Legacy in the French Prerevolution," in Keith Baker, ed., *The Political Culture of the Old Regime* (London: Pergamon Press, 1987), pp. 169–201; Shanti Singham, "'A Conspiracy of Twenty Million Frenchmen': Public Opinion, Patriotism, and the Assault on Absolutism during the Maupeou Years, 1770–1775" (Ph.D diss., Princeton University, 1991), chap. 2; Roger Bickart, *Les Parlements et la notion de souveraineté nationale au XVIIIe siècle* (Paris: Felix Alcan, 1932); Elie Carcassonne, *Montesquieu et le problème de la constitution française au XVIIIe siècle* (Paris: Presses Universitaires de France, 1927).

the remonstrances of the eighteenth-century parlements, the writings of Jansenist lawyers, and the tradition of political theory that stretched from Locke to Montesquieu and Rousseau. The Maupeou crisis simply served as a catalyst, impelling those in the eye of the political storm to synthesize these ideas and to demonstrate their relevance to contemporary developments. But how could such ideas as "public interest" or "the Nation" be given the sort of concrete expression that could make them intelligible to an ever-widening reading public? It was easy enough, in the course of the crisis, to find embodiments for the negative pole of reference, "despotism," which described the actions of Maupeou and his ministerial colleagues and, it was hinted, the monarch whom they served. It was more difficult, however, to give a concrete form to "the Nation," which above all needed to be distinguished from the person of the monarch, even one as benevolent (it was hoped) as the young Louis XVI.

It was at this juncture that the rosière appeared, the perfect symbol, in her pristine femininity, of the nation reborn. The rosière was not a specific woman, since her identity differed from year to year; rather, she embodied a moral principle, virtue, and her yearly election by the villagers and the seigneur made her a symbol of consensual community politics. Since antiquity, of course, the female form had served as the most common iconographic motif for representing such abstractions as Justice, Prudence, or Fortitude, and political symbolism had made abundant use of the figure of the armed and helmeted Minerva, the warlike goddess born of man alone, whose embattled chastity stood for the purest form of patrilineage.[132] The lawyers who wrote briefs in the Salency case drew upon this iconographic and symbolic tradition to make the rosière's virginity into an emblem of public interest and integrity, not just for the Salenciens, but for the entire nation.

To stress the political implications of the Salency case is not, however, to deny that the mémoires also carried a social message. As in the Morangiès affair, the most explicit theme of the briefs in this case was the attack on the social pretensions of certain members of the nobility. As we have seen, the denunciation of the lord of Salency is in part symptomatic of the eighteenth-century spread of litigation into the rural world and of the experience gained by barristers like Target in disputes involving questions of feudal law. But it is also likely that, as in the Mo-

132. Marina Warner, *Monuments and Maidens: The Allegory of the Female Form* (New York: Atheneum, 1985), pp. 87–125.

rangiès case, the barristers were drawing on and combining the two major and antagonistic themes of the Maupeou-era pamphleteering: the attack on "despotism" by *patriote* polemicists, and the denunciation of aristocratic selfishness by ministerial writers. In the combining of these themes the Salency case, like the Morangiès affair before it, prefigured the explosive ideological syncretism of the late 1780s.

The case of the rosière of Salency was not one of the major causes célèbres of prerevolutionary France; pitting France's premier trial lawyers against an unpopular and obscure country squire, it was easily won and, in the volatile climate of opinion of the mid 1770s, soon forgotten. It has been singled out here, however, as a salient example of the ways in which a public ceremonial event, the *fête de la rose,* could take on an entirely different set of meanings as it was appropriated by different social groups for different purposes. Beginning in the 1760s, the rosière served as the iconic center of celebrations held in villages, on stage, and in villages on stage, where effusions of virtuous sentiment served to buttress the self-image, and thus the moral authority, of an enlightened ruling class. But prior to 1789, the actual enactment of a festival bringing together—as Rousseau had dreamed—a whole nation as opposed to a remote and fictionalized village, seemed as yet inconceivable. "There is a place where [virtue] is crowned," lamented Delacroix. "Why must this place be only a village?"[133]

The young lawyer could hardly have imagined that his wish was to come true less than twenty years later, as the grandiose festivals engineered by revolutionary groups and leaders centered on virginal females much like the rosière, who like their predecessor embodied moral and political abstractions. The Festival of Reason held on 10 November 1793 in Notre-Dame, for instance, culminated in the appearance in the midst of the cathedral of the Goddess of Reason, a woman clad, like the rosière, in blue and white, but who also wore a red Phrygian cap and carried a pike.[134] The tricolor sported by this new divinity stood for one

---

133. Delacroix, *Mémoire*, p. 2.
134. Alphonse Aulard, *Le Culte de la raison et le culte de l'Etre Suprême* (Paris, 1892), pp. 52–55. For general discussions of female allegories in the Revolution, see Mona Ozouf, *La Fête révolutionnnaire, 1789–1799* (Paris: Gallimard, 1976), pp. 114–121; Maurice Agulhon, *Marianne into Battle: Republican Imagery and Symbolism in France,* trans. Janet Lloyd (Cambridge: Cambridge University Press, 1981), chap. 1; Lynn Hunt, *Politics, Culture and Class in the French Revolution* (Berkeley: University of California Press, 1984), chaps. 2 and 3.

of the central tenets of radical republican ideology, the merging of private virtues (suggested by the rosière's Marian colors) with public political beliefs.

The rosière case thus serves as an illustration of the process whereby the courtroom was becoming an arena for forging a new language and imagery of public life. As we saw in the previous chapter, the forensic rhetoric of the 1770s and 1780s often drew its inspiration from the moral polarities and sentimental expressivity of the new "drame" or "genre sérieux." The Salency case, however, suggests that the language of the courtroom can also be read as a repudiation of more traditional courtly and aristocratic theatricality, of the vacuous prettiness and complacent hedonism of established genres favored by the ruling elites such as the pastorale and the opéra-comique. The growing numbers and increasing activity of segments of the legal profession, the political crisis of the early 1770s, and the very function and language of trial briefs, all contributed to the rise of courtroom rhetoric as a powerful new molder of public sentiment.

The Salency case also offers us a first perspective on the gendered nature of the politico-cultural transformations taking place in late-eighteenth-century France. Within *le monde,* the closed world of the Old Regime top elites, *l'opinion* had long been an extralegal tribunal—an informal consensus often governed by women, whose function was to regulate and judge the morality of other women. (One thinks here inevitably of the social banishment of Mme de Merteuil at the end of *Les Liaisons dangereuses,* a sentence carried out by and before the public at the Opera, and one more final and more terrible to her than the concurrent loss of her lawsuit.) What the Salency case represents is the masculinization and politicization of "public opinion," as men of law now appropriated the function of judging female virtue in the person of the village maiden.[135] The culmination of this trend would come about a decade after the Salency case, with a trial whose implicit agenda was to judge the morality of the queen of France.

During the course of the Salency trial, a writer named Blin de Sainmore composed a thoroughly insipid poem whose subject was a plea addressed by the maidens of Salency to the young queen, Marie-Antoinette. "I imagined," he wrote in the preface to the piece, "this address by the young girls of Salency to the young Sovereign, so de-

135. I wish to thank Dena Goodman for the central idea of this paragraph, which she develops in more detail in her forthcoming book on the Republic of Letters.

servedly adored by all Frenchmen, and who graces the throne with all of the virtues."[136] The author's initiative certainly made sense, since Marie-Antoinette was at this time building her own version of Salency at Trianon: an outdoor theater called Le Hameau (the Hamlet), decorated by the painter Hubert Robert and furnished with cottages, hayricks, and dove-cotes.[137] The historical irony of Blin de Sainmore's dedication is hard to miss, if one knows that a decade or so later Marie-Antoinette was to become in the eyes of many people the exact antithesis of what the rosière stood for, an embodiment of female corruption at the dead center of the political sphere. As the following chapters will illustrate, the causes célèbres of the prerevolutionary decades used images of female sexuality as well as of male authority as central parables for the decaying public culture of the Old Regime.

136. Blin de Sainmore, *Requête des filles de Salency à la reine* (Paris: Delalain, 1774), p. 7.

137. Stefan Zweig, *Marie-Antoinette: The Portrait of an Average Woman,* trans. Eden and Cedar Paul (New York: Garden City, 1933), pp. 111–113.

3

Private Lives and Public Affairs

Upper-Class Scandal, 1774–1778

The death of Louis XV in May of 1774 and the accession of his twenty-year-old grandson ushered in a period of hope and good feelings. The young Louis XVI was, if not very bright or energetic, benign and easygoing, as different as could be from his autocratic predecessor, and the nineteen-year-old queen was beautiful and popular. Most important, in the months following the old king's death, his trio of hated ministers, d'Aiguillon, Maupeou, and Terray, were forced out of office, and the old Parlement was restored.[1] To most observers of the political scene, the mid-1770s seemed to offer the promise of an entirely new deal.

The ideological tensions that had come to the fore during the difficult years between 1771 and 1774 did not disappear, however, or even go into abeyance for long. The most clear-sighted critics of the regime were well aware that despite the advent of a new king, a new ministry, and a restored sovereign court, the system of government had not been fundamentally altered. The oppositional ideas that had crystallized during the Maupeou crisis survived the demise of the ministerial "despots" and spilled over into the new reign: in June of 1775, the very month that Louis XVI was crowned at Reims, the restored Parlement ordered the burning of two "seditious" and "subversive" works, Jacques Martin

---

1. For a survey of the political upheavals at the beginning of the reign of Louis XVI, see Edgar Faure, *La Disgrâce de Turgot* (Paris: Gallimard, 1961), chaps. 1 and 2; and Joseph Droz, *Histoire du règne de Louis XVI*, 3 vols. (Paris: Renouard, 1860), vol. 1, chap. 1.

de Mariveaux's *L'Ami des lois* and Guillaume Saige's *Le Catéchisme du citoyen*. Both authors were lawyers and exponents of a Rousseauean version of the *patriote* ideology that had taken shape during the Maupeou crisis, and both works forcefully articulated the *patriote* thesis of the sovereignty of the nation over its monarchical rulers.[2]

In the mid-1770s, the hope for thoroughgoing administrative and governmental reform was fueled both by residual anger at the high-handed practices of the former reign and by the expectations raised by the advent of a new regime. In the preceding chapter, we saw how, in the early months of the new reign, lawyers sympathetic to the *patriote* cause came to construe a rather ordinary dispute between villagers and their lord into a parable of national regeneration. Several months later, in May of 1775, the fifty-five magistrates of the Paris Cour des Aides, the court of appeals for fiscal matters attached to the Parlement, presented the new monarch with a far more explicit set of grievances and demands.[3]

The *Remontrances* of the Cour des Aides of 1775 were written by the court's president, Chrétien de Lamoignon de Malesherbes. A friend of the philosophes and faithful but enlightened servant of the monarchy, Malesherbes, as director of royal censorship in the 1750s, had been the person most responsible for protecting and ultimately saving from its enemies that monument of the French Enlightenment, Diderot and d'Alembert's great *Encyclopédie;* as both an official censor and a man of letters (he was elected to the Académie Française in 1775), Malesherbes recognized and respected the power of the printed word. The text that he wrote and presented to the king on behalf of his colleagues on the court in 1775 was a vigorous indictment of the "despotic" abuses that over the course of the Old Regime had crept into the entire judicial and administrative system, especially where fiscal matters were concerned. Although Louis XVI had at first accepted to receive and read the court's remonstrances, he and his advisers judged the document's contents to

2. Keith Michael Baker, "French Political Thought at the Accession of Louis XVI," *Journal of Modern History* 50 (June 1978): 279–282.

3. The *cours des aides* were special law courts whose function was to judge on appeal disputes relating to the levy of taxes, such as the *taille, aides, gabelles,* and so on. There was one such court in Paris, made up of three chambers, each one headed by three *présidents,* and twelve courts in the provinces attached to the local parlements. Although the *cours des aides* were frequently in dispute with their local parlements, that of Paris sided with the Paris Parlement during the Maupeou crisis and was disbanded by the chancellor from 1771 to 1774. See Marcel Marion, *Dictionnaire des institutions de la France aux XVIIe et XVIIIe siècles* (1923; reprint Paris: Picard, 1984), pp. 156–157.

be incendiary and forbade its publication. It was published abroad three years later, however, and soon circulated illegally within France.[4]

The *Remontrances* written by Malesherbes were ostensibly a specific critique of the fiscal policies of the royal administration, an indictment of the arbitrary, erratic, and secret procedures used by tax-farmers and royal officials in the levying of taxes throughout the realm. But in fact Malesherbes aimed his shafts beyond the tax system, at the very heart of the monarchy's administrative and governmental practices.[5] The royal administration, he charged, was taking on the characteristics of an "oriental despotism"; it had silenced and suppressed all of the nation's traditional forms of national and local representation, including the Estates-General of the realm, the provincial estates, and the representative organs of communities and corporate bodies; it had stifled the protests of these bodies and of the parlements and other courts. In their place, the monarchy had allowed the development of an administration whose practices were secret, arbitrary, and tyrannical.[6]

What could be done to reverse this slide toward despotism and restore the health of the French body politic? In the first place, Malesherbes prescribed a restoration of traditional rights of representation, so that the king could have access once more to the wishes of his subjects by taking counsel directly from the Estates-General and its provincial counterparts.[7] In 1775, however, a convening of the Estates-General must have seemed like a remote ideal, not an actual possibility, as that body had not been assembled since 1614. More realistically, perhaps, the political system could be made more equitable and less oppressive in the short run if its workings were systematically opened up, made public: in Malesherbes' mind, as in that of many of his contemporaries, since occlusion and secrecy characterized "despotic" or "tyrannical" governments, openness and publicity, conversely, would be among the central principles of a free and humane political order.

This explains the crucial role that liberal thinkers such as Malesherbes accorded to the printing press and the printed word in the creation of a new, open and enlightened, political system. The kings of France, Malesherbes explained, had once dispensed justice in public, in front of

4. Elisabeth Badinter, ed., *Les "Remontrances" de Malesherbes, 1771–1775* (Paris: Union générale d'éditions, 1978), pp. 104–113, 136–144.

5. Ibid., pp. 110–129; Baker, "French Political Thought," p. 291.

6. Badinter, *"Remontrances" de Malesherbes,* pp. 115–136; Baker, "French Political Thought," pp. 291–293.

7. Baker, "French Political Thought," p. 293.

their assembled subjects; in subsequent centuries as the laws were written down and the legal code became more complex, the administration of justice had become an increasingly specialized and secret process. The long-term effects of the print revolution could, however, usher in a return to something like the golden age when subjects directly witnessed and condoned the dispensing of justice by their kings. Not only did printing make for better-educated citizens; it could also re-create, in a much larger and geographically dispersed nation, a "public" similar to the one that had once physically assembled in the Champ de Mars to hear the verdicts of rulers: "The art of printing has thus given to the written word the same publicity which the spoken word once enjoyed in the midst of the Nation assembled."[8]

Was this vision of a nation bound together and communicating with its rulers thanks to the printed word a dream, a wholly utopian attempt to duplicate for the French political order what the Protestant reformers had achieved thanks to the printed word of the Bible? Not quite, for Malesherbes pointed out that one category of printed texts had already, for several years, been used to this effect; and these were none other than mémoires, or trial briefs. Individuals involved in litigation could appeal their sentences to the higher courts, or even to the ruler, by publishing a mémoire; and while objections to this practice, and especially to its recent proliferation, were frequently voiced, Malesherbes believed that far from being a "dangerous innovation," the escalating use of trial briefs signaled "the reestablishment of the ancient judicial order of the realm" to something closer to "the primitive constitution of the Monarchy."[9]

This development, Malesherbes believed, had already made for much more openness and equity in the dispensing of justice. And why, he asked, could the printing of appeals not be extended to other areas of the administration? Why could a subject not use a printed, public mémoire to appeal to the government against a provincial governor, or *intendant?*[10] Malesherbes, then, singled out the use of trial briefs by private individuals involved in litigation as a development fraught with promising political implications. Thanks to the endless possibilities of the print medium, *mémoires judiciaires* had reached out to, and were

---

8. Badinter, *"Remontrances" de Malesherbes*, pp. 270–273; quote p. 273. Baker, "French Political Thought," p. 294.

9. Badinter, *"Remontrances" de Malesherbes*, p. 270.

10. Ibid., pp. 273–274.

creating, a new "public." Their use was a first example of, and a model for, the opening up and transformation of the public sphere.

In 1775, Malesherbes was not the only person to view the increasing popularity of trial briefs as a significant political development. That very same year, apologias for this medium were written by two young lawyers whom we have already encountered as successful authors of mémoires, Ambroise Falconnet and Jacques-Vincent Delacroix. Falconnet wrote his *Mémoire pour M. Falconnet* as a justification and defense of his own writings and behavior in a case that is discussed later in this chapter, a sensational judicial duel between the French ambassador to London and his secretary; this piece was censored by the Parlement, but Falconnet had it reprinted after the Revolution.[11] Delacroix's *Réflexions sur les mémoires,* a somewhat less incendiary statement, was often cited by contemporaries; the author also chose to reprint it as the coda to the article "Factum" that he wrote in the early 1780s for the *Encyclopédie méthodique.*[12]

Like Malesherbes, Falconnet argued that trial briefs served crucial functions in molding a free citizenry: they defended people while educating them in the workings of the law. "What is a mémoire?" Falconnet resoundingly began. "Here is how I define it. A mémoire establishes the rights of a citizen by explaining them to the judges and to the public."[13] At the same time, he continued, such writings performed for the benefit of the state an important task of public education. The laws might be excellent, but they were arcane and inaccessible, consigned to fat volumes that only specialists could comprehend. The prevailing ignorance of the law was breeding a "cowardly indifference" and an "alarming pyrrhonism" among laypersons. But a good mémoire "brings one back to the law, shows its origins and nature; it underscores [the law's] necessity; it reproduces it, so to speak, and brings it to light in the best way."[14]

The principal virtue of a mémoire was its openness, publicity, and accessibility. As such, it served as the best weapon against the most dan-

11. Ambroise Falconnet, *Le Barreau français, partie moderne,* 2 vols. (Paris: Gueffier, 1806–1808); pp. xvi–xxxii are a reprint of the author's *Mémoire pour M. Falconnet, avocat en la cour, appelant d'une sentence rendue au Châtelet de Paris,* originally published in 1775.

12. Jacques-Vincent Delacroix, *Réflexions sur les mémoires* (n.p., 1775); reprinted in vol. 4 of the articles on jurisprudence of the *Encyclopédie méthodique* (Paris: Panckoucke, 1784), pp. 457–458.

13. Falconnet, *Mémoire pour M. Falconnet,* p. xvi.

14. Ibid., p. xvii.

gerous aspect of the judicial process, namely, its secrecy. There might be dangers in the use of trial briefs, wrote Delacroix, but these were negligible compared with the evils that resulted from "the dark intrigues, silent maneuvers, secret defamations, the art of disfiguring and altering facts in the judges' chambers."[15] Such obscure and corrupt dealings would become impossible if a case were fought out "in the open field, under the eyes of a crowd of spectators"—in other words, in print.[16] Both lawyers, like Malesherbes, couched their argument for the importance of *mémoires judiciaires* within the framework of an opposition between occlusion and openness; and this was a line of thinking that could easily be extended from the judicial process to the entire system of government.

Indeed, the very terms used by these and other champions of judicial publicity, words like "nation," "citizen," and "the public," were hardly innocent; they suggested that much more was at stake here than the publicizing of private disputes. Falconnet articulated the political implications of the argument most explicitly and at the same time promoted his own role as a lawyer. Every court case, he suggested, came down to a negotiation between the sovereign power and the citizenry; if the judge's function was to represent the majesty of government, the lawyer, for his part, acted as "deputy of the entire people." "What is the judge? The voice of the sovereign. What is the lawyer? The voice of the nation."[17] For all of their bombast and self-promotion, Delacroix and Falconnet had grasped and were arguing an important point: that trial briefs were one of the few forms of licit printed matter to both emanate from and reach a wide and scattered public. The lawyer who properly availed himself of this medium could claim to be, as Falconnet immodestly put it, "the beacon of all powers, the legislator of his compatriots, and the benefactor of the human race."[18]

The argument in these lawyers' writings, then, in part follows that of Malesherbes in his bold indictment of administrative secrecy and cor-

---

15. Delacroix, *Réflexions,* p. 9. See also Falconnet, *Mémoire pour M. Falconnet,* p. xxxii.

16. Ibid., p. 10.

17. Falconnet, *Mémoire pour M. Falconnet,* p. xxi. The lawyers thus added their own claim to those of other individuals and groups portending to "represent" the French nation—the monarchy, the parlements, and the landed/propertied elites: see Keith M. Baker, *Inventing the French Revolution* (Cambridge: Cambridge University Press, 1990), chap. 10.

18. Ibid., pp.xvii-xviii.

ruption. But the other main theme in these two texts was one that Malesherbes had not touched on: for Delacroix and Falconnet, mémoires were not just a tool for forcing open the *arcana imperii,* but also, and more important still, a means of equalizing social conditions. "The more social conditions become uneven," wrote Delacroix, "the more justice must bring them closer to equality"; and Falconnet concurred that justice must, "like the sun, shine for everyone without distinction."[19] They argued that a secret process worked to the advantage of the wealthy and powerful, who, behind the scenes, could bribe judges and coerce witnesses with impunity. In a public dispute, however, "there will be no inequality between the adversaries but that established by right."[20]

Both lawyers, it must be remembered, had recently achieved success in defending commoners against oppressive seigneurs: Falconnet, as we have seen, was one of the lawyers of the Véron family, and Delacroix had pleaded for the villagers of Salency against their lord. Perhaps inevitably, they capitalized on their recently acquired reputations as Robin Hoods of the bar. Both of them imagine conversations in which a fearful associate advises them to back down: "What are you thinking of . . . this is no way to express oneself! Observe the difference in conditions. Your antagonist is a Grand Seigneur."[21] But trial briefs precisely allowed one to resist such blandishments by resting one's case on the two principles that no seigneur, however grand, could challenge: publicity and the law.

Mémoires judiciaires were the best defense of the weak, the oppressed, the obscure, against those who threatened to exploit them; they protected the merchant from the insolvent gentleman, the artisan from the grasping merchant, the citizen from the greedy tax collector. And they did so not just by demonstrating the legal rights of the underdog, but also by simply bringing such cases out into the open. Delacroix's argument here takes an interesting turn: "Are you seeking," he wrote, "in a nation where honor means everything, and virtue is counted for nothing, to put a brake on iniquity? Threaten to unveil it, to expose it to daylight in all of its ugliness." (The opposition of "honor" to "virtue" echoes Montesquieu's argument in *The Spirit of the Laws* that the former was the central principle of monarchies, the latter

19. Delacroix, *Réflexions,* p. 5; Falconnet, *Mémoire pour M. Falconnet,* p. xx.
20. Delacroix, *Réflexions,* p. 5.
21. Falconnet, *Mémoire pour M. Falconnet,* p. xx; see also Delacroix, *Réflexions,* p. 14.

that of republics.) Delacroix followed this up with the story of a gentleman who had swindled a creditor, and who, when threatened with the publicity of a mémoire—already written and printed, but not yet made public—took fright and paid up.[22] This was a society, as the lawyer aptly pointed out, in which power and social standing were contingent upon appearances and reputation, and these were uniquely vulnerable to the adverse publicity of a trial brief. In such a world a printed public mémoire was the best defense of the oppressed, the weak man's most effective answer to the "honor" of the powerful. Trial briefs, then, were considered much more than just another type of pamphlet. Certainly, the last two decades of the Old Regime saw a proliferation of ephemeral printed matter. In the years between the Maupeou crisis and the Revolution, one could find just about anything, and increasing quantities of it, on the streets of Paris: official newspapers and uncensored foreign gazettes, the handwritten newssheets called *nouvelles à la main,* and pamphlets that ranged from arid political tracts to heretical "philosophy" and pornographic slander.[23] There can be no doubt that all of these contributed, in different ways, to the political education of the French nation. Why, then, should trial briefs enjoy a special status amidst this profusion of printed words?

The answer to that question may at first appear paradoxical. Unlike the most politically influential books, newspapers, and pamphlets, *mémoires judiciaires,* as we have seen, circulated legally and openly. They were not an attack on the system from without, like the censored material that flowed from underground or foreign presses, but a legitimate part of it. Their very existence, sanctioned by law and practice, had evolved into a challenge to the system from within, a major but unintended breach in the Old Regime's hierarchical and repressive control of public expression. Their subversive, or at least reforming, potential took on somewhat different meanings, however, for different people. To an enlightened official like Malesherbes, a man battling the vices of the administration, but also a powerful member of the sociopolitical

---

22. Delacroix, *Réflexions,* pp. 9–10.

23. See Robert Darnton, *The Literary Underground of the Old Regime* (Cambridge, Mass.: Harvard University Press, 1982); Jack Censer and Jeremy Popkin, eds., *Press and Politics in Pre-Revolutionary France* (Berkeley: University of California Press, 1987); Robert Darnton and Daniel Roche, eds., *Revolution in Print: The Press in France, 1775–1800* (Berkeley: University of California Press, 1989); and Jeremy Popkin, *News and Politics in the Age of Revolution: Jean Luzac's "Gazette de Leyde"* (Ithaca: Cornell University Press, 1989).

elite, the growing use of trial briefs held out the possibility above all of political improvement. But to ambitious barristers of undistinguished origins like Delacroix and Falconnet, the promise of such documents was social as well, for they were touted as the nonprivileged's best answer to the great and influential. Those outside of the elite wanted to make trial briefs into the vehicles of *égalité* as well as *liberté*.

The remainder of this chapter will offer further proof of the multivalence of the trial brief medium in the public culture of prerevolutionary France, through further instances of cases in which social and political messages overlapped in these texts: the playwright Beaumarchais's courtroom struggle with a dishonest magistrate; the sensational public dispute between a peer of the realm and his aristocratic onetime mistress; and a financial scandal involving a French ambassador and his personal secretary. Men of middling birth and high ambition, like Beaumarchais, Delacroix, and Falconnet, continued to inject trial briefs with egalitarian images and arguments. But paradoxically, the cases presented here also show the growing popularity of the *mémoire judiciaire* among the upper classes as a means of entertainment and information, and its use for the increasingly public settling of scores among the traditional social and political elites.

The argument for the importance of trial briefs rested upon the premise that these documents somehow reflected the rights and interests of a "public" that they simultaneously represented and molded: the authors of mémoires routinely claimed that they were speaking for "the public" and also acknowledged that they could influence and educate their audience. Recent studies of the birth of the notion of "public opinion" in prerevolutionary France argue that this entity was above all an abstraction, as Keith Baker puts it, "an abstract category of authority, invoked by actors in a new kind of politics to secure the legitimacy of claims that could no longer be made binding in the terms . . . of an absolutist political order"; in a similar argument Mona Ozouf describes this new political term as referring to "an impersonal and anonymous tribunal," "an imaginary authority."[24]

---

24. Keith Michael Baker, "Politics and Public Opinion," in Censer and Popkin, *Press and Politics*, p. 213. Mona Ozouf, "L'Opinion Publique," in Keith Michael Baker, ed., *The Political Culture of the Old Regime* (Oxford: Pergamon Press, 1987), pp. 424–425; English translation as "'Public Opinion' at the End of the Old Regime," *Journal of Modern History* 60 (Supplement, September 1988): S9–S13.

While acknowledging that the appearance of the term is undoubtedly linked in some fashion to long-term sociological transformations, such as the growth of literacy and the increasing commercialization of the printing industry, Baker and Ozouf suggest nonetheless that we resist the impulse to connect this term to a precise social referent: by *opinion publique* contemporaries meant, not the actual opinion of any discernible group in society, but a transcendent category that served as the functional replacement for the waning authority of a "desacralized" and increasingly unpopular monarchy.

This analysis holds true for trial briefs, inasmuch as their authors regularly claimed to be expressing the opinion of a "public" that had never, of course, been consulted: as we have seen, appeals to "public opinion" in mémoires went back at least as far as the 1720s and 1730s, and Voltaire had followed suit in the briefs he wrote for the Calas family and others in the 1760s. This ritual invocation of the "voice" or "opinion" of a wholly abstract "public" was not as arbitrary or empty as it might seem to us today. Most eighteenth-century thinkers equated public opinion with rational evidence and believed that no properly informed, rational person could hold an opinion that flew in the face of logical demonstration.[25] It followed that those who articulated a truth based on what they considered solid evidence and flawless reasoning could feel justified in claiming the sanction of *l'opinion publique*. This, then, was one of the bases on which authors of trial briefs claimed to be speaking for "the public"—including, of course, in those many cases in which two lawyers presenting contradictory and mutually exclusive points of view claimed to enjoy the total support of "the public."

Nonetheless, substantial evidence exists to prove that in the 1770s and 1780s there *was* a real, and growing, public of readers eagerly awaiting the publication of important legal briefs. Although one might be tempted to argue that the rhetorical use of terms like "the public" or "public opinion" eventually brought into being the real public of mémoire readers, the relationship between real and rhetorical publics probably took the form of a more complex dialectic. Authors of trial briefs—and indeed of newspapers and pamphlets—were aware of the growth of literacy and the gradual opening up of political debate, which in turn increased the strength and ubiquity of claims to speak for "the public," and so on. But whatever the origins of their popularity, all of the evidence about the production, dissemination, and sale of trial briefs

25. Ozouf, "L'Opinion Publique," pp. 426–427.

suggests that they were one of the most important, possibly the single most popular, form of ephemeral literature circulating in Paris in the two decades before the Revolution.

Mémoires judiciaires could be bulky objects; their length varied from a few pages to several hundred, most usually ranging between fifty and one hundred. They were usually published in a large quarto format, and indeed a circular from the royal director of publications to printers in 1774 made this an official requirement.[26] This attempt at controlling the size of trial briefs probably stemmed from the fact that during notorious or controversial trials lawyers sometimes arranged for the publication of briefs in smaller duodecimo editions, which were cheaper to produce and looked suspiciously like popular or libelous pamphlets: we have seen that the seigneur of Salency had complained bitterly that Delacroix's first brief attacking him was circulating in this smaller format. Quarto editions, being larger and more expensive, were probably easier for the authorities to monitor and preserved some of the formality and respectability that was deemed appropriate to this sort of legal document.

Despite their bulky, formal appearance, mémoires were printed in large, sometimes enormous quantities. In eighteenth-century France the printing of a book usually ranged between 500 and 3,000 copies, which were sold, in most cases, over a number of years or even decades. The average edition for books published by the Avignon presses ran to 2,000 copies, for instance, while printings of Voltaire's successful history of the reign of Charles XII attained runs of 3,800.[27] Newspapers enjoyed similar press runs, although these were, of course, immediately sold: the staid *Mercure de France* had a circulation of about 2,000 in the late 1770s, the unofficial *Gazette de Leyde* sold between 1,500 and 2,500 copies of each issue in France at about the same time, other foreign-based gazettes had press runs of 7,000 to 8,000 in the 1780s, while the government-backed *Gazette de France* reached printings of 15,000 on the eve of the Revolution.[28]

A trial brief published in the context of a cause célèbre circulated at

26. Letter from the police lieutenant Sartine to the printers' and booksellers' guilds, 17 August 1774, Bibliothèque Nationale, Collection Anisson 22179, folio 326.

27. Wallace Kirsop, "Les Mécanismes éditoriaux," in Henri-Jean Martin and Roger Chartier, eds., *Histoire de l'édition française*, vol. 2: *Le Livre triomphant, 1660–1830* (Paris: Fayard, 1990), pp. 28–29.

28. Jean Sgard, "La Multiplication des périodiques," in Martin and Chartier, *Histoire de l'édition* 2:205; Jeremy Popkin, "The Gazette de Leyde under Louis XVI," in Censer

least as widely as a successful book or major newspaper. We know this in large part thanks to the journal of Siméon-Prosper Hardy, a chronicler of current events, who was also a bookseller by trade and took a professional interest in quantities and prices of printed matter. Thus, we learn from Hardy that in 1772 3,000 copies were printed of Vermeil's *Mémoire pour Geneviève Gaillard,* that very successful mémoire that first introduced the Véron-Morangiès case to the Parisian public.[29] In the course of that same case, Delacroix boasted that 3,000 copies of his first brief for the Véron family "could not satisfy the public's burning curiosity."[30] Interest in the case apparently did not flag over the next two years: in April of 1774, a staggering 10,000 copies were reportedly printed of François Dujonquay's appeal of the case to the Parlement.[31]

It is true that one finds cases much earlier in the century—most notably the great Jansenist *affaires* of the twenties and thirties—that provoked similar press runs of mémoires; and of course there were plenty of much less publicized cases, like that of a Mlle Peloux in 1776, in which only 300 copies of a brief were printed.[32] But throughout the 1770s, printings of 3,000 to 6,000 copies continued to be the norm for mémoires published in the context of sensational court cases. One of Linguet's more notorious pieces was printed up in 3,000 copies in 1774; the following year Falconnet's first brief against the comte de Guines reached either 4,000 copies (according to Hardy) or 6,000 (according to its author), while an eagerly awaited mémoire by the playwright Beaumarchais had a press run of 6,000.[33] We shall see in a later chapter that in the 1780s, the number of mémoires per printing contin-

and Popkin, *Press and Politics,* p. 86; Gilles Feyel, "Réimpressions et diffusions de la Gazette dans les provinces: 1631–1752," in Pierre Rétat, ed., *Le Journalisme d'ancien régime* (Lyon: Presses Universitaires de Lyon, 1981), pp. 76–77; Jean Sgard, "Les Souscripteurs du *Journal étranger,*" in Hans Bots, ed., *La Diffusion et la lecture des journaux de langue française sous l'Ancien Régime* (Amsterdam: Holland University Press, 1988), pp. 97–98.

29. Hardy's journal, which covers the years 1764–1789, is entitled *Mes Loisirs;* it makes up volumes 6680 to 6687 of the Manuscrits français collection in the Bibliothèque Nationale; here, Ms. Fr. 6681, 4 November 1772.

30. Jacques-Vincent Delacroix, *Mémoire pour le sieur Dujonquay et la dame Romain contre le comte de Morangiès* (Paris: P. G. Simon, 1772), p. 34.

31. Ms. Fr. 6681, 20 April 1774.

32. David Bell, "Lawyers and Politics in Eighteenth-Century Paris (1700–1790)" (Ph.D. diss., Princeton University, 1990), pp. 150–157; Ms. Fr. 6682, 26 January 1776.

33. Ms. Fr. 6681, 9 February 1774; Ms. Fr. 6682, 21 February 1775; Falconnet, *Mémoire pour M. Falconnet,* p. x; Ms. Fr. 6682, 22 January 1775.

ued to increase: printings of 10,000 or more were frequent in the great cases of the eighties, such as the so-called Diamond Necklace and Kornmann affairs.

Trial briefs were printed in quantities that were extremely large by eighteenth-century standards. And in addition to the size of press runs, one must remember that a big case like the Véron-Morangiès affair could generate several dozen trial briefs over a year or two, although apparently only the mémoires designed to make a big impact, like the *Mémoire pour Geneviève Gaillard,* were issued in thousands of copies. Not only were these documents plentiful, they were also easily accessible: one of the most remarkable facts about mémoires is that these extremely popular pamphlets could often be obtained free of charge. In theory, as we have seen, trial briefs were internal memoranda destined for the judges and the relatives of the feuding parties; as such, they were not supposed to be for sale. A royal edict of March 1774 spelled this out, in an attempt, no doubt, to contain the proliferation of such documents touched off by the Morangiès case: mémoires, it stated, could not be sold until a year after the final verdict had been handed down in the case to which they pertained.[34]

In many cases, mémoires were indeed given out free: Hardy frequently used the terms "distributed" or "distribution" in describing the initial dissemination of a trial brief, and sometimes he was even more specific. On 17 February 1775, he noted that a brief for the duc de Richelieu against his adversary Mme de Saint-Vincent had been written by the lawyer Tronchet, "who was distributing it free of charge to all those who asked for it."[35] Not surprisingly, litigants who were on the losing side of a case appear to have been more likely to give out their mémoires free: in 1773 the magistrate Goezman, who was being routed by Beaumarchais, had a copy of his defense given to all those who cared to write their names on a roll kept by his doorman; in the 1780s, the countess de La Motte, in jeopardy for her unsavory role in the Diamond Necklace scandal, showered Paris with free copies of the brief written for her.[36]

Nonetheless, it was even more common, especially in important or

34. François Isambert et al., *Recueil général des anciennes lois françaises depuis 420 jusqu'à la révolution,* 29 vols. (Paris, 1821–1833), 20:561.

35. Ms. Fr. 6682, 17 February 1775.

36. Ms. Fr. 6681, 27 November 1773; Ms. Fr. 6685, 26 November 1785.

sensational cases, for trial briefs to be sold, and the law of 1774 seems to have made no significant difference in this respect. Some lawyers, like Delacroix, waxed self-righteous about this: "I strongly disapprove of the sale of mémoires," he grumbled. "A litigant must not display on the stalls of booksellers that which is meant to be distributed generously to all those who take an interest in his case." [37] He and Linguet had traded insults on this subject during the Véron-Morangiès case; in the course of the affair Delacroix wrote that Linguet "accuses us of selling our trial briefs, but there has not yet been one of his which we have not been obliged to buy; the booksellers from whom he gets money must be having a good laugh about his little notes." [38] The booksellers would be smirking because they, as well as the authors who wrote the briefs, stood to make a profit from the sale of mémoires. In 1786 the advocate-general of the Paris Parlement complained that trial briefs, published in ever greater numbers, "have become less the defense of clients than an object of curiosity and amusement for the public, much more a matter of trade for booksellers and a financial speculation for lawyers." [39]

No doubt, a profit could be made from the sale of a mémoire, although how much of the proceeds went to paying the lawyer's fee is not known. Sometimes the profits were allegedly put to good use: in 1786, the lawyer Dupaty's defense of three paupers unjustly condemned to be broken on the wheel was sold for the high price of four livres and four sous, with the proceeds to be donated to the three men, who were languishing in prison. [40] Usually, mémoires sold for considerably less than this. According to Hardy's numerous notations, the price of a trial brief, which seems not to have varied over the course of two decades, was twenty, twenty-four, thirty, or thirty-six sous, depending on its length. [41] (In the French monetary system, as in the English one, the basic monetary unit, the livre, or pound, was made up of twenty sous, and the sou of twelve deniers.) Only in special cases involving censored or manuscript briefs did the prices rise much higher. Hand-written copies of Tar-

37. Delacroix, *Réflexions sur les mémoires*, p. 12.

38. Jacques-Vincent Delacroix, *Examen du résumé général du comte de Morangiès* (Paris: P. G. Simon, 1775), p. 1.

39. *Mémoires secrets* 32:215.

40. Ms. Fr. 6685, 15 March 1786.

41. The numerous notations in Hardy's journal show that in the seventies and eighties a twenty- to thirty-page brief sold for twenty sous, one of sixty to eighty pages for twenty-four sous, and one of one hundred pages or more for thirty-six sous.

get's defense of the Cardinal de Rohan, for instance, were peddled, before its publication, for the astronomical sum of thirty-six livres.[42] In the normal course of things, however, the author of a brief could expect to share with its printer a sizable profit of several thousand livres. The profit motive should not be ignored if one seeks to explain the increasing publicity that surrounded court cases in the later eighteenth century.

Where would a person go to read about the latest developments in a case, perhaps at the cost of one or two livres? Trial briefs could be purchased from booksellers, of course, especially those who kept stalls in the area known as the *enclos du Palais de Justice,* around the main law court, where a brisk trade in printed matter went on. Even inside the great hall of the law court, the legally established *marchands du Palais* faced stiff competition from peddlers and even clerks and refreshment sellers, who illegally hawked briefs and printed decrees while dodging the authorities.[43] But lawyers and litigants often played an important role in seeing to it that their trial briefs reached a large audience; a hot mémoire could often be picked up at the very home of the lawyer who had just written it. The popularity of these items in a big case was so great that their appearance on a bookseller's stall or at a lawyer's doorstep could provoke mob scenes. We have seen that when Target produced his eagerly awaited brief for the rosière of Salency, both his publisher's stall and his own house were looted. In the mid-1780s, the publication of briefs relating to the Diamond Necklace scandal occasioned even bigger presses of avid mémoire seekers; when the lawyer Jean-Charles Thilorier made available his mémoire for the shady Cagliostro, the police authorities had to position eight soldiers from the Paris guard at his door to contain the crowds that had assembled there.[44]

If readers did not come to a trial brief, it would sometimes come to them thanks to the efforts of enterprising lawyers and their clients. In 1785 in Rouen, a young servant named Marie Cléreaux was facing death on the gallows for a theft she had not committed. The lawyer who took on her defense, Louis Froudière, orchestrated an elaborate campaign to ensure that his mémoire defending her was widely read.

42. Ms. Fr. 6685, 13 March 1786.

43. Official attempts to control the trade of printed matter in the *enclos du Palais* are recorded in the decrees of the Bibliothèque Nationale's Anisson Collection, 22114, items 21, 27, 28.

44. Ms. Fr. 6685, 20 February 1786.

He had his own servants, and even his client, place bundles of it in shops and private homes throughout the town and had a colleague send 150 copies to the Paris newspaper *La France littéraire;* the brief was dispatched to the capital and other cities, 6 or 12 copies at a time, stuffed in with the bundles of merchandise that were shipped out of the town's port.[45]

Finally, mémoires often reached their readers thanks to the efforts of the *colporteurs,* or peddlers, who either shouted advertisements for their wares in public places, or went from door to door. During the Diamond Necklace Affair, *colporteurs* often publicized a fresh crop of printed news about the case by bellowing in the streets: "Voilà du nouveau!" ("Fresh news!").[46] In other cases, peddlers would be hired to push trial briefs on potential readers by going from door to door. Beaumarchais himself described a *colporteur*'s visit to his home in a fictional but evocative scene dripping with sarcasm—all the more so since it heads off his response to the mémoire that was being forced upon him by the peddler. An exhausted, panting *colporteur* appears at Beaumarchais's door bearing the most recent brief for the comte de La Blache—who happens to be the playwright's antagonist in a case that is the talk of the town. Beaumarchais asks the man if he knows to whom he is talking: "No, sir; but it doesn't matter: there are three of us running from door to door, with orders to go everywhere, even to the convents and shops—I am not curious, my friend, spare me—ah, do please accept it, sir, so many people have turned it down!"[47]

It was easy enough, then, to get one's hands on a trial brief if one wanted to; but who exactly did want them, and who read them? The questions as to how many people actually read mémoires and who these readers were are the hardest of all to answer, since solid evidence on this is extremely scarce. To begin with, the number of readers cannot, of course, be equated with the number of briefs that were printed. Studies of reading practices in Old Regime towns have demonstrated that any

45. Hans-Jürgen Lüsebrink, "L'Affaire Cléreaux (Rouen 1785–1790): Affrontements idéologiques et tensions institutionnelles sur la scène judiciaire de la fin du XVIIIe siècle," *Studies on Voltaire and the Eighteenth Century* 191 (1980): 895, and "Mémoire pour la fille Cléreaux (Rouen 1785)," *Studies on Voltaire and the Eighteenth Century* 208 (1982): 327.

46. Ms. Fr. 6685, 12 July 1786.

47. Pierre-Augustin Caron de Beaumarchais, "Réponse ingénue de Pierre-Augustin Caron de Beaumarchais à la consultation injurieuse que le Comte Joseph-Alexandre Falcoz de La Blache a répandue dans Aix," in Beaumarchais, *Oeuvres complètes,* 7 vols. (Paris: Leopold Collin, 1809), 4:153–154.

given piece of printed matter, especially one that aroused great interest, would reach several readers.[48] Like newspapers and pamphlets, mémoires were certainly passed from hand to hand; they might be made available in cafés and reading rooms (*cabinets de lecture*); excerpts, at least, would be read aloud at outdoor gatherings and in private homes.[49] Hardy praised one of Beaumarchais's trial briefs by calling it "a piece of literature that deserves to be kept not only in the reading rooms of people of taste, but in all the public libraries."[50] Starting with the Diamond Necklace Affair in the mid-eighties, trial briefs reached an even greater audience as foreign-based newspapers such as the *Gazette de Leyde* began to print extensive excerpts, and occasionally the entire text, of mémoires relating to news-making cases.[51]

The number of readers of an important, well-publicized trial brief would certainly amount to several times the three, five, or ten thousand copies in circulation. The internal evidence of the texts, however, as well as their price when sold, strongly suggest that these items would not reach the barely literate or the laboring poor. The contents of mémoires might be vivid or gripping, aimed at readers who had little technical expertise in legal matters; but they were also written in a high literary style akin to that of contemporary novels, and the arguments they presented usually took place on a level of abstract reasoning inaccessible to those with little schooling. Mémoires would be indigestible fare to people who had only experienced the printed word in chapbooks and almanacs. Besides, at a time when a laborer earned one livre per working day and a skilled artisan two, and half of a working family's income was spent on bread, it is hard to imagine that any worker would even think of spending one or two livres on such ephemeral reading matter.[52]

There were cases when the contents of mémoires seem to have reached, directly or indirectly, a large and socially mixed audience. Louis Froudière's printed defense of Marie Cléreaux was so effective, it seems, that it provoked acts of violence against Cléreaux's master and accuser,

---

48. For a good recent synthesis of this work, see Roger Chartier and Daniel Roche, "Les Pratiques urbaines de l'imprimé," in Martin and Chartier, eds., *Histoire de l'édition française* 2:521–558.

49. Ibid.

50. Ms. Fr. 6681, 22 December 1773.

51. Jeremy Popkin, "The *Gazete de Leyde* Under Louis XVI," in Censer and Popkin, eds., *Press and Politics*, p. 100.

52. On wages and prices, see George Rudé, *The Crowd in the French Revolution* (Oxford: Oxford University Press, 1959), pp. 20–21.

Thibault; on one occasion an angry crowd shouting invectives surrounded his house and threatened to burn it down.[53] But the sparse information available suggests more generally that the "public" of the mémoires was more restricted and mostly upper-class. We saw that the editor of the *Causes célèbres* collection, Gayot de Pitaval, described his readers as members of the bar and men and women of high society. Delacroix used almost the same phrase when describing the reception of one of his briefs: "Judges and *gens du monde*," he wrote, "seemed to welcome my mémoire."[54] Falconnet described a scene in which a "lady of quality" praised his trial briefs to the keeper of seals Miromesnil, who was disparaging them.[55] And Hardy reported that after the publication of one of Linguet's pieces, "one could see today in a Paris café a clique of priests in the midst of whom the aforementioned mémoire was being read with enthusiasm."[56]

In sum, the appeal in *mémoires judiciaires* to the sanction of "public opinion" was undoubtedly a rhetorical convention shaped by political struggles over the course of the century; increasingly, however, the convention overlapped with the growing social reality of the mémoire readers. In the city of Paris, which on the eve of the Revolution counted about half a million inhabitants, five or ten thousand, maybe more, of the most educated, prosperous, and influential people had access to briefs that were sold, given out free, hawked by peddlers, read in cafés, and summarized or reprinted in newspapers. On occasion that public sprang into visible existence, mobbing the houses of lawyers or the stalls of the Palais de Justice after the publication of an eagerly awaited brief. Lawyers, litigants, judges, and public officials were keenly aware of the existence and importance of that public: why else would the authorities have attempted to forbid the publication of more than one hundred copies of the briefs in the lawsuit between the count de Guines and his secretary—no doubt, wrote Hardy, "to prevent the public from knowing of different arguments in the case."[57]

The readers of mémoires could not, of course, exert any direct influence on the course of a trial. None of the magistrates involved in the

53. Lüsebrink, "Mémoire pour la fille Cléreaux," p. 326.

54. Pitaval, cited in Hans-Jürgen Lüsebrink, "Les Représentations sociales de la criminalité en France au XVIIIe siècle" (thesis, Université de Paris-I, 1983), p. 136; Delacroix, *Mémoire pour le sieur Dujonquay,* p. 34.

55. Falconnet, *Le Barreau français,* p. xiv.

56. Ms. Fr. 6682, 31 January 1775.

57. Ms. Fr. 6682, 5 February 1776.

case were elected officials, and the official fiction survived that what went on in the courtroom was a private dispensing of justice in the name of a divine-right monarch. But as Malesherbes, Delacroix, and Falconnet so aptly pointed out, the increasing use of the print medium to publicize court cases was utterly transforming the nature of the relationship between the secluded space of the courtroom and the public arena beyond it. By opening up the secret proceedings of the courtroom to public scrutiny, by tearing the veil of secrecy that had traditionally protected the rich and powerful, and above all by assuming that their readers were endowed with an opinion that mattered, trial briefs were playing a major role in helping to shape a protodemocratic public sphere.

As we have seen in the previous chapters, it was the Maupeou crisis that first began to invest seemingly mundane court cases with a broad political resonance: thus, in the early 1770s the Véron-Morangiès case was construed as a parable about the abuse of social and political power, and the defense of the rosière of Salency became a vision of national regeneration. These cases became infused with political meaning in large part as a result of the personal ambitions and ideological leanings of younger barristers, such as Target, Vermeil, Falconnet, and Delacroix; these were men whose beliefs and behavior were shaped both by their awareness of Voltaire's remarkable success as a judicial crusader and by their own fierce opposition to Chancellor Maupeou.

The young *patriote* lawyers who have figured so prominently in the great cases of the Maupeou years had little to do, however, with the case that more than any other came to symbolize the resistance to the chancellor and his "servile" courts. From April of 1773 to February of 1774, an energetic, multitalented, and until then relatively obscure playwright named Pierre-Augustin Caron de Beaumarchais became embroiled in a highly publicized dispute with a pompous and unpleasant judge from the Maupeou courts named Goezman and the latter's (apparently) dim-witted wife. The four mémoires that Beaumarchais wrote against the Goezman couple have been canonized as the highest literary achievement reached by any author of mémoires, and much quoted as the perfect illustration of the political struggles which in the late eighteenth century pitted talented but downtrodden men against a rigidly inegalitarian social system. But the so-called Goezman Affair, it will be argued here, was less of a culmination than a turning point. With the verbal brio that was soon to become his trademark, Beaumarchais made trial briefs into a form of literature agreeable and acceptable to the elites of town and court, who soon took to using them as weapons against one another in their own internecine disputes.

In the two centuries since the Revolution, the life-story of Beaumarchais has been many times told and retold as a parable of the declining Old Regime.[58] Beaumarchais's first and best biographer, however, was himself: the son of the clockmaker Caron displayed considerable genius in the narration of his own destiny, working hard to merge his identity with that of his most famous character, Figaro, or "le fils Caron," the worthy, witty, and lovable social climber. As a result, biographers have often recounted the life of Beaumarchais within the terms set by their subject himself, as a story of laborious, often thwarted, but ultimately successful upward mobility within the stiflingly hierarchical social world of late-eighteenth-century France.

Were we less influenced by the image of the clever valet, Figaro, railing at his aristocratic master, it would be easier to see the glass as more than half-full, and read the story of Beaumarchais's life as an illustration of the ease rather than the difficulty of social mobility in the late ancien régime. Pierre-Augustin Caron did not exactly start out as a nobody, since he was born the cherished only son (he had five sisters) of a skilled and established Parisian artisan. Young Caron was clever and charming,

---

58. There have been since the nineteenth century an enormous number of biographies of Beaumarchais, not only because of the intrinsic interest presented by the life of this writer, adventurer, parvenu, and man of the world, but also because he has long been considered the embodiment both of the elegance and wit of the late eighteenth century and of a "timeless" French or Parisian spirit—hence the profusion of popular works with titles such as *Beaumarchais: Adventurer in the Century of Women* (by Paul Frischauer; New York: Viking Press, 1935) or *Beaumarchais: Le parisien universel* (by Patrice Boussel; Paris: Levrault, 1983). The classic and most exhaustive biography remains one of the earliest, Louis de Loménie, *Beaumarchais et son temps: Études sur la société en France au XVIIIe siècle*, 2 vols. (Paris: Michel Levy, 1856); other reputable biographies include Eugène Lintilhac, *Beaumarchais et ses oeuvres* (Paris: Hachette, 1887); Louis Latzarus, *Beaumarchais* (Paris: Plon et Nourrit, 1930); Marcel Pollitzer, *Beaumarchais: Le Père de Figaro* (Paris: Vieux Colombier, 1957); René Pomeau, *Beaumarchais ou la bizarre destinée* (Paris: Presses Universitaires de France, 1987); and Frédéric Grendel, *Beaumarchais: The Man Who Was Figaro*, trans. Roger Greaves (New York: Thomas Crowell, 1977). For a full bibliography of works on Beaumarchais, see Bernard Morton and Donald Spinelli, *Beaumarchais: A Bibliography* (Ann Arbor, Mich.: Olivia and Hill, 1988). Such remains the mystique of Beaumarchais as a quintessential representative of his time and place that, so far as I can tell, most biographies continue to defend and romanticize a man who was in fact much reviled in his day. The following section draws mainly on Loménie and Grendel.

an able musician and inventor; by the age of twenty-six, he was a regular visitor at court, having endeared himself, as music teacher, to several members of the royal family; he had also acquired a veneer of ersatz nobility by adopting the name of a small property, Beaumarchais, which had belonged to his first, prematurely deceased, wife.

Obviously, one of Beaumarchais's great assets was a knack for meeting and cultivating the right people. His greatest success in this regard was the close friendship he formed, while in his late twenties, with the wealthy financier Joseph Pâris-Duverney. The latter, one of the richest men in France, probably recognized in Beaumarchais a kindred spirit: Pâris-Duverney was an *arriviste* himself, an innkeeper's son who, like the younger Caron, had clawed his way up the social scale in record time. Starting in about 1760, the seventy-six-year-old banker took on the young man as a business associate and close personal protégé, training him in the ways of the financial world, forking out large sums of money to buy him a patent as royal secretary, and engaging with him in a series of complex business ventures.

It was the death of Pâris-Duverney in 1770 that touched off the lengthy, tortuous court case that was to dominate Beaumarchais's life for the next eight years. To summarize a complicated story, the settlement of accounts between Beaumarchais and Pâris-Duverney was challenged, after the latter's death, by his grandnephew and heir, a rapacious nobleman named Alexandre Falcoz de La Blache. The count de La Blache charged that his great-uncle's signature on his last settlement of accounts with Beaumarchais was a forgery; he maintained that far from being a creditor to the old man's estate, Caron was in fact a major debtor. In February of 1772, after six months of arduous litigation, an initial decision by a lower court found in favor of Beaumarchais and dismissed his opponent's summons for forgery.

La Blache immediately appealed the case to the Parlement of Paris; as bad luck—or bad judgment—would have it, Beaumarchais managed at this time to get into an altercation with a powerful grandee, the duc de Chaulnes, a matter that resulted in his being thrown into the prison of Fort-L'Evêque. In February of 1773, a few weeks before the case was to be judged by the Parlement's magistrates, Beaumarchais was a ruined man and a prisoner; it was in this situation, with his fortunes at an unprecedented nadir, that he came to lock horns with the judge Goezman, the magistrate entrusted with reporting the case to his colleagues in preparation for the final verdict.

Beaumarchais attempted to approach and bribe Goezman, following in this the dictates of contemporary custom, which demanded that defendants present *épices* (a sort of customary bribe) to the magistrates presiding over their cases. He was allowed out of prison for this purpose, and after several fruitless attempts finally managed to present Goezman's wife with payments consisting of a diamond-studded watch, one hundred livres, and fifteen gold louis. The outcome of these efforts was bitterly disappointing. The Goezmans were a venal pair who seemed to have taken some sadistic pleasure in playing games with their victim: Goezman knew that the verdict would go against Beaumarchais and informed him of this with cruel casualness in the course of the one short interview he finally granted him. Indeed, on 6 April 1773, the Parlement charged Beaumarchais with forgery and ordered him to pay fifty-six thousand livres, a very large sum, to his archenemy La Blache.

It was at this juncture that Beaumarchais managed somehow to summon up the courage and ingenuity to turn the whole situation around, armed only with his skill as a polemicist and writer. The Goezmans had at least had the good grace—as custom and prudence dictated—to return most of the *épices* Beaumarchais had offered them. But Mme Goezman, a woman not noted for her disinterestedness, failed to restitute the last and smallest payment of fifteen louis, which she had demanded as a sort of afterthought. It was this ultimate act of dishonest greed that spurred Beaumarchais to counterattack in a series of four hugely successful mémoires aimed at the Goezmans and their associates. Since Goezman was a judge in the highly unpopular Maupeou courts, contemporaries read Beaumarchais's pieces not only as exposures of a venal and heartless magistrate, but also as indictments of the judicial system under Maupeou: "Louis XV toppled the old parlement," ran a popular quip of the day, "fifteen louis will bring down the new one." [59]

By the fall of 1773, Beaumarchais had had the case reopened, charging Goezman with dishonesty, while the latter shot back accusations of "corruption and calumny." Between October of 1773 and February of 1774, the four trial briefs that Beaumarchais wrote in his own defense transformed him from a moderately successful playwright and minor celebrity into a nationally acclaimed writer. Beaumarchais's mémoires against the Goezman couple probably circulated more widely than any other trial briefs in the 1770s, with printings of up to 10,000 copies

---

59. Grendel, *Beaumarchais,* p. 88.

selling out within days of their publication.[60] The reasons why these pieces had such broad appeal is as obvious now as it was when they appeared. Beaumarchais deliberately avoided the ponderous, complicated technicalities that were included in even the most gripping of contemporary mémoires, and reduced the conflict between himself and the Goezman couple to a few points that could be easily grasped, and no less easily judged, by the lay reader: was he wrong to have offered money to the magistrate, not in order to influence his judgment, but merely to be granted the hearing that he, as beleaguered defendant, so desperately needed? And how could his conduct as an isolated, desperate man be compared with the lies and evasions of the powerful judge and his grasping wife?[61]

Around these central questions Beaumarchais set up a dark-hued comedy, featuring himself as protagonist, the courageous, energetic, witty everyman standing up alone to a corrupt establishment: "The necessity of writing against a powerful man is my passport to my readers. I do not deceive myself: for readers this is less a matter of my own justification than of seeing how an isolated man goes about sustaining so great an attack and repulsing it on his own."[62] Those readers were in any case not likely to be bored by the mémoires, whose style is obviously related to that of the playwright's comic masterpieces, and especially of his recently completed—but as yet unperformed—Barber of Seville.[63]

The fast-paced narrative, at the beginning of Beaumarchais's first brief, of his frantic trips to try to approach Goezman, of repeated door-slamming in his face by the latter's servants, of hasty palavers with his family and friends, and of the shifty role played by his two-faced enemies Marin and Baculard d'Arnaud, builds "into a helter-skelter worthy of

60. Ibid., p. 93; Gaudry, *Histoire de Barreau*, p. 285; this figure of 10,000 is probably based on a claim made by Beaumarchais's enemy Marin, to which Beaumarchais alludes repeatedly in the fourth mémoire in the series: see "Quatrième mémoire à consulter pour Pierre-Augustin Caron de Beaumarchais," in Beaumarchais, *Oeuvres* (Paris: Gallimard, 1988), p. 891.

61. These points are driven home forcefully in all four briefs and neatly summarized in the *requête d'atténuation* that closes the third mémoire, "Addition au supplément du mémoire à consulter pour Pierre-Augustin Caron de Beaumarchais"; see *Oeuvres*, pp. 835–844. A *requête d'atténuation* was a plea by the defendant for a reduction in the counts of indictment against him or her.

62. "Mémoire à consulter pour Pierre-Augustin Caron de Beaumarchais" (the first in the series), in *Oeuvres*, p. 707.

63. See John Hampton, "The Literary Technique of the First Two *Mémoires* of Beaumarchais against Goezman," *Studies on Voltaire and the Eighteenth Century* 47 (1966): 177–205.

his comedies."[64] Beaumarchais's characterizations of his enemies range from the elaborate to the pithy and are also the stuff of classic satire. Thus the famous evocation, in the fourth mémoire of Marin, the corrupt censor and gazetteer who helped the Goezmans: "Marin with his sleeves pushed back to the elbows, fishing for evil in muddy water; saying aloud what he wishes, doing quietly what he can; making on one side reputations he tears down on another . . . if he walks, he slithers like a serpent; if he rises, he falls like a toad."[65] This fulsome denunciation of Marin—it goes on for several bilious but funny paragraphs—is hardly more evocative, however, than an earlier rapid sketch of the cold-hearted Goezman peering down into the street from behind his curtains at the desperate Beaumarchais being once again turned away from his door.[66] Finally, there are dialogues aplenty between all of the characters in the mémoires—as well as between Beaumarchais and his reader—including the celebrated account in the second mémoire of the playwright's confrontation in court with the choleric Gabrielle Goezman.

This literary triumph only resulted, for Beaumarchais, in an ambiguous judicial outcome. The Parlement's judges were at least sufficiently aware of his growing popularity to apportion the blame evenhandedly: both Beaumarchais and Mme Goezman were sentenced to a public reprimand, and although the four mémoires were condemned to be burned and lacerated "as containing bold and scandalous imputations, insulting to the magistracy in general," Goezman was also struck from the rolls of the Parlement, and two of his accomplices were publicly admonished.[67] Nonetheless, there can be no doubt of the success of Beaumarchais's four briefs, which contemporaries greeted with "enthusiasm" or "avidity" as established "masterpieces."

It would be a mistake, however, to conclude from the wide circulation and warm reception of the Goezman briefs that these made Beaumarchais into a hero to those middling groups in society—the artisanal and commercial classes—to which he belonged by birth. Indeed, what is remarkable about the reception of his mémoires is the degree to which they seem to have appealed to high society, to the elites of fortune and taste that he had frequented since early adulthood. The bookseller Hardy, for instance, used expressions such as *la cour et la ville* or *les gens*

---

64. Hampton, "The Literary Technique," p. 189; *Oeuvres,* pp. 677–698.
65. Oeuvres, p. 894.
66. In the first mémoire: *Oeuvres,* p. 678.
67. Grendel, *Beaumarchais,* p. 106; B.N. Ms. Fr. 6681, 26 February 1774.

de goût when referring to Beaumarchais's most enthusiastic public, and echoed those readers' praise of the briefs' "style," "wit," and "elegance."[68] Those who joined in the chorus of praise included such luminaries as Voltaire, Rousseau, Mme du Deffand, and, outside of France, Walpole and Goethe: the eminences of the Republic of Letters, as well as the elites of court and town, clasped the new prodigy to their collective bosom.[69]

Within France, the select company in Parisian salons, and even the king's mistress Mme du Barry at Versailles, quickly recognized the dramatic qualities of the mémoires and amused themselves by acting out scenes from them as society playlets: a contemporary piece of salon doggerel praised Beaumarchais as the man "qui trois fois avec gloire / Mit le mémoire en drame et le drame en mémoire."[70] It should be noted, in this context, that Beaumarchais's very first dramatic productions were *parades,* the short, lewd farces written in pseudopopular style that became fashionable among the wealthy in the first half of the century.[71] In the early 1760s, Beaumarchais had cemented his links with the world of aristocratic high finance by writing and acting in such *parades* at the country home of the financier Charles Le Normand d'Etiolles—on the very theater where Mme de Genlis and the marquise de Pompadour had made their acting debuts when young.[72] If one keeps in mind Beaumarchais's early social trajectory, it is hardly surprising that his mémoires became drawing room entertainment. For all of the personal and political passion that informed them, they served to cast him once again in the role that had initially made his fortune: that of court jester to the high and mighty.

The single most celebrated passage in the four mémoires is also the one that provided fodder for salon theatricals at Versailles and elsewhere, the section in the second brief in which Beaumarchais recounts his confrontation in court to Mme Goezman. This episode, punctuated with lively comic dialogue, builds up to a culminating moment in which

---

68. Ms. Fr. 6681, 21 November 1773, 22 December 1773, 13 February 1774.

69. Loménie, *Beaumarchais et son temps* 1:357–359; Grendel, *Beaumarchais,* p. 104; Clément de Royer, *Etude sur les mémoires de Beaumarchais* (Paris: J. Claye, 1872), p. 20.

70. Royer, *Mémoires de Beaumarchais,* p. 20; Loménie, *Beaumarchais et son temps* 1:358.

71. See Pierre-Augustin Caron de Beaumarchais, *Parades,* ed. Pierre Larthomas (Paris: S.E.D.E.S., 1977), introduction; see also Thomas Crow, *Painters and Public Life in Eighteenth-Century Paris* (New Haven: Yale University Press, 1985), pp. 53–54.

72. See Beaumarchais, *Parades.*

the lady adamantly denies ever having heard of, much less received, the famous fifteen louis: "Would there have been any sense in offering fifteen louis to a lady of my quality! to one like me, who had refused a hundred of them on the very eve!—To what eve do you allude, Madam?—Eh, Begod, sir, the eve of the day . . . (she stopped short, biting her lip)—The eve of the day, said I, when you never heard of those fifteen louis, was it not?"[73] Passages such as this one caused the chronicler Hardy to wax enthusiastic: "This Supplement, or new mémoire, which contained the confrontation of M. Caron to the Dame Goezman, was written with as much wit as the first, but was found even more interesting, both because of the clever and satirical shafts dispersed within it, and of the fine and delicate irony that marked it from beginning to end, and which made it most suitable as an amusement for town and court."[74]

The episode featuring Mme Goezman was indeed the stuff of superior "amusement." The situation offered Beaumarchais excellent material for comedy, which he molded into shape by accentuating the contrast between Mme Goezman's clumsy defensiveness and his own poise and wit. He showed some fairness in making it clear that the hapless lady was but a pawn manipulated by her husband and others, "pushed into the arena by those who do not have the courage to appear there themselves."[75]

The comic impact of the scenes between Mme Goezman and Beaumarchais arises most obviously from the sharp contrast in their characters and situations. The judge's wife, as presented by her antagonist, is trying to cover up her husband's and her own wrongdoings; this puts her on the defensive and exacerbates her naturally choleric disposition: "Every time a witness came forward, Mme Goezman began by challenging him, objecting to him, and insulting him before he even spoke; then she let him speak."[76] Her sharp, short responses invariably miss the point of the questions that are put to her. Did she know Beaumarchais? "My goodness, no, said Mme Goezman, I don't, nor do I ever want to know him."[77] Beaumarchais's response is condescendingly orotund: "I have not the honor of knowing madame either, but

73. Beaumarchais, *Oeuvres,* p. 723.
74. B.N. Ms. Fr. 6681, 21 November 1773.
75. Beaumarchais, *Oeuvres,* p. 718.
76. Ibid., p. 710.
77. Ibid., p. 713.

after seeing her I cannot resist forming a wish much different from hers."[78] The tone of suave urbanity that is Beaumarchais's throughout the exchange also highlights the sexual difference between the playwright as man-of-the-world, and the quasi-hysterical woman who, when pushed into a corner, resorts to the argument that she cannot in fact remember what happened, because she was suffering at the time from her monthly discomfort.[79]

But the contrast between these ill-matched interlocutors goes beyond differences in sex and character; the disparity is also and most importantly a matter of style and language, as these relate to social class. Beaumarchais triumphs over Mme Goezman not only through the force of his personality and arguments, but also because he has mastered aristocratic arts of poise and social grace and uses these to crush a woman of lower social status. Mme Goezman's responses in court make it painfully clear that despite her husband's elevated position, she is nothing of a *grande dame*. In the manner of a true parvenue, she refers to herself as a "lady of quality" and is given to bragging about the trappings of her upper-class life: "Write down, write down please that monsieur, who spoke to my lackey, does not even know that I have my own livery, I who have two of them, one for winter and another for summer."[80] For all of her pretensions, however, her view of the world is narrowly domestic, as she herself admits: "I mean to say, sir, that I don't look to my husband's business or his hearings, only to my housework."[81]

Most damningly—from the point of view of Beaumarchais and his readers—Mme Goezman speaks like a woman of the people. Her easy recourse to proverbs—"A stupid question deserves no answer"[82]—is a recognizably plebeian habit of speech. Where upper-class speakers cultivated abstraction, she uses concrete, even earthy imagery, as in her alleged comment that she and her husband knew "the art of plucking a chicken without making it squawk."[83] Finally, she tends to preface her remarks with a ringing "Pour cela" or "Ah, pardi," interjections that evoke the marketplace, not the salon.

In response to her outbursts, Beaumarchais adopts a tone of unflap-

---

78. Ibid.
79. Ibid., p. 720.
80. Ibid., p. 715.
81. Ibid.
82. Ibid., p. 727.
83. Ibid., p. 711; the comment also appears in a slightly different version in the first mémoire, p. 679.

pable and mocking gallantry: "I have no reproach to make to madame, not even with regard to the little temper that dominates her at this moment; I can only express regrets that a criminal case is my first occasion to pay her my homages."[84] He destroys her testimony, not only by exposing her lies and contradictions, but also by refusing to take her seriously. He dismisses her, explicitly on the grounds of her sex ("these confrontations, all of these virile debates are not made for women: one feels that they are out of place in the midst of them"),[85] but implicitly on the grounds of class. He speaks to her in the upper-class language of *politesse*, with its subjunctives, symmetries, and circumlocutions; it is a language that Mme Goezman can barely understand, much less respond to: "With all of your nasty roundabout phrases," she bursts out, "you are just trying to tangle me up and cut me off."[86]

To stress the class-bound nature of Beaumarchais's language in his briefs is not to deny their overt political content. In the last *mémoire* especially, no doubt emboldened by the enthusiastic response to his earlier writings, Beaumarchais freely attacked the president of the Parlement, Judge Nicolai, and asserted his right as a "citizen" to argue his case before "the nation": "Each one of us Frenchmen has the honor of being a citizen in the courtroom: that is the only place where we can uphold the rights of equality."[87] He threw in some of the familiar rhetoric about citizens being the judges of judges, and of his own case being that of the nation; these were statements that in the Maupeou years, as we have seen, were recognizably close to *patriote* sentiment.

There can be no doubt of Beaumarchais's links to anti-Maupeou circles. Far from being an isolated nobody, as he liked to portray himself, he was encouraged and helped by some very important somebodies: the lawyers Target and Falconnet, the prince de Conti, and even, at a distance, the duc de Choiseul—in short the staunchest and most powerful enemies of Louis XV's "triumvirate."[88] Beaumarchais thrived on attacking the powerful when their power was misused, but he always took

84. Ibid., p. 713.
85. Ibid., p. 718.
86. Ibid., p. 723.
87. Ibid., p. 887.
88. Grendel, *Beaumarchais,* pp. 55–56; on the prince de Conti's role in the opposition to the Maupeou crisis, see Dale Van Kley, *The Damiens Affair and the Unraveling of the Ancien Régime, 1750–1770* (Princeton: Princeton University Press, 1984), pp. 144–147, and Nina Gelbart, *Feminine and Opposition Journalism in Old Regime France: Le Journal des Dames* (Berkeley: University of California Press, 1987), pp. 113–114.

pains to make it clear that he respected the social hierarchy that had served him so well. At the end of his fourth mémoire, addressing President Nicolai, he protested: "In all of this, monsieur, I am far from attacking the nobility and the dignities which in you are the mark of your ancestors' virtues."[89] It stands to reason that Beaumarchais would not challenge the principle of aristocracy; the style he cultivated was that of the upper-class *frondeur*, not that of the low-born Grub Street radical. As he had done in writing farces for the wealthy, with titles like *Jean-Bête à la foire* or *Zizabelle mannequin*, he found it easy and profitable to write the script for upper-class mockery of social inferiors.

Beaumarchais's briefs in the Goezman case continued the trend inaugurated at the start of the Maupeou crisis, toward using trial briefs as vehicles for political education and propaganda. Like Malesherbes and Falconnet (the latter was his personal friend and lawyer), Beaumarchais believed that trial briefs and public hearings would promote greater equality before the law and make for a healthier, English-style, judicial system.[90] At the same time, the playwright's literary and social skills contributed to increasing the popularity of the medium among the population at large, but especially among the social elites.

By the mid-1770s, then, the use of trial briefs in some of the most sensational cases of the age was often presented as a challenge to the social and institutional—and hence the political—status quo. Enlightened critics of absolutism like Malesherbes saw in mémoires the beginning of a corrective to the secret, arbitrary, and erratic nature not only of the judicial system, but of the political system as a whole. At the same time, the most sensational use of such documents had occurred in cases that seemed to pit the poor and the powerless against powerful individuals or institutions. How else but through the dissemination of printed briefs could the Vérons or the villagers of Salency have taken on wealthy and well-connected noblemen, or could the humble Calas family or the impoverished Beaumarchais have secured justice in the courts?

As we have seen, however, in many instances apparently downtrodden defendants were neither as poor nor as vulnerable nor, obviously, as blameless as they were portrayed by their defenders. But by the mid-

---

89. Beaumarchais, *Oeuvres*, pp. 887–888.
90. Ibid., pp. 869–870.

1770s, the struggle of the "little man" against his betters had become irreversibly established as a central motif of the cause célèbre—often as a transposition into the realm of social relations of tensions that were mostly political. Such was the rhetorical power of this theme that it carried over into the post-Maupeou era, at a time when the struggle against "despotic" ministers and their allegedly venal law courts had temporarily subsided.

In the early reign of Louis XVI, however, many causes célèbres continued to revolve around themes of social inequality; the purpose of the social typecasting in these pieces was, however, somewhat different than before. From the mid-1770s to the end of the decade, the theme of the "little man against his superiors," and the denunciation of power based on wealth and lineage, continued to pervade the rhetoric of the *mémoire judiciaire*, even as the latter was used to settle scores among the elites of town and court.

Among the many court cases of the immediate post-Maupeou years, two are especially worthy of attention because of the high status of their protagonists and the amount of contemporary commentary they generated. From 1774 to 1777 a peer of the realm accused a noblewoman of fraud and forgery, in a case rife with tales of sordid financial and sexual intrigue. During the same years, a sensational case involving mutual accusations of illegal stock-jobbing pitted the French ambassador in London against his own secretary—and the latter's high-ranking protectors. The central figures in these cases were not, as in previous trials, obscure country squires or penurious army officers, but were among the highest of France's high society: the elites of the realm had taken, it seemed, to washing their dirty linen in public.

In early August of 1774, one chronicler announced with evident relish "a singular trial, rather similar to that of the count of Morangiès," although several days later he detailed the differences between the two cases.[91] The bookseller Hardy, ever avid for the latest gossip, also likened the case of Mme de Saint-Vincent and the duc de Richelieu to the Morangiès case.[92] But while this new cause célèbre resembled the Morangiès affair in that it too revolved around accusations of financial skullduggery on a large scale, it was different in that both of the main

91. [Pidansat de Mairobert], *Journal historique de la révolution opérée dans la constitution de la monarchie française par M. de Maupeou,* 6 vols. (London, 1776), 6:134, 148.
92. Ms. Fr. 6681, 21 August 1774.

protagonists were of very high rank.[93] Julie de Vence-Villeneuve belonged to an illustrious family of the Provençal nobility of the robe; most of her male relatives were judges or high magistrates in the parlement of Aix—as well as substantial landholders—and she was the great-granddaughter, on her mother's side, of the marquise de Sévigné of letter-writing fame. At the age of fifteen, Julie had been suitably married to the marquis de Fauris de Saint-Vincent, a *président* in the parlement of Aix, but she subsequently committed indiscretions that resulted in her being confined, at the behest of her father and her husband, to a convent in the southwestern town of Millau.

While in the convent, she began a correspondence with her relative the aging and imperious Louis-François-Armand du Plessis, maréchal-duc de Richelieu. Richelieu, a peer of France and member of an illustrious family, had since 1755 served as governor of Guyenne and Gascony; from Paris or from the governor's mansion in Bordeaux, Richelieu ruled over southwestern France "like a viceroy."[94] The purpose of Mme de Saint-Vincent's letters to him, at least initially, was to ask for sums of money with which to supplement the allowance granted to her by her family; although the nature of the relationship between the two at this point remains unclear, the duke apparently complied with her requests. Richelieu was also instrumental in securing Mme de Saint-Vincent's transfers from one fashionable convent to the next—to Tarbes, then Poitiers, and finally Paris. At some point Saint-Vincent and the duke became lovers, but there were other men in her life as well, among them a middle-aged officer, Vedel de Montel, and a shady businessman from Languedoc named Benaven. (Mme de Saint-Vincent's reputation for dissoluteness was to weigh heavily against her in the subsequent court case.)

Since Mme de Saint-Vincent made no secret of her intimate relations with Richelieu, nobody seems to have been surprised when in June of 1773, in Paris, she and her friends began to negotiate money orders for large sums bearing the duke's signature. Since it would have been

93. The following account of the background and unfolding of the case is based on J. B. Mary-Lafon, *Le Maréchal de Richelieu et Madame de Saint-Vincent* (Paris: Didot et Cie, 1863). For brief accounts of the trial, see Henri Carré, *La Noblesse de France et l'opinion publique au XVIIIe siècle* (Paris: Champion, 1920), pp. 285–290; and Jean-Louis-Girard Soulavie, *Memoirs of the Duke of Richelieu*, 3 vols. (New York: Baker and Merrill, 1904), 3:144–157.

94. William Doyle, *The Parlement of Bordeaux and the End of the Old Regime, 1771–1790* (London: Ernest Benn, 1974), pp. 4–5.

DAME JULIE DE   VILLENEUVE
VENCE DE   St VINCENT.

Petite Fille de   *Mme de Sévigné.*

3. Julie de Saint-Vincent, in a portrait done at the time of her suit against the duc de Richelieu. The caption identifies her as the granddaughter of Mme de Sévigné, and the artist has no doubt deliberately emphasized her "lasciviousness." (Phot. Bibl. Nat. Paris)

LOUIS FRANCOIS ARMAND DUPLESSIS DUC DE
RICHELIEU ET DE FRONSAC.
Pair et premier Marechal de France &c.a &c.a &c.a
Dedié a Mgr. le Duc de Richelieu son Fils
Pair de France &c.a.

D'après le modele en terre Par son très humble et très
fait en 1785. par Deseine respectueux Serviteur L.Bouteloup
Sculpteur Lourd et muet. Graveur de S. A. S.Mgr. le P^{ce} de Condé.
rue St. Hyacenthe n° 17.

4. The duc de Richelieu. The model for the engraving was a terra-cotta bust
   sculpted in 1785. (Phot. Bibl. Nat. Paris)

unseemly for a woman of Saint-Vincent's rank to peddle the *billets* herself, she did so through the intermediary of Vedel, Benaven, and her nephew, the abbé de Villeneuve-Flayosc. The money orders came to the very large sum of 425,000 livres, some 300,000 of which she had already negotiated. Some of the bills were cashed, but most of them were traded against hard goods; the single largest sum, 55,000 livres, was paid to a Jewish dealer in secondhand clothes and furniture, named Rubit or Ruby.

It was the latter who exposed the whole affair by entering in contact with Richelieu's steward in June of 1774. Rubit was immediately detained, and a few days later the duke himself rushed back from Bordeaux to confront Saint-Vincent and her associates, who insisted that the money orders were authentic. The Paris police chief, Sartine, was alerted, and on 24 July 1774 Saint-Vincent, Vedel de Montel, and Benaven were arrested on charges of fabricating over 300,000 livres worth of money orders bearing the forged signature of the duc de Richelieu. In the course of preliminary interrogations by the police authorities, Mme de Saint-Vincent insisted that the duke had given her presents of large sums of money, not only because she was his mistress, but also because during her stay in Poitiers she had become pregnant by him.[95]

The matter was originally investigated by the lower jurisdiction of Paris, the Châtelet court. In the fall of 1774, however, upon the restoration of the pre-Maupeou Parlement, Saint-Vincent appealed to the high court on the grounds that Richelieu had illegally ordered her arrest. This tactic proved successful, and in May of 1775 the Paris Parlement annulled part of the previous procedure and took over the whole affair.[96] Initially, public sentiment seems to have favored the marquise, or at least to have been hostile to the aging and authoritarian marshal-duke. At the very start of the case, Hardy wrote that it was to be feared "that Mme de Saint Vincent, guilty or not, should become the victim of that lord's ill-deserved influence, however discredited he might be in the minds of all honest people."[97] Over a year later, the *Mémoires secrets* re-

---

95. Mary-Lafon, *Le Maréchal de Richelieu*, pp. 109–110. The outcome of the alleged pregnancy is not mentioned in the sources; if it was real, one can only presume that Mme de Saint-Vincent miscarried or had an abortion, since there is no subsequent mention of a child in the sources.

96. *Nouvelles extraordinaires*, 19 August and 30 August 1774; Carré, *La Noblesse de France*, 287.

97. Ms. Fr. 6681, 21 August 1774.

ported that "all of the public, at least the less prejudiced portion of it, is beginning to side with the présidente."[98]

Support for Mme de Saint-Vincent began to fall off, however, when handwriting experts were brought in on the case. It was persuasively demonstrated that the duke's handwriting and signature on the bills had been forged; someone had traced the letters on the bills from an authentic sample of the duke's handwriting, probably by placing the original under a blank sheet of paper and holding both sheets up against a window.[99] Since Mme de Saint-Vincent was in correspondence with Richelieu and therefore possessed numerous samples of his handwriting, suspicions were bound to fall heavily on her. But even so, the case was far from clear: not only did the role of the marquise's friends Vedel and Benaven remain obscure, but Saint-Vincent also counterattacked by suing the duke, no doubt with good reason, for having had her illegally arrested and detained, and also charged him with bribing witnesses and judges.[100] The elaborate and ambiguous verdict finally handed down by the Parlement in May of 1777 reflected the confusion and conflicts rampant among the magistrates, as among the public at large. The bills were declared to be false, and Mme de Saint-Vincent was condemned to repay those she had already negotiated, although the duke's charges of forgery against her, and hers of bribery against her opponent, were both thrown out of court; all of the marquise's associates were cleared of charges, but Richelieu was ordered to pay heavy damages to them, and was also charged for the printing and posting of the final verdict.[101]

Parisian readers and gossips may not have cared very much that the outcome of the case was so messy. For over three years they had been regaled with stories and speculations about the private lives of two rather unsavory aging libertines. There were plenty of mémoires to read, and Richelieu was wealthy enough to have his given out free of charge.[102] Better still, the marshal had also arranged for the publication of transcripts of the cross-examinations of Saint-Vincent and her associ-

98. *Mémoires secrets* 8:318, December 1775; see also [Pidansat de Mairobert], *Journal Historique* 6:148, 244, 339.

99. Soulavie, *Memoirs* 3:146–147.

100. Ms. Fr 6682, 17 March 1775; [Pidansat de Mairobert], *Journal Historique* 7:143, 27 February 1775; Soulavie, *Memoirs* 3:152.

101. *Nouvelles extraordinaires,* 16 May 1777.

102. The *Gazette de Leyde* alluded, near the end of the case, to the "quantité extraordinaire de mémoires qui ont paru dans cette cause célèbre" (*Nouvelles extraordinaires,* 9 May 1777); for Richelieu's briefs, see Ms. Fr. 6682, 17 February 1775 and 30 January 1776.

ates, a move that was technically illegal but was applauded as bringing the French judicial system closer to its much-admired British counterpart.[103]

The trial itself was sensational, not least because Richelieu was a peer of France, and as such would be judged not only by the magistrates of the high court, but also by the forty or so peers of the realm who joined them on these occasions. Such was the excitement over this matter that the prince de Conti, who held for Richelieu, had himself carried to the Palais de Justice throughout the winter of 1775–1776 even though he was terminally ill and attendants had to rush bowls of hot broth into the courtroom to restore him. When warned that he was endangering his life, Conti grandly retorted: "Gentlemen, I must die somewhere, and I would just as soon die among you as at home."[104] Best of all, of course, was the spectacle of the marquise and the duke, she in her mid-forties and he in his late seventies, former lovers slinging mud at each other. Richelieu denied, of course, that he had ever paid off his erstwhile mistress with money orders: "But madame," he burst out, "have a look at your face. Would one pay such an exorbitant sum for it?" To which came the acid rejoinder: "But you, monsieur, have a look at your own, and ask yourself if one could endure it for less."[105]

Sensationalism alone, however, does not account for the wide resonance of the case. The deliciously scandalous rumor that a high-born lady was making purchases with promissory notes bearing the forged signature of a dissolute grandee might, in other circumstances, have caused a stir for only a few days. But the judicial struggle between the marquise and the duke represented much more than just another morsel for the delectation of the gossips of town and court. To their supporters and detractors, the two protagonists of the affair were the embodiments of several overlapping sets of tensions among the titled elites of the late ancien régime: tensions between aristocratic families, between nobles of the robe and of the sword, and political animosities carried over from the previous reign.

For all of the innovative uses to which trial briefs could be put, they could still serve as vehicles for extremely traditional causes such as the

---

103. [Pidansat de Mairobert], *Journal Historique* 7:115, 17 February 1775, and 7:174, 11 March 1775.

104. *Mémoires secrets* 8:343, 29 December 1775; Ms. Fr. 6682, 17 March 1775 and 7 February 1776.

105. *Mémoires secrets* 8:22, 22 May 1775.

defense of aristocratic lineage and honor. Although Julie de Saint-Vincent certainly qualified as the black sheep of her family, the extended clan of her Provençal relations rushed to her defense as soon as the scandal broke out. In August of 1774, a gazetteer reported that Mme de Saint-Vincent was related to "many people of quality, whose warm support she enjoys in this affair."[106] Indeed, as a Villeneuve, she belonged to one of those select families of the Provençal nobility that could trace their lineages back to the thirteenth century.[107] And once the trial had been transferred before the Parlement, an incendiary and much-publicized brief was presented to the judges, and then circulated among the public, signed by the cream of the Provençal aristocracy: the Villeneuves, Castellanes, Forbins, Simianes, and others.[108]

The relatives of Mme de Saint-Vincent were in the embarrassing position of having to defend a woman whose conduct had been such as to warrant her confinement in a convent. They did so by stigmatizing the duke as a subverter of aristocratic honor and family loyalty: who was he, after all, to "tear her from the asylum that her family's prudence had prepared, in order to protect her from her own weakness," to "violate a judgment pronounced by the authority of her kin"? Such family justice, they argued, was the very basis of "a nation governed by honor."[109] And yet another brief, written by Mme de Saint-Vincent's nephew, railed in the strongest of terms against Richelieu's affront to the house of Villeneuve in the person of a woman who was "a hundred times above him by her birth."[110]

Thus, the Richelieu–Saint-Vincent case reflected, on one level, a struggle between members of the French high nobility, fought out in the name of such traditional aristocratic values as lineage, family honor, and the protection of their womenfolk's reputations. The *Gazette de Leyde* picked up on this in a discussion of the brief: "It is not really the case between M. le Maréchal and his relative that they lay out in their mémoire; it is the affront to themselves and their family which they wish

106. [Pidansat de Mairobert], *Journal Historique* 6:141, 8 August 1774.

107. Michel Vovelle et al., *Histoire d'Aix-en-Provence* (Aix-en-Provence: Edisud, 1977), p. 193.

108. *Mémoire à consulter pour les parens de Madame de Saint-Vincent* (Paris: P. G. Simon, 1775). Rumors about the brief circulated long before its publication in December of 1775; Richelieu was so offended by its tone that he requested unsuccessfully that it be censored as a *libelle*. See *Mémoires secrets* 8:325, 14 December 1775, and *Nouvelles extraordinaires*, 18 August 1775.

109. *Mémoire à consulter pour les parens*, pp. 2, 7.

110. Cited in *Mémoires secrets* 10:131, 29 April 1977.

to avenge."[111] The novelty of it was that a matter that might have been settled in the not too distant past by means of a duel was now fought out in print and before a much wider public.

It was not irrelevant, either, that Richelieu as a peer of the realm claimed descent from the great feudal lords of medieval France, while the family and milieu of his opponent were that of the high nobility of the robe. A nineteenth-century chronicler of the case asserted that this was in reality "another guise of the struggle between the Parlement and the court, a personal quarrel between the judges and the princes."[112] And indeed, contemporary sources suggest that while most of the dukes and peers supported Richelieu, many magistrates, especially the younger ones, championed Mme de Saint-Vincent.[113]

The Parlement's magistrates were hardly less elevated than courtiers and peers in the social hierarchy of the Old Regime. There is no doubt much truth to the classic argument that the French robe and sword no-bilities gradually merged over the course of the eighteenth century, be-coming less and less distinct in their lineages, fortunes, modes of living, and ideologies.[114] Certainly the aristocratic magistrates of the Parlement of Paris always upheld the traditional social order and systematically de-fended the fiscal interests of the nobility as a whole.[115] But, as Bailey Stone has demonstrated, long-standing tensions between robe and sword did endure up to the end of the Old Regime, finding their clear-est expression, right up to the 1780s, in judicial affairs in which parle-mentary magistrates opposed high-ranking aristocrats.

Five years after the end of the Saint-Vincent case, for instance, a triv-ial dispute over a theater seat broke out in Paris between the arrogant young comte de Moreton-Chabrillant and a *procureur* named Du-plessis. Was it a coincidence that Duplessis's attorney, who handily won the case by denouncing the count's contumelious behavior, was the same Jean Blondel who had defended Vedel de Montel against Riche-lieu in the 1770s? Nobody missed the social implications of the Chabril-

111. *Nouvelles extraordinaires,* 18 August 1775.

112. Mary-Lafon, *Le Maréchal de Richelieu,* p. viii.

113. *Mémoires secrets* 8:343, 29 December 1775; Carré, *La Noblesse de France,* p. 289.

114. The classic statement of this case is Franklin Ford, *Robe and Sword: The Regroup-ing of the French Aristocracy after Louis XIV* (Cambridge, Mass.: Harvard University Press, 1953). See also François Bluche, *Les Magistrats du Parlement de Paris au XVIIIe siècle* (Paris: Les Belles-Lettres, 1960).

115. Bailey Stone, *The Parlement of Paris, 1774–1789* (Chapel Hill: University of North Carolina Press, 1981), pp. 93–100.

lant case when Blondel contrasted Duplessis, "dressed in the customary fashion of his estate, in black with long hair," to the count "in rose-colored coat, with sword and plumed hat"; they certainly understood in Bordeaux, where parlementary families could intermarry freely with middling nobles of the sword, but could never hope for a match with the great Versailles-connected families of the region, the Richelieus, d'Aiguillons, or La Tour du Pins.[116] Only two years later, in 1784, it was the Paris magistrates who found themselves openly at war with Riche-lieu (now aged eighty-eight, but ever cantankerous) who, as governor of Guyenne and leader of the marshals of France, was defying the authority of the parlements by subjecting the mayor of Bordeaux to a military trial.[117]

Intranobiliary quarrels, however, were not the only underlying factors in the Richelieu–Saint-Vincent case. As we have seen, many of the great causes célèbres of the 1770s reflected the political tensions of the Maupeou crisis. In this case, the connections were more obvious than usual, for Richelieu was deeply involved in the chancellor's show of force and may indeed have been one of its instigators.[118] It was the authoritarian marshal-duke who was dispatched to handle the crisis in Bordeaux, and who presided over the dismantling of the courts there by having *lettres de cachet* handed to most of the magistrates; it was he, also, who recruited the personnel for the new courts and implemented locally such reforms as the abolition of office venality and of customary bribes (*épices*).[119] Although Richelieu continued to earn the respect of some Bordelais magistrates, who never lost their admiration for his effectiveness and high sense of duty, to many others he represented locally what Maupeou was nationally, a symbol of hated despotism (in the aftermath of the crisis the story circulated in Bordeaux that one angry magistrate had disrupted a dinner party by apostrophizing, and then slicing the ears off, a plaster bust of the marshal-duke).[120]

When the affair with Mme de Saint-Vincent was brought before the Parlement of Paris, many of the magistrates were only too happy to have this occasion to get back at the man who had ridden roughshod over their provincial colleagues. It did not help Richelieu's case that he had

---

116. Ibid., p. 102; Doyle, *The Parlement of Bordeaux*, p. 16.
117. Stone, *The Parlement of Paris*, pp. 100–111.
118. Mary-Lafon, *Le Maréchal de Richelieu*, p. v.
119. Doyle, *The Parlement of Bordeaux*, pp. 144–148.
120. Ibid., pp. 162–170, 175 n. 95, 219.

a widespread reputation for abusing his personal authority, that he was known to have had individuals summarily imprisoned, on a whim. The relative harshness of the sentence against him at the end of the case has been plausibly attributed to the Paris Parlement's desire to exact revenge on the imperious old man.[121] Given the duke's past history and the fact that Julie de Saint-Vincent was connected to the high provincial magistracy, the case was bound to have political as well as social implications for the ruling elites of the 1770s.

We have seen how, earlier in the decade, personal and political animosities connected to the Maupeou crisis were translated, in the judicial arena, into striking descriptions of social asymmetry and of the abuse of power, as was the case in the Véron-Morangiès and Beaumarchais-Goezman affairs. But in the trial that concerns us now, the fact that the protagonists were both members of the high nobility might seem to exclude such a scenario. Such was not, however, the case. Richelieu's prominent involvement in the political crisis of the early 1770s once again gave issues of arbitrary power a central place in the trial briefs that recounted the affair. In this instance, however, the case pitted a man against a woman; as a result, issues of gender came to complement— and in some ways to displace—the discussion of sociopolitical inequality.

Mme de Saint-Vincent had been illegally detained by a powerful grandee, and the latter had appealed to be judged by his fellow dukes and peers; all of this made the matter of social rank an inescapable issue. To the rank and file of the Paris Parlement, the social difference between a noblewoman of the robe and a peer of France would be quite obvious. This much was implicit in the response to Richelieu of one of the magistrates' spokesmen, Rolland de La Challerange—a *parlementaire* activist with close links to the eminent Jansenist Adrien Le Paige. According to Hardy, Rolland had countered Richelieu's insults to the marquise by stoutly declaring that "in the eyes of justice, red heels and clogs, the man of the lowest station and the commander of armies, were the same thing." Since the duke no more commanded armies than the marquise wore clogs, Hardy translated this for his readers as meaning that the *parlementaires* intended to extend no special considerations to Richelieu on account of his elevated station.[122] But if the difference in social position between the duke and the marquise was obvious to members

121. Soulavie, *Memoirs* 3:152–157.
122. Ms. Fr. 6682, 4 July 1775.

of the high social elite, it would be much less evident to the wider audience of mémoire readers. And yet, issues of rank and social inequality were in fact made central to the case, thanks to the efforts of barristers eager to capitalize on what was fast becoming a central motif of the cause célèbre; such issues were simply displaced from the protagonists of the case onto secondary figures. In all cases, however, the most rhetorically accomplished briefs were those that attacked Richelieu—as high nobleman, as courtier, and as predatory seducer.

One of the most striking briefs in the case, for instance, was that written for Saint-Vincent's lover, François Vedel de Montel, by a forty-two-year-old lawyer named Jean Blondel. The keen sense of rank and the resentment of social injustice that infuse the florid prose of Blondel's brief were perhaps a reflection of the barrister's own rapid upward mobility: although a member since 1760 of the prestigious Ordre des Avocats—on his way to occupying high posts in the royal administration— Blondel was the son of a baker.[123]

Blondel's *Défense de François de Vedel Montel,* published in 1775, was a first-person narrative in his client's voice—not a sprightly *recitativo* in the style of Beaumarchais, but a melodramatic autobiography that began: "What irresistible power governs the destiny of men!"[124] The *Mémoires secrets* suggest that the brief was well received: "It is very well done, clear, methodical, but verbose and sometimes emphatic in style."[125] Like Vermeil's briefs for the Vérons, Blondel's was organized antithetically, around a contrast between a respectable family man and an isolated, manipulative seigneur. Vedel, however, was a nobleman, the last male descendant of a dynasty of military officers; his lawyer capitalized on both Vedel's fatherlessness and his military ancestry to inject plenty of pathos-with-dignity into the mémoire: "Proud and generous father, venerable ancestors," Blondel/Vedel intoned, "you who died bearing arms for the defense of the nation, arise from your graves and come testify for me."[126]

Since Vedel happened not to have a close-knit family to drape around himself, he and his lawyer invented one by evoking the officers who cared for the young man after the battlefield deaths of his father and

123. Albert Poirot, *Le Milieu socio-professionnel des avocats du Parlement de Paris à la veille de la Révolution (1760–1790),* 2 vols. (thesis, Ecole des Chartes, Paris, 1977), 1:29.
124. Jean Blondel, *Défense de François de Vedel Montel, chevalier de l'ordre royal et militaire de Saint-Louis* (Paris: P. G. Simon, 1775).
125. *Mémoires secrets* 8:39.
126. Blondel, *Défense de Vedel Montel,* p. 5.

brother. Left on his own, "Vedel" writes, he was taken on by the regiment in a sort of "military adoption," which he evokes, curiously, by stepping outside of himself: "I have never forgotten the sublime and touching spectacle of a young orphaned officer, always surrounded by his adoptive fathers, by those aged and respectable warriors, keeping at bay from him the licentiousness of the camps, and setting up around his person a sort of incorruptible guard of advice, understanding, and experience." [127]

This world of warm but martial camaraderie is described as a foil to Richelieu's natural environment, the court—a place of intrigue, deception, and illusion. The duke is at ease with the ways of court life, of which Vedel claims total innocence: "I am a warrior, not a courtier; I know only how to serve my prince and my country, and I do not understand the language of the court, which is said to be more given to flattery than to truth." [128] The words that recur in reference to Richelieu are such terms as *crédit, intrigue,* or *illusion;* these are the tools with which power is wielded at court and which can be used to ruin a simple *citoyen* ignorant of the ways of Versailles. Although Vedel was neither a commoner nor, it seems, poverty stricken, the lawyer managed in his brief to create an artificially wide social gap between the two men. Thus, although writing in a dispute between two noblemen, Blondel managed to make the egalitarian rhetoric of his brief sound like a very apt illustration of Falconnet's and Delacroix's argument that the best use of the publicity of mémoires was as a defense of the weak and poor against the wealthy and powerful: "We are now, my adversary and I, two perfectly equal men both appearing before that which the French people find most imposing and worthy of respect, before the first and most equitable of tribunals, before which all ranks, decorations, dignities and fame disappear." [129]

Vedel and his lawyer denounced Richelieu for abusing his status and power not just as a wealthy nobleman but as a courtier and grandee (*un grand du royaume*), a statesman with direct access to the center of power at Versailles: the terminology used was one in which social and political categories overlapped. This conflation of high social status with unjust authority can also be found in other briefs in the case, such as the defense of the clothes dealer Rubit (accused of complicity with Vedel and

127. Ibid., p. 9.
128. Ibid., p. 16.
129. Ibid., p. 6.

Saint-Vincent) by François de Neufchâteau. (Neufchâteau was a dis-barred lawyer, originally from the east of France, who went on to have an active career in public life under the Revolution, culminating in his election to the Legislative Assembly in 1791).[130] Neufchâteau's brief was also written in the first person, in the voice of the Jewish merchant who takes pride in "the virtuous obscurity of a modest trade."[131] Rubit's main line of defense was to assert his utter ignorance of the falsity of the bills. But his lawyer also had him trying desperately to see the duke in order to clear his name, and being repulsed from the door by Riche-lieu's henchmen—which prompted the following tirade: "Truth is fated always to present itself at the door of the mighty, and always to be turned away. These illustrious captives, locked up in the splendid prisons which they call palaces, seem to be deprived of all communication with human beings; or, if one prefers, these deities hidden within their temples place at the doors of their sanctuaries inflexible guards whose constant duty is to turn away the profane."[132]

An obscure but honest tradesman, Rubit defends himself (through the pen of his lawyer) by pointing less to Richelieu specifically than to the general victimization of the poor by the capricious, but carefully concealed, power of the great. And once again, the appeal to social jus-tice shades into a commentary on arbitrary authority; at the end of the brief, Neufchâteau waxes eloquent about "the legitimate alarm felt by citizens if the name of a grandee is enough to cause their ruin." But thankfully, he concludes, "there are today magistrates who judge cases without making personal exceptions: there is a tribunal before which the inequality of rank disappears."[133]

The now familiar themes of social inequality and arbitrary power were thus displaced, in this case, onto the briefs for secondary characters in the affair; given Richelieu's personal reputation and the recent mem-ory of his role in the Maupeou crisis, it is likely that readers understood clearly the political implications of the way he was portrayed in the mémoires against him. But, one may ask, what of the briefs pertaining to the two protagonists in the case? Given that Richelieu and Mme de

130. On Neufchâteau's career, see Mary-Lafon, *Le Maréchal de Richelieu,* pp. 167–168.
131. François de Neufchâteau, *Mémoire pour le sieur Rubit l'aîné, marchand mercier, pr[emier] tailleur du roi, contre M. le maréchal-duc de Richelieu* (Paris: Clousier, 1775), p. 3.
132. Ibid., p. 11.
133. Ibid., pp. 13–14.

Saint-Vincent were both wealthy, privileged types, could their mémoires against each other raise points that transcended the simple ad hominem attack?

The briefs written for Mme de Saint-Vincent, however, are similar to those for Vedel and Rubit in that they too attack Richelieu by transforming him into a symbol of authority misused; the difference is that where the other briefs couch their case in class terms, those for the marquise make a central issue of the sexual power exercised by the old roué over the allegedly vulnerable Julie. As we have seen, the mémoire issued by Mme de Saint-Vincent's relatives was couched as a family defense of her injured honor. But the terms used in this denunciation of Richelieu as sexual predator specifically emphasize the imperious, arbitrary nature of the power he wields: he is an "active and powerful man," "an oppressor who rises over us, overturns the laws, forces open our homes, takes possession of our persons." [134] The behavior and language described are similar to those attributed to Morangiès: Richelieu sends the police commissioner Chenon to seize the marquise, accompanied by "twenty henchmen"; the reported speech attributed to the duke is peppered with such verbs as *il exige* or *il veut*.[135] And what this aristocratic bully wants is the ruin, not of a social inferior, but of "a weak, frivolous, thoughtless woman," a trusting creature whom he made into "the companion and victim of [his] vices." [136]

In sum: the Richelieu–Saint-Vincent case offers us an example of the ways in which a scandal purely internal to the high aristocracy was adapted to the new conventions of public discourse of the post-Maupeou years. Because of the duc de Richelieu's prominent (and mostly unpopular) role in the Maupeou coup, the case can be viewed as one of the many aftershocks of that crisis. But just as the Maupeou crisis had brought forth an unprecedented amount of open and polemical discussion of political matters, so the personal scandals touching participants in that crisis also became, through the proliferation of mémoires, a matter of intense public concern. This argument is not meant to suggest that scandals concerning the rich and powerful were never widely broadcast before the 1770s. As we saw in the previous chapter, the lives of the French elites were often acted out in public—as was, indeed, the life of the monarch at Versailles. But the audience before

---

134. *Mémoire à consulter pour les parens de Madame de Saint-Vincent,* pp. 1–2.
135. Ibid., pp. 4–5.
136. Ibid., pp. 1, 9.

which one's life was displayed was originally a small group of insiders—
le monde, la cour, et la ville. The case we have just examined suggests
some of the ways in which the peculiar conditions of the early 1770s,
as well as the longer-term evolution of judicial practices, bestowed a
novel and growing amount of publicity upon an intranobiliary scandal,
thereby widening the audience before which the wealthy and powerful
played out their financial and sexual intrigues.

The final case that we examine in this chapter began, like so many others, with an arbitrary arrest and imprisonment.[137] On 28 April 1771, a
young man named Barthélemy Tort de La Sonde was thrown into the
Bastille at the request of his employer, the count de Guines. The latter
was a well-connected courtier and, since November of 1770, the French
ambassador to London, where Tort served as his personal secretary. Tort
was incarcerated under charges of fraudulent dealings on the London
stock market. He had allegedly been passing inside information from
the French embassy to various associates, including substantial London
bankers, who could thus anticipate international developments that affected the value of government stocks. In 1771, however, the diplomatic situation was extremely volatile, with war between England and
Spain over the Falkland Islands averted in extremis thanks to mediation
by the French. When Tort's failure to predict this last development led
to enormous losses for his English associates, he fled precipitously to
France, where he was promptly arrested.

Needless to say, the whole affair was a great embarrassment to the
French government, and to Guines in particular, who insisted that Tort
be punished for having used his employer's name in carrying out his
shady transactions. Meanwhile, after a few months in prison, Tort suddenly began to renege on some of his previous statements and to
assert that he had carried out all of his financial transactions on behalf
of Guines, and that it was at the latter's behest that he had fled to
France. Suddenly turning accuser, he entered charges of calumny
against Guines before the supreme jurisdiction of the Conseil du Roi.
In January of 1772, Tort was released from the Bastille for lack of
proof against him.

137. The following summary of the case is based on these accounts: Jacob-Nicolas
Moreau, *Mes Souvenirs*, 2 vols. (Paris: Plon, 1898), 2:125–142; Carré, *La Noblesse de
France*, pp. 289–292; Faure, *La Disgrâce de Turgot*, pp. 330–334; P. Girault de Coursac,
Marie Antoinette et le scandale de Guines (Paris: Gallimard, 1962).

Under pressure from Tort's English creditors, and fearing for the reputation of the whole French diplomatic corps, the foreign minister La Vrillière allowed Tort to take his case against Guines to the lower jurisdiction of Paris, the Châtelet court. In 1773 Guines was recalled from his post in London, and, many months of procedure later, in June of 1775, the Châtelet judges returned an ambiguous verdict; to be sure, the judgment seemed to go against Tort, who was condemned to make public amends to his former employer and to pay a fine of three hundred livres for court expenses. But although Guines's supporters engaged in great shows of celebration, Paris gossips noted that the former ambassador had also been ordered to contribute to court costs, and that if Tort had indeed cheated and slandered, the sentence he received was suspiciously light. Guines went back to London after the trial, only to be recalled early in the following year because Tort had appealed the case before the Paris Parlement. The verdict in the second trial, handed down on 31 March 1777, was remarkably similar to the first. Tort was given a *blâme*, a shaming admonition, and once again fined three hundred livres, while Guines's name was cleared. Clout, if not justice, had once again prevailed. There was more to the Tort-Guines case, however, than first met the eye, and this was hardly a secret. Just about everyone among the literate Parisian public knew that this was a political affair; in this instance, however, the power struggle that underlay the case had less to do with the ideological conflicts of the Maupeou era than with good, old-fashioned court politics.

At the beginning of the reign of Louis XVI, the French court was polarized around two factions, holdovers from the previous reign whose antagonism had been exacerbated by the Maupeou crisis. On one side was the group of courtiers who had, under Louis XV, gravitated around the duc de Choiseul, the omnipotent grandee who for twelve years had directed French foreign policy before being ousted from office by his enemies in 1770. Even after his banishment, Choiseul retained a strong group of supporters at court, who continued into the next reign an unsuccessful campaign to get him back into power. Support for Choiseul made for strange political bedfellows. On the one hand, Choiseul and his partisans were backed by Marie-Antoinette, both before and after she became queen, since Choiseul had been the architect of the alliance with Austria that had resulted in her marriage in 1770 to the future Louis XVI. On the other hand, the Choiseulist group had connections with the leaders of the Paris Parlement, including some of its radical *patriote* elements, whom it backed during the dark years of the

Maupeou crisis.[138] One of the reasons for the hubbub created by the Tort-Guines case was that Guines was a *créature* of Choiseul, and a close friend of Marie-Antoinette's bosom friend, the duchesse de Polignac, and so enjoyed the queen's support; but thanks to the peculiar logic of court politics, the affable and dim-witted courtier Guines also received legal assistance from such famous *patriote* lawyers as Target and Elie de Beaumont.[139]

What cemented the links between the disparate elements that came under the Choiseulist umbrella in the early 1770s was hatred of a common enemy or, rather, of three common enemies, the notorious triumvirate Maupeou, Terray, and d'Aiguillon. The Choiseulist camp was especially hostile toward d'Aiguillon for as many reasons as the faction had constituencies: d'Aiguillon had, as we have seen, been locked in acrimonious dispute with the parlements of Paris and Brittany in the late 1760s; he had probably masterminded the ousting of Choiseul, whom he succeeded, in 1771, as foreign minister; and the queen had conceived a bitter personal dislike for him. Right from the start of the affair, it had become clear to everyone that Tort's extraordinary counterattack against his employer in 1771 was in fact the work of the then-powerful duc d'Aiguillon.[140]

The Tort-Guines case, then, was a direct emanation of long-standing factional struggles at court, struggles that spanned two reigns and outlived the rise and fall, first of Choiseul and then of d'Aiguillon. The ins and outs of the case were difficult even for well-informed contemporaries to follow; the author of the *Mémoires secrets* concluded the account of a particularly tricky maneuver on the part of d'Aiguillon's enemies by writing that "one must be a courtier to understand the full subtlety and wickedness of such a scheme."[141] The affair represented an important

138. Faure, *La Disgrâce de Turgot,* chap. 1; Girault de Coursac, *Marie-Antoinette,* passim.

139. Durand Echeverria, *The Maupeou Revolution: A Study in the History of Libertarianism* (Baton Rouge: Louisiana State University Press, 1985), p. 43; [Pidansat de Mairobert], *Journal historique* 7:106–110, 11 February 1775. Target and Elie de Beaumont signed the *consultation* that concluded Guines's first and most important brief in the affair, *Mémoire pour le comte de Guines, ambassadeur du roi contre les sieurs Tort et Delpech, ci-devant ses secrétaires* (Paris: Louis Cellot, 1774); although the mémoire itself is signed by the count and an attorney named Letourneau, the quality of the prose suggests that either Target or Elie de Beaumont was its true author.

140. Moreau, *Mes Souvenirs* 2:137; [Pidansat de Mairobert], *Journal historique* 7:107, 11 February 1775.

141. *Mémoires secrets* 8:58, 29 May 1775.

new departure. Earlier in the 1770s, cases that began as courtroom disputes were sometimes invested with broader political meaning by the
writers and lawyers who took them up; in this case, however, the dispute
between Guines and his secretary only became a cause célèbre when and
because the d'Aiguillon faction began to manipulate Tort for their own
political purposes. At least one clear-sighted contemporary wrote that
"this ministerial affair, arbitrated by the king, has become a criminal
trial, and one that has yet to be judged."[142]

Connected to these factional struggles were animosities and alliances
held over from the Maupeou years, as is suggested by the identities of
the lawyers on either side of the case. Guines's barristers were two prominent, unequivocally *patriote* men who had steadfastly boycotted the
Maupeou courts, Target and Elie de Beaumont; their involvement on
Guines's side was logical given their history of *parlementaire* activism
and their probable connections with the Choiseulist camp. On the
other side of the case, however, we find lawyers whose allegiances were
more ambiguous. The identity of one of them will come as no surprise:
Jean-Baptiste Gerbier was Target's long-standing rival, and his public
capitulation to Maupeou had placed him in a situation of de facto alliance with the "ministerial" party.

But Tort also found defenders in two men well known to us by now,
whose position was a good deal more ambiguous—Ambroise Falconnet
and Jacques-Vincent Delacroix. Although both of them seem to have
harbored some *patriote* sympathies (as suggested by Delacroix's role in
the Salency case and Falconnet's support for Beaumarchais in the Goezman affair), they were *avocats rentrants* who had worked for the
Maupeou courts. Several overlapping factors can explain these two barristers' defense of Barthélémy Tort. Their identity as *rentrants* aligned
them, albeit perhaps uncomfortably, with the d'Aiguillon faction at
court; and as we have seen in previous cases, their attacks on the titled
and privileged (Morangiès and Danré) may have drawn on the antiaristocratic themes characteristic of "ministerial" propaganda. In the
Tort-Guines affair Delacroix and Falconnet remained allied with a political faction unpopular with the public at large, and this perhaps explains
their need to court public popularity by trumpeting their concern for
the "little man" in the writings on mémoires analyzed earlier in this
chapter.

And indeed, the lawyers who took on Tort's case were in what could

142. Ibid., 8:42, 18 May 1775.

be termed a situation of "narrative advantage," defending an obscure and vulnerable everyman against his high-ranking employer. Gerbier was one of the first to collaborate in Tort's defense, hoping, among other things, to repair his damaged reputation while continuing to side with the "ministerial" party. The brief he wrote in response to accusations of dishonesty flung at him by Guines is laced with the usual leveling rhetoric: "What would become of the laws, of morality, of our ministry, if every time an unfortunate comes to beg us for our help, we must, before deciding to defend him, take the measure of the credit and power that oppress him? . . . Approach, my fellow citizens, my fellow men. Your poverty will not rebuff my zeal, your misfortune will only increase it."[143]

In order to bolster such claims, Gerbier alluded to his role—in reality quite minimal—in the defense of the Véron family. He drew a suitably tear-drenched tableau of the Véron clan—grandmother, children, grandchildren—arriving at his country house in an open cart and falling on their knees before him, stammering their pleas for help (there are clear echoes here of Voltaire's role in the Calas case).[144] The Morangiès affair was also the main point of reference for Delacroix who, as we have seen, specialized in sentimentalized defenses of the oppressed, having made his name by championing the Vérons and the villagers of Salency. Delacroix's brief in defense of Tort's associate and co-accused, the cloth-merchant Delpech, also sounded the obligatory notes. When a man comes to us for help, he began, and denounces as his opponent a man of stature, whose character and position command respect, we are naturally suspicious, not wanting to believe that a man of high rank could betray the trust that society places in him. "But, arrested by such considerations, will we betray the most sacred of our duties? Will we forget that we are even more the defenders of the feeble and the oppressed than of the wealthy and powerful? No."[145]

The most successful briefs published in conjunction with the case, however, were those written for Tort himself by Falconnet. When Falconnet's eagerly awaited first mémoire for Tort appeared, newspapers and other periodicals summarized its contents for their readers; the

---

143. Jean-Baptiste Gerbier, *Mémoire pour Me Gerbier, ancien avocat au parlement* (Paris: Didot, 1775), p. 37.

144. Ibid., p. 34.

145. Jacques-Vincent Delacroix, *Mémoire pour le sieur Delpech, marchand d'étoffes de soie, en réponse à celui du comte de Guines* (Paris: P. G. Simon, 1774), pp 1–2.

diligent Hardy reported that four thousand copies of it were being distributed all over Paris. Hardy identified Falconnet as a man "whose talents were already known thanks to productions of the same sort," and went on to report that his style in this new piece was judged to be overly vehement and somewhat inappropriate to the style of the bar.[146]

Falconnet did, indeed, let out all the stops in the mémoires he wrote for this case. Both briefs were written in the first person, in Tort's voice; they were impassioned, dramatic, direct. The first mémoire against Guines struck some familiar chords: like Vedel and Rubit, the lower-class defendants in the Saint-Vincent case, Tort began by emphasizing the loneliness and courage of the man who stands up to the mighty, pointing to the almost insurmountable obstacles he must face. When a man tries to demand justice of a grandee, wrote Falconnet, "a most terrifying loneliness descends upon him"; his friends avoid him, while swarms of the evil and the opportunist conspire to persecute him.[147] And, again like Vedel and Rubit, Tort speaks of the barriers of complaisance, servility, and brute force that protect the rich and powerful from their victims, while "the hand of a terrible prejudice erects around the public a triple wall that forbids humble truth from access to all hearts"; even the judges, he pursues, "seem to fear using a vigorous arm to rip off the veil that conceals the iniquities of an illustrious culprit."[148]

Two familiar themes recur many times in both of Falconnet's briefs, the denunciation of unfair social privilege, and the sovereignty of the law and its ministers as the best defense against such injustice; these ideas, however, are stated more fully and forcefully here than had ever been done before. Like Morangiès before him, Guines is depicted not only as dishonest and tyrannical, but as sadistic in the very exercise of his iniquity: "But still, what sort of a man are you?" asks Tort. "It is not with anger, not in cold blood, but laughing heartily that you make every effort to drag me to the scaffold by accusing me of crimes against the Prince."[149] Fortunately, the legal system and its ministers are there to

146. Ms. Fr. 6682, 21 February 1775; for other reports about the brief, see [Pidansat de Mairobert], *Journal historique* 7:129–130, and *Mémoires secrets* 8:45.

147. Ambroise Falconnet, *Premier mémoire contre le comte de Guines, ambassadeur du Roi en Angleterre, par le sieur Tort, ci-devant son secrétaire* (Paris: P. G. Simon, 1775), pp. 3–4.

148. Ibid., p. 4.

149. Ambroise Falconnet, *Second mémoire contre le comte de Guines, ambassadeur du Roi en Angleterre* (Paris: P. G. Simon, 1775), pp. 23–24.

protect the weak; the legal system, in fact, does more than correct social iniquities, it *constitutes* society and the state: "A judge is the most interesting personage in the state. He holds both ends of the important chain that links subjects to the sovereign, by dispensing justice in the name of the latter. For without justice, no law; without law, no society; and without society, no empires."[150] It is this legal system, the bulwark of the common man, that has allowed Tort to exercise against his high-ranking employer "the rights of a citizen injured by a citizen."[151]

All of this was vigorously stated, but, in the mid-1770s, hardly un-precedented; and yet Falconnet's writings for Tort were judged suffi-ciently offensive to be singled out for admonition in both of the verdicts rendered in the case. In 1775 the Châtelet forbade him "to write any more briefs of this sort, on pain of whatever penalty may apply," and in 1777 the Parlement stepped up the warning (no doubt delighted with this occasion to get back at d'Aiguillon through Tort and his lawyers), denouncing Falconnet's writings as "full of sarcasm" and threatening the barrister with an "exemplary punishment."[152] Falconnet's briefs were, indeed, incendiary; but the real departure was not in their con-tents but in their style.

Lawyers and writers who cast their clients in the role of the oppressed victim usually adopted the lachrymose style of the *drame:* the appro-priate stance for a Pierre Calas or a François Dujonquay was to wring one's hands, shed tears aplenty, and appeal with a quivering voice to the justice of the magistrates or of the "Public." Tort did none of this. The voice that Falconnet invented for him was very different—the voice of a proud, angry, defiant man. This was evident from the first page of the first mémoire, which begins by citing a rhetorical question drawn from an earlier brief for Guines: "What, showing rare generos-ity, Tort would have made himself into my willing victim? He would have sacrificed his reputation to mine, and I would have rewarded him with a prison cell and shackles?" The answer to this comes back like a whiplash: "Yes, monsieur le comte, *tu es ille vir;* you are that [sort of] man."[153]

Many previous trial briefs for the underdog were written in the first

---

150. Ibid., p. 41.
151. Ibid., p. 38.
152. *Nouvelles extraordinaires*, 13 June 1775; *Gazette d'Utrecht*, 28 March 1777.
153. Falconnet, *Premier mémoire*, p. 3.

person, but the narrator usually described the actions of his or her tormentor in the third person: he had me thrown in prison, he made false accusations, and so on. Falconnet's writings for Tort flamboyantly broke with that convention; in both mémoires, Tort addressed the count directly, verbally grabbing him by the shirtfront and shaking him: "Now dare to complain. Will you reproach me with having made use of your privilege? Eh, but you allowed me to! Will you insist [that I] committed the crime of smuggling? But you did so yourself. Oh, yes, monsieur le comte, you did so yourself." [154] Tort, the victim, in this way, thanks to a stylistic trick, turns the tables on Guines; Tort's monologue is really a cross-examination that purports to make clear the motives and reasoning of his onetime employer: "Nothing was simpler; have me flee abroad and then repudiate me. Say that I am a disloyal secretary, a knave, and you're in business. If they believe you, so much the better. If they don't, what matter? I can counter you neither with titles nor with witnesses; everything that went on between us was done in the greatest secret. . . . Ah, yes, monsieur le comte, that was your reasoning, was it not?" [155]

The rhetoric attributed to Tort in Falconnet's briefs was all the more effective in that it was coupled with another device, the creation of a bond of complicity between the narrator and his readers. Tort pauses from his haranguing of Guines only to imagine and guide his reader's reactions: "At this point, my brief falls from the hands of the reader; he wonders, if these facts are proven true, what madness makes you present [me] as a cheat and impostor." [156] He goads the reader on with promises of ever-more scandalous revelations of Guines's villainy: "I said that I had presented you in my first brief only sketched in profile; was I lying? Readers, you are not yet done." [157] In fact, the briefs almost become something like a serial, with one mémoire ending with intimations of better things to come in the next one: "I will show in [my next brief] the bold accuser, the tireless persecutor, merge with the sly courtier who, to conciliate one party, presents himself as the victim of the other." Or again, posing as the considerate author: "My readers' time is precious, I must spare it, so enough for now." [158] In short, Falconnet's briefs

154. Falconnet, *Second mémoire,* p. 5.
155. Falconnet, *Premier mémoire,* p. 31.
156. Falconnet, *Second mémoire,* p. 66.
157. Ibid., p. 24.
158. Ibid., pp. 80–81.

were particularly effective—and as a result particularly offensive to the judicial authorities—first because of the sarcastic, irreverent tone attributed to the narrator, and also because of the sense of immediacy created by the dialogue between Tort and his opponent and between Tort and his readers.

The simultaneous dialogue with readers and opponent, the feisty and sarcastic tone, and the lively, informal pace of the mémoires for Tort—all of these, as used by a barrister on behalf of a social nobody and directed against a court grandee, had the potential to fascinate and shock contemporaries. But the use of such stylistic devices had an obvious precedent and model. Falconnet, as we have seen, was a friend of Beaumarchais, and had served as his legal counsel during the business with Goezman, had literally stood by his side as the venal magistrate and his wife played cat-and-mouse games with the playwright.[159] Beaumarchais attained celebrity as a mémoire writer in late 1773 and early 1774, when he published the four briefs against Goezman, just about the time of the beginning of the Tort-Guines case; there can be little doubt that the defiant tone and stylistic daring of Falconnet's pieces derived from the example of Beaumarchais's recent trial briefs—although the lawyer never came close to equaling the verbal virtuosity of Beaumarchais.

The influences may have been reciprocal, however. By 1777 Beaumarchais was deeply embroiled in the second phase of his protracted lawsuit, this time writing briefs directly aimed at the count of La Blache. In Beaumarchais's mémoires against La Blache one finds as a recurrent motif the apostrophe "monsieur le comte" and a sustained contrast between the social stations of the playwright and his antagonist. One may well wonder whether readers in 1777 made the connection between the Tort-Guines dispute, which was approaching a conclusion, and passages in Beaumarchais such as this one: "Such cries! Such fury! Ah, but you are hotheaded, rude, and cavalier with poor commoners, monsieur le comte! It's quite plain that you are quality! But patience!"[160] By now,

159. Grendel, *Beaumarchais,* pp. 80–84.

160. Beaumarchais, "Le Tartare à la légion," in *Oeuvres complètes,* 7 vols. (Paris: Léopold Collin, 1809), 4:313. The other 1777 brief, which contains passages in the same style, is "Réponse ingénue de Pierre-Augustin Caron de Beaumarchais," in ibid., pp. 153–311. Beaumarchais's first important brief against La Blache, published in 1775, is a more conventional piece of writing, which contains little of the verbal brio and confrontational stances characteristic of the Goezman pieces and the 1777 briefs: see "Réponse au mémoire signifié du comte Alexandre-Joseph Falcoz de la Blache," in ibid., pp. 22–153.

of course, the main literary legacy of the Tort-Guines case—if one accepts the hypothesis of this filiation—will already have come to mind. By the end of 1778, Beaumarchais had finished writing a play that drew heavily on some of the themes of his trial briefs; he had penned the famous monologue in act five of *The Marriage of Figaro,* including these oft-quoted lines: "Nobility, fortune, rank, position! How proud they make a man feel! What have *you* done to deserve such advantages? Put yourself to the trouble of being born—nothing more!"[161] The most famous passage in Beaumarchais's oeuvre thus stands as a testimony to the reciprocal influences of the stage and the courtroom in the twilight years of the Old Regime.

In the first years of the reign of Louis XVI, trial briefs served an increasingly diverse set of social and ideological functions. From the Maupeou years the briefs disseminated during causes célèbres had inherited a twofold mission, one vigorously endorsed in 1775 by Malesherbes, Delacroix, and Falconnet: their use was promoted both as a blueprint for the reform of government that was hoped for under the new reign and as a means of combating in the judicial arena the social inequity that arose from differences in wealth, status, and power.

In the years after 1774, muckraking mémoires connected to great court cases continued to circulate widely. But like other forms of printed propaganda in this age of reform—the writings of enlightened authors, the political or pornographic productions flowing from the underground presses—subversive or critical trial briefs were absorbed into the culture of the social and political elite. Beaumarchais's role in this evolution was pivotal precisely because it was ambiguous. Certainly, the playwright's very public struggle against the judge Goezman and his wife was the quintessential literary expression of the resistance to the administrative tyranny of the Maupeou years. But Beaumarchais's literary brilliance and successful adoption of the style and language of high society also made his mémoires more attractive to the elites of town and court than to a broader oppositional public; it is for this reason that denizens of the salons of Mme du Deffand or Mme du Barry took such pleasure in reenacting, as society playlets, the scenes in which Beaumarchais trounced the vulgar Mme Goezman.

With the two great court cases of the later 1770s, the use of trial

161. Pierre Augustin Caron de Beaumarchais, *The Barber of Seville and the Marriage of Figaro,* trans. John Wood (London: Penguin Books, 1964), p. 199.

briefs became even more closely enmeshed with the culture of the elites, as these pamphlets served to publicize the internal conflicts of the ruling classes. The protagonists of the highly publicized Richelieu–Saint-Vincent case both belonged securely in the world of the titled elites, but in fact they embodied and acted out, in print, conflicts between different groups within the aristocracy. Conversely, although a wide social gap appeared to separate the comte de Guines from his secretary Tort, *their* struggle was really the expression of a dispute between court factions. But even within such "aristocratic" cases, the language and motifs of the Maupeou era survived. The theme of confrontation between grandee and commoner seemed always to make its way into salient court cases, because it reflected the beliefs and ambitions of the most successful barristers and because it continued to prove an effective theme for a sensational mémoire.

Thus, the resonance of the causes célèbres of the later 1770s came from the convergence between long-standing tensions at the level of the elites—between robe and sword, parlement and court, or, within the court, between factions—on the one hand, and, on the other, the newly fashionable conventions of the *mémoire judiciaire*. Antagonists within the nobility continued to square off as they had for generations, but their struggles were now played out before the audience of tens of thousands that could be reached thanks to the mémoire. By the later 1770s, trial briefs gave unprecedented publicity to the scandalous underside of upper-class life, while the emplotment of a successful brief frequently included a debunking of aristocratic morgue and power. Thanks to court cases and mémoires the private theater of upper-class life had been forced open: *le public* was well on its way to becoming *l'opinion publique*.

4

The Diamond Necklace Affair, 1785–1786

If Jean-Jacques Rousseau is sometimes called a writer of "genius," one of the reasons for this was his uncanny ability in his own age to predict and shape cultural trends that came into their own long after he had discerned them. A case in point is the Genevan writer's polemical discussion, in several of his works, of the role played by upper-class women in the society and polity of late-eighteenth-century France. Rousseau expounded his views on women in many of his major works, including *La Nouvelle Héloïse* (1761), *Emile* (1762), and especially the *Lettre à M. d'Alembert sur le théâtre* (*Letter to M. d'Alembert on the Theatre*), written in 1758. Rousseau's views of contemporary women have been denounced, with good reason, by feminists in every generation since Mary Wollstonecraft; criticizing the social and sexual freedom and the intellectual ambitions of French society women, Rousseau argued that the health of the body politic demanded the confinement of women, as chaste wives and mothers, to the domestic sphere.[1] Whatever one thinks of such ideas, there is no denying Rousseau's prescience: one of the most striking developments to affect French political culture in the 1780s and 1790s was a growing clamor, among those who criticized

1. The following discussion of gendered metaphors in Rousseau's social and political writings, and especially of the *Lettre à M. d'Alembert*, is indebted to two excellent recent discussions of the subject: Joel Schwartz, *The Sexual Politics of Jean-Jacques Rousseau* (Chicago: University of Chicago Press, 1984), especially chap. 3; and Joan Landes, *Women and the Public Sphere in the Age of the French Revolution* (Ithaca: Cornell University Press, 1988), especially chap. 3.

the old order, for the exclusion of women from public social and political activity. A brief analysis of Rousseau's ideas on the subject is the best introduction to the cultural forces that shaped the growing resentment of "public women" in the final decades of the Old Regime. These same trends in turn explain many aspects of the most sensational trial of the Old Regime, the notorious Diamond Necklace Affair, which forms the core of this chapter.

Rousseau wrote his *Letter to M. d'Alembert on the Theatre* in response to d'Alembert's article "Geneva" in the *Encyclopédie*, which, while praising the enlightened religious tolerance of the Genevans, deplored the city's puritanical ban on theatrical entertainment. The article prompted Rousseau to spring to the defense of his native city, producing the extended missive that marked his decisive break with the mainstream Enlightenment represented by the *Encyclopédie*. Beyond d'Alembert, Rousseau's polemic was aimed at Voltaire, whose lifelong passion for the theater revealed his profound cultural kinship with the literate—in Rousseau's view, corrupt—French upper classes. Rousseau's discussion of women in the *Letter* must be understood in relation to his critique of the theater, and specifically of actors as beings who teach deceit and who forsake their selfhood for money: "What is the talent of the actor? It is the art of counterfeiting himself, of putting on another character than his own, of appearing different than he is, of becoming passionate in cold blood. . . . What is the profession of the actor? It is a trade in which he performs for money, submits himself to the disgrace and affronts that others buy the right to give him, and puts his person publicly on sale." [2] If this is the case for actors, it will be all the more so for actresses, whose very profession violates what Rousseau sees as the reserve and chastity "natural" to the female sex; a woman who displays herself in public becomes, in fact, a "public woman" no better than a prostitute in Rousseau's view, since "any woman who shows herself off disgraces herself." [3]

Just as Rousseau's indictment of the theater and of actors in reality constitutes a critique of the alienation and hypocrisy rampant in contemporary society, so the charges he levies at actresses extend to all women involved in the very public life of the Old Regime elite, as host-

2. Jean-Jacques Rousseau, *Politics and the Arts: Letter to M. d'Alembert on the Theatre,* trans. and ed. Allan Bloom (Ithaca: Cornell University Press, 1960), p. 79.

3. Ibid., p. 83.

esses, articulate *salonnières*, and pampered, overdecorated objects of desire: "With us . . . , the most esteemed woman is the one who has greatest renown, about whom most is said, who is the most seen in society, at whose home one dines the most, who most imperiously sets the tone, who judges, resolves, decides, pronounces, . . . and whose favor is most ignominiously begged for by humble, learned men. On the stage it is even worse."[4]

For Rousseau, the theatrical world is emblematic of contemporary society; the playhouse is merely a stylized version of the social world of the elites, where communication is laced with deceit and a person's being is inseparable from his or her appearance, adornment, and role. Since both the theater and high society are realms of the spectacular, the beauty and desirability of women in such settings invests them with unnatural amounts of authority: "Look through most contemporary plays; it is always a woman who knows everything, who teaches everything to men."[5] As the preceding quotes suggest, one of the most insistent themes in Rousseau's discussion is that the power invested in women in such settings has as its inevitable corollary the weakening of men, who are reduced by female authority to the level of adoring eunuchs: "Every woman at Paris gathers in her apartment a harem of men more womanish than she."[6]

Rousseau's critique of contemporary culture (the theater) and society (feminized high society) builds up, as one might expect, to a political argument. The demonstration is set up as a series of equivalences, which might read as follows: the theater equals high society equals the court equals absolute monarchical government, or *despotisme*. Each term in the succession of equivalences is a feminized world of display and deceit, and in each the power of the female principle dictates the weakening of the male. The metaphor that recurs, explicitly or implicitly, in the discussion of these confined and feminized worlds, is that of the harem. Students of French history and literature need no reminder that in eighteenth-century political discourse the substantive "despotism" routinely conjured up the adjective "oriental," and that some forty years earlier Montesquieu had, with great success, used the harem in his *Persian Letters*, a world of women and eunuchs governed by an absent lord,

4. Ibid., p. 49.
5. Ibid.
6. Ibid., p. 101; Schwartz, *Sexual Politics,* pp. 45–46, 60–67.

as a metaphor for the declining autocracy of Louis XIV.[7] Finally, Rousseau's denunciation of the corrupting effects of women on the public or political sphere proceeds by way of antithesis as well. His text is laced, not surprisingly, with admiring references to the republics of antiquity where women "appeared rarely with men," "did not put themselves on display," and where "there was no common place of assembly for the two sexes."[8]

Rousseau's discussion of the dangerous authority wielded by women in the theater builds into an implicit critique of absolute monarchy, which he equates with "despotism." The visibility and power of women, he suggests, are a sure sign of impending political degeneracy. Republics are grounded in the political participation of males, while monarchies are at best gender-neutral; the sex of a citizen matters, that of a subject does not: "Whether a monarch governs men or women ought to be rather indifferent to him, provided that he be obeyed; but in a republic, men are needed."[9]

Rousseau's fears of female power, and his dream of a republic of male citizens, while grounded in his particular psychosexual makeup, were also symptomatic of the slow but profound transformation of French political culture that began to take shape in the 1750s. Since gender, as Joan Scott reminds us, "is a primary way of signifying relationships of power,"[10] Rousseau used gendered images and arguments to build a case about power in the society and polity, a case that concerns men just as much as women. As Joel Schwartz points out, Rousseau "associates women with personal and particularly with informal rule," that is, with the arbitrariness of monarchical rule—with political styles that are dangerously effective because they are easy to succumb to.[11]

In Rousseau's view, absolute monarchy is based upon—and promotes—the power of women, who in a system of personal and informal rule can freely exert their sexual and emotional power over men. Conversely, a monarchical system symbolically emasculates men by implicitly

7. For a perceptive analysis of the seraglio as a central metaphor in seventeenth- and eighteenth-century French thought, see Alain Grosrichard, *Structure du sérail: La Fiction du despotisme asiatique dans l'Occident classique* (Paris: Seuil, 1979), especially the section on women and eunuchs, pp. 175–206.

8. Ibid., pp. 88–89, 101.

9. Ibid., pp. 100–101.

10. Joan Scott, *Gender and the Politics of History* (New York: Columbia University Press, 1988), p. 42.

11. Schwartz, p. 45.

reducing all men who serve the monarch to the status of personal attendants or domestics. In sum, Rousseau uses the prism of gender to demonstrate that absolute monarchy is a corrupt political form because it
distorts "natural" gender roles by feminizing men while promoting
women into masculine positions of authority.[12] What can be done, then,
to rectify this bad, and worsening, state of affairs in the polity? To this
question Rousseau offers an answer that is mostly utopian. He exhorts
contemporary woman to retrieve the virtue of her classical forebears by
retreating to the private sphere and to the duties of mother and mistress
of the home, which alone invest her with true dignity and beauty.[13]

While full justice cannot be done here either to the complexity of
Rousseau's ideas on this subject or to their controversial implications,
their historical importance should be evident. When Rousseau wrote
these pages in the late 1750s, nobody thought of challenging the role
of society women as cultural mediators and as symbols of hedonistic
elegance at court, in salons, and on stage. (The extent to which such
women wielded *effective* as opposed to *symbolic* power is a large question, which will not detain us here; Rousseau, of course, is dealing in
the realm of the symbolic.) And yet, some three decades later the French
revolutionaries, especially those of the more radical Jacobin persuasion,
carried out Rousseau's program more brutally and more completely
than he could ever have envisioned.

Although at the start of the Revolution women joined men in voicing
their (singular and collective) opinions in pamphlets and patriotic clubs,
by the early 1790s the rights of women to petition and assemble were
curtailed and then abolished altogether. With the advent of the Jacobins
in the summer and fall of 1793, the silencing of women became more
systematic and more violent. In October of 1793 the government
closed down the most active women's club, the Society of Republican
Revolutionary Women, and from July to November of 1793 the National Convention sent to their deaths a number of conspicuous women
who ran the gamut of political allegiances: the *ci-devants* Marie-
Antoinette and Mme du Barry, the Girondins Charlotte Corday and
Marie-Jeanne Roland, and the feminist Olympe de Gouges.[14] In the re-

12. Landes, *Women and the Public Sphere,* p. 87.
13. Rousseau, *Politics and the Arts,* pp. 87–89.
14. Significant works on the role of women in the French Revolution and the revolutionaries' attitudes toward women include: Paule-Marie Duhet, *Les Femmes et la Révolution, 1789–1794* (Paris: Julliard, 1971); Jane Abray, "Feminism in the French Revolution,"
American Historical Review 80 (February 1975): 43–62; Darline Levy, Harriet Ap-

port that closed down female political clubs in 1793, the deputy André Amar justified the measure in language that could have been straight out of Rousseau: "If we consider that the political education of men is at its beginning, that all its principles are not developed, and that we are still stammering the word liberty, then how much more reasonable is it for women, whose moral education is almost nil, to be less enlightened concerning its principles? . . . Let us add that women are disposed by their organization to an over-excitation which would be deadly in public affairs, and that interests of state would soon be sacrificed to everything which ardor in passions can generate in the way of error and disorder."[15]

It could be argued, of course, that highly visible and influential women are often the targets of public anger in periods of political upheaval, regardless of time and place: English revolutionaries of the 1640s resented Henrietta Stuart's French and Catholic allegiances, just as their Russian counterparts in the early twentieth century fastened upon the mystical excesses of Alexandra Romanov, and the media in the 1980s made Imelda Marcos, first lady of the Philippines, into the principal symbol of the corruption of her husband's regime. But the denunciation of female action or even mere presence in the public sphere, which gathered increasing strength in France in the last decades of the Old Regime, was symptomatic, it will be argued here, of a specific, and major, turning point in French political culture.

The late eighteenth century in France, and later periods throughout Europe, witnessed the gradual demise of royal and aristocratic courts modeled on households, in which female rulers, relatives, and mistresses played a major—if limited—role, and the ascendancy of entirely masculine representative bodies. In other words, the male-female world of familial and sexual bonds represented by Versailles was overpowered by the all-male contractual universe of the revolutionary assemblies. It was

---

plewhite, and Mary Johnson, eds. and trans., *Women in Revolutionary Paris* (Urbana: University of Illinois Press, 1979); Linda Kelly, *Women of the French Revolution* (London: Hamish Hamilton, 1987); Annette Rosa, *Citoyennes: Les Femmes et la révolution française* (Paris: Messidor, 1988); Dominique Godineau, *Citoyennes tricoteuses: Les Femmes du peuple à Paris pendant la révolution française* (Paris: Alinéa, 1988).

15. Levy et al., *Women in Revolutionary Paris,* p. 216. For discussions of the background to such fears of female "unruliness," see Natalie Zemon Davis, *Society and Culture in Early Modern France* (Stanford: Stanford University Press, 1975), chap. 5, and Carole Pateman, *The Disorder of Women: Democracy, Feminism, and Political Theory* (Stanford: Stanford University Press, 1989), esp. chaps. 1 and 2.

the tensions relating to this crucial transition that Rousseau foresaw and expressed in his writings about public womanhood. This major shift in political culture, as Joan Landes perceptively argues, concerned not only forms of government (from absolute monarchy through constitutional monarchy to democratic republic) but also systems of representation. Rousseau sets up an implicit opposition between femininity and theatricality, on the one hand, and masculinity and textuality, on the other, "between the iconic spectacularity of the old regime and the textual and legal order of the bourgeois public sphere."[16] Rousseau's critique of the public functions of femininity and theatricality is aimed at what he sees as absolutism's "narcissistic overinvestment in the image," its localization of the symbolics of power in the realm of the spectacular, rather than in the abstract language of the law.[17]

If it is true that the protests against the political culture of monarchical absolutism included prominently the clamor to remove women from the political sphere, where, beyond the writings of Rousseau, is this visible? Most obviously, one must look to writings about women who were indeed conspicuous and powerful in late-eighteenth-century France. Among women who wielded power, or at least seemed to, in the second half of the eighteenth century one would count the two official mistresses of Louis XV, Mme de Pompadour and Mme du Barry (that monarch's wife, Marie Lecszinska, led a pious and withdrawn life); most conspicuous, however, was the wife of Louis XVI, the ill-fated Marie-Antoinette, whose narrow-minded frivolity and clumsy political meddling earned her early on in her reign such unflattering nicknames as "l'Autrichienne" and "Madame Déficit."[18] For our purposes here, the

16. Landes, *Women and the Public Sphere,* p. 67.
17. Ibid., p. 72.
18. The question of Marie-Antoinette's reputation has waxed and waned in importance along with historiographic trends. It figures prominently in older accounts that give pride of place to individual personality as a determining factor in historical developments; this approach has survived in anecdotal accounts such as Claude Manceron's *Les Hommes de la liberté,* 4 vols. (Paris: Robert Laffont, 1972–1979). The French *Annales* tradition of social and economic history, which goes back as far as the 1930s and was adopted in the 1960s and 1970s by English and American scholars in the field, made the topic seem frivolous and gossipy. Accordingly, Marie-Antoinette is either not mentioned or barely mentioned in such standard overviews of the origins of the Revolution as Georges Lefebvre, *The Coming of the French Revolution* (1939; trans. R. R. Palmer, Princeton: Princeton University Press, 1967); Pierre Goubert, *L'Ancien Régime* (Paris: Armand Colin, 1969); William Doyle, *Origins of the French Revolution* (Oxford: Oxford University Press, 1980); and (despite its title) Michel Vovelle, *La Chute de la monarchie (1787–1792)*

increasingly nasty attacks aimed at that queen—culminating in a particularly vindictive trial and execution in 1793—are especially interesting because her name was mixed up in what has remained the most famous cause célèbre of the Old Regime, the so-called Diamond Necklace Affair.

A word must be said here about the chronological gap between the cases examined in the preceding chapter and the affair that will occupy us here. As we have seen, the great cases of the mid- to late seventies (the Goezman, Saint-Vincent, and Guines affairs) can all be read as expressions of the ideological and political fallout from the Maupeou crisis of the early seventies. The period from the mid-1780s to the outbreak of the Revolution witnessed a multitude of overlapping causes célèbres, including besides the Diamond Necklace Affair a series of cases used to dramatize the need for judicial reform and a spate of highly publicized marital cases. But sources covering the period from 1777 to 1784, such as the *Mémoires secrets* and Siméon-Prosper Hardy's journal, report almost no cases, and certainly no big ones, between about 1777 and 1784. How can we explain this puzzling gap? This question cannot be answered with any certainty until we know more about the heretofore mostly neglected political history of the early reign of Louis XVI; but some answers are suggested in Jeremy Popkin's explorations of the coverage of French news during these years in one of Europe's most popular newspapers, the *Gazette de Leyde*. First, it must be noted that the outbreak of causes célèbres usually accompanied periods of domestic political ferment, and, for reasons explored in earlier chapters, this was especially true when the Parlement of Paris was in the eye of a political storm. In the late seventies and early eighties the Parlement was unusually quiescent, and in fact ceased to publish *remontrances* altogether during those years. Its activity was only to resume when worsening financial crises and ever-louder calls for re-

---

(Paris: Le Seuil, 1972). Very recently, the topic has regained importance because of the growing interest both in gender studies and in the history of political culture: see Chantal Thomas, *La Reine scélérate: Marie-Antoinette dans les pamphlets* (Paris: Le Seuil, 1989); Lynn Hunt, "The Many Bodies of Marie-Antoinette: Political Pornography and the Problem of the Feminine in the French Revolution," in Lynn Hunt, ed., *Eroticism and the Body Politic* (Baltimore: Johns Hopkins University Press, 1991), pp. 108–131, and Lynn Hunt, *The Family Romance of the French Revolution* (Berkeley: University of California Press, 1992), chaps. 4 and 5; Jacques Revel, "Marie-Antoinette and Her Fictions: The Staging of Hatred," in Bernadette Fort, ed., *Fictions of the French Revolution* (Evanston, Ill.: Northwestern University Press, 1991), pp. 111–129.

form began once more to galvanize the internal political scene in the mid-eighties.[19]

The second reason for the discontinuity has to do with the *reporting* of cases, which may have fallen off for several reasons. One of these is that French domestic political life offered little of interest (Popkin observes that French politics in the early eighties were duller than at any time since the refusal-of-sacraments controversy in the 1750s); in contrast, there was considerable interest in foreign affairs, principally in France's involvement in the American War of Independence, which dominated news reporting in those years.[20] Once again, the link between domestic turmoil and the publicizing of sensational cases may explain the dearth of the latter at this period.

Perhaps most important, the years after 1776 saw a tightening of censorship laws and a general crackdown on dissenting journalists and pamphleteers. The toppling of the liberal ministry of Turgot in 1776 was accompanied by the rise to power of men determined to stamp out political dissent—the censor Coqueley de Chaussepierre, for instance, and Le Camus de Neville, who replaced Malesherbes as director of the book trade. Under this new regime, radical journalists like Louis-Sébastien Mercier and Jean-Pierre Le Fuel de Méricourt were harassed, newspaper offices ransacked, and papers seized. (In 1777 an angry mémoire denouncing such practices was published; one of its two signers was Ambroise Falconnet.) Several journalists known for their irreverence, including Le Fuel and Linguet, fled to London.[21] Much of this crackdown was instigated by the foreign minister, Vergennes, who wanted to conduct the American war free from domestic criticism or interference.[22] Thus, the political climate of the late seventies and early eighties was inhospitable, to say the least, to the publicizing of controversial views, and this must to some measure explain the lack of sensational mémoire-spawning cases in those years. It was not until after the

19. Jeremy Popkin, "The *Gazette de Leyde* under Louis XVI," in Jack Censer and Jeremy Popkin, eds., *Press and Politics in Pre-Revolutionary France* (Berkeley: University of California Press, 1987), pp. 92–97.

20. Ibid., pp. 94–95.

21. Nina Rattner Gelbart, *Feminine and Opposition Journalism in Old Regime France: Le Journal des Dames* (Berkeley: University of California Press, 1987), pp. 233–247.

22. Popkin, "The *Gazette de Leyde*," pp. 95–98; see also Popkin's *News and Politics in the Age of Revolution: Jean Luzac's "Gazette de Leyde"* (Ithaca: Cornell University Press, 1989), pp. 149–157.

end of the war in 1783 that oppositional voices, including that of the Parlement of Paris, were once again heard loud and clear. The Parlement was to reenter the political scene with a bang, when the queen of France became the hapless victim of an unprecedented scandal.

Although the Austrian princess who married Louis XVI, and who was seen from the start as a pawn in the unnatural alliance between Hapsburg and Bourbon dynasties, was not popular with her subjects for very long, open attacks on the queen were very rare before the mid-1780s.[23] It has long been a commonplace of traditional historiography to attribute the demise of the queen's public reputation to a particularly sordid and complicated scandal later dubbed the Diamond Necklace Affair, which burst into the open in 1785–86. And yet to anyone acquainted with even the bare facts of the case, then and now, it was and remains patently obvious that Marie-Antoinette was innocent of any connection with the gang of bold schemers who used her name to pursue their goals. And in fact, the vast majority of the pamphlets and reports circulating at the time of the affair loudly proclaimed the queen's innocence and expressed outrage at the idea that her "august name" had been defamed. Standard accounts of the affair usually argue that the queen was believed to be somehow implicated in the affair, partly because her personal reputation was worsening, and partly because of political animosities at court.[24]

This conventional assessment is not so much wrong as insufficiently documented; the severity of the blow that the affair dealt to the queen's reputation, as well as her total lack of involvement in it, begs questions that a narrow biographical or political explanation cannot begin to explain. This chapter argues, first, that the queen's vulnerability to even

---

23. Henri d'Alméras, *Marie-Antoinette et les pamphlets royalistes et révolutionnaires* (Paris: Albin Michel, n.d.), chaps. 7 and 8; Hector Fleischmann, *Les Pamphlets libertins contre Marie-Antoinette* (Paris, 1908; reprint Geneva: Slatkine, 1976). Both authors' evidence comes overwhelmingly from material published after 1789. Jacques Revel indicates that several important pamphlets attacking the queen were published from as early as 1779 but were successfully hunted down and destroyed by the monarchy, "Marie-Antoinette," pp. 114–115.

24. For instance, Alfred Cobban, *A History of Modern France* (Harmondsworth: Penguin Books, 1957), 1:117–120. Cobban's summary in what is still the most widely used textbook on this period is probably drawn from the classic, exhaustively documented study by Frantz Funck-Brentano, *L'Affaire du collier* (Paris: Hachette, 1901). For a similar and equally popular account, see Stefan Zweig, *Marie-Antoinette* (New York, 1933), chaps. 14–17.

the most implicit attacks upon her reputation is comprehensible only if the events of 1785–86 are replaced within the context of late-eighteenth-century political culture, with reference to earlier pamphlet literature denouncing the activities of women in the public sphere; and second, that the literature that appeared in connection with the case in the form of pamphlets and especially of *mémoires judiciaires* managed to indict the queen without naming her openly. Whether they knew it or not, the lawyers who penned these documents delivered an implicit message to their readers, one that made the female sovereign central to a sordid intrigue in which she actually had played no role.

Before the details of the affair are laid out, it is necessary to mention again some of the features of later-eighteenth-century political life in France that may explain the unpopularity of the prerevolutionary monarchs and the impact of the case on public opinion. A broad array of causes—including the personal unpopularity of Louis XV, the military fiascoes of the Seven Years' War, the writings of the philosophes, and especially the impact of the protracted struggles over Jansenism—contributed to the onset as early as the 1750s of what historians have termed the "desacralization" of the French monarchy.[25] We have already seen the role played by the parlements, especially that of Paris, in resisting royal decrees and claiming for themselves the role of true representatives of the nation. The magistrates and lawyers of the sovereign courts were highly influential in the Diamond Necklace scandal, as in others, in bringing general principles to bear on a particular court case.

Challenges to royal and ministerial authority came not only from competing centers of political activity, such as the Parlement of Paris, but from within the rarefied milieu of the court itself. In the preceding chapter, we saw that one of the most sensational court cases of the 1770s, the Tort-Guines affair, was a reflection of the long-standing struggle between Choiseul and his supporters (including Marie-Antoinette), on the one hand, and the so-called *dévôt* party around the triumvirate, on the other. Because of structural developments affecting court politics after 1774, these conflicts began to reverberate loudly far beyond the confines of Versailles or of the Parisian elites. Whereas earlier in the century, under Louis XV, disgraced ministers were exiled from

---

25. Dale Van Kley, *The Damiens Affair and the Unraveling of the Old Regime, 1750–1770* (Princeton: Princeton University Press, 1984); Jeffrey Merrick, *The Desacralization of the French Monarchy in the Eighteenth Century* (Baton Rouge: Louisiana State University Press, 1990).

the court and the capital, under Louis XVI they were allowed to remain in Paris, where some of them organized effective oppositional networks: such were the parties that coalesced around Choiseul after his fall in 1770 and around Jacques Necker after 1781.[26] Taking their cue from the parlements and the underground pamphleteers, these factions flooded court and city with everything from scurrilous libels to high-minded appeals to "the public" or the "tribunal of the nation."[27]

Political strife within France's governing circles probably spawned most of the literature against Louis XV and his mistresses that began to circulate widely after that monarch's death in 1774. The late king's notorious debauchery, the power wielded by his mistresses Mme de Pompadour and later Mme du Barry, the existence of a private brothel called the Parc aux Cerfs, where the monarch was provided with an un-ending series of nubile young women, were widely known secrets long before his death. Many a subject of Louis "le Bien-Aimé" shared the feelings of Jean-François Le Clerc, a veteran arrested in 1757 for calling the king a "bugger" and complaining that the kingdom was governed "by two whores."[28] As Jules Michelet wrote hyperbolically but not inac-curately of Louis XV: "The philosophers pull him to the right, the priests to the left. Who will carry him off? Women. This god is a god of flesh."[29]

The two titular mistresses of Louis XV, the marquise de Pompadour and the comtesse du Barry, played pivotal roles in the court intrigues of the reign, each of them supporting one of the two warring parties at court. Mme de Pompadour lent her support to Choiseul until her death in 1764—as did Marie-Antoinette, even though her marriage to the future Louis XVI in 1770 coincided with Choiseul's dismissal from office. Mme du Barry, on the contrary, was an ally of the so-called *parti dévôt*, which sided with the unpopular triumvirate of Maupeou, d'Aiguillon, and Terray.[30] As we saw in the preceding chapter, these two main court factions carried their struggle into the reign of Louis XVI:

26. Doyle, *Origins of the French Revolution*, pp. 56–58.

27. Keith Baker, "Politics and Public Opinion Under the Old Regime," in Jack Censer and Jeremy Popkin, eds., *Press and Politics in Prerevolutionary France* (Berkeley: University of California Press, 1987), pp. 208–213. See also Keith Baker, *Inventing the French Revolution* (Cambridge: Cambridge University Press, 1990), chap. 8.

28. Van Kley, *The Damiens Affair*, pp. 3, 239.

29. Jules Michelet, *History of the French Revolution*, trans. Charles Cocks (Chicago: University of Chicago Press, 1967), p. 54.

30. Cobban, *History of Modern France* 1:90–99; Edgar Faure, *La Disgrâce de Turgot* (Paris: Gallimard, 1961), chap. 1.

the Choiseulist group, hoping to engineer the return of their leader to power—in which they proved unsuccessful—kept up a rearguard action in the form of a pamphlet war against the three ministers and the "royal whore" who had patronized them.[31] The content of these pamphlets appears to confirm Jeremy Popkin's argument that in the later eighteenth century most political pamphlets, although usually written by impoverished hacks, were commissioned and paid for by members of the elite: Choiseul's followers were probably responsible for much of the abundant underground literature circulating in the 1770s and 1780s that described in detail the political intrigues and sexual exploits of Louis XV, his ministers, and Mme du Barry.[32] Even in a provincial town such as Troyes, as Robert Darnton has shown, the clandestine bookseller Mauvelain kept his shelves well stocked with volumes bearing such titles as *Anecdotes secrètes sur Madame du Barry*, *Correspondance de Madame du Barry*, and *La Vie privée de Louis XV*.[33]

By far the most successful of these *libelles* (as they were called) was a fat volume entitled *Les Fastes de Louis XV*, published in 1782, a collection of anecdotes cobbled together from other similar accounts, published across the border in Switzerland, and which Mauvelain ordered for his provincial readers on eleven occasions in the 1780s.[34] The opening pages of the book identify it clearly as emanating from the Choiseulist camp. The duke, intones the anonymous author, was Louis XV's only good minister, a man of "genius and perspicacity," who attracted followers because he was "lovable, generous, imposing, and sensitive," but who could not alone "stem the waters of the flood of profligacy that was washing over the court and the town."[35] A model of political integrity, Choiseul was brought down by "the tyrant Maupeou, the brigand Terray, the despot d'Aiguillon, . . . ministers, slaves crawling at the feet of a prostitute who had ascended in one leap from the brothel to the throne."[36]

The scandalous tales that make up *Les Fastes de Louis XV* add up to

31. Doyle, *Origins of the French Revolution*, p. 557.

32. Jeremy Popkin, "Pamphlet Journalism at the End of the Old Regime," *Eighteenth-Century Studies* 22 (Spring, 1989): 351–367.

33. Robert Darnton, *The Literary Underground of the Old Regime* (Cambridge, Mass.: Harvard University Press, 1982), p. 146.

34. Ibid., pp. 139, 145–146.

35. *Les Fastes de Louis XV, de ses ministres, généraux, et autres notables personnages de son règne* ("A Villefranche, chez la Veuve Liberté," 1782), pp. xl–xlix.

36. Ibid., p. lvi.

a description of what might variously be termed the feminization, eroti-
cization, or privatization of the political sphere under Louis XV. The
style of *Les Fastes* is hardly evocative of Rousseau. The prose of the pamphlet is workmanlike, studded with the clichés about *corruption* and *séduction* that one finds in any *libelle* of the 1770s or 1780s; its substance
is a series of crude character-sketches of courtiers and courtesans along
with details of their proclivities and tastes, especially in matters sexual.
But while the manner of *Les Fastes,* at once world-weary and titillating,
could hardly be further from the impassioned rhetoric of the *Lettre à
d'Alembert,* many of its themes are strikingly reminiscent of Rousseau:
the description of the court as a theater, at once claustrophobically
closed and very public; the ascendancy of women thanks to their sexual
power over men; and the emasculation of men at court, as they take on
increasingly feminine traits and tastes.

The beginning of the feminization, and hence weakening, of the
French monarchy in the eighteenth century is ascribed to Louis XV's
tutor, Cardinal Fleury, who plotted to distract the young monarch from
his political duties and thus to ensure his own power, by pushing the
young man into the arms of his first mistress, Mme de Mailly.[37] The
advent of Mme de Pompadour coincided with the conclusion of the
War of Austrian Succession, and the author identifies the peace of 1748
as the shameful moment when the king "put down his armor" and
handed over the reins of his kingdom to his titular mistress. Under
the "reign" of Mme de Pompadour, the Parc aux Cerfs over which she
presided became the dark center of the realm, "an abyss for innocence
and simplicity, which swallowed up throngs of victims and then spat
them back into society, into which they carried the corruption and taste
for debauchery and vices that necessarily infected them in such a
place."[38] Female sexuality run amok had taken over, it seemed, the very
heart of the monarchy.

The empire of women in Louis's court dictated the feminization of
men, especially those closest to the center of power. A surprising passage in *Les Fastes* describes Chancellor Maupeou not only as a supple,
scheming, protean courtier, but also as a sort of she-man: his dwelling
contained "elegant furnishings and delicious boudoirs in which the
most fastidious courtesan would not be out of place."[39] Maupeou's

37. Ibid., pp. 106–107.
38. Ibid., pp. 351–352.
39. Ibid., p. 382.

power was based on his ability to seduce, a talent he enhanced by paint-ing his face white and powdering it with rouge.[40] (As Lynn Hunt ar-gues, following René Girard, cultural crises that culminate in ritual vio-lence directed at a scapegoat—in this instance, the Old Regime monarchy and its "public women"—are usually accompanied by fears of gender confusion, by anxieties arising from the perceived masculin-ization of women and feminization of men.)[41]

The man most thoroughly feminized by the rise of female power was, of course, the monarch himself. The most public individual in the realm gradually withdrew from his designated sphere, we are told, and re-treated into "the private, slothful, and voluptuous life for which he had been yearning," his conversation turning increasingly to trivia and gos-sip.[42] The later advent of Mme du Barry further un-manned the mon-arch. "The king's scepter," the author slyly concluded, "a plaything in turn for love, ambition, and avarice became in the hands of the countess the rattle wielded by folly."[43] The pamphlet's themes are strikingly remi-niscent of Rousseau's admonitions two decades earlier: Jean-Jacques had also warned his contemporaries that the ascendancy of women would cause men to lose their physical vigor "in the indolent and soft life to which our dependence on women reduces us" and to forget their public mission by turning to private concerns.[44]

In *Les Fastes*, the privatization of the king of France had as its coun-terpart the growing public role of the women who ruled over him, and not surprisingly, for Pompadour and du Barry had begun their careers as public women. (And here, as in Rousseau, the confusion of the two meanings of the expression "public woman" is deliberate and telling.) According to the *libelliste*, the marquise's mother had risen in the world by trading on her charms, a talent she passed on to her daughter, and "la du Barry"—as she was scornfully called—had first plied her trade in the dark streets of Paris and under the arcades of the Palais-Royal.[45] The displacement of unbridled female sexuality from its normally interstitial position in society to the center of power both reflected and generated social disorder. Both Pompadour and du Barry had clawed their way up

40. Ibid., p. lvi.
41. Lynn Hunt, "The Many Bodies of Marie-Antoinette," pp. 123–124, and *Family Romance*, pp. 10–11, 114–116.
42. *Les Fastes*, pp. lvii–lviii.
43. Ibid., pp. 381, 566.
44. Rousseau, *Letter*, pp. 102–103; Schwartz, *Sexual Politics*, pp. 59–61.
45. *Les Fastes*, p. 705.

the social scale and into the king's bed, the first from *la classe la plus infime* (she was in fact the daughter of a prosperous wholesale merchant), the second from the slums of the capital.[46] As their sexuality propelled these women into the highest spheres, it sent the king tumbling down the social scale as he moved from highborn mistresses to the middle-class Jeanne Poisson (later de Pompadour), to the vulgar du Barry, while his subjects, we are told, died of hunger. "It is indeed essential," the author acidly concluded, "for a prince to get to know each one of his estates."[47]

Les Fastes de Louis XV thus summarizes most of the themes of the illegal pamphlet literature that chronicled the decay of the French monarchy under Louis XV: the anomalous ascendancy of women, the privatization of the public sphere, the role of female sexuality in breeding social and political disorder. On the face of it, the shafts aimed at the likes of Mme du Barry might seem to have little to do with the ruling queen of France: Marie-Antoinette was no ambitious shop-girl but the well-bred scion of one of Europe's oldest dynasties and the wife of a popular king. And yet the connection between Louis XV's mistresses and Louis XVI's wife was one that revolutionary pamphlets were to draw repeatedly. One of the most popular pamphlets of the late 1780s, the *Essais historiques sur la vie de Marie-Antoinette,* began with a lengthy parallel between du Barry and the queen, alleging that they shared the same taste for power and the same debauched "effervescence of passions." Du Barry even came out ahead of the queen, since she "almost honored a dishonorable position while [Marie-Antoinette] prostituted an estate that seemed invulnerable."[48]

No party or political group, of course, held a monopoly on antifemale literature. Since the queen remained blindly loyal to the Choiseulist party at court, it is highly unlikely that they were responsible for any of the later literature attacking her. But the anti–du Barry literature described above was sufficiently widespread and well-known to give special resonance to the scandal that erupted in 1785. By accidentally linking the queen's name to those of two adventuresses whose careers closely resembled that of Mme du Barry, the Diamond Necklace Affair

46. Ibid., pp. xcviii, 263.
47. Ibid., pp. 664, 698.
48. *Essais historiques sur la vie de Marie-Antoinette d'Autriche, reine de France* (London, 1789), pp. 2, 70.

greatly facilitated the transition from attacks on the morals of Louis XV and his mistresses to slander of the reigning queen.

The fact that in the eyes of the public the queen became closely implicated in the affair can be attributed to two causes: first, two of the most interesting protagonists of the affair were female, and second, Louis XVI committed the egregious blunder of turning the affair over to the judges and lawyers of the Parlement of Paris instead of settling it privately.[49]

At the center of the scandal was a woman named Jeanne de Saint-Rémi, whose talents for breathtakingly complex plotting—in both senses of the word—matched those of the fictional characters of Laclos and Beaumarchais. Although her family was of provincial and utterly ruined nobility (her father had died in the poorhouse in Paris), she styled herself Jeanne de Valois, claiming descent from the French royal family through a bastard line. By dint of charm and hubris, and by playing on her alleged royal origins, the destitute young girl managed to secure the help of wealthy protectors, notably the marquise de Boulainvilliers, who provided her with a good education. In 1780, she married a penniless young officer of dubious nobility, Count Nicolas de La Motte.

It was three years later, through Mme de Boulainvilliers, that this talented con woman met the man whose gullibility was to ensure her a seemingly endless source of revenue. The fifty-year-old Louis de Rohan was a prominent member of the old and powerful Rohan-Soubise family, bishop of Strasbourg, Grand Almoner of France, and former ambassador to Vienna. His prodigious wealth, and the fact that he was already

49. The following summary of the events leading up to the trial is based on the two most comprehensive and reliable accounts of the affair, Funck-Brentano, *L'Affaire du collier,* and Frances Mossiker, *The Queen's Necklace* (New York: Simon and Schuster, 1961); for a brilliantly evocative discussion of the case in relation to prerevolutionary culture, see Simon Schama, *Citizens: A Chronicle of the French Revolution* (New York: Knopf, 1989), pp. 203–227. Mossiker provides a useful survey of different accounts of the affair: see pp. 594–598. The affair was in fact more complicated than is suggested by the following summary. For the sake of clarity, I have omitted many details of the case, in particular the two main subplots of the story, which contemporaries found equally fascinating. One of these concerns the notorious "count" Cagliostro and his wife, who were exercising their talents as Mesmerist charlatans upon the cardinal; the other revolves around Jeanne's lover Bette d'Etienville and his friend, a certain baron de Fages-Chaulnes, both of whom attempted to blackmail Rohan, published best-selling mémoires, and were fully acquitted of complicity in the main theft.

the prey of the notorious adventurer and con artist Cagliostro, marked him out to the countess as an ideal target. Better still, Rohan was driven by a powerful obsession that could be put to good use: he yearned for high political office and was convinced that only the queen, whom he had alienated years before at the Austrian court, stood between him and his ambitions. Mme de La Motte had already tried her hand successfully at trading on entirely fictitious connections with her "cousin" the queen for substantial sums of money. Soon the cardinal was composing missives to the queen begging her to forget the past, and paying high prices for evasive replies elegantly forged by Jeanne's accomplice and sometime lover, Rétaux de Villette.

Well aware that even the gullible Rohan might soon tire of this ineffective strategy, Jeanne and her husband decided to feed his fantasies with heartier fare. They searched the streets of Paris, eventually locating in the gardens of the Palais-Royal a young woman of easy virtue named Nicole Le Guay, whose features approximated those of the queen. It was on a summer's night in 1784, in the gardens of Versailles, that Rohan finally met his queen, the carefully dressed and coached Nicole, who stammered a few words at him before being whisked off by her mentors.

The time was ripe for Jeanne de La Motte's finest hour, for her most ambitious coup. The most famous jewel in France, a diamond necklace made up of 647 flawless gems and worth over one and a half million livres, was the masterpiece of the jewelers Boehmer and Bassange. Louis XV had commissioned it for Mme du Barry, and then backed down before the jewel's price. In 1778 the necklace was offered to Louis XVI for his queen, but the latter turned it down with the noble (though no doubt apocryphal) statement that the realm needed ships more than necklaces. By 1785, however, Mme de La Motte was able to persuade Rohan that the queen had her heart set on this expensive bauble, the purchase of which would ensure the cardinal's political fortune. A purchase order duly approved and signed by the queen was produced, and on the night of 1 February 1785 the object was delivered to Rohan and the countess and handed over to a man purporting to be the queen's valet. The necklace, which Rohan was to pay for in installments over the next several years, was promptly picked apart, and the gems sold on the black markets of Paris and London.

The La Mottes' good luck was not to last for long, however. In July, the jewelers sent Marie-Antoinette a cryptic note that mentioned "the most beautiful jewel in the world," and on August 3 the whole business came to light in a conversation between Boehmer and the queen's first chambermaid, Mme Campan.[50] On August 15 the nation was stunned to hear of the arrest of Cardinal Rohan at Versailles as he was preparing to conduct Assumption services, clad in full pontifical regalia. A few days later the countess, Nicole Le Guay, and a few others were rounded up (Nicolas de La Motte was still in London), and preparations began for the most sensational trial of the reign.

Nine months of feverish anticipation elapsed between the arrests and the trial. Despite attempts by the countess and her lawyers to shift the blame for the swindle onto the shady Cagliostro, hardly anyone doubted her role in masterminding the swindle. The forgeries and theft of the necklace added up to a common criminal matter that could easily be disposed of. The real issue, as contemporaries quickly realized, lay elsewhere: should the cardinal be charged with "criminal presumption" and "lèse-majesté" for believing that the queen would stoop to dealing with the likes of Mme de La Motte and to assigning a nocturnal rendez-vous? Or should he be acquitted, on the implicit grounds that such be-havior on the part of Marie-Antoinette was not at all implausible?

The trial of a high-ranking courtier such as Rohan was bound to rouse passions within the social and political elites, and indeed factions immediately aligned themselves for and against the cardinal. This was inevitable given Louis XVI's extraordinary decision to take the matter to court rather than settle it as quietly as possible. Even Rohan's personal secretary, the abbé Georgel, later lauded the king's decision as "a solemn homage to the great influence of the laws which protect a citizen's honor," and a testimony to "the sublime empire of reason in a well-ordered monarchy"[51]—and indeed such a combination of naive prin-ciple and mind-boggling obtuseness would not have been atypical of Louis XVI. But in fact it is also the case that Louis's arm was twisted by others.

As soon as she heard of the scandal, Marie-Antoinette consulted not her husband but her closest allies and protégés at court, most notably the man she had made minister of the Royal Household and who was at the center of the queen's faction, the baron de Breteuil. Breteuil may have gotten wind of the scandal before it even broke out into the open,

50. Jeanne-Louise Campan, *Mémoires sur la vie privée de Marie-Antoinette,* 2 vols. (London, n.d.), 2:8–10.
51. Jean-François Georgel, *Mémoires pour servir à l'histoire des événemens de la fin du dix-huitième siècle,* 6 vols. (Paris, 1820), 2:70, 98–99, 131, 150.

and saw in it an occasion to get even with Rohan, whom he detested for having bested him in a competition for the post of ambassador to Vienna. Breteuil was convinced, and so persuaded the queen, that the publicity caused by the trial could harm only the cardinal. Marie-Antoinette, wanting to see Rohan punished, prevailed upon the king to have the case tried before the inner court, or Grand'Chambre, of the Paris Parlement.[52]

Aligned against Rohan, then, were the queen and her main allies at court, including the baron de Breteuil and the extended clan of relatives of her close female friend, the duchesse de Polignac; within the Parlement the monarchy had staunch supporters in many of the senior magistrates, including the court's First President, d'Aligre, and the Royal Prosecutor, Joly de Fleury.[53] Despite Louis XVI's personal support of his wife, patterns of alliance were further complicated by the fact that the king and queen stood at the center of different, competing parties, and that as a result members of the "king's party" were antagonistic to the queen's supporters.[54] The controller-general, Charles-Alexandre de Calonne, for instance, a member of the "king's party," supported Rohan out of hatred of Breteuil. The queen's position was therefore compromised because the support she enjoyed was never sufficient to counterbalance the broad array of forces aligned in defense of the cardinal.

Rohan naturally enjoyed the support of many members of the high nobility, including prominently the extended and powerful Rohan-Soubise clan, indignant at this affront to their family honor; many members of the French high clergy also rushed to the defense of one of their own. Although the magistrates of the Parlement were divided, many of the younger and more progressive members of the court, such as the fiery Jean-Jacques Duval d'Eprémesnil, were glad of this occasion to act out their long-standing resentments of royal prerogative.[55] Further-

52. The other main instigator of the trial on the queen's side was the abbé de Vermond, who bore a similar grudge against Rohan. Georgel, *Mémoires* 2:70, 98–99; Joseph Droz, *Histoire du règne de Louis XVI*, 2 vols. (Paris: Jules Renouard), 1:333–334; Alfred Cobban, *History of Modern France* 1:118–119.

53. Georgel, *Mémoires* 2:70, 98–99, 131, 150; Bailey Stone, *The Parlement of Paris, 1774–1789* (Chapel Hill: University of North Carolina Press, 1981), pp. 74–75.

54. Munro Price, "The 'Ministry of the Hundred Hours': A Reappraisal," *French History* 4 (September 1990): 318–319.

55. Funck-Brentano, *L'Affaire du collier*, pp. 244, 251, 323–324; Alméras, *Marie-Antoinette*, p. 281; Droz, *Histoire du règne de Louis XVI* 1:335–336; Stone, *The Parlement of Paris*, pp. 74–75.

more, Rohan agreed to be tried by the Parlement as a peer of the realm, rather than by an ecclesiastical court, thereby ignoring the papacy's wishes and emerging, somewhat incongruously, as a hero to those in the Parlement who supported "Gallican liberties."[56] The number and diversity of Rohan's supporters explain some of the resonance of the case. The "public" at large, those literate elements of the population who, thanks in part to such causes célèbres, were quick to denounce acts of arbitrary authority, seem to have espoused the cardinal's side in large numbers. The bookseller Hardy, himself an enemy of ministerial authority, indicated as much in the immediate aftermath of Rohan's arrest: "There were universal protests against the imprisonment of his eminence as an act of absolute despotism and arbitrary authority," he wrote, adding that "some people" saw it as an act of pure vindictiveness on the part of Breteuil.[57]

The first verdicts in the case, handed down on 31 May 1786, proved neither surprising nor controversial. Jeanne de La Motte was condemned to whipping, branding, and life imprisonment, her husband in absentia to a life sentence on the galleys. Their accomplices suffered lesser penalties, such as exile, and Nicole Le Guay, who produced for the occasion a newborn child and a convincing tale of beleaguered innocence, was fully acquitted. But a furor erupted in court over the sentencing of Rohan, against whom the prosecutor requested a sentence of exile on the grounds of "criminal temerity" and disrespect for the monarchs. After hours of bitter dispute, the Grand'Chambre of the Parlement returned a verdict of not guilty by a vote of thirty to twenty. While Rohan left the Palais de Justice to the roars of a cheering crowd, the queen at Versailles wept tears of anger and humiliation.[58]

There can be no doubt that the Diamond Necklace Affair (which contemporaries called, more pointedly, *l'affaire du cardinal*) was the greatest cause célèbre of the Old Regime, and that only the trials of the sovereigns themselves, less than a decade later, outstripped in importance that of Rohan and Mme de La Motte. It was also a new departure, a culmination of the changes in the relationship between the French government and its "public" that had been taking shape over the preceding decades. Unlike most of the great cases of the 1770s, the affair

56. Popkin, "The *Gazette de Leyde*," pp. 99–100.
57. B.N. Ms. Fr. 6685, 30 August 1785.
58. Funck-Brentano, *L'Affaire du collier*, pp. 301–314; Mossiker, *The Queen's Necklace*, chap. 22.

of the necklace was not a true judicial contest. The Véron-Morangiès case, for instance, or that between the duc de Richelieu and Mme de Saint-Vincent, were sensational because guilt and innocence were genuinely undetermined, and the expectation of a verdict—with which, of course, one could disagree—was what built suspense into the lengthy procedure.

L'affaire du cardinal was different. Despite the vigorous efforts of Rohan and Mme de La Motte to incriminate each other, their respective degrees of responsibility in the swindle were never in doubt to most people. Furthermore, most of the previous causes célèbres had been publicized because individuals or groups did their best to create and galvanize their audience: *patriote* lawyers in the Morangiès and Salency cases, court factions in the Tort-Guines case, a fame- and fortune-seeking writer in the Beaumarchais-Goezman case. The Diamond Necklace Affair, by contrast, became a public scandal almost in spite of itself, because nobody, except perhaps Breteuil, had any interest in seeing the case brought out into the open: paradoxically, its impact was all the greater. In this case, which came closer than any previous one to the hidden centers of power, publicity was no longer sought after, it was inevitable.

Publicity around the case took many forms. The most important vector of information about the case was undoubtedly word of mouth; the rumors that flew around cafés and drawing rooms, up and down the halls of Versailles, or from house to house in Paris, are only known to us from the brief notations in the daily chronicles known as *nouvelles à la main*. On 18 August 1785, just after the case had broken: "Although the story is very improbable, it is so widely spread about, and sworn to by people so well placed and so trustworthy, that it is very difficult not to believe it." On 24 August: "They say that Cagliostro, who lived in great style but accepted money from nobody, was in fact kept by the cardinal." On 23 October: "Every day there are new anecdotes concerning the cardinal and his adventure. Here is a new one, given out by people who seem so placed as to be well informed."[59] And so on, day after day, month after month.

The case naturally spawned many pamphlets arguing this or that position, taking a stand for or against the cardinal, accusing Jeanne de La Motte or Cagliostro, denouncing arbitrary arrest, or pitying the young

59. *Mémoires secrets* 29:213, 222; 30:29.

queen.[60] The story of the necklace so resembled a novel that it also rapidly produced fictional spin-offs in the form of (mostly invented) biographies of the main characters. The *Histoire véritable de Jeanne de Saint-Rémi, ou aventures de la comtesse de La Motte,* published in 1786, for instance, was an underground production that seems to have come from the same source as *Les Fastes de Louis XV,* since it bears, like the latter work, the fanciful imprint "A Villefranche, chez la Veuve Liberté." The *Histoire véritable* includes not only the story of Jeanne herself, but also the lives of her parents and siblings, and its style wavers between that of sentimental melodrama and that of cautionary fairy tale. There are lachrymose subplots: Jeanne's brother is rescued from poverty and obscurity by his aristocratic employer, Jeanne's sister Marianne finds true love with a peasant boy named Colas, and so on. The parts of the story concerning Jeanne follow a rise-and-fall pattern, from her degraded beginnings to the extraordinary wealth she briefly enjoyed immediately post-necklace (there is an elaborate description of the bed of velvet, gold, and pearls she slept in at the time), to her downfall and punishment: "Most of those who saw her suffer the punishment she deserved [whipping and branding] exclaimed like Candide, all is well, it couldn't be better!"[61] A similar work concerning Cagliostro, the *Mémoires authentiques pour servir à l'histoire du comte de Cagliostro* (the terms *authentique* or *véritable* in titles of this sort tip the reader off that this is mostly invention), contains even more unwieldy tales of the origins, travels, and evil dispositions of Cagliostro and his Italian prostitute wife.[62]

The public's interest in the case seemed to be limitless: the cardinal's daily walk around the battlements of the Bastille had to be given up because of the crowds that came to gawk at him.[63] Portraits of the twenty-two principal actors in the case were sold both before and after the verdict to collectors who added them to their other memorabilia pertaining to the affair. Customers either did not know or did not care that these pictures bore no resemblance to the persons they purported

60. Funck-Brentano, *L'Affaire du collier,* p. 287. See, for instance, *Lettre d'un garde du roi pour servir de suite aux mémoires sur Cagliostro* (London, 1786) and *La Dernière pièce du fameux collier* (n.p., n.d.).

61. *Histoire véritable de Jeanne de Saint-Rémi ou les aventures de la comtesse de La Motte* ("A Villefranche, chez la Veuve Liberté": 1786), p. 72.

62. *Mémoires authentiques pour servir à l'histoire du comte de Cagliostro* (Paris, 1786).

63. *Mémoires secrets* 30:4, 8 October 1785.

to represent: a popular print showing Mme de La Motte displaying most of a voluminous bosom was in fact a portrait of Mme de Saint-Vincent that had been withdrawn from circulation ten years earlier, and the images of her husband were recycled portraits of a minister, the prince de Montbarey. The ultimate commercialization of the case came with the launching of fashionable hats for ladies of scarlet on gold, a style that was dubbed "cardinal on straw." [64]

But the main source of information about the case, as well as the main source of profits from it, was of course the mass of *mémoires judiciaires* that it generated. Predictably, the Rohan case provoked an outpouring of trial briefs, an avalanche whose speed and volume increased as the trial approached. Four thousand copies of the first brief for Jeanne de La Motte by her lawyer, Doillot, were quickly snatched up in November of 1785; by the following March, printings of briefs for even minor defendants in the case were published in the thousands, and by the time the trial got under way in May one or two were appearing each day.[65] In fact, the Diamond Necklace Affair saw a leap in the numbers of mémoires circulating in connection with a judicial case. In the 1770s, as we have seen, very popular briefs, such as that of Vermeil for the Véron family or those of Beaumarchais against the Goezmans, reached—according to Hardy's notations—printings of six thousand at most. While Jeanne de La Motte's first brief had a press run of four thousand, her lawyer got thousands of letters asking for copies of subsequent briefs and started publishing them ten thousand at a time.[66] It was also in this case that the single largest run of a trial brief in the eighteenth century was reported, the twenty thousand copies that were printed of the first brief for Nicole Le Guay.[67] There is no lack of other evidence to suggest the unprecedented demand for trial briefs provoked by the case. While the first mémoire for Jeanne de La Motte seems to have been given out free, subsequent briefs for all of the principals in the case sold briskly at prices of one livre or more; manuscript versions of the first brief for Rohan written by the celebrated Jean-Baptiste Target were peddled sub

---

64. Funck-Brentano, *L'Affaire du collier,* p. 288; *Mémoires secrets* 9:130, 23 May 1776 (on the original portaits of Mme de Saint-Vincent); 31:206, 26 March 1786; B.N. Ms. Fr. 6685, 5 June 1786.

65. The publication of mémoires in the Diamond Necklace Affair can best be followed in Hardy's journal, in the volume covering the years 1785–1786, B.N. Ms. Fr. 6685.

66. Funck-Brentano, *L'Affaire du collier,* pp. 279–280.

67. Ibid., p. 283; B.N. Ms. Fr. 6685, 22 March 1786.

rosa months before its publication for the astronomical sum of thirty-six livres.[68] But whether these mémoires were sold or distributed free, their appearance often provoked veritable stampedes around the houses of the lawyers and their clients: on the day that the lawyer Thilorier produced his first mémoire for Cagliostro, the police had to position eight guards at his door to stave off the crowd.[69]

Both the volume of mémoires produced and descriptions of the crowds of avid buyers suggest that these briefs were reaching a broader and more varied cross section of the population in Paris and elsewhere than had been true in previous affairs of this sort. The author of an anonymous pamphlet published in 1786 describes himself strolling one morning in the vicinity of the house of Maître Doillot, the lawyer of Mme de La Motte. Suddenly, he is caught up in a frantic bustle, and an onlooker informs him that the crowd is there waiting for an imminent distribution of mémoires. A clerk collars him, yelling: "Monsieur, do you have any? Monsieur, do you have any?" Attempting a getaway, the author is nearly knocked over by the coach of a doctor who bellows: "Coachman, coachman, stop at that door!" Only after escaping the clutches of several other people, including a loud surgeon from Gascony, does he escape, "sending to the devil both the lawyer and his brief." "In truth, dear reader," he concludes, "I believed at that moment that [the onlookers] had misled me, and that they were giving out not a trial brief but gold, to all Frenchmen who have none."[70]

If one takes the details in this text at face value—and there is no reason for the author to have invented the social and occupational status of the mémoire-seekers—it suggests, along with the higher circulation figures, that trial briefs were reaching a broader and more varied population of readers. In the 1770s, as we saw, the readership of mémoires was described by contemporaries as a mixture of members of the legal profession and members of high society; the text cited above indicates that mémoires in the Diamond Necklace Affair appealed to members of other professional groups (the medical profession), while several descriptions of rambunctious crowds suggest that their readership now included people of more diverse and less "polite" backgrounds.

68. See the entries in B.N. Ms. Fr. 6685 for 1786. The mémoires for Bette d'Etienville, La Motte, and Le Guay sold for 24 or 36 sous (one or one and a half livres); on the manuscript version of Target's brief, see 13 March 1786.

69. B.N. Ms. Fr. 6685, 20 February 1786.

70. *Observations de P. Tranquille sur le premier mémoire de madame la comtesse de La Motte* ("A La Mecque," 1786), pp. 3–6.

Finally, the trial briefs in the Diamond Necklace scandal reached many more readers by indirect means. In a pamphlet written several years after the affair, Mme de La Motte recounted some of the adventures that befell her husband as he was in flight in the British Isles during the months leading up to the trial. In this passage of the pamphlet Nicolas de La Motte describes the circumstances under which he was able to read the first mémoire written in his wife's defense. He was in Scotland residing with a friend when he struck up a conversation with a French language-teacher. The latter, ignorant of his companion's identity, gives him a garbled account of the case and its reverberations, mentioning in particular the trial briefs written for Rohan, Cagliostro, and Jeanne de La Motte.

Avid for information, Nicolas rents a carriage and rushes off to Glasgow, where he had noticed that a certain café had a subscription to the *Gazette de Leyde*. That newspaper had begun, during the affair, to reprint substantial excerpts (and sometimes the full text) of the mémoires relating to the scandal. La Motte feverishly goes through back issues of the gazette, locates the reprinted excerpts of the briefs for his wife, and is aghast at the incompetence and dishonesty of his wife's lawyer. He spends two days and two nights copying down passages from the briefs in order to confront the barrister.[71] The *Gazette de Leyde* was the most successful of the foreign-based gazettes that reported on French news while (most of the time) escaping the censorship mechanisms of the French government. At its peak in the mid-1780s the paper had a European-wide circulation of 4,200. As the *Gazette*'s most prominent historian notes, however, tens of thousands of readers in fact had access to the paper or at least to excerpts of it, through public lending institutions such as the Glasgow café, private hand-to-hand circulation, and authorized or pirated reprints; in its heyday in the 1780s, the contents of the *Gazette de Leyde* may have reached between 50,000 and 100,000 readers.[72] Thanks to the *Gazette de Leyde*, in short, the "public" of the

71. *Mémoire justificatif de la comtesse de Valois de La Motte, écrit par elle-même* (London, 1789), pp. 106–111. This pamphlet, to which we will return, is obviously not a trustworthy account of the case or of Jeanne's involvement in it; but while there is ample reason to suspect that the central narrative of the piece is distorted, the details mentioned unself-consciously, such as Nicolas's reading portions of the briefs in the newspapers kept in a Glasgow café, are much more likely to be accurate or at least very plausible to a contemporary audience.

72. Jeremy Popkin, *News and Politics in the Age of Revolution*, pp. 194–195, 120–126. Popkin shows that the Diamond Necklace Affair was in fact a turning point for the paper, since in the course of the case the *Gazette* freed itself from the residual control

affair, which had expanded socially within France, also expanded geographically. The combined circulation of the trial briefs and the *Gazette*
ensured that an audience of at least 100,000 readers had access to the
most important publications in the case. Both the crowds that swarmed
at the doorsteps of lawyers and the *Gazette de Leyde*'s reprints of the
briefs suggest that with *l'affaire du cardinal* the trial brief as a genre
and a medium had reached its apex: mémoires no longer just *conveyed*
news, they had also *become* news.

The authorship of one of these briefs could make or break a barrister's reputation, whether he was a novice or a pillar of the Parisian legal
milieu. Those who took the gamble and staked their reputations on the
case varied a great deal in age, experience, and reputation. The best
known by far was the ubiquitous Guy-Jean-Baptiste Target, who headed
the team of four barristers working on the cardinal's defense, and who
personally penned both of the principal briefs written for Rohan.[73] Rohan's choice of Target is hardly surprising, for the latter's reputation as
France's finest barrister had been recently crowned by his election in
1785 to the Académie Française. Target's acceptance of the delicate task
of defending the cardinal is equally easy to understand: the Rohan-
Soubise were one of the most wealthy and powerful families in the
realm, and there was an excellent case to be made for Rohan's technical
innocence—if not for his integrity or good judgment—provided one
were careful to sidestep the issue of the queen's reputation. It is possible,
however, that the barrister's enduring reputation as a *patriote* firebrand
contributed to the politicization of the case by associating the cardinal
with other victims of "despotism" previously defended by Target. That
perception was probably reinforced by the fact that the second most
famous lawyer on Rohan's team was the eminent François Denis Tronchet, age sixty, who also had taken a stand against ministerial authority
during the political crisis of the early 1770s.[74]

Other defendants had to content themselves with the services of
much lesser luminaries. One of these we have already met: Jean Blondel,
the upwardly mobile barrister who in the Saint-Vincent case had written

---

exercised over it by the French state. The *Gazette* had originally espoused the French
court's anti-Rohan version of the case, but it soon shifted to a pro-Rohan position more
in line with the paper's generally oppositional stance to the ministry and the court.

73. *Mémoires secrets* 29:270, 16 September 1785; Ms. Fr. 6685, 30 August 1785.

74. Albert Poirot, "Le Milieu socio-professionnel des avocats du Parlement de Paris
à la veille de la révolution (1760–1790)," 2 vols. (thesis, Paris: Ecole Nationale des
Chartes), 2:189.

briefs for the marquise's paramour François Vedel du Montel, now took on the defense of the young Nicole Le Guay. As we have seen, the fifty-three-year-old lawyer's briefs were hugely successful: not only did they attain unprecedented printings of 20,000, they also resulted in a complete acquittal for his client. Jeanne de La Motte probably had a harder time securing the services of a barrister: despite the lure of high profits to be garnered from the sale of mémoires, the overwhelming evidence of her guilt and the danger of antagonizing both the Rohan family and the monarchs were probably enough to scare off most prospective candidates. It is for these reasons, no doubt, that the man who took on the task, Maître Doillot, was a competent but obscure barrister nearing retirement.[75] Finally, the perplexing task of defending the slippery Cagliostro fell to Jean-Charles Thilorier, an unknown thirty-year-old barrister from the provinces.[76]

These were the men from whose pens the French public initially learned of the case, and for all of their differences they had a good deal in common. Except for Doillot they were all members of the Parisian Ordre des Avocats, and as such connected to *parlementaire* circles. Ranging in age from their thirties to their sixties, most of them had experienced the Maupeou crisis of fifteen years earlier as adults and had learned from it to mistrust the court and the ministry. It is interesting to note that, with the exception of the elusive Doillot, all of them later opted for active involvement in the political ferment of the first years of the Revolution. Blondel and Thilorier both became electors for the city of Paris prior to the convening of the Estates-General and went on to hold public office under the Revolution.[77] Target became a member of the "Society of Thirty," the group of liberal nobles and commoners whose political propaganda is credited with triggering the revolt of the Third Estate, then was prominent in the National Assembly as the head of the committee that drafted France's first constitution. Tronchet, also later a member of the Assembly, served on the Judicial Committee that was responsible for the Criminal Code of 1791.[78] Discussing the best strategy for Rohan's defense in 1786, Target and Tronchet could never

75. Hardy could only identify Doillot with reference to his residence on the rue des Maçons (B.N. Ms. Fr. 6685, 26 November 1785). See also Funck-Brentano, *L'Affaire du collier,* pp. 278–279.

76. Poirot, "Avocats" 2:186; Funck-Brentano, *L'Affaire du collier,* p. 281.

77. Poirot, "Avocats" 2:29, 186.

78. On Target and Tronchet's roles in the Revolution, see Roger Caratini, *Dictionnaire des personnages de la Révolution* (Paris: Belfond, 1988), pp. 516, 525.

have imagined that a mere seven years later they both would be asked to perform the awesome task of defending their *ci-devant* king, Louis XVI, before the stern-faced deputies of the National Convention: Target turned down the job, Tronchet accepted it.[79]

In sum, the lawyers in the case were for the most part men whose position (as lawyers attached to the Parlement) and experience (the Maupeou crisis) suggest a great awareness of political realities and perhaps a predisposition to oppositional stances. They were dealing with a case in which, as in the Tort-Guines affair, underlying political stakes were obvious to most reasonably well informed people: none of these lawyers could have been unaware of Rohan's political ambitions, of his feud with the queen, of the latter's declining reputation, of Breteuil's vendetta against the cardinal, and so on. But the reader who expects to find any of these explicitly addressed in the trial briefs written by these men will be disappointed: just as the dog in Conan Doyle's story did not bark, the trial briefs in the Diamond Necklace scandal did not bite.

The most eagerly awaited brief in the case, for instance, was the first one written by Target in defense of Rohan; Target was as famous for his *patriote* allegiances as for his skill as a barrister and writer, and the man he was defending was in open conflict with the queen and her allies at court. No doubt there was hope that Target would produce one of his bravura pieces, a denunciation of court intrigues, perhaps, laced with resounding appeals to "citizens" and "the Nation." If so, those hopes were quickly dashed: as his first mémoire for Rohan (and subsequent ones as well) the lawyer produced instead of his usual flights of rhetoric a tightly reasoned but mostly technical piece of writing. Soon there was doggerel verse circulating in town and at court, which poked fun at the "verbose eloquence" and "dry reasoning" of the brief and at its central argument that Rohan was entirely misled and manipulated; as the versifiers gleefully pointed out, Target's argument implied that the Grand Almoner of France was not only a dupe but also an utter fool.[80] The reticence of Target and his colleagues to address any of the political issues implicit in the case is of course entirely understandable. They all knew that the question of the queen's personal reputation was a matter far too delicate to be addressed explicitly in works whose authors were known.

---

79. David Jordan, *The King's Trial: Louis XVI vs. the French Revolution* (Berkeley: University of California Press, 1981), chap. 6.

80. Georgel, *Mémoires* 2:158; B.N. Ms. Fr. 6685, 19 May 1786.

But if political issues in the narrow sense were never mentioned in the briefs, broader questions of political culture were addressed, albeit indirectly. The remainder of this chapter argues that a close reading of some of the trial briefs does indeed reveal the existence of a political subtext, especially in the briefs written for Jeanne de La Motte and Nicole Le Guay. The implied message of the briefs becomes clear if one keeps in mind the issues of gender and politics discussed earlier in this chapter: the involvement of Marie-Antoinette in factional politics and the resulting deterioration of her personal reputation; the increasingly popular pamphlet literature that blamed the rise of debauched and power-hungry "public women" (Pompadour and du Barry) for the decay of the French monarchy; and the idea, precociously formulated by Rousseau, that the corruption of a political society could be measured by the freedom and power that it granted to women in the public sphere. The facts that a woman of intrigue reached her goals by claiming royal descent and that she carried out her trickery by having a prostitute masquerade as the queen of France were enough to convince alert readers of mémoires that female powers of deceit were indeed corrupting the monarchy.

There is a good deal of evidence to suggest that what fascinated contemporaries most about Jeanne de Saint-Rémi de La Motte-Valois (as she preferred to call herself), besides her mind-boggling audacity and unqualified wickedness, was her claim to royal descent. When in November of 1785 the bookseller Hardy reported on the first brief written for her by her lawyer, Doillot, he stated, first, that it was reputed to be poorly written and argued and, second, that it presented "a clear and precise table of the noble and illustrious origin of the damsel Jeanne de Saint-Rémy de Valois."[81] Doillot began his brief with a predictable description of the contrast between the high-and-mighty Rohan and his antagonist, a woman born to poverty and obscurity but whose lineage, it was stressed, ranked higher than his.[82] A full three pages were then devoted to Jeanne's genealogy in order to establish her (apparently authentic) descent from the house of Valois. Doillot concluded, however, in the best of enlightened language, that "it is not on the basis of privilege deriving from her birth that she wishes to confront her adversary,

---

81. B.N. Ms. Fr. 6685, 26 November 1785.
82. Doillot, *Histoire du collier ou mémoire de la dame comtesse de La Motte* (Paris, 1786), pp. 3–5.

but on the grounds of natural law, which surpasses all human institutions."[83]

Doillot's odd rhetorical strategy, which consisted in heavily emphasizing his client's royal origins only to deny their explicit bearing upon the case, was echoed time and time again in his and other people's writings in defense of the countess.[84] An intriguing detail in one of Doillot's later writings for his client shed more light on his purpose in arguing the case on these terms. What of the bill of sale for the necklace that she produced, signed with the words "Marie-Antoinette of France"? Doillot reminded his readers that newspapers all over Europe had initially reported that Mme de La Motte's real first name was Marie-Antoinette, and that since a Valois could claim to be part of the royal house "of France," the countess had innocently affixed her own signature to the document.[85] Although Doillot then went on to argue that Mme de La Motte had in fact not signed the document at all, his purpose in dragging this red herring across the path of his readers must have been related to his repeated stress on Jeanne's lineage: although explicitly arguing that Cagliostro and possibly Rohan were responsible for the swindle, he was implicitly making the point that Jeanne's identity was interchangeable with that of the queen, that her royal descent should partly exonerate her from blame, that the queen's misconduct, in sum, spawned and legitimated other forms of female misconduct. (It is interesting to note, in this context, that genealogical anxieties—were the queen's children really fathered by Louis XVI?—recur as a central motif in the prerevolutionary pamphlet literature against Marie-Antoinette.)[86]

This theme of interchangeable female identities attains even greater complexity in the briefs written for the young lady of the Palais-Royal, Nicole Le Guay. In his two briefs for the young woman, the lawyer Jean Blondel made use of the devices that had served him so well in his defense of Vedel du Montel during the Saint-Vincent case: the first-person narrative, the portrayal of beleaguered innocence, the dignity and

83. Ibid., pp. 7–10.
84. See also Doillot, *Sommaire pour la dame comtesse de La Motte* (Paris, 1786), pp. 49–51.
85. Ibid., pp. 9–11.
86. On this and other aspects of the pamphlet literature against the queen, see Revel, "Marie-Antoinette"; and Chantal Thomas, *La Reine scélérate*.

pathos of the defendant. The first brief opens with the plaintive self-description of the accused, arrested, thrown into a state prison, caught between a powerful lord and a collection of diabolical crooks, "I, a young woman, weak, ignorant and timid, knowing nothing of procedure, inexperienced in juridical matters." [87] Against such a formidable array of obstacles, Nicole Le Guay can muster only her utter innocence: "My account will be simple, naive, and artless, as are my character and the strange role I was made to play by my seducers." [88]

It is through the eyes of this impressionable creature—the real Nicole Le Guay was anything but innocent—that we hear of Jeanne de La Motte's first attempt at recruiting Nicole to assist in her designs. Blondel's account, in his client's voice, of Mme de La Motte's first visit to the young woman is a consummate piece of dramatic writing, in which the artful La Motte is seen entrapping her future accomplice by playing upon a combination of social authority and dangerous female intimacy: "I offer a seat to Mme de La Motte; she herself draws it closer to mine. She sits down. Then she leans toward me with an air of both mystery and confidence, gives me a look that seems to suggest both the concern and the intimacy of friendship, tempered however by the dignified bearing of a lady of high rank about to confide an important secret in her protégée, and utters in low tones the strange words that follow." [89] La Motte immediately brings up her close connection to the queen ("we are like two fingers on a hand") while reassuring her companion by means of seductive blandishments: "Trust me, *mon cher coeur*," she murmurs, "I am a woman of rank [*une femme comme il faut*] attached to the court." [90] The impressionable Nicole soon consents to assist the La Mottes in carrying out what she believes to be the queen's wishes.

The alliance between La Motte and Le Guay is cemented by refashioning the latter's identity. Having introduced herself as the countess de Valois, the older woman announces that if her young friend wishes to move in circles connected to the court, she too must have *une qualité*. And so in Blondel's account as well as in many others we learn how Nicole Le Guay (no stranger in reality to multiple identities, since she

87. Jean Blondel, *Mémoire pour la demoiselle Le Guay d'Oliva* (Paris: P. G. Simon, 1786), p. 4.

88. Ibid., p. 8.

89. Ibid., p. 14.

90. Ibid., p. 58.

5a and b. The female protagonists of the Diamond Necklace Affair, taken
from one of the collections of prints that were sold with mémoires
or on their own during the affair. On the left Nicole Le Guay, on
the right, Jeanne de La Motte. The *cartouches* under the portraits
represent pivotal scenes in the affair: Under Le Guay, Nicolas de La
Motte making the young girl's acquaintance in the Palais Royal;
under La Motte, the countess recruiting Le Guay for the intrigue.
(Phot. Bibl. Nat. Paris)

plied her trade as a courtesan under the nom de guerre Mme de Signy)
became in the hands of her mentors the baroness d'Oliva. There was
nothing random about the choice of this name d'Oliva (sometimes
spelled d'Olisva) by Mme de La Motte for her young protégée, for it
was an anagram of Jeanne's own "royal" name, Valois.[91] What's in a
name? A great deal in this case, since it was the Valois name that had
connected the trickster to the queen in the first place, and its anagram

91. Jean Blondel, *Second mémoire pour la demoiselle Le Guay d'Oliva* (Paris: P. G. Simon, 1786), p. 16; Droz, *Histoire du règne de Louis XVI* 1:336; Funck-Brentano, *L'Affaire du collier,* p. 150.

that closed the circle linking prostitution to female sovereignty. Having made herself into the sovereign's doppelganger, Jeanne de La Motte created her own double to masquerade as the queen. Another woman briefly entered the picture: the countess's chambermaid Rosalie assisted her mistress in dressing Nicole Le Guay for her appearance at night in the gardens of Versailles. The young woman was decked out for the occasion in an informal white shift. Le Guay had no idea, or so her lawyer claimed, of whom she was impersonating, no notion that this costume, known as a *robe en gaule,* was identical to the one sported by Marie-Antoinette in a recent portrait by Elisabeth Vigée-Lebrun.[92] While Rosalie arranged Le Guay's hair, the countess dressed her with her own hands, stooping for the occasion, Blondel stressed, to playing second chambermaid to a young woman innocently masquerading as the queen. "Once the two women had finished serving as maids," Blondel went on, "Mme de La Motte resumed her rank of countess and the dignified mien of a protector."[93]

This insistence on the fluid character of Mme de La Motte's social identity served to underscore her vocation for intrigue: she was the exact female equivalent of the protean Cagliostro, though her femininity made her the more dangerous of the two. She and her husband had gathered around themselves a *demi-monde* of fake counts, barons, and marquis, all of whom pursued social promotion by means of sexual and financial intrigue.[94] It was exactly this sort of world, a degraded replica of high society, that had generated a Mme du Barry, fully equipped with ersatz nobility and threatening sexual powers.

As Mary Douglas has argued, groups and individuals that exist at the margins of society are usually perceived as profoundly menacing, for they continually threaten to alter the shape of the social order by taking over its center.[95] Tricksters whose skills enable them to impersonate a wide range of social types, and female prostitutes whose sexual powers give them access to an equally broad cross section of society, appear as recurrent examples of such "liminal" types. The power-wielding mis-

92. Blondel, *Mémoire pour Le Guay,* pp. 18–19; this scene is described again in his *Second mémoire pour Le Guay,* pp. 16–17.

93. Blondel, *Second mémoire pour Le Guay,* p. 16.

94. Funck-Brentano, *L'Affaire du collier,* chap. 13; *Histoire véritable de Jeanne de La Motte,* pp. 48–49.

95. Mary Douglas, *Purity and Danger: An Analysis of Concepts of Pollution and Taboo* (London: Routledge and Kegan Paul, 1966); see also Victor Turner, *The Ritual Process: Structure and Anti-Structure* (Ithaca: Cornell University Press, 1969).

tresses of Louis XV had carried pollution and disorder to the center of political power by making their way directly to the king's bedroom. Under the reign of a more virtuous monarch, a La Motte had to operate indirectly, merging her identity and that of her double, d'Oliva, with that of the king's wife. In either case, the sexual power wielded by "public women" over the sacred body of the king was perceived as the breach through which chaos was overtaking the realm.

The pivotal scene in Blondel's two trial briefs, as in many other accounts of the affair, was the nocturnal episode known as *la scène du bosquet,* the scene in the grove, in which Nicole Le Guay impersonated the queen for Rohan's benefit. The lawyer argued, predictably enough, that Le Guay was kept ignorant of the meaning of the intrigue and of whom she was to represent in the scene for which she was coached—although she was told that she was carrying out the wishes of the queen, who would be nearby watching the proceedings.[96] Blondel then launched into a dizzying spiral of argumentation, the purpose of which was to demonstrate that since Nicole Le Guay was persuaded that the queen would be present at the scene, she could not have suspected that she was impersonating her. "When one sets about representing a person, assuredly that person must not be present. Otherwise, the disguise becomes impracticable, and the man whom one wishes to make the dupe of this fraud sees through it and is not taken in; and the person in charge of its execution [Nicole Le Guay] cannot believe that she is playing the role of a person who is present."[97] Convinced of the queen's presence at the nocturnal rendezvous, Le Guay could not have imagined, or so the argument goes, that she was playing the role of a character who stood nearby. The reader, meanwhile, is asked to identify with the young woman, to share her belief that Marie-Antoinette could very well have been present at a midnight tryst set up by a woman of intrigue. The triumphant acquittal of Le Guay testifies to her lawyer's skill in convincing the judges and the public that the absent queen was present at least in spirit on that fatal night in the groves of Versailles.

Nearly everyone who wrote about the affair at the time seemed to assume that the core of the matter lay in what happened at the *scène du bosquet.* Had Jeanne de La Motte not set up this encounter, much of what followed would not have occurred: Rohan might not have been

---

96. Blondel, *Mémoire pour Le Guay,* p. 31; Blondel, *Second mémoire pour Le Guay,* p. 36.

97. Blondel, *Second mémoire pour Le Guay,* p. 41.

convinced, Nicole Le Guay would not have become involved, the queen would not have been insulted, the necklace never purchased. Much of the affair, in short, depended on Jeanne de La Motte's ability to set up and direct the nocturnal scene—for the events of that night are always labeled a *scene*, rather than an episode or an event. Contemporaries, from whatever perspective they were writing, always focused on the theatrical moments in the Diamond Necklace Affair.

Much of Target's sober defense of Rohan, for instance, hinges on what he called "the criminal scene executed in the gardens of Versailles."[98] The terms "illusion," "artifice," and "scene" recur at every twist and turn of the brief—not surprisingly, since Target's strategy was to emphasize Jeanne de La Motte's diabolical cleverness as both an actress and a producer in order to explain how fully duped his client had been. Writing from a similar point of view, but some years later and without a case to build, Rohan's secretary, the abbé Georgel, also singled out the theatrical aspects of Jeanne de La Motte's enterprise. Georgel evokes another "scene" of the affair, the moment when Rohan witnessed the handing over of the fabulous necklace to the man he was told was the queen's valet: "Mad with joy at the prodigious success of her extraordinary scheme, [Jeanne de La Motte] had prepared, in her apartment at Versailles, the theater where the delivery of the necklace was to take place. . . . It was truly a scene, a performance." Georgel goes on to describe La Motte's preparations for the scene. She selects a room onto which opens a small alcove with a glass-paneled door, and it is in the alcove that "this clever actress placed her spectator"; from there the cardinal witnesses the handing over of the necklace in the darkened room, to a man whose features he cannot distinguish, but who announces himself as the queen's emissary.[99]

Nicole Le Guay's lawyer, Jean Blondel, also made heavy use of the theatrical terms (*scène, jouer, représenter, personnage*) in defending his client. The core of his defense, as we have seen, was the argument that the young Nicole had no knowledge that she was impersonating the queen: "I did not know then, have never known, and still do not know what character I was made to play, and what character I was to ad-

98. Guy-Jean-Baptiste Target, *Mémoire pour Louis-René-Edouard de Rohan, Cardinal de la Sainte-Eglise Romaine, Evêque de Strasbourg* (Paris: P. G. Simon, 1786), p. 19.
99. Georgel, *Mémoires* 2:61–62.

dress."[100] Like the abbé Georgel, the barrister Blondel showed his readers the countess masterminding, with consummate skill, a performance for which she has written the script, while keeping her actors, literally as well as figuratively, in the dark: "A scene that was imagined, ordered, directed by Mme de La Motte was performed by night in one of the garden walks."[101]

Not everyone was convinced that Le Guay was quite the pristine innocent that her lawyer portrayed in the brief. The author of a muck-raking pamphlet published during the case pointed out, aptly enough, that a person who was offered 15,000 livres for a few minutes' work must have suspected that something foul was afoot; he suggested that d'Oliva's impersonation of the queen was a bit too skillful to make her innocence credible.[102] The young woman's protestations of innocence leave him cold: "Do we not see our actresses representing upon our stages the noblest of virtues, while conducting themselves [in private] in ways that are completely opposite?"[103] The author's broad banter in the pamphlet plays upon contemporary assumptions that were grounded in reality: if, as everyone knew, most successful actresses in Paris were also highly paid courtesans, was it unlikely that a prostitute should turn actress to play a role in this sleazy plot? Rousseau had surmised that a woman who sold the pleasure of watching her onstage might as well be selling her sexual favors; the reverse could very easily be imagined.

In short, the Diamond Necklace Affair was often presented in contemporary accounts—trial briefs, pseudomemoirs, or polemical pamphlets—as an elaborate play, with a producer and director (Jeanne de La Motte), actors in leading and supporting roles (some of whom may not have known the purpose of the plot), and a single spectator, Rohan, whose belief in the reality of the performance was crucial to the furthering of La Motte's schemes. But what sort of play was it? Not a melodrama or *drame*, to be sure, despite the lawyer Blondel's attempts at presenting his client as a young innocent entrapped by evil seducers. Those who were not cynical might have found the young Nicole's story

100. Blondel, *Mémoire pour Le Guay*, pp. 31–32.
101. Blondel, *Second mémoire*, p. 21.
102. *Suite des observations de Motus sur le mémoire de Melle d'Oliva* (n.p., 1786), p. 67.
103. Ibid., p. 70.

touching, but it was, after all, marginal to the central intrigue plotted out by Mme de La Motte.

The Diamond Necklace Affair, and especially its central "scene in the grove," was not a lachrymose drama but something much closer to the opéra-comique we encountered in chapter two as a form of upper-class diversion. The Diamond Necklace Affair offered a complicated plot, disguises and mistaken identities, purloined letters, elegant settings, and luscious female characters. It had all the elegant shallowness of a light (and late) rococo comedy, and its main "intertext" is not difficult to discover. In Blondel's first brief for Le Guay, the young woman mentions that one of the rewards she received for the role she had played was to be taken by Mme de La Motte to see a performance of the runaway success of 1784, Beaumarchais's *Marriage of Figaro*.[104] Mme de La Motte's taste for such fashionable theatrical entertainment is hardly surprising, given both her predilection for aping the high society that flocked to these events and her talents as an actress and producer.

The success of the briefs in the Diamond Necklace Affair, with their printings in the tens of thousands, was a literary phenomenon that can only be compared, in the 1780s, to the popularity of Beaumarchais's play, with its unprecedented sixty-eight consecutive performances.[105] But the similarities between the mémoires and the play do not end there. *The Marriage of Figaro* does include a trial scene in act three, complete with references to lawyers and their briefs; beyond that, however, spectators of the play might well have recognized in Blondel's briefs for Nicole Le Guay some startling reminders of Beaumarchais's plot. The lawyer's depictions of the "highborn" La Motte and her maid, Rosalie, decking out the ambiguously innocent Nicole in lace and muslin was oddly reminiscent of the sexually charged scene in act two of the play, in which the page-boy Chérubin (played on the contemporary stage by a girl) is dressed in female clothing by the countess and her maid, Suzanne. The last act of the play (and of Mozart's opera, which follows it closely) takes place in an elegant park studded with kiosks and pavilions; in this setting the countess and her maid, having exchanged clothes for the occasion, take advantage of the shadows and of their disguises to teach their respective husbands a lesson in trust and fidelity.

104. Blondel, *Mémoire pour Le Guay,* p. 41.
105. See Félix Gaiffe, *Le Mariage de Figaro* (Paris: Nizet, 1926).

Both the play and the lawyers' briefs, then, recount elaborately theatrical plots masterminded by women, of which highborn and powerful men (Rohan and Almaviva) are the dupes. One should not be misled by *Figaro*'s posthumous reputation as a politically subversive paean to the ambitions of talented commoners, for, as we shall see in a later chapter, Beaumarchais was perceived in the 1780s as an ally of the forces of political and stylistic conservatism.[106] Nor were contemporaries unaware of the forces that had made possible the play's opening in Paris in April of 1784, after years of protracted struggles with the censors. It had first been staged in private some months earlier on the estates of the count de Vaudreuil, a member of the queen's inner circle and the lover of her most intimate friend, Mme de Polignac.[107] So enamored, in fact, was the queen of Beaumarchais's talent, that she was rehearsing to play the female lead, Rosine, in a private production of his earlier *Barbier de Séville* at about the time that the scandal erupted.[108] At Versailles, or more precisely in her intimate residence, the Trianon, the queen inhabited a world that was not very different from the worlds of Beaumarchais's comedies and of the Diamond Necklace tragicomedy; worlds of gallantry and intrigue, of disguises and mistaken identities, and above all, worlds that were ruled by women.

With Beaumarchais's *Marriage of Figaro* we have come full circle back to Rousseau's fulminations against "public women." The Genevan writer, it will be remembered, had already articulated in the late 1750s the cultural kinship between high society, court society, and the contemporary stage: "Look through most contemporary plays. It is always a woman who knows everything, who teaches everything to men."[109] Had Rousseau lived to witness the Diamond Necklace Affair or to see *The Marriage of Figaro*, he would have found his irate masculinist prognosis amply confirmed. In Beaumarchais's most famous play, Figaro, for all of his self-dramatizing insolence, is duped in the end by a conspiracy of women. As for the Diamond Necklace Affair, it too was a woman's business, down to its central object: in eighteenth-century licentious parlance, jewels, *les bijoux,* meant female genitalia.[110] Both the play and

106. See below, chapter 6.

107. Frédéric Grendel, *Beaumarchais,* trans. Roger Greaves (New York: Thomas Y. Crowell, 1977), chap. 14; Zweig, *Marie-Antoinette,* pp. 157–158.

108. Zweig, *Marie-Antoinette,* p. 156; Almeras, *Marie-Antoinette,* p. 32.

109. Rousseau, *Politics and the Arts,* p. 49.

110. Diderot's most frankly pornographic work, *Les Bijoux indiscrets,* has the eponymous *bijoux,* female genitalia, recounting their adventures. The licentious connotations

the scandal provided dramatic illustrations of the dangers of "public womanhood" to those who shared Rousseau's dim view of the sexual politics of the Old Regime elite.

The Diamond Necklace Affair was from the start rife with erotic innuendo and scandalous gossip, none of which was stated explicitly in the trial briefs. But the rumors were there from the beginning, fueled by the pamphlets from the literary underground: that the women in the case were all dissolute, that all of them were Rohan's lovers, and, yes, that Rohan was or aspired to become one of the queen's paramours; but rumor, and muckraking pamphlets, also had it that Marie-Antoinette's sexual tastes ran more to women, which of course explained the mysterious link between the queen and her debauched "cousin" Jeanne de Valois. A pamphlet of 1786, for instance, *Suite des Observations de Motus,* revels in sarcastic innuendo directed at all the characters in the case, including prominently the queen. Questioning the veracity of Nicole Le Guay's account as presented by her lawyer, the author argues that she must have skillfully imitated the queen's very voice in order to dupe Rohan, since "the sound of *adorable Antoinette's* voice was not unknown to M. de Rohan" [emphasis in text]; and again, with ironic sanctimoniousness: "Did that prince conceive the bold and sacrilegious hope (for he must have known the sovereign to be incapable of such baseness) of plucking a rose from the most sacred rose-bush in France?" Finally, the author suggests that d'Oliva would have had to be very credulous to believe that the queen needed her services, since she must have known as well as anyone of the queen's fashionable taste in sexual pleasures: "But could d'Oliva, who has only worked *pour homme,* who, as I have already said, does not know how to do anything *pour femme,* have believed that the queen had need of her ministry?"[111]

Such muckraking was, however, comparatively rare in 1786. But with the explosion of political pamphleteering in the late 1780s the scurrilous innuendo of the case came out into the open. Whisked out of the

---

of the famous necklace as *bijou* were made most explicit in a well-known revolutionary caricature, *Enjambée de la Sainte-Famille des Thuilleries à Montmidy* (c. 1791). The print shows Marie-Antoinette stepping from the roof of the Tuileries palace to the émigré outpost of Montmidy on the northeastern frontier, carrying the royal family on her back. Mme de La Motte, Rohan, and one of the queen's alleged lovers, the duc de Coigny, stand directly below the queen's open legs and stare up as La Motte holds the necklace aloft. *French Caricature and the French Revolution, 1789–1790* (Catalog, Grunwald Center for the Graphic Arts, University of California at Los Angeles, 1988), pp. 185–186.

111. *Observations de Motus,* pp. 35, 47, 27.

Salpêtrière prison and over to London thanks to the efforts of the queen's enemies, Jeanne de La Motte eventually produced (with the help, it was rumored, of the exiled Calonne), her own "candid" account of the events of 1784–85.[112] Her *Mémoire justificatif* of 1789 announces most of the themes that were played out ad nauseam in the pamphlets of the 1790s: Marie-Antoinette was a cold-blooded *politique* whose principal aim was to undermine the kingdom and turn it over to her brother, the Austrian emperor; her political corruption was matched only by the personal debauchery made evident by her indiscriminate passion for women as well as men, with Mme de Polignac and Mme de La Motte herself figuring prominently among the queen's many female lovers.[113] Well into the 1790s, Jeanne de La Motte was a recurrent figure in pamphlets that presented her as the archetypal plebeian victim of the evil political designs and sexual excesses of the queen and Mme de Polignac.[114]

The antifemale legacy of the Diamond Necklace Affair is abundantly visible in the volley of obscene literature aimed against the queen that began to appear in 1789.[115] Sometimes the connection with the scandal of 1785–86 was explicit. *La Reine dévoilée*, for instance, a 1789 pamphlet in the form of letters that purport to reveal Marie-Antoinette's bisexual lusts, was advertised as a sequel to Mme de La Motte's "candid" memoir of the same year; one of the letters it contains is from Mme de La Motte, claiming once again that she was forced to serve as scapegoat for the queen's sexual misconduct.[116] In other cases, the link with the themes of the Rohan scandal are implicit, but still visible. The phenomenally successful *Essais historiques sur la vie de Marie-Antoinette*—first published and suppressed in 1783, then a runaway success in 1789 and after—picks up the queen's alleged fondness for nighttime walks in the gardens of Versailles in the company of her

112. Funck-Brentano, *L'Affaire du collier*, chaps. 37–38.
113. *Mémoire justificatif de la comtesse de Valois-La Motte, écrit par elle-même* (London, 1789).
114. For instance, *Suplique [sic] à la Nation et requête à l'Assemblée nationale par Jeanne de Saint-Rémi de Valois* (n.p., 1790); *Adresse de la comtesse de La Motte Valois à l'Assemblée nationale pour être déclarée citoyenne active* (London, 1790); *Le Capitaine Tempête à Jeanne de La Motte* (n.p., n.d.); *Les Lettres de cachet presque ressuscitées* (n.p., n.d.).
115. For a chronological listing of the main pamphlets, see d'Alméras, *Marie-Antoinette*, pp. 395–421.
116. *La reine dévoilée ou supplément au mémoire de Madame la comtesse de La Motte* (London, 1789), pp. 81–82.

ladies-in-waiting; these nocturnal pastimes, according to the author, soon degenerated into orgies with the young princess and her friends and attendants swapping lovers in the gardens of the palace. "Women from all walks of life all had a role to play in this endless course in de-bauchery. Women of the court, chambermaids, the wives of high offi-cials, of bourgeois, of the palace servants, and even *grisettes*, all of them intermingled for these promenades in the dark."[117] To readers in 1789, these erotic encounters in the moonlit alleys of the palace gardens, and the mingling of women of all social stations who partook of them, would no doubt bring to mind the famous *scène du bosquet*.

The attacks against Marie-Antoinette were eventually broadened into general condemnations of female rule as the worst, most corrupt form of power spawned by the Old Regime. A grand synthesis on the subject, a five-hundred-page volume entitled *Les Crimes des reines de France,* appeared in 1791; its author, ironically, was a woman (albeit of Jacobin leanings), Louise de Keralio.[118] Keralio's chronicle of the iniqui-ties of female power begins in the dark ages, with the mind-boggling crimes of early queens like Frédégonde and Brunehaut, moves on to the "Italian vices" of Catherine and Marie de Médicis, and culminates in a denunciation of the worst of them all, the Austrian monster Antoinette. The introduction to the volume warns readers that if absolute power corrupts, absolute female power does so with a vengeance: "A woman for whom all is possible is capable of anything."[119] The publication of Keralio's book coincided with the escalation in early 1791 of antimonar-chical agitation both in political clubs and in the radical press.[120]

With the execution of Marie-Antoinette in October of 1793, the Revolution brought to a horrible culmination the ideas set forth in Rousseau's *Letter to d'Alembert.* From the 1760s to the 1790s, female power was seen by many as the embodiment—quite literally—of the worst of personal, hereditary, and despotic rule. Feminine nature, char-acterized by deceit, seduction, and the selfish pursuit of private interest,

---

117. *Essais historiques,* p. 34. For a fuller discussion of this pamphlet, including its publishing history, see Hunt, "The Many Bodies of Marie-Antoinette," pp. 117–118.

118. [Louise de Keralio], *Les Crimes des reines de France depuis le commencement de la monarchie jusqu'à Marie-Antoinette* (Paris, 1791); the volume bears the name of Louis Prudhomme, the editor of the newspaper *Les Révolutions de Paris.* I am grateful to Lynn Hunt and to Carla Hesse for pointing out to me the real authorship of the book. (See also the article on Louise de Keralio in Michaud's *Biographie Universelle.*)

119. Keralio, *Les Crimes,* pp. vii, ix.

120. Jack Censer, *Prelude to Power: The Parisian Radical Press, 1789–1791* (Balti-more: Johns Hopkins University Press, 1976), pp. 96–98, 111–115.

6. The frontispiece of [Louise de Keralio] *Les Crimes des reines de France* (1791). The Newberry Library, Chicago.

was construed as the extreme antithesis of the abstract principles of reason made law that were to govern the public sphere. Femininity, in
short, became radically incompatible with the new definition of the
polity.[121]

None of these ideas, of course, were explicitly articulated in the
mémoires published during the *affaire du cardinal*. Even as late as
1786, open criticism of the king's wife in a signed work was, if not unthinkable, at least extremely dangerous. There can be little doubt, however, that the Diamond Necklace Affair played a crucial role in setting
the stage for the brutal misogyny of the Jacobin revolution—if only
through the introduction of the French public to Jeanne de La Motte,
a symbol of female cunning and debauchery whose dogged claims to
royal descent forever tainted, by association, the unpopular queen of
France.

In the cultural context of the later eighteenth century, the greatest
cause célèbre of the Old Regime accentuated the gendered nature of
prerevolutionary political discourse. "Despotism" had once been mostly
male, incarnated in the figure of Chancellor Maupeou and his fellow
ministers, d'Aiguillon and Terray, reincarnated, in the judicial arena, under the traits of a Morangiès, a Goezman, a Guines. It was Rousseau's
great insight, for better or for worse, that the corruption of the polity
could be symbolized most dramatically by the conspicuous presence of
women in the public sphere. In the second half of the eighteenth century, the power attributed to Louis XV's mistresses seemed to confirm,
far more than the debauchery of the old king himself, that something
was rotten in the state of France; the authority of such women, as revealed in salacious gossip and pamphlets, pointed to the emasculation
of male power and the unhealthy privatization of the state. Like the Parc
aux Cerfs, the underworld of the Diamond Necklace Affair evoked a
powerful eighteenth-century phantasm—that of the oriental harem, the
dwelling of innumerable and interchangeable women driven by insatia-
ble lust, whose very multiplicity served to define the irreducible oneness
of the despot.[122]

The Diamond Necklace Affair significantly promoted the emerging
contrast drawn by many writers between the public sphere of the monarchy and the aristocracy (gendered female) and the new public sphere
defined by law, justice, and publicity (gendered male). With its curious

121. Landes, *Women in the Public Sphere,* chaps. 4–6.
122. Grosrichard, *Structure du sérail,* pp. 177–178.

game of interchangeable female identities, the Necklace scandal seemed to confirm the fear that women of lascivious temperament and with a disposition to intrigue had open access to wealth and public power, while the unprecedented diffusion of information relating to the case drove the message home to growing numbers of people. If the integrity of the secular French state found one of its first symbolic incarnations, in 1773–1774, in the radiant figure of the virgin of Salency, the corruption of the monarchy, conversely, was given female form in the antiheroines of the Necklace scandal. It remained for a series of domestic dramas of the mid-to-late 1780s, the subject of a later chapter, to bring closer to home for most readers the private meaning of the contrast between the healthy political "virtue" of men and the destructive designs of "public women."

5

"Innocent Blood Avenged"

Emplotting Judicial Reform, 1785–1786

We have seen how the increasing popularity of trial briefs contributed to transforming the structure of public life in the last two decades of the Old Regime. Not only did mémoires personalize and publicize sensational disputes among the upper classes and factional strife at court, they also often carried political messages—albeit with varying degrees of explicitness. Sometimes the narratives in trial briefs castigated "despotic" authority in the persons of tyrannical grandees like Morangiès and Richelieu; in other cases they celebrated a positive political ideal, as in the allegorization of Salency and of its virginal queen of virtue; the narratives of the sensational Diamond Necklace Affair, by contrast, demonized real women, the mistresses and wives of kings, whose presence and activities were said to corrupt the public sphere. But the political messages buried in these accounts had one thing in common: they were critical but not constructive, descriptive rather than prescriptive. Although the lawyer-authors all strove, rhetorically, to enlist the support of their readers, that support was sought for no practical end beyond the legal victory of their clients.

All of this changed in the mid-1780s, with a cluster of very similar cases in which the defense of beleaguered clients seemed a mere pretext for pressing calls for reform. The timing of this development will come as no surprise to those familiar with the history of a period that in textbooks is commonly labeled "the Age of Reform." Throughout the reign of Louis XVI, programs for reform succeeded one another like lemmings, only to drown, ultimately, in a sea of political opposition. Such was the fate of Turgot's physiocratic and anticorporatist economic measures (1774–1776) and of attempts by Necker (1776–1781), Joly de Fleury (1781–1783), and Calonne (1783–1787) to impose new taxes and to reshape local administrations. Such large-scale reforms, which threatened the economic interests of powerful groups, met with little success, as is well known, before the very late 1780s. The reforms that *were* achieved prior to the Revolution were mostly symbolically charged measures in the direction of greater humanitarianism and tolerance that cost little, politically, but looked good; most of these came about in the 1780s. In 1779, Jacques Necker abolished the *mainmorte*, the last major legal holdover from serfdom in France, and in 1780 he did away with the "preparatory" torture that was applied to the accused in order to extract a confession (the torture of convicted criminals prior to execution for the purpose of getting them to name their accomplices was not abolished until 1788). Throughout the 1780s there was recurrent concern about conditions in royal prisons and about arbitrary arrest. In 1787, nine years after Voltaire's death, *l'infâme* was finally crushed by means of the Edict of Toleration that granted civil rights to Protestants.

The issue that surfaced in the mémoires of the mid-1780s was that of the long-overdue reform of France's criminal justice system. Calls for the reform of the realm's costly and inefficient judiciary system long antedated the 1780s. In the first half of the eighteenth century, administrators such as the abbé de Saint-Pierre, Chancellor d'Aguesseau, and the marquis d'Argenson had drawn up elaborate plans for reforming the realm's notoriously complex and corrupt system of justice. They articulated suggestions that would be echoed by others right up to the Revolution: reducing the number of overlapping lower jurisdictions, equalizing the very uneven areas served by the regional parlements, decreasing the number and length of lawsuits, simplifying the laws and reducing their number, modifying and abolishing the venality of judicial offices.[1] Many of these proposed reforms were in fact carried out later in the century: we should not forget that Maupeou's unpopular initiatives of 1771 were not just a settling of political scores, but a heavy-handed, hence short-lived, implementation of many of these suggestions.[2]

The ministers and other officials who throughout the eighteenth century proposed reforms, or even acted upon them, saw the problems from their own perspective, as administrators concerned primarily with

1. John Carey, *Judicial Reform in France before the Revolution of 1789* (Cambridge, Mass.: Harvard University Press, 1981), chap. 2.
2. Ibid., chap. 4.

matters of efficiency or cost. Lawyers, of course, would see things from a different angle, as representatives of individuals caught in the creaking and cumbersome machinery of the Old Regime judicial system. By the mid-1780s, it was also plain to ambitious members of the profession that a strikingly *pathétique* defense of an oppressed person could make a barrister into a local or national celebrity. Careerist considerations along with, no doubt, sincere humanitarian convictions caused several lawyers simultaneously to produce mémoires that dramatically indicted the Old Regime's criminal law system, for it was in the area of criminal justice that the most glaring abuses were to be found: the accused confronting his or her judges in secret, with no knowledge of the charges or of the witnesses' depositions; given no time to prepare defenses when subsequently confronted with the witnesses, and granted only in certain cases limited access to counsel; a procedure that routinely included the use of torture to extract confessions, and in which it was left to the judge's discretion to choose among an array of penalties, including barbarically cruel forms of physical punishment and execution, the one that fit the crime at hand; inefficient and erratic investigations that kept the accused languishing in prison for years, while executions followed upon sentencing with dangerous haste—these were only some of the vices of the procedure set up by the Ordinance of 1670.[3]

The cases we look at in this chapter—the defenses of Marie Cléreaux, of Victoire Salmon, and of the three men known as the Trois Roués—resembled less the judicial scandals of the 1770s and the 1780s than they did Voltaire's *infâme*-crushing cases of the 1760s. The causes célèbres of the 1770s usually pitted against each other two antagonists, each of whom claimed to be asserting a true version of the facts; the political or prescriptive message of the brief was mostly implicit in the defense of one character and one version of the story, and in the critical portrayal of an identifiable opponent. The Calas affair, by contrast, was a case of miscarriage of justice. It was not an individual who brought about the torture and execution of Jean Calas or the mutilation and beheading of the chevalier de La Barre, but a system of officially sanctioned religious zealotry and prejudice.

In the mid-1780s a group of lawyers named Froudière, Lecauchois,

3. Ibid., and Edmond Seligman, *La Justice en France pendant la Révolution,* 2 vols. (Paris: Plon, 1901–1913), 1, chap. 2. For a convenient summary, see the article "Justice criminelle" in Marcel Marion, *Dictionnaire des institutions de la France aux XVIIe et XVIIIe siècles* (Paris, 1923; reprint Paris: A. and J. Picard, 1981), pp. 316–318.

Fournel, and Dupaty picked up the Voltairean torch and threw themselves, invoking the name of the Patriarch of Ferney, into the battle against judicial iniquity. Like Voltaire, they took on clients out of sincere compassion for individual victims (unlike Voltaire's most famous protégés, their clients were still alive) and also with the broader aim of exposing the great flaws in the criminal justice system and calling for its reform. Their purpose was as explicitly political as Voltaire's had been and, if anything, more geared to immediate, concrete, reforming action. The fact that it was lawyers, some of them obscure men, who revived the Voltairean tradition of explicit *engagement* in the trial brief may well suggest the displacement of men of letters by men of law as leaders of the prerevolutionary ideological crusade.

Finally, these cases of the mid-eighties show a qualitatively different concern for social justice than we have seen in any of the previous cases, including Voltaire's. Yes, a Falconnet or a Delacroix could claim to enter the fray with his pen to protect the "little man" from the tyranny of the powerful; but the underdog in previous cases had been, at worst, a literate, fairly prosperous member of the middle or lower-middle classes. It would have been unthinkable, after all, for a Morangiès, a Guines, or a Goezman to enter the lists against an illiterate laborer. But with the 1780s this changed, as progressively-minded barristers took up the cudgels for the truly wretched of their society. In this new crusade it was no longer a matter of using mémoires to redress the inequality between socially mismatched antagonists, but one of protecting the dispossessed against a legal system designed by and for their social "betters."

The three cases that form the core of this chapter cannot be addressed chronologically, for, although they stretched out over several years, all three came to a climax at exactly the same time. The case of Marie Cléreaux unfolded very quickly in 1785, although polemical fallout from it continued into the revolutionary years; the Victoire Salmon affair, which began in 1781, did not reach a judicial conclusion until 1786, with the public controversy around it taking place entirely between 1784 and 1786; finally, the case known as the affair of the Trois Roués stretched from 1783 to 1787, but only attained national celebrity in 1786. These cases therefore all made their greatest impact in 1785 and 1786, playing themselves out as a sort of counterpoint to the Diamond Necklace Affair and raising an entirely different set of issues.

The first two cases, the Cléreaux and Salmon affairs, present a number of striking similarities. Both started in Normandy, in the towns of Rouen and Caen (the proximity to Paris of these towns most likely played a role in the cases' celebrity). In both cases the protagonist was a female servant accused wrongly (it seems) by her masters, facing the death penalty, and rescued in extremis by a local barrister. The salient mémoires in each case were striking narratives that melodramatically contrasted the innocence and vulnerability of the accused with the evil natures and motives of her accusers. The narratives of both cases circulated widely and did much—albeit with different degrees of explicitness—to publicize the urgent need for a reform of the kingdom's criminal justice system.

Compared with all of the other cases analyzed in this book, that of Marie Cléreaux was remarkably short and simple; but it was also as sensational as any other and as suited to a dramatic account.[4] The bare bones of the case are as follows. In the fall of 1784 in Rouen the servant Marie Cléreaux sued her employers of four months, a wealthy merchant named Thibault and his son, claiming that they had taken from her a sum of 504 livres, her lifetime's savings. It turned out that Thibault had recently fired Cléreaux, accusing her of stealing a bottle of Malaga wine, some silk kerchiefs, and the money, which he claimed as his own: in May of 1785 he brought these accusations before the lower court of Rouen, the *bailliage*. By virtue of an ancient law framed for the protection of employers, the death penalty was, on the books, the punishment for domestic theft.[5] Although by the late eighteenth century this anomalously harsh provision was rarely applied, Marie Cléreaux was condemned in July of 1785 to death by hanging, and the *bailliage*'s sentence was confirmed by the parlement of Rouen. At this juncture a young lawyer of the town, Louis Froudière, leapt to the young woman's defense (he had been alerted by her father-confessor). With remarkable speed, he produced a trial brief defending Cléreaux and carefully orchestrated its dissemination; this proved so effective that there were demonstrations in town against the verdict, and witnesses came forward

---

4. The following discussion of the case draws heavily on Hans-Jürgen Lüsebrink's excellent presentation of it in an article and an annotated edition of the main brief by Froudière, which includes a helpful introduction: "L'Affaire Cléreaux (Rouen 1785–1790): Affrontements idéologiques et tensions institutionnelles sur la scène judiciaire de la fin du XVIIIe siècle," *Studies on Voltaire and the Eighteenth Century* 191 (1980): 892–900, and "Mémoire pour la fille Cléreaux (Rouen 1785)," ibid. 208 (1982): 322–372. For another account, see the *Gazette des Tribunaux 1785*, no. 45.

5. Sarah Maza, *Servants and Masters in Eighteenth-Century France: The Uses of Loyalty* (Princeton: Princeton University Press, 1983), pp. 100–102.

to corroborate Cléreaux's version of the facts, forcing the parlement to reconsider. On 12 August 1785 the parlement annulled its own verdict, although it made no further statement as to Cléreaux's innocence or guilt and it condemned the lawyer's mémoire to be suppressed as libelous. This decision effectively ended the case, although Thibault and his housekeeper, Marianne Delaunay, kept up until 1791 a running campaign in the courts for Froudière's arrest.[6]

Reading Froudière's account, one is hardly surprised at Thibault's persistence in prosecuting him: the lawyer's tale reveals the household's damning secrets, evoking a world of sordid provincial domesticity worthy of Balzac—spiced up with a touch of the marquis de Sade. Marie Cléreaux, of a "poor but honest family," worked first as a servant in the country, then made her way to Caen where she served two families over five years.[7] When she moved to Rouen, she found employment with the widower Thibault and his grown son; their housekeeper, Marianne Delaunay, under whose orders she was placed, was mistress of more than the household: "By day she dominated the household; by night the younger Thibault looked to her virtue by having her sleep in his room."[8] But Delaunay confided in Cléreaux that she actually felt repugnance for Thibault the younger, and only satisfied his lust because of practical considerations; her heart belonged to the household's gardener, whom she entertained twice a week. Cléreaux at first helped out by lending the couple her bedroom for those two nights a week, but moral qualms, she said, led her eventually to withdraw her help. This, she claimed in her mémoire, explained that Delaunay began to hate her and poisoned her employers' minds against her.

In the meantime, the consequences of Marianne Delaunay's active sex life were becoming manifest. Unaware, of course, that the child she was carrying might not be his, the younger Thibault moved his mistress out to the country to give birth, taking Cléreaux along to help. Cléreaux was not supposed to know what was going on, but the cries she heard one night—Delaunay's and a child's—left little room for doubt. The next day, although the housekeeper lay half-conscious in blood-stained sheets, no doctor was called; and there was no child to be seen.

---

6. For a complete list of the later publications relating to the case, see Lüsebrink, "L'Affaire Cléreaux," p. 894, n. 6.

7. Lüsebrink, "Mémoire," pp. 336–337.

8. Ibid., p. 337.

Cléreaux's final ordeal in this unsavory household occurred after their return to town. Since Delaunay was still in no condition to satisfy her master's lust, the latter turned to his other female employee. He pressed her and she resisted until one day he aggressed her physically, stark naked and wielding a knife. As one might expect, this unpleasant scene prompted Cléreaux to leave the household; that very evening she gave two weeks' notice and asked for her wages. But the Thibaults and their housekeeper could not let her go abroad and tell tales of what she had seen in the household; they decided that accusing the maid of theft would get her expelled from Rouen and keep her at a safe distance. To this end, they tricked her into putting the wine bottle in her pocket and planted the kerchiefs among her belongings; they beat her when she denied having stolen them, and they refused to give her either her savings or her wages.

This, then, was the lawyer Froudière's rendering of Marie Cléreaux's account of the events that led up to her arrest and conviction. Of the success of Froudière's brief, there can be no doubt, however one defines the success of a piece such as this. It saved Marie Cléreaux from the gallows, for one, even if the parlement's decision left some doubt as to its opinion of her guilt; and if the court censored and condemned it, what better proof, in the 1780s, of its author's admirable daring? Of its impact on readers there can be no doubt either: as was mentioned in an earlier chapter, inhabitants of Rouen were so incensed by its contents that they took to the streets, surrounding the Thibaults' house and threatening to attack them.[9] Finally, Froudière seems to have known that the brief would sell; although concern for his client was perhaps his main preoccupation, he also hoped, when he advanced her a thousand livres to have it printed, that he would not only break even but make a profit.[10]

The authors of previous successful mémoires sometimes had to take liberties with the facts in order to present their clients as destitute, vulnerable, or innocent. In this case there was no need to tamper with reality, for Marie Cléreaux was genuinely isolated and poor. There is plenty in the historical record to show that female servants were usually at great risk, both materially and sexually, and an eighteenth-century literary tradition extending from Richardson's *Pamela* to the marquis

9. Lüsebrink, "L'Affaire Cléreaux," p. 893.
10. Ibid., p. 327.

de Sade can only have reinforced the perception of their vulnerability.[11] Readers of the mémoire could be expected to respond to the overlapping of myth with observable social realities.

This is not to say that readers accepted Froudière's brief for what it claimed to be, Cléreaux's own first-person narrative of her predicament. By the 1780s, the conventions of the trial-brief genre were established and accepted. Certainly the fact that a woman who blindly affixed her "rustic signature" to a document she did not understand because, she said, "I cannot read anything manuscript," was supposed to be the author of the eloquent brief did not bother them; it did not even matter that this barely literate peasant quoted Latin phrases from Tacitus, the capitularies of Charlemagne, and the ordinances of Francis I, or that she described her first employment in the countryside in incongruously Rousseauean terms: "These simple men, closer to nature, who drew their wealth directly from its fruits, brought me back to original equality by sharing in my labors."[12]

No, what mattered was not plausibility in a narrow technical sense, but the moral coherence of this drama of good and evil. Indeed, the defense of Marie Cléreaux comes closer than any previous mémoire to the mode of pure melodrama. There were several scenes whose sensationalism may have been unprecedented in a trial brief—for instance, Cléreaux's description of her employer's attack on her: "One day as I was alone with him at home, sewing in an upstairs room, he appeared to me *naked from head to foot* and explained to me energetically, through gesture and words, what he demanded of me. I cried out in surprise and fear, and promptly took flight. He tried to stop me to obtain by force what he could not get through my consent. Then, armed with a knife, seizing me around the waist, he threatened to plunge it into my breast if I did not comply with his will [emphasis in text]."[13] The literary technique of this passage is exactly that of Richardson's great novels of female virtue besieged: the on-the-spot recording by a woman of a violent sexual threat to her body. Froudière also made shameless use of dramatic suspense and revelation. The episode of the suspected infanticide by

11. Maza, *Servants and Masters,* chap. 2; Cissie Fairchilds, *Domestic Enemies: Servants and Their Masters in Old Regime France* (Baltimore: Johns Hopkins University Press, 1984), chaps. 3, 6.

12. Lüsebrink, "Mémoire," pp. 334–336, 343.

13. Ibid., pp. 340–341.

Thibault and Delaunay opens thus: "What horrors, great gods, I saw in just a few days! And why did master Thibault make it impossible for me to remain silent about them! He wanted to quell the very memory of them in my blood; but I still live, and must tell of them." But despite this premonitory heavy breathing, the account of the night when the child was heard ends on a narrative tease: "I went up a few steps to make them think that I was gone; but I immediately came down again quietly; I put my eye to the keyhole, the room was lit and I saw . . . I heard . . . but I must only reveal this to the court."[14]

The function of scenes like these within the melodramatic mode goes beyond their obvious appeal to readers' or viewers' hunger for strong sensations. As Peter Brooks argues, "Melodrama needs a repeated use of peripety and coups de theatre because it is here that characters are best in a position to name the absolute moral attributes of the universe, to say its nature as they proclaim their own."[15] And indeed Froudière's account is a fine example of the melodramatic urge to assign unambiguous moral labels. From the very start, Cléreaux introduces herself as "moi, créature foible et malheureuse"; she calls her former employer a "monstre souverainement odieux," and later addresses him as "homme d'immense et profonde perversité."[16] In the world of melodrama, people do not commit good or bad actions; they *embody* virtue and vice. To arguments whitewashing Thibault, Cléreaux scornfully responds: "No, no, do not credit this: vice does not, in one instant, become virtue"; and to attempts to have her change her testimony she responds with the impossibility "of having me pass suddenly from virtue to vice."[17]

Not everyone was happy with Froudière's deft manipulation of dramatic form. The lawyer's most prominent opponent, the Parisian lawyer Tronson du Coudray, who defended the Thibaults, accused him of pandering to the tastes of different categories of readers in order to "have partisans in every class of society": "noble and brilliant tableaux" for persons of quality and taste, sarcasm, moral posturing, and criticism of the law for those who dabbled in *philosophie,* licentious story and vulgar expressions for the lower classes.[18] Tronson singled out precisely what

14. Ibid., p. 339.

15. Peter Brooks, *The Melodramatic Imagination: Balzac, Henry James, Melodrama, and the Mode of Excess* (New Haven: Yale University Press, 1976; reprint New York: Columbia University Press, 1985), p. 40.

16. Lüsebrink, "Mémoire," pp. 334, 347.

17. Ibid., pp. 348, 354.

18. Lüsebrink, "L'Affaire Cléreaux," p. 896.

made the mémoire most effective, its ability to make legal argument into fiction and to give it the gripping immediacy of stage melodrama: "The author makes this novel into a veritable *drame;* he animates the actors and makes them come alive. You see the scene unfolding before your very eyes; you see it; you witness everything; you are close to it all, watching it all; you tremble at every gesture, at every look. The cries of the servant, the cries of the child; the anxiety of Marie Cléreaux; her haste in rising from her bed, in running to the room from which those cries are coming, in questioning, in looking. . . . The glow that lights the theater of the crime and testifies to the evil deed, what the Cléreaux girl sees, what she hears, in her very words, the gesture of the assassin, the heart-rending cry of his victim, it is all there, described or imagined with incredible artifice, and already the reader has in spite of himself seen it all, heard it all, like the Cléreaux girl herself." [19] Although this was meant as a diatribe against Froudière's manipulation of his readers, Tronson's grudging admiration nonetheless comes through. What he could not accept, though, was the exchange of legitimation between factual account and fictional creation that had taken place over the course of the century. In the early 1700s, writers of novels had sought to heighten the pleasure of their readers by claiming that the story they told was a real one, a miraculously found set of letters or a memoir; by the later eighteenth century, conversely, readers of "factual" trial briefs more easily believed them if their authors borrowed the themes, language, and techniques of fiction. We will return to this paradox at the end of the chapter.

Since Tronson du Coudray was a member of the Parisian Order of Barristers, he may for that reason have resented the attention-grabbing techniques of the young upstart provincial Froudière. Tronson's accusations of opportunism may not, in fact, have been undeserved, since it seems clear that it was the Cléreaux case that launched the thirty-four-year-old Froudière's subsequent political career (he later was elected one of the sixteen deputies of his department to the Legislative Assembly in 1791).[20] But beyond what the case did for Froudière, it also suggests some new developments in the public role that lawyers sought for themselves.

As Hans-Jürgen Lüsebrink argues, Froudière's careful orchestration of the case was aimed at establishing the lawyer's role of "double media-

19. Lüsebrink, "Mémoire," p. 329.
20. Lüsebrink, "Mémoire," p. 370, nn. 48–49.

tion": between defendants and their judges, and between the judicial arena and the public sphere.[21] But Froudière stopped short, at the time of the affair, from making the more radical claims he would articulate some years later. In his original brief of 1785, Froudière did not attack outright the criminal code, he merely argued that legal procedure had been severely violated. "Marie Cléreaux" points out that all of those whose depositions charged her with the crime were either relatives or close friends of her accusers, and that their accounts were mutually contradictory; on both counts, according to the Ordinance of 1670 and the commentaries of jurists, the testimonies should have been invalid.[22] Only four years later, as political change was sweeping the land, did Froudière come forth with more radical statements challenging the existing legal code and promoting the role of lawyers as champions of the defenseless poor.[23] By 1789, many others had entered the fray, arguing more explicitly than Froudière had done for the need to recast the inquisitorial procedures of the courts. But the Cléreaux case, a curtain-raiser to reform, had done much to make visible and palpable, as well as clearly legible, the need for the laws to protect the accused from their judges, and the poor from the rich.

In the dark hours just before dawn on 1 August 1781, a young woman in her early twenties walked on the road to Caen.[24] Like Marie Cléreaux or any other laborer's daughter, Marie-Françoise-Victoire Salmon worked to earn her keep and to save the dowry that would get her a good husband. Work as a farm servant in the country and then as a seamstress in Bayeux had not been particularly lucrative; Bayeux had yielded savings of forty-eight livres, a bundle of bonnets, skirts, and stockings, and a broken engagement. And so on to Caen, a bigger town, and, she hoped, better wages. Victoire Salmon could not possibly have imagined the extraordinary events that were to unfold a mere week after her arrival in that town, or the upheavals in her life over the next five years.

---

21. Lüsebrink, "L'Affaire Cléreaux," pp. 898–899.
22. Lüsebrink, "Mémoire," pp. 354–355, 359–361.
23. Ibid., pp. 327–329; Lüsebrink, "L'Affaire Cléreaux," pp. 898–900.
24. The following summary of the case is based on Armand Le Corbeiller, *Le Long Martyre de Françoise Salmon* (Paris: Perrin, 1927). Le Corbeiller's account owes a great deal to the mémoires cited below, but draws on archival sources as well. Salmon's first names were Marie-Françoise-Victoire. The fact that contemporaries called her either

By what seemed a stroke of good luck, Salmon found work on her very first day in Caen. A Mme Huet-Duparc offered her employment as maid-of-all-work, doing housework for a family of seven (the master and mistress, the latter's parents, M. and Mme Paisant de Beaulieu, and three children) and caring for the master's horse. (The family seem to have been petit-bourgeois landowners.) The work load was heavy, but Salmon accepted the job, although word of mouth had it that the family had dismissed five or six servants in the last dozen days.

On the first Monday after she was hired, 6 August, Salmon prepared a porridge of milk and flour for the eighty-eight-year-old grandfather, as she had been ordered. She saw her mistress throw salt, or something else, into the old man's *bouilli*. When she returned from errands later that morning, she learned that M. Paisant had a violent colic and that a doctor and priest had been summoned; the old man died that evening at six. Salmon later professed to have been surprised at the family's callousness about Paisant's death. The daughter of the household had remarked that her grandfather had been of late a burden on the family and that he wanted too much wood on the fire; the others seemed similarly unmoved. Salmon was to stand guard over the body that night.

On the following morning, Mme Huet-Duparc berated her servant for her carelessness: Salmon was still wearing the new calico pockets she had donned on Sunday and was told to change them for the striped ones she wore every day. This was before she helped Mme Huet-Duparc and her daughter prepare the midday meal: a fresh soup for the masters, a leftover one for herself and another servant, and a plate of cherries for dessert. The story at this point gets somewhat muddled: it seems that several family members felt ill after the meal, and that Mme Huet-Duparc, on entering the kitchen, had exclaimed that she smelled burned arsenic and that they had all been poisoned. The rumor that a servant had poisoned her masters was in any case circulating in town that very day; a police officer and a surgeon who came to investigate the matter found a white and glittery substance presumed to be arsenic in the pockets that Victoire Salmon was wearing. She was arrested on the spot.[25]

Thus began Victoire Salmon's long ordeal in the prisons and courts

Françoise or Victoire may reflect the preferences of her different employers. I call her Victoire here because she herself seems to have used that name habitually.

25. Ibid., pp. 28–41; for another account see Pierre-Noël Lecauchois, *Justification de Marie-Françoise-Victoire Salmon* (Paris: Cailleau, 1786), pp. 3–5.

of Caen, Rouen, and Paris. Arrested in early August of 1781, she was not to recover her freedom until May of 1786. The first investigation of the case was conducted by the *bailliage,* or lower court, of Caen, and lasted over eight months. Thirty-five witnesses were heard from, and Salmon herself was examined and cross-examined countless times; only by virtue of the previous year's change in the law did she escape the ordeal of "preparatory" torture that would most likely have forced a confession from her. On 18 April 1782, the officers of the Caen *bailliage* accepted the recommendation of their public prosecutor, Roland Revel de Bretteville: charged with poisoning her masters with the intention of robbing them, Victoire Salmon was sentenced to be tortured (for the names of her accomplices), to beg forgiveness in public carrying a torch, barefoot, and with a rope around her neck, and to be burned at the stake. When the case went on appeal to the parlement of Rouen— as did automatically all cases involving capital punishment—the latter body upheld, on 17 May 1782, the lower court's judgment.

From then on the case for a while turned into a series of cliffhangers. The execution date was set for 30 May, and the prisoner was transferred back to Caen where she was to be burned. But when Salmon was brought into the room where she was to submit to the "question," she did the one thing that could stave off torture and execution: she declared that she was pregnant. The judges did what they had to do by law: they deferred the execution until the accused could be examined by midwives for proof of her condition two months later. It was at this truly harrowing juncture that Victoire Salmon's savior appeared on the scene. Three priests who had spoken to the young woman in prison convinced the Rouennais lawyer Pierre-Noël Lecauchois to examine documents relating to the case; having done so, the barrister agreed to take on her defense. He immediately petitioned the king for a stay of execution, which was duly granted, although the royal order barely got to Caen in time, on 27 July 1782, just a few days before Salmon was to be examined and executed. For a second time a stake had been built for her in Caen, and for a second time it was dismantled.

In the following weeks, the hundreds of bundles of documents pertaining to the Salmon case were shipped off to Paris, where the king's private court of justice, the Conseil Privé, was to consider Lecauchois's petition for a retrial. This phase of the case lasted for close to two years, at the end of which, on 18 May 1784, the Conseil agreed to a revision and lobbed the case back to the parlement of Rouen. It was while the case was being once again examined by the Rouen magistrates that Lecauchois published the first of several trial briefs that were to make the case nationally famous; it was printed up in thousands of copies and sent all over France. Its eloquence convinced the parlement's chief prosecutor, the marquis de Godard de Belbeuf, not only of Victoire Salmon's innocence but also of her employers' guilt. Although Belbeuf then entered a charge against all of the members of the Huet-Duparc family, his colleagues were not entirely convinced and rendered a mixed verdict. On 12 March 1785, the Rouen parlement annulled the original verdict of the Caen lower court; it did not follow up on Godard de Belbeuf's accusations, however, and it also decreed that Victoire Salmon should remain in jail until further evidence had been gathered. Thanks largely to the efforts of Lecauchois and a colleague of his named Turpin, the case was transferred seven months later to the Paris Parlement. It was in the capital, then, that the case entered its last and shortest phase; the ever-more voluminous bundles relating to the case were once again trundled up to Paris, this time accompanied by Salmon herself. By the winter of 1786, the case had become a full-fledged cause célèbre, and Salmon herself something of a heroine. Lecauchois produced a new, longer, and more eloquent mémoire, as did a gifted and well-established Parisian barrister named Jean-François Fournel. It would have been difficult for the Paris Parlement to render any verdict other than a full acquittal, and this indeed occurred on 23 May 1786. Victoire Salmon emerged from the courtroom that day at the top of the great staircase of the Palais de Justice to find Paris both literally and figuratively at her feet. She had been in prison for five years, but that summer dawn when she had walked on the road to Caen must have seemed light years away.

The two men who became most prominently involved in the defense of Victoire Salmon were lawyers in their early forties. One was provincial, and more of an activist; the other, a Parisian, had most conspicuously devoted himself to written work. Pierre-Noël Lecauchois was born in Rouen and mostly lived and worked there, except for a few years' residence in Paris in the early 1770s. Although he only became an *avocat au parlement* in Rouen in 1776, he had already been involved, as a very young man, in cases that earned him a local reputation as a champion of the poor and unprotected. In 1762 he had successfully defended a soldier named Savary, wrongly accused of rape and theft; two years later he rescued another soldier from a life sentence on the galleys. His subsequent cases in the 1770s and 1780s confirmed his renown as a man of integrity and compassion; Lecauchois's reputation in Rouen was very similar to that developed in the 1780s in the northern town of Arras by the young Maximilien de Robespierre.[26] The man who helped Lecauchois during the last stages of the Salmon case belonged by birth to a Parisian family with important connections in the judicial world. Jean-François Fournel joined the Parisian Ordre des Avocats in 1771, at the age of twenty-seven; in his prime he became a lawyer respected for the conscientiousness and deep learning he brought to the preparation of his cases, and was known for his authorship of successful legal treatises on adultery (1778), seduction (1781), and injuries (1785); unlike most prominent Parisian lawyers, however, Fournel was to take a stance against the Revolution from the moment of its inception.[27]

Between them, these two men wrote three mémoires for Salmon— as we have seen, Lecauchois's first was composed in 1784, during the Rouen parlement's second examination of the case, and each of them published an important brief in 1786 while the Paris Parlement was making its final appraisal of the affair. Like Froudière in the Cléreaux case, Lecauchois and Fournel relied heavily, in making their case, on the dramatic presentation of a sensational story. Much more prominently than Froudière, however, they employed rhetorical strategies destined to alter the function of the mémoire from the simple vehicle of an emotionally gripping account to a springboard for reforming action. First, they appealed in specific ways to the judgment of readers by explaining the rules of evidence in the judicial process and by challenging their audience to evaluate and weigh the evidence in the case at hand. Second, the lawyer as champion of the accused, crusader for reform, and even as man of sentiment appeared more prominently than before in at least one of the briefs. And third, the Salmon mémoires represented a further escalation of explicit demands for the reform of the criminal justice system.

The account of Victoire Salmon's ordeals could easily be pressed into the familiar mold of tales of innocent femininity besieged and betrayed. Like Jean Blondel's briefs for Nicole Le Guay, or Louis Froudière's for Marie Cléreaux, Lecauchois's first effort is a first-person narrative that plays up its narrator's candor and vulnerability. "Unfortunate maid!" exclaims the narrator; "aged only twenty-one; a defenseless young girl! But forgive me, reader, if I stray from my account: my situation, my sex,

26. Le Corbeiller, *Victoire Salmon,* pp. 91–94. On Robespierre, see J. M. Thompson, *Robespierre,* 2 vols. (New York: D. Appleton, 1939), 1:17–40.
27. Le Corbellier, *Victoire Salmon,* pp. 165–167.

my age, deserve some consideration."[28] In this initial account Lecauchois made use of a technique that will be familiar to readers of eighteenth-century fiction in the female voice: rather than assert Salmon's innocence, virtue, and attractiveness, he has her describe herself as she is perceived by (usually male) others—as do, for instance, the female narrators in works by Richardson, Marivaux, and Diderot.

All of the mémoires, for instance, report an incident earlier in Victoire's life which, it is heavily hinted, may have had a great impact on the case: the Caen prosecutor, Revel de Bretteville, the same man who in 1782 pushed for and obtained the harshest sentence against Salmon, had met her at her first employer's and had made an unsuccessful pass at her. The meeting is described thus: "He saw me there; my youth, my figure, and my bearing struck him; he had the kindness to tell me that I should come and serve in Caen."[29] Or there is Salmon's account of her reaction to the old grandfather's death: "Young as I am, I shed tears at the sight of that head, still venerable although deprived of life; his gentleness toward me, his sufferings, had aroused my concern for him. And so I weep."[30] Although Salmon never quite engages in explicit self-promotion, the reader is not allowed to forget for long that she is young, tenderhearted, and innocently alluring.

Nor did the lawyers skimp on relating the most wrenching episodes of Victoire Salmon's ordeals. One of the strongest scenes in Lecauchois's second, and most celebrated, mémoire occurs in the prison at Rouen, as Salmon is waiting for the outcome of the appeal of her case before the parlement. One of the warders tells her that she is to be taken back to Caen and, perhaps out of compassion, adds that the death sentence has been annulled and that the case is going to be retried. Giddy with relief, she goes back to her cell and makes herself a cabbage soup, the first meal she has been able to swallow in days. But a fellow prisoner knows the truth and brutally informs her that she is being misled: the journey to Caen will take her to the stake. "At this terrible news, the touching features of this unfortunate girl took on a deathly hue; her eyes rolled back, she cried: 'Ah! Great God! Horrors!' And then fell to the ground senseless."[31]

28. Pierre-Noël Lecauchois, *Mémoire pour Marie-Françoise-Victoire Salmon* (Rouen: Oursel, 1784), p. 17.

29. Ibid., p. 11.

30. Ibid., p. 19.

31. Pierre-Noël Lecauchois, *Justification de Marie-Françoise-Victoire Salmon*, pp. 6–7.

Jean-François Fournel's account of the same scene describes and ana-
lyzes Salmon's reactions in greater detail. He prefaces his account with
the observation that the guilty and the innocent react differently to the
news of imminent execution: the former lose all courage and implore
the judges and the heavens for mercy, while the latter are galvanized
into furious outcries against human injustice, and when they implore
God, "it is less to ask for mercy than to demand justice."[32] Salmon's
reactions, her gestures, and the terms she uses, spell out her innocence
in signs that cannot be mistaken by those who witness the scene: "She
appeals, with loud cries, to *Divine Justice;* she calls upon all the heavenly
judges against her persecutors; she *cites* them before the Tribunal of the
Sovereign Judge; now with her brow to the ground which she drenches
with her tears; now on her knees with her hands out to the heavens as
the source of all justice, she begs for an act of their almighty power to
rescue *innocence* [emphases in text]."[33] Among those who are present
at Salmon's outburst are three priests who will be moved by the scene
to go and secure Lecauchois's help. To them, Salmon's words and gestures leave no doubt as to her guiltlessness; the priests "do not recognize in the accents of the Salmon girl the usual language of the guilty."[34]

In Lecauchois's initial first-person narrative, the narrator stages
her purity of heart for the reader; in the third-person narratives, the
assembled prisoners, the three priests, and later the lawyer Lecauchois
stand in for the reader as witnesses to the gestures and words that signify
the young woman's virtue and innocence. Salmon's bowed head and her
tears over the old man's deathbed, her anger, imploring gestures, and
howling for divine justice, all belong to the gestural and linguistic reper-
toire of melodrama, which is, writes Brooks, "about virtue made visible
and acknowledged, the drama of a recognition."[35] In short, readers of
the trial briefs for the Salmon case were mobilized as spectators to the
first act of a melodrama, of the sort of drama "that has as its true stakes
the recognition and triumph of the sign of virtue."[36] The presumed, the
necessary outcome was written into these narratives of the affair.

Like Froudière's brief for Marie Cléreaux, but in more thorough and
sophisticated fashion, the mémoires for Victoire Salmon make use of

32. Jean-François Fournel, *Consultation pour une jeune fille condamnée à être brûlée
vive* (Paris: Cailleau, 1786), p. 74.
33. Ibid., p. 7.
34. Ibid.
35. Brooks, *The Melodramatic Imagination,* p. 27.
36. Ibid., p. 49.

titillation, sentiment, and dramatic scenes that reveal the signs of innocence. But they are also more complex than this, for they function on several levels of persuasion. In Lecauchois's second, and most important, brief, the reader's conviction of the young woman's innocence, and concern for her fate, is established by means of another device: the presence in the mémoire of the lawyer himself as mediator between the protagonist and the reader. Lecauchois makes his first appearance on page 7 of this 117-page text, and he then becomes a presence within the story as no previous author of mémoires—with the exception of Beaumarchais—had been.

The lawyer's espousal of Salmon's cause is made all the more convincing in that, first, he has never seen the girl or witnessed the "signs" of her innocence; and second, he describes himself as initially reluctant to take on the case at all. When approached by the three priests, Lecauchois describes himself as reacting, despite his reputation for *sensibilité*, as a firm upholder of the judicial system: "All of this, I answered rather brusquely, is of no use, two courts have already found the girl guilty; let justice take its course." [37] Having agreed, at last, to review the case, the lawyer struggles to prevent his natural penchant toward compassion from biasing his reading of the records: "The duties of my estate on one side, my sensibility on the other: would they be in struggle, or in accord?" [38] His careful examination of the documents reveals a multitude of suspicious contradictions, biases, and procedural flaws, and it is then, before he has even met Victoire Salmon, that he decides to champion her cause. The prologue to the substantive discussion of the case turns into an account of the lawyer's appeals to higher authorities, of the opposition and even threats he encounters, of the support, too, that he receives from all over the realm. [39] The presence of the lawyer-narrator as an actor in the drama of the case thus serves two purposes. It deliberately gave center stage to the mémoire's author as the person whose initiative—as well as integrity and sensibility—changes the course of a judicial case, and of a person's life; this, as we shall see, is symptomatic of the evolution that gave certain members of the legal profession increasing authority and visibility on the eve of the Revolution. But it also served as an effective rhetorical ploy: Lecauchois's initial reluctance to question the courts' rulings, and his change of heart when confronted

37. Lecauchois, *Justification*, p. 8.
38. Ibid., p. 10.
39. Ibid., pp. 10–18.

with the evidence, drew readers into the process of judging the case by challenging them to do likewise.

But the readers were not asked to take the lawyer's conclusions on faith; they were presented not only with all of the relevant facts—as assembled by the defense, of course—but also with the rules by which to weigh that information and its bearing on the ultimate decision. This had always been the function of the mémoire: to lay out the facts of the case (*faits*) and the technical bases for judgment (*moyens*) for the benefit mostly of the judges. As we have seen, however, with the broadening of the audience of trial briefs to categories of persons outside of the legal profession, the skillful, dramatic presentation of the *faits* had become the essential means for drawing the reading public over to one side of the case, while the usually abstruse and forbidding *moyens* were aimed at the legal specialists reviewing the case. With the Salmon case, how-ever, we are in the presence of a new departure: the translation into simple terms, for the benefit of the lay public, of the rules for weighing evidence and for determining guilt.

This was Lecauchois's explicitly stated intention from the very mo-ment that he took the case. Along with his first mémoire, he published a separate *Introduction aux défenses de la fille Salmon,* which begins thus: "Since this brief will be coming before the eyes of a number of persons of different estates, the greater number of whom are not instructed in the points of departure from which criminal justice proceeds in order to acquire proof. . ."[40] He goes on to explain that the accused in a crim-inal case can be charged on the basis of written proof, testimony of wit-nesses, confession, or clues (*indices*—what we would call circumstantial evidence), and that documents and objects can have the status of *té-moins muets,* or "mute witnesses." But Lecauchois's object here is more than just definitional, in that he articulates a disagreement with contem-porary judicial practice. Truth, he asserts, is necessarily one and indivis-ible, and anything that establishes truth can be considered a "proof." *Indices,* however, do not constitute a proof—they merely indicate a

---

40. Pierre-Noël Lecauchois, *Introduction aux défenses de la fille Salmon, accusée de crimes de poison et de vol domestique* (n.d., n.p.). My belief that this was a companion piece to the first mémoire rests, first, on the facts that it directly precedes the 1784 mémoire in the collected papers of the Paris Parlement's prosecutor Joly de Fleury (B.N. Ms. Fr. Joly de Fleury 2087), and that the short account of the case that it contains goes only to the stay of execution ordered by the king in 1782. The *Introduction* may well have been writ-ten and published some time after the first brief, but internal evidence suggests that it was intended in any case as its companion piece.

route that can, in some cases, lead to the discovery of solid evidence, but they cannot in themselves be construed as proof. The use in some cases of cumulative *indices* as *semi-preuves* is patently absurd in the context of a unitary definition of truth—for how can one speak of a quarter, or an eighth, of truth?[41] Lecauchois later inserted this very same passage aimed at laypersons near the beginning of his second brief for Salmon.[42]

Besides passages such as this, which explicitly instruct readers in the rules for establishing guilt, all of the briefs contain demonstrations of the lack of solid proof against Salmon, and in varying degrees highlight evidence that suggests who the real culprit, or culprits, might be. (The suggestion is of course that the Huet-Duparc family wanted to rid themselves of their cumbersome aging relative, and that after poisoning him they staged the tainted-dinner episode in order to frame Salmon. Modern readers may find this counterplot problematic: would anyone at the time have found the death of a very old man from apparent food-poisoning suspicious in the first place?) As we have seen, Victoire in the first brief insists on the fact that the family members seemed relieved, rather than distressed, at the old man's death; she maintains several times that it was the mistress and her daughter, rather than she herself, who prepared the famous "poisoned" dinner, and points to other clues and suspicious occurrences.[43]

In the second brief, Lecauchois exposes in great detail the sloppiness and partiality with which the case was investigated in the hours after the alleged poisoning, the complacency with which the surgeon, lawyer, and police officer who arrived upon the scene accepted the Duparcs' version of the facts and may even—for obscure reasons—have aided in planting evidence damaging to Victoire.[44] Lecauchois mounted his case for the defense on the widest possible array of grounds: forensic evidence from the autopsy of the old man, procedural flaws in the investigation, contradictions in the testimonies of the witnesses who charged Salmon, the suspicious behavior of the Duparcs, lack of solid evidence against the accused and of plausible motive for the crime, bias on the part of the prosecution (in the person of the onetime spurned Revel de Bretteville), and the character and behavior of the accused.[45] Fournel, in his

41. Ibid., pp. i–v.
42. Lecauchois, *Justification,* pp. 27–28.
43. Lecauchois, *Mémoire,* pp. 19–30.
44. Lecauchois, *Justification,* pp. 45–54.
45. Ibid., passim. See the summary of his arguments, "Résumé des moyens de justification," pp. 96–100.

brief, echoed many of these points; although he was less thorough in lining up his arguments, he more explicitly charged the Duparc family with having fabricated the case against their servant.[46]

To the modern reader of the Salmon briefs, accustomed to courtroom fiction and to jury trials, these sorts of arguments will seem very familiar. In their late-eighteenth-century context, however, the Salmon briefs reveal a further important change in the presumed audience for forensic argument. Only a few years earlier, the legal argument in briefs (as opposed to the dramatized account aimed at a wider public) had been a highly technical discussion of juridical texts, commentaries, and precedents. Now, the technicalities were almost absent from the briefs; the arguments for Victoire Salmon's innocence were couched in such a way as to be intelligible to anyone equipped with good common sense and average education. In short, the process of determining guilt had been shifted, rhetorically, from the judges to something like a jury of readers.

Like Froudière, however, Lecauchois and Fournel stopped short of articulating the broader institutional implications of the story, the need to reform a system that made possible such a shocking miscarriage of justice. Indeed, the fact that it was the monarch himself who had saved Salmon from the stake by an act of mercy made it easy for the lawyers to praise the absolutist status quo while reserving their wrath for the lesser institutions and individuals responsible for her mistreatment.[47] Most of their denunciations of the ways in which the case was conducted had to do with the ignoring or flouting of the existing criminal laws.

Other arguments, however, strongly suggest a need to change those laws in order to prevent scandals like the Salmon case from occurring. As we have seen, Lecauchois strongly objected to the use of *indices,* or circumstantial evidence, in lieu of solid proof. Elsewhere he advocated measures that implied a recasting of legal practice—for instance, the need for the accused's counsel to have access to the actual trial records.[48]

---

46. Fournel also devotes the last section of his brief to an analysis of the grounds for a countersuit for damages by Salmon against the Duparc family and the authorities who investigated the case: see pp. 120 ff.

47. See, for instance, Fournel, *Consultation,* pp. 77–78: "Ah! que l'autorité qui se manifeste par de pareils actes a de grands droits à notre respect! Bénissons cette glorieuse portion du gouvernement français qui attache à la main de nos rois cette superbe prérogative d'arrêter d'un seul signe le glaive de l'exécuteur."

48. Lecauchois, *Justification,* p. 116.

Furthermore, the argument is punctuated with references to other famous contemporary victims of judicial error: the case of the recently exonerated Marie Cléreaux is brought up in Lecauchois's second brief, and some of her less fortunate fellow victims are invoked in a ghoulish passage: "Ghosts of LeBrun, of the Danglades and Fourrés, join that of the unfortunate Calas. . . . Bring forth your grief-stricken, ruined families; uncover your bloody·corpses, some cruelly mangled by torture and mutilated on the gallows, others crushed with blows, crawling, expiring on the galleys."[49] Only at the very end of the piece does the author explicitly suggest that the French criminal justice system should be reformed to bring it closer to its English counterpart, as described in Blackstone's *Commentaries*.[50] But was there a need for a frontal attack on the system when so much had been accomplished in the very writing of a brief which, the *Mémoires secrets* tell us, was avidly sought out and read by contemporaries?[51] The familiar mode of melodrama had been pressed into service to interest readers in the fate of an obscure woman, to have them identify with her terrors and bear witness to the signs of her innocence. The story also demonstrated how much hinged on the role of a lawyer of integrity who had access to the records in the case; without Lecauchois's fortuitous, indeed miraculous intervention, an innocent would have been tortured and burned. Finally, melodrama was conflated with a primitive form of detective fiction that let readers evaluate the evidence of guilt and take an educated guess at who the real culprits might be. In short, the emplotting of the Salmon briefs gave the story at least three implications that flew in the face of the theory and practice of contemporary criminal justice: the need to protect the weak, the need for barristers to play as great a role in the process as prosecutors and judges, and the idea that laypersons should have the right and the responsibility to determine innocence or guilt.

In the Cléreaux and Salmon briefs, then, attacks on the Criminal Ordinance of 1670 were muted and mostly indirect; they were implicit in these stories of bungled and biased prosecutions that very nearly culminated in tragedy, and in the roles assigned to lawyers and their readers in sensational briefs that exposed judicial error. But preoccupation with the flaws in the Old Regime criminal justice system cannot have been

49. Ibid., p. 33.
50. Ibid., p. 117.
51. *Mémoires secrets* 31:277.

very far from the minds of those who wrote and read these works: by the mid-1780s, the need for reform in this area had been of growing concern to many people for over two decades.

The challenge to absolutist judicial systems throughout Europe in the eighteenth century grew out of the spread of natural law theories of government and society among intellectuals, and the accompanying critique of theologically based institutions. The need to rationalize and simplify the legal system, and to make punishment both more socially effective and more humane, was articulated in France at mid-century by such prominent philosophes as Montesquieu in *The Spirit of the Laws* and Jaucourt in the article "Crime" of the *Encyclopédie*.[52] But the work that more than any other galvanized the philosophes and their followers was Cesare Beccaria's treatise *Dei delitti e delle penne*, published in Italy in 1764 and soon after popularized in France by Voltaire.[53]

Beccaria's ideas had a profound influence on the sage of Ferney, and through him on a generation of French reformers whose efforts spanned the last two decades of the Old Regime and carried over into the Revolution. The Milanese reformer took a staunchly utilitarian view of criminal justice, arguing that crimes should be judged, not by arbitrary ethical criteria, but according to their effects on society, and that the logic of punishment should be preventive rather than retributive. One of the corollaries of Beccaria's view that the criminal justice system should reflect the will and interests of all citizens was his impassioned defense of the rights of the accused; he denounced the secret, inquisitorial procedures in use in most European law courts, objected to long imprisonments prior to trial, argued for the availability of counsel, and advocated trial by jury. Most famously, he proposed a rational and predictable congruence between crimes and their punishments and awoke countless contemporaries to the barbarity of institutionalized torture and cruel punishments.[54] Beccaria's zeal for humanitarian reform had been aroused by his reading of the French philosophes, and the latter in turn, beginning with Voltaire, drew copiously on his work in their campaigns for reform.[55]

52. Peter Gay, *The Enlightenment: An Interpretation*, vol. 2, *The Science of Freedom* (1969; reprint, New York: W. W. Norton, 1977), pp 423–437; David Jacobson, "The Politics of Criminal Law Reform in Late Eighteenth-Century France" (Ph.D. diss., Brown University, 1976), pp. 59–71.
53. Gay, *The Science of Freedom*, pp. 437–447.
54. Ibid.; Jacobson, "Criminal Law Reform," pp. 71–83.
55. Gay, *The Science of Freedom*, pp. 437–438, 445–447.

As Michel Foucault brilliantly argues in *Discipline and Punish*, the campaign to reform criminal law in the eighteenth century had far-reaching implications; beyond a sincere concern with the rights of the accused and the convicted, such efforts also pointed to a profound shift in European mentalities.[56] The logic of Old Regime torture and execution, of the public *amende honorable,* and of protracted torturings-to-death of notorious criminals was, according to Foucault, that of vengeance and expiation. Within the premodern penal system, the body of the condemned criminal was the locus upon which the heinous nature of the crime was first affirmed and then obliterated. A criminal was considered to have offended, not his or her fellow subjects, but the divinely ordained society and polity incarnated in the monarch. And just as power was invested in, and displayed through, the body of the king, punishments that spelled out the hideous nature of a crime were performed in public upon the body of the criminal—a branded letter for theft, a severed tongue for blasphemy, a chopped-off wrist (followed by death) for parricide, a body reduced to ashes on the stake for crimes like sodomy or incest that defiled society.[57] "The sentence," writes Foucault, "had to be legible on the body of the guilty man."[58]

Both the criminal and the public assembled for the execution of a sentence were to participate actively in a ritual of expiation thanks to which a crime was "manifested and annulled"[59]—the condemned by (ideally) showing remorse and begging for forgiveness, the crowd by witnessing a drama of physical agony and spiritual redemption that washed away the crime. There were no prison sentences, except for debtors: the purpose of Old Regime penology was not—or was only incidentally—to protect individual subjects by preventing the repetition of a crime, but to cleanse symbolically the social, political, and religious order that had been tainted by sin.

Within this explanatory framework, the growing campaign against the traditional penological system reflects much more than just the rise of liberal humanitarian sentiment. In arguing for the rights of the ac-

---

56. Michel Foucault, *Surveiller et punir: Naissance de la prison* (Paris: Gallimard, 1975); American ed., *Discipline and Punish: The Birth of the Prison,* trans. Alan Sheridan (New York: Random House, 1979). The following synopsis is based on part 1 (pp. 3–69).

57. Foucault, *Discipline and Punish,* pp. 43–47; Charles Prud'homme, *Michel de Servan (1737–1807): Un Magistrat réformateur* (Paris: Larose et Tenin, 1905), pp. 103–115.

58. Foucault, *Discipline and Punish,* p. 43.

59. Ibid., p. 55.

cused, in displacing the rationale of punishment from the vengeance of the sovereign to the defense of society, in repudiating baroque ceremonials of cruelty, criminal-law reformers were issuing a challenge to the entire cultural system of which divine-right monarchy was the political embodiment.

The crusade to reform France's criminal law was a movement that spanned three decades, accelerating sharply on the eve of the Revolution. According to David Jacobson, no fewer than 108 books on criminal law were submitted to the censors between 1760 and 1789, their numbers increasing steadily over time.[60] Initiated by such high priests of the French Enlightenment as Montesquieu and Voltaire, the campaign was later taken up by younger, lesser-known acolytes, men of considerable talent and achievement who carried it into the 1770s and 1780s.

The prerevolutionary criminal law reform movement offers yet another illustration of the crucial role played by men of law as critics and propagandists in the closing decades of the Old Regime. David Jacobson's study of the prerevolutionary reform movement shows it to have been overwhelmingly centered in the legal profession: of the two dozen most prominent reformers active in the mid-1780s, thirteen were *avocats* and nine were magistrates.[61] Some of these men, such as the barristers Jean Blondel and Jean-Baptiste Target, are already known to us. Others were to achieve lasting fame in the Revolutionary years—Bergasse, Brissot, Condorcet, Lacretelle, Robespierre, and Valazé. (Eleven of Jacobson's twenty-four prominent reformers were later to sit in revolutionary assemblies.)[62] In the eighties, most of these men knew each other and made up a network bound together by common experiences and goals. They were mostly in their thirties and forties, successful professionals, prominent members of a generation that had grown up revering the philosophes and longing to emulate them; they all read and responded to each other's writings, many of them frequented each other socially, some were even united by family ties.[63]

The elder statesmen in this group were figures of considerable stature and reputation: Malesherbes (born in 1721), enlightened statesman and friend of the philosophes, took an active interest in criminal law reform,

60. Jacobson, "Criminal Law Reform," p. 294.
61. Ibid., pp. 101–110.
62. Ibid., p. 104.
63. Ibid., chap. 3.

as did Target (born in 1733), the hero of the Maupeou years. One of the standard-bearers of the movement, whose name and works were constantly invoked by reformers in the 1770s and 1780s, was a magistrate from Grenoble, four years Target's junior, named Michel de Servan. A brilliant young *conseiller* at the parlement of Grenoble, friend of Voltaire and disciple of Beccaria, Servan first made his mark at the age of thirty with a resounding *Discours sur l'administration de la justice criminelle* (1767), in which he argued that the punishment of criminals should be "an example for the future rather than a vengeance for the past. . . . A chastisement is nothing but a political act whose object is the conservation of [public] morality."[64]

For the next two decades, Servan continued to sound Beccarian themes, joined by a growing chorus of other voices. Most of the significant work on this subject was published in the form of essays written in response to competitions organized by provincial academies in France and abroad.[65] A few of these appeared in the 1770s, such as the young lawyer Pierre-Louis de Lacretelle's 1773 essay on the causes and prevention of crimes, written for a contest sponsored by the Academy of Mantua; in 1777, the French academician Guillaume-François Letrosne published his influential *Vues sur la justice criminelle*. But it was in the years around 1780 that the trickle of publications grew into a torrent.

A competition organized by the Société économique of Berne in 1777 spawned both Jean-Paul Marat's *Plan de législation criminelle* (1780) and Jacques-Pierre Brissot's *Théorie des loix criminelles* (1781). That same year, Brissot won a prize for a pamphlet that argued for the need to compensate those unjustly accused and detained, *Le Sang innocent vengé*. In 1778 and 1781 there appeared works on these themes by two of the lawyers who had defended the Véron family—Jacques-Vincent Delacroix's *Réflexions philosophiques sur l'origine de la civilisation* and François Vermeil's *Essai sur les réformes à faire dans notre législation criminelle*. In 1783 the Academy of Metz proposed a topic dealing with the so-called *peines infâmantes* (degrading punishments) and their effects on the families of those who suffered them; Lacretelle's entry won the first prize, while that submitted by one Maximilien de Robespierre came in a close second.[66]

---

64. Michel de Servan, *Discours sur l'administration de la justice criminelle* (Geneva, 1767), p. 33; Charles Prud'homme, *Michel de Servan*.

65. Jacobson, "Criminal Law Reform," chap. 7; Prud'homme, *Servan*, pp. 83–88.

66. Jacobson, "Criminal Law Reform," pp. 102, 305–322.

Although the reformers addressed a wide range of specific issues and differed from one another on a number of points, they were in fundamental agreement about the major vices and abuses in both the Ordinance of 1670 and the actual practice of criminal law in the courts. Their basic objections were always the same: that the Ordinance of 1670 ratified "inquisitorial" practices such as the secrecy of judicial proceedings and the absolute power granted to prosecutors and judges; that this lopsided situation was accentuated by the multiplicity and complexity of laws and the absence of clear directives as to the relationship between crimes and punishments; that the accused was left utterly vulnerable, having no access to counsel or to the incriminating evidence, and because of the cumbersome inefficiency of the judicial process was often made to languish for months or years in prison awaiting trial; and that the legal system condoned the use of torture and of degrading and shockingly cruel punishments.[67] Most of these issues, as we have seen, were implicit in the narratives of the Cléreaux and Salmon cases.

That there were strong political undertones to all of this criticism is undeniable. The reformers were well aware that the "inquisitorial" procedures of the Old Regime reflected the assumptions of an absolutist political culture in which all-powerful judges served as extensions of a monarch who had originally dispensed justice in the name of God. They, in contrast, framed their criticisms and proposals with contractual theories of society and government. Servan's 1767 *Discours*, for instance, opens with pristinely Rousseauean prolegomena, with man emerging from the state of nature and giving up his natural rights to acquire the higher freedom that comes from submission to the will of all made manifest through the law.[68] It followed that punishment should be dispensed according to fixed laws that were the expression of the will of society, and that the only function of the magistrate was that of conveyor and executor of those laws: "The law is nothing but the public will, and even if shaped and presented by a single legislator, it must nonetheless be regarded as the emanation and expression of all individual wills."[69] A magistrate should therefore be able to say to the man

67. Jacobson, "Criminal Law Reform," chap. 4.

68. Servan, *Discours*, pp. 7–9; Prud'homme, *Servan*, pp. 139–41. See also Jacques-Vincent Delacroix, *Réflexions philosophiques sur l'origine de la civilisation et sur les moyens de remédier à quelques-uns des abus qu'elle entraîne* (Amsterdam, 1778), pp. 10–22. François Vermeil, *Essai sur les réformes à faire dans notre législation criminelle* (Paris: Demonville, 1781), pp. 24–25.

69. Ibid., p. 111.

whom he punished: "I am no longer your judge, it is the law that condemns you."[70]

Throughout these discussions runs a keen awareness that the principles of a criminal justice system are a direct reflection of the type of political system in which it exists. If the ideal criminal code was that of the Rousseauean contractual polity, the most convenient contemporary model was the English one. Although eighteenth-century British criminal law practices were in fact harshly repressive and rife with abuses, French reformers were understandably impressed by such formal features of the system as the trial by jury and the publicity of proceedings.[71] Vermeil, for instance, hailed the English system as the glorious outcome of a century of political storms: "One radiant day, humanity came to be respected there; every citizen acquired the right to be judged by his peers and to have a defender; he could only be condemned to death by a unanimous vote; proceedings were public and seemed to be based on the presumption of innocence."[72] Beyond this, however, reformers made cautious references to still more radical models or possibilities, contrasting the workings of justice in a republic to those of monarchical governments. Penalties will be less drastic in a republic, Delacroix wrote, since the legislator knows that they apply to him as to his fellow citizens; and Servan pointed out that arbitrary arrest was a far more serious matter in a republic than in a monarchy—not being, in the latter case, a crime against the sovereign.[73]

The criticism of contemporary law and procedure had, if not revolutionary, at least thoroughly reformist implications. The reformers were no doubt sincerely appalled by the authoritarian and cruel treatment meted out to those accused or even suspected of crimes by contemporary French courts, and they were well aware of the crying social iniquity built into a system in which upper-class magistrates had free rein in dealing with destitute, uneducated defendants. Servan's portrayals of such encounters are chillingly effective: "They are brought an unknown man, haggard, disfigured, white from hunger and fear, his face covered with hair like that of a wild beast. . . . Who is this being? None of his judges know—he is a shadow, a specter, appearing from the depths of a prison-

70. Ibid., p. 113.

71. Gay, *The Science of Freedom*, pp. 426–427; Douglas Hay et al., *Albion's Fatal Tree: Crime and Society in Eighteenth-Century England* (New York: Random House, 1975).

72. Vermeil, *Essai sur les réformes*, p. 8.

73. Delacroix, *Réflexions*, p. 30; Prud'homme, *Servan*, p. 155.

cell before judges whose power terrifies him. Of his interests, his character, his morals, who can know anything? Who even asks?"[74]

The likes of Vermeil and Delacroix, authors of mémoires in defense
of the underdog, fully realized that secrecy and the excessive authority
granted to prosecutors were features of the system that mostly victimized those without money, education, and connections—Delacroix, as
we have seen, had spoken vigorously to this issue in his *Réflexions sur
les mémoires* of 1775. The writings on criminal law reform of the 1760s
through 1780s contained, then, some radical challenges to Old Regime
society and politics as these were reflected in judicial institutions. There
was, however, as Foucault aptly points out, a darker side to the humanitarianism of eighteenth-century reformers. The desire expressed by
most of them to make the system more uniform and efficient, to make
punishment more socially effective, if less barbaric, can be interpreted
in Foucauldian terms as an urge for greater social control. Servan's arguments for swift punishments to serve as deterrents, for instance, hardly
comes across as benevolent or humane: "Here is the moment to punish
crime, do not let it escape, make haste in convicting and judging, erect
scaffolds, set stakes aflame, drag culprits into the public squares, call the
People with loud cries. . . . You will see joy exploding, and that virile
insensibility that comes from the love of peace and the horror of
crime."[75]

Foucault argues that such calls for rapid, certain, and socially exemplary chastisement reflected a shift away from a central preoccupation
with exceptional, violent criminality—such as the act of the would-be
regicide François Damiens—toward greater concern with more mundane but increasingly numerous crimes against property. As a result, reformers argued for stricter methods of surveillance, greater efficiency in
obtaining information, "a closer penal mapping of the social body."[76]

The logic of Foucault's argument does lead him to downplay the sincere concern for fellow creatures at work in the reformers' calls for jury
trials, adequate counsel, and their opposition to lengthy detention prior
to trial. It is nonetheless remarkable how much energy these writers invested in devising new, minutely detailed classifications of crimes and of

74. Cited in Prud'homme, *Servan,* p. 167.
75. Servan, *Discours,* p. 36. In all of his writings Servan argued that in order to be
effective deterrents, punishments should be both swift and certain; see Prud'homme, *Servan,* pp. 141–145.
76. Foucault, *Discipline and Punish,* pp. 75–81; quote p. 78.

their corresponding penalties—and no less striking how barbaric these new prescriptions often were. The most common argument used in setting up such taxonomies was that put forward, for instance, by Vermeil, that a punishment should exactly fit the nature of the crime committed; the penalty, he wrote, should be that "most contrary to the vicious predisposition that produced the crime . . . the most suited to repress it and the most efficacious."[77] Thus, those who love or hate excessively, adulterers, rapists, polygamists, should be banished from the community by deportation or exile; crimes of "idleness" like theft, forgery, or illegal profiteering should be punished by forced labor. In Vermeil's discussion of more serious offenses, however, this preoccupation with strict congruence between crime and punishment turns into a sadism as lurid as that practiced by the Old Regime authorities. Arsonists should be thrown alive into the flames, poisoners have a cup of poison tossed at them before being thrown into a vat of boiling water; as for the parricide, he would have his eyes put out and be hung above ground in a cage, wearing nothing and fed only bread, "condemned to no longer see the heavens he has outraged, nor to inhabit the earth he has defiled."[78]

At first sight this might seem like no more than a slight modification of traditional penology, which had also, as was mentioned above, relied heavily on the symbolic nature of public punishment. But, as Foucault argues, the code suggested here is in reality quite different; the purpose of classifications like Servan's or Vermeil's is not public symbolic expiation but didacticism, the penalty being calculated "not in terms of the crime but of its possible repetition."[79] The symbolism at work in traditional forms of punishment was ideally a "symmetry of vengeance" aimed mostly at violent crime—the biblical "eye for an eye" enacted upon the body of the guilty man or woman by the hand of the monarch. In the new codes, by contrast, chastisement took on the more abstract qualities of a language, a decipherable set of signs that were not replicas of the crimes but compressed narratives of the action committed and its effects upon society. In a society ruled by law rather than absolute power, in which control over citizens had to be less violent but more

77. Vermeil, *Essai sur les réformes*, p. 30.
78. Ibid., pp. 66–157; quote p. 149. See also the many examples of these sorts of taxonomies of crimes and punishments given in Foucault, *Discipline and Punish*, pp. 109–114.
79. Foucault, *Discipline and Punish*, p. 93.

widespread and effective, punishment was reimagined as a language, a fable, an open book from which all could learn.[80] In short, in matters of crime and punishment we encounter once again the cultural transition from image to sign, from icon to abstract representation.

Reformers and critics had always argued that judicial proceedings should be public—the purpose of this being partly, but not only, the protection of the accused. They also never challenged the idea that punishments should take place in public; in fact they vigorously reasserted the principle: this was not yet the heyday of the prison system. Their aim was didactic, and they explained their purpose with arguments similar to those used by Diderot and other dramatists in promoting the *genre sérieux*. Vermeil evoked the public's jubilation in hearing a judgment clearing an innocent of erroneous charges, their righteous anger and satisfaction in witnessing the conviction of the guilty: "Prepared for either one of these events by an illuminating report and a wise discussion, the Public would find in this exposition a moral lesson all the more persuasive in that example and precept would be conjoined, and punishment would follow closely upon crime."[81]

And who better than lawyers to frame and deliver such a lesson? Servan called upon members of the bar to take on cases that could be made into occasions for the education of the people and the reform of criminal justice—and would boost their own careers, to boot: "Do you not see the path that opens up to take you to fame? Only take on the defense of an innocent, and you will soon have the human race as client."[82] By the mid-1780s, in the wake of two decades of concern with the criminal justice system, a recent proliferation of critiques and proposals, and several well-publicized cases of miscarriage of justice, the time was ripe for a cause célèbre that would dramatize the issues while educating the French people and their rulers. To paraphrase Voltaire, if the Trois Roués case had not existed, it would have had to be invented.

One of the most remarkable features of the so-called Trois Roués affair was how slight an event the actual case was, especially compared with the other causes célèbres of the Old Regime. Compared with the Diamond Necklace Affair, which, unfolding at about the same time, had all the twists and turns and deceptions of a play like *The Marriage of Figaro*,

---

80. Ibid., pp. 104–114.
81. Vermeil, *Essai sur les réformes*, pp. 236–237.
82. Servan, *Discours*, pp. 147–148.

the case of the three men convicted in Chaumont seems like *Waiting for Godot*—with the waiting, in this case, done in prison.[83] It was a case of simple, if nasty, break-in and burglary. On the night of 29–30 January 1783, three men forced their way into the house of a couple named Thomassin, farmers in the village of Vinet near Troyes in Champagne. They tied up the couple, then terrified and brutalized them into revealing the whereabouts of their most valuable possessions; they left with about one hundred livres in cash, a silver cross, and a bundle of linen.

The essence of the case, however, was not what took place on that freezing night in the Thomassins' farmhouse, but what happened in the following weeks, months, and years. The local constabulary was immediately alerted and set about tracking down the criminals. They first picked up an epileptic vagrant named Guyot—he was to die in prison before the case came to trial. Then, on the strength of the Thomassins' descriptions, they arrested three other suspects, a laborer named Nicolas Lardoise and two horse and cattle traders who were brothers-in-law, Charles Bradier and Jean-Baptiste Simare. The three men had been seen drinking together the day before the crime, Bradier wore a red jacket like one of the couple's assailants, and Simare had a small silver cross in his pocket.

To this day it remains unclear whether the three men were indeed innocent of the crime, as their defenders so staunchly proclaimed.[84] But unquestionably they became, like Victoire Salmon, the victims of rank administrative sloth, procedural bungling, and total contempt for the fate of the accused. The usual shifting of prisoners from one local jail and jurisdiction to the next took four months, until in May of 1783 they landed in the prison of Chaumont, seat of the regional *bailliage*. It was perhaps scandalous, but alas not atypical, that it took the *bailliage* authorities over two years even to begin to investigate the case. In June of 1785, twenty-eight months after the crime was committed, the royal prosecutor and other Chaumont officials finally set off for Vinet with the prisoners, on the very cold trail of the evidence.

---

83. The following summary of the case is based on the following accounts: Edmond Seligman, "L'Affaire des Trois Roués," *Revue de Paris,* 15 March 1901, pp. 413–425; Adolphe Wattine, *L'Affaire des Trois Roués: Étude sur la justice criminelle à la fin de l'ancien régime (1783–1789)* (Macon: Protat Frères, 1921); William Doyle, "Dupaty (1746–1788): A Career in the Late Enlightenment," *Studies on Voltaire and the Eighteenth Century* 230 (1985): 82–106.

84. The most thorough chronicler of the case, Adolphe Wattine, admits that the evidence is inconclusive either way, and that the fact that Lardoise was picked up again for

The bulk of that evidence consisted in the Thomassins' formal recognition of the prisoners as their aggressors. Beyond that, precious little could be found; one woman claimed to have seen the thieves at dead of night, others bore witness to the couple's state after the break-in, most of the physical traces of the crime had, predictably, disappeared. The *bailliage* court reviewed and then judged the case that summer, and the verdict was handed down on 11 August 1785. The *procureur du roi* requested a harsh sentence against the men, that they be *roués,* broken on the wheel. Lardoise, Bradier, and Simare had from the start vehemently protested their innocence, although the alibis they presented were at this point hard to confirm. It was perhaps for this reason that the four judges in Chaumont opted for a lesser sentence, condemning the three to life terms on the galleys.

But worse was to come for the three accused. The case went up to the Parlement of Paris—this, as we have seen, was routine for cases that potentially involved capital punishment—allowing the Chaumont prosecutor to lodge an appeal for a harsher sentence. If the lower court had proceeded with glacial slowness, the Parlement reviewed the case with unseemly haste. In half a day, the twelve judges of the Tournelle court were ready to vote: nine of them supported the royal prosecutor in asking for the death penalty, two upheld the condemnation to the galleys, one requested that the case be further investigated. On 20 October 1785 Lardoise, Bradier, and Simare were condemned (though they did not yet know it) to ghastly death on the wheel—merciful strangulation by the executioner, but only after their limbs had been shattered by means of a steel bar. Though they were not, in the end, executed, the case became known elliptically as the Trois Roués—the three who were sentenced to die on the wheel.

Salvation came to the three in the person of Charles-Marguerite Dupaty, a magistrate from Bordeaux residing in Paris in the home of his brother-in-law, the councillor Emmanuel Fréteau de Saint-Just. Fréteau had been one of the dissenting judges in the case, and he illegally granted his relative access to the trial documents. Dupaty quickly became convinced of the three men's innocence and had Fréteau petition the keeper of seals, Miromesnil, for a stay of execution while the case went on appeal to the Royal Council. As in the Salmon case, this tactic allowed time for the mobilization of the new, increasingly weighty force

---

theft and violence a few months after the conclusion of the Trois Roués case does cast some doubt on the men's innocence: *L'Affaire des Trois Roués,* chap. 19.

of "public opinion." By February of 1786, Dupaty produced a long mémoire in defense of the three men, *Mémoire justificatif pour trois hommes condamnés à la roue,* which was received by the public with "the warmest applause," but which set its (anonymous, but well-identified) author on a collision course with the Paris Parlement.[85] The brief explicitly and insistently used the case as an occasion to argue for the need to reform the criminal law code. It was first given out free, then, as its popularity increased, sold for six livres to benefit the three prisoners; the queen herself and three princes of the blood were said to have purchased it.

Dupaty had taken great care to aim his attacks at the legal system only, and not at the magistrates who had handled the case, but the Parlement felt nonetheless that its professional integrity had been challenged. Through the spring and summer of 1786, while the Royal Council delayed on reaching a decision, the conservative wing of the high court geared up for a counterattack. In June, the liberal philosophe Condorcet (who was at the time courting Dupaty's niece) further envenomed the debate by publishing a pamphlet, *Réflexions d'un citoyen non-gradué sur un procès très connu,* which accused the magistrates of carelessness, intolerance, and aristocratic morgue.[86] The long-awaited counterblast came on 11 August 1786, in the form of a formal charge or *réquisitoire* delivered by the notoriously conservative advocate-general, Louis-Antoine Séguier; this served as a prelude to the court's vote on 18 August that the mémoire be publicly torn and burned. The Ordre des Avocats expressed its support of the Parlement's decision by striking from its rolls the young advocate Louis-Augustin Legrand de Laleu who had officially signed the mémoire.

It took almost another year for the government to reach a decision on the case. For reasons that remain unclear, the Royal Council seemed disinclined to throw its weight behind Séguier's blistering *réquisitoire* and the Parlement's vote.[87] It may be that the public's boisterous response to Victoire Salmon's recent acquittal made the authorities wary of moving against men who had been similarly cast as martyrs to the abuse of judicial power. The event that most decisively affected the outcome of the case was undoubtedly the fall from power in April of 1787

85. *Nouvelles extraordinaires,* 27 March 1786.

86. [Marie-Jean-Antoine de Condorcet], *Réflexions d'un citoyen non-gradué sur un procès très-connu* (Frankfurt, 1786). See esp. pp. 12–14.

87. Doyle, "Dupaty," pp. 93–94.

of the keeper of seals, Miromesnil—for reasons unrelated to the case—and his replacement by a minister committed to the cause of judicial reform, Lamoignon. On 30 July 1787 the Council quashed the Chaumont verdict on the grounds that the documentary evidence was inadequate. Rather than clear the accused, however, it ordered a retrial by the parlement of Rouen. The latter proceeded briskly—albeit not without controversy—and in December of 1787 Bradier, Simare, and Lardoise were declared innocent and allowed to sue their accusers. On 19 January 1788, in response to an appeal by Dupaty against the condemnation of his mémoire, the Royal Council quashed that sentence as well. With Lamoignon in power and already at work on the criminal justice system, the triumph of the reforming movement seemed complete.

The instigator of this stunning reversal of the Trois Roués case was, in many respects, a paradoxical figure—not least in that the man who found himself taking on the conservative establishment of the Paris Parlement was himself a high-ranking magistrate, a *président à mortier.* In many ways Charles Dupaty appears the quintessential insider.[88] Born in 1746 to a family of wealthy merchants of La Rochelle, his life initially followed a textbook pattern of ancien régime upward mobility, as he inherited an office in the local financial administration, made a socially advantageous marriage, and furthered his ambitions by moving to Bordeaux after purchasing an office of advocate-general in that town's parlement. Much of Dupaty's substantial income came from plantations he inherited from his father on Saint-Domingue, but it apparently never struck him as problematic that, as William Doyle points out, his campaigns on behalf of dispossessed victims in France "were paid for, at least in part, out of the labor of black slaves."[89]

A bust of Dupaty sculpted after his death by Houdon suggests an uncanny air of kinship with Voltaire—the same taut, high-cheekboned face, piercing eyes, and mischievous half-smile—and a contemporary description reinforces the impression: a small, frail man, he exuded a mixture of affability, disdain, and causticity and was especially supercilious when dealing with his social superiors. Dupaty's engagement with public affairs and his budding penchant for well-publicized controversy kept him in the eye of the storm during the Maupeou crisis in Bordeaux,

88. The following account of Dupaty's life prior to the Trois Roués case is from Doyle, "Dupaty," chaps. 1–4.
89. Ibid., p. 14.

when he emerged as one of the leading spokesmen of the anti-Maupeou parlement. Arrested for publishing an incendiary *arrêté* against the ministry and subsequently exiled for three and a half years, he was to deliver, to great applause, the opening speech when the Bordeaux parlement was reinstated in 1775.[90]

By the time he was thirty, Dupaty seemed poised for unqualified success as a liberal luminary in the France of Louis XVI. A hero of the Maupeou years, prominent provincial magistrate with distinguished connections in Paris, he also successfully cultivated the obligatory second career as a man of letters. While in his twenties he had belonged to the literary academy of La Rochelle, published a eulogy of Henry IV, corresponded with and been praised by Voltaire, frequented the fashionable literary salon of Mme Necker, and had significant social contact with Diderot, d'Alembert, and Beaumarchais.[91] In the late seventies and early eighties, however, a series of events occurred that jeopardized his flawless rise to social prominence and significantly altered his view of the world.

In 1777, Dupaty initiated negotiations for the acquisition of a charge of *président à mortier,* but was brutally rebuffed by the president of the Bordeaux parlement, Le Berthon (who had designs on the position for his son) and a sizable faction of the latter's partisans. To make matters worse, Le Berthon justified his opposition on the grounds of Dupaty's undistinguished social origins. The crisis lasted for two and a half years, punctuated by bitter dispute and passionate oratory; it seemed resolved in March of 1780 when a royal order secured by Miromesnil forced a majority of the magistrates to vote their colleague into his new office. Ostensibly, Dupaty had won the day, and his triumph seemed complete when, the following summer, another royal decree ordered the obdurate Le Berthon into exile. But Dupaty's was, in fact, a Pyrrhic victory. For the next two years a majority of his colleagues, embittered and humiliated by the government's intervention in their affairs, ostracized him and interfered with his conduct of business in the court. By then the internecine dispute within the Bordeaux parlement had become nationally famous, earning the embattled *président à mortier* even more fame and widespread support. But although the government once again weighed in on his side, Dupaty had had enough. In 1782 he turned his

90. Ibid., pp. 32–35.
91. Ibid., pp. 16–21, 66–67.

back for good on his career in Bordeaux and moved to Paris with the intention of devoting himself to the issue that had long been on his mind, the reform of the criminal justice system.

Dupaty's troubles in Bordeaux had a profound impact on his outlook and the course of his life. A critical spirit by temperament, his de facto exclusion from the high court soured him against the magistracy and aristocratic pretensions in general. In 1775, when he delivered the speech that marked the reinstatement of the Bordeaux parlement, Dupaty had argued in true Montesquieuian style that the best bulwark against "despotic anarchy" in a monarchic state was an irremovable, permanent judiciary, as established by the French "constitution": "When magistrates become movable in monarchies and permanent in republics, the world will be enslaved."[92] And the highest calling of the magistracy was to guide and enlighten the "invincible, fearsome" forum of public opinion, "more powerful than evil laws and evil princes."[93] A decade later, full of distrust for the same courts he had so eloquently championed, his celebrity much increased by his troubles, Dupaty was ready to go straight to the higher tribunal of *l'opinion.*

That *l'opinion* in general responded favorably to Dupaty's *Mémoire justificatif pour trois hommes condamnés à la roue* is beyond doubt. Shortly after its publication, Hardy noted that its "fiery style," "impetuosity and zeal" had caught the public's attention, and that readers were responding warmly to its description of the huge procedural flaws in the case.[94] The *Gazette de Leyde* echoed this prognosis, noting both the Parlement's displeasure and the widespread enthusiastic response to the mémoire, and happily anticipating another sensational *affaire:* "Thus everything seems to announce that this affair will be examined and conducted on a scale proportional to the sensation and trouble it has occasioned in the Palais de Justice."[95] Dupaty's daring and style contributed much to the piece's success; so did his recent notoriety, his profuse and systematic distribution of the mémoire to well-placed friends and connections, and the topicality of the subject as other cases such as the Salmon affair were unfolding. Soon after its publication he wrote to a colleague in Bordeaux that he was being besieged by visitors of all social

92. *Discours prononcé par M. Dupaty, avocat-général, le 13 mars 1775 à la première audience de la Grand'Chambre après le rétablissement du Parlement* (n.p., n.d.), pp. 3–5, quote p. 3.
93. Ibid., p. 9.
94. Ms. Fr. 6685, 20 March 1786.
95. *Nouvelles extraordinaires,* 27 March 1786.

ranks from all over France asking him to intervene for their unjustly condemned relatives.[96]

The Paris Parlement's violently hostile reaction to the mémoire from the moment of its publication had to do mostly with one of the subtexts of the case—Dupaty's recent battles with the magistracy. In the text of the brief, he carefully avoided framing his arguments as an attack on the magistrates of Chaumont or Paris. In the very first pages he went out of his way—although it must have cost him—to praise the nation's magistrates as scrupulous, fair, hardworking but overburdened, and hamstrung by defective legislation: "Our magistrates are enlightened, but in spite of their wishes and that of the Sovereign our criminal jurisprudence is so barbaric!"[97] If the mémoire did contain attacks on the *parlementaires,* these were oblique, implicit in Dupaty's striking indictments of the social iniquity built into the nation's laws.

Dupaty's mémoire was rhetorically brilliant but, compared with practically any other of the great trial briefs we have examined, curiously abstract. Lardoise, Bradier, and Simare only appear in one brief prison scene as human beings—for the most part they are never described or given a voice. This choice on the author's part was both politic—unlike the touching Marie and Victoire, the three men seem to have been decidedly unsavory characters—and germane to the point he was making. This case is not about "the brilliant misfortunes of passion," but about "the obscure misfortunes of need," he warned his readers, "since these three men I am defending are only men."[98] Nothing mattered about the three except their innocence, their poverty, and their victimization by the legal system.

For it was not primarily individuals who had brought the three hapless peasants so close to an undeserved death on the wheel, although a number of people had contributed to this outcome out of habit, laziness, cowardice, or heartlessness. After analyzing at great length the variations and inconsistencies in the Thomassins' account of the night of the crime, Dupaty skillfully reconstructed the couple's motives in formally recognizing three men who were not in fact their assailants: a vague description of the men to the *maréchaussée,* which is anxious to pick up suspects because it needs to justify its pay; a rash agreement that,

96. Doyle, "Dupaty," pp. 86–87.
97. [Charles Dupaty], *Mémoire justificatif pour trois hommes condamnés à la roue* (Paris, 1786), p. 3.
98. Ibid., p. 4.

yes, these must be the culprits, and then panic when the time comes for a formal recognition; then the fear of having to pay *réparations,* which leads to ever more adamant confirmations of the story; and so on until the terrible logic of events leads to a tragic outcome.[99] But Dupaty carefully shied away from laying the blame of what happened at the door of any particular person or persons. The culprits were not the Thomassins, who lied to save face, or a constabulary hell-bent on bringing in anyone fitting a vague description, or the judges of Chaumont, who forgot about three paupers rotting in jail for months on end. The real author of this tragedy was a legal system that allowed for principles such as that of *témoins nécessaires*—that if witnesses to a serious crime could not be found, the word of interested parties, such as the victims themselves, could send suspects to their death.

The ultimate message of the mémoire was, predictably, an explicit, point-by-point critique of the "vices and rigors" of the Ordinance of 1670. The arguments implicit in the Cléreaux and Salmon briefs were here brought out in full force: the "inquisitorial" origins and nature of the law, the potent criticisms directed at it by such eminent and respected jurists as Montesquieu, d'Aguesseau, and Lamoignon, the leeway granted to prosecutors and the vulnerability of the accused, the lack of just proportion between crimes and punishments.[100] But Dupaty, echoing more forcefully and more pointedly the arguments advanced by the likes of Servan, also stressed that the problem was not just with the Ordinance, but with the socially iniquitous way in which its provisions were applied in reality. The laws in fact *seemed* just, in that they allowed a defendant to appeal to a higher jurisdiction; and had things been different, these three men could have done so to their advantage: "How? By what means? Shall I say it? If they had not been poor. Alas! yes, had they not been poor; like the rich, they could have appealed; like the rich they would have known the secrets of the procedure at the hearing, or bought them from the clerk, they would have presented petitions, published mémoires; finally, can anyone believe that the judges of Chaumont would have buried three rich men in their gaols for thirty months?"[101]

In the second mémoire he wrote for the men, *Moyens de droit pour Bradier, Simare, Lardoise,* Dupaty pushed these points further still, this

99. Ibid., pp. 206–214.
100. Ibid., pp. 234–239.
101. Ibid., p. 236.

time coming closer to an outright attack on the magistrates as uphold-
ers of "aristocratic" social tyranny. He noted that those who championed the law as it existed, including its laxity about securing proper
proof, were generally the powerful, those who fear crimes and rarely
commit them, who are the accusers and so seldom the accused: "O you,
men who are powerful through wealth, talent, or position! You who
make up a sort of aristocracy within monarchical governments! You for
whom the laws have done so much that it is hard for you to do anything
against them." [102] It would have been difficult for the magistrates of the
parlement not to recognize themselves in this description. In both of
his briefs he proclaimed insistently that the law's primary function
should be as safeguard of *les peuples,* of the millions without money and
connections. The novelty of his approach to the Ordinance lay in his
lucid recognition that the "inquisitorial" procedures of the courts reflected not so much administrative "despotism" as social injustice—an
insight he perhaps derived from his own experience of the elitism of the
Bordeaux parlement. But whatever its origin, what Dupaty developed
was a startlingly modern analysis of the socially hegemonic nature of the
legal system.

Dupaty's *Mémoire justificatif* and *Moyens de droit* capped a whole
generation's worth of widely read trial briefs that purported to protect
the poor and vulnerable from their social "superiors"; but they also carried the genre, and the discussion, in a whole new direction. The classic
sensational mémoire of the prerevolutionary decades showed its readers
an everyman (or woman) victimized by the Great. Both the victim
and his or her oppressor were vividly portrayed as individuals, and
the former was not necessarily a pauper; François Véron-Dujonquay,
Barthélémy Tort, Beaumarchais, and even the Virgin of Salency were
classless or middling sorts whose identity as *petits* derived primarily from
the persecution visited upon them by *un grand.* (Even a great lady like
Mme de Saint-Vincent could present herself, on those grounds, as a
victim of social injustice.) For all of its effectiveness, the social typology
in most mémoires was more theatrically Manichaean than convincingly
sociological. Even in the Cléreaux and Salmon cases there had been
sharply drawn villains, the lewd Thibault and the scheming Huet-
Duparc family. Dupaty's innovation lay in his use of the Trois Roués case
to demonstrate that judicial persecution derived from structural factors,

---

102. [Charles Dupaty], *Moyens de droit pour Bradier, Simare, Lardoise condamnés à
la roue* (Paris, 1786), p. 42.

not from the random caprice of any given grandee, village lordling, judge, or master. Drawing ammunition from previous cases such as the Salmon affair, invoking the "innocent blood" of the Calas, Montbaillis, and other victims of the law, he mounted a powerful argument, which exposed the "banality of evil" and its origins in legislation that reflected the injustices of contemporary society.

The radical implications of Dupaty's mémoire, the vigor with which it brought the issue of reform out of the salons of the intelligentsia and before a wide public, were not lost on contemporaries, certainly not on the advocate-general of the Paris Parlement, Louis-Antoine Séguier. The *réquisitoire* that Séguier delivered on 7 August 1786—later printed and widely read—was equally remarkable for the lucidity and force with which it denounced rash innovation, the irresponsible use of trial briefs as propaganda, and the conventional appeal to the sanction of *l'opinion publique*.[103] Indeed, the confrontation between Dupaty and Séguier, capping fifteen years of growth in the popularity of *mémoires judiciaires,* is neatly emblematic of the clash between partisans of authority and those who sought to mobilize *l'opinion*.

Séguier devoted some of his oration to justifying the procedure in the case and upholding the Parlement's verdict as correct, but the bulk of his lengthy speech concerned broader, indeed fundamental, political issues. He defended the existing criminal laws on the grounds that they were intrinsically just (secrecy, for instance, protected the accused) and best suited to the French polity. Then, in Burkean tones, he warned of the dangers of sudden and radical change, which might well "topple the political constitution" and begin a revolution: "Let us cast afar those systems of general reform whose proposals are all the more dangerous in that they always are heralded in the name of Humanity."[104] He warned his fellow Frenchmen against "the cries of those citizens, foreigners in their own land, who admire only the laws of states neighboring on France, of reformers solely occupied with overthrowing our laws under pretext of bringing them closer to the code of nature."[105]

Much of the danger Séguier saw in the meddling by nonspecialists in

103. Wattine, *L'Affaire des Trois Roués,* chap. 14; Doyle, "Dupaty," pp. 8–92; Jacobson, "Criminal Law Reform," pp. 350–355.

104. M. Clair and A. Clapier, *Le Barreau français: Collection des chefs d'oeuvre de l'éloquence judiciaire en France,* 16 vols (Paris: Pancoucke, 1823–1824), 4:299.

105. Ibid.

matters of legislation he attributed, correctly, to the new popularity of mémoires and their departure from their original and proper functions. His lengthy denunciation of the new mémoires is a particularly interesting testimony to their growing commercialization: "Mémoires, which originally were allowed only for the purpose of instructing the judges and the bar, are now more than ever an object of amusement and curiosity for the public, and one can even say, a matter of commerce for booksellers and a commercial speculation for the parties. They are peddled in squares and public promenades, sold at the entrance to parks and spectacles, laid out on the quays and in the bookstalls. They are carefully decorated with epigraphs announcing their spirit, and extravagance has gone as far as to have them include the portraits of the unfortunate souls for whom they are written."[106] This commercial success stemmed directly from the style in which popular trial briefs were written, which Séguier, like many another opponent of a sensational mémoire, denounced as mendaciously novelistic—with particular reference to the trial brief at hand. Dupaty, claimed Séguier, had gotten caught up in his own "seduction" of his readers: "In the heat of composition, objects loom larger before his dazzled eyes; his imagination invents specters to combat them. In the solitude of his retreat, he sees beside him humanity trembling and reaching out to him, a dishevelled fatherland showing him its wounds, the whole nation taking on his voice and commanding him to speak in its name."[107]

If these were delusions, Séguier heatedly concluded, they were dangerous ones, leading to a solipsistic view of "public opinion" as a reflection of one's own desires. In a remarkable passage, the advocate-general vigorously indicted the rhetorical conventions that allowed the likes of a Dupaty to claim universal sanction for a personal crusade. What was, after all, this public opinion that Dupaty invoked? Should it be a particular belief arbitrarily erected into the will of all? No, he pursued, public opinion was "the meeting of all reflexions, the result of general suffrage, a gathering of general feeling . . . a voice composed of all voices . . . a wish widely expressed."[108] Rather than rejecting the notion of "public opinion" as dangerously seditious, as a less intelligent conservative might have done, Séguier attacked the conventionally rhetorical use of

106. Ibid., pp. 513–514.
107. Ibid., p. 476.
108. Ibid., pp. 518–519.

the term by critics of the establishment and countered it surprisingly by invoking a more modern, democratic usage.[109] The *Réquisitoire Séguier* aroused nearly as much interest as had the mémoire itself, and indeed by the following fall both texts were sold bound together.[110] Such was the force of Séguier's counterattack that it apparently succeeded in dividing public sentiment, which had initially been strongly behind Dupaty. But while there were now rumblings against the reformers, the *Mémoirs secrets* also reported truculent indignation when the *Réquisitoire* was published, on the part of "the public which also likes to judge, is no more forgiving than any other tribunal, and does not care for attempts to restrict its jurisdiction."[111]

More than any other previous case, the Trois Roués affair had laid open for debate the competing claims of established authority and of "public opinion." It also appeared to have as direct an effect on government policy as any case of the age. As we have seen, the outcome of the Roués case was linked to the advent in the spring of 1787 of a new ministry headed by Archbishop Loménie de Brienne with, as keeper of seals, a magistrate who had long agitated within the Parlement for judicial reform, Chrétien-François de Lamoignon.[112] Although the case in no way brought about the change in ministry, Dupaty had invoked Lamoignon's name repeatedly in his trial briefs, and the new minister had substantial contacts within the very milieu of enlightened reformers to which Dupaty belonged. Lamoignon immediately set up a commission of jurists to draw up new legislation and also sought help from Dupaty's reforming brothers-in-arms—Malesherbes, Target, Blondel, Lacretelle—and probably from Dupaty himself.[113]

The reforms that Lamoignon brought before the Parlement in an edict in May of 1788, although they stopped short of such radical proposals as complete publicity and trials by jury, incorporated many of the demands of the reform movement, including a lengthening of the delay between sentencing and execution, the printing and publicizing of ver-

---

109. See Mona Ozouf's discussion of archaic and modern understandings of "public opinion" in "Public Opinion at the End of the Old Regime," *Journal of Modern History* 60 (Supplement, September 1988): S1–S21.

110. Doyle, "Dupaty," pp. 95–96.

111. Doyle, "Dupaty," p. 96. *Mémoires secrets* 33, 16 September 1786.

112. On Lamoignon's role in the Parlement, see Bailey Stone, *The Parlement of Paris, 1774–1789* (Chapel Hill: University of North Carolina Press, 1981), pp. 26–27, 46–52.

113. Doyle, "Dupaty," pp. 104–105; Jacobson, "Criminal Law Reform," pp. 391–394.

dicts, a greater majority of votes for capital convictions, and the abolition of all torture. Lamoignon's attempted inroads into the old legal system were hamstrung by predictably vociferous resistance from the magistrates and by the fall of the ministry in September of 1788.[114] Little did any minister or magistrate at the time imagine how drastic an overhaul of the judicial system would be accomplished a mere three years later when the Constituent Assembly voted into effect a new code of criminal justice that would have been any eighteenth-century reformer's dream. If Dupaty's mémoires had not been shots fired at the old order, they had at least provided a good deal of the ammunition.

In a famous article published some two decades ago, Robert Darnton suggested that one of the difficulties in attempting to link the Enlightenment to the French Revolution was generational. The great philosophes, the Voltaires, Montesquieus, Rousseaus, and others, were mostly of a generation, born in the early decades of the eighteenth century or earlier, at the peak of their powers at mid-century, declining or dying off in the 1770s and 1780s. In order to explain the transmission of the *lumières* and their transformation into the more radical ideologies of the 1780s and 1790s, Darnton pointed to the bipolarization of the literary world after mid-century: on the one hand, an establishment of second-rate professional men of letters, such as Suard, Marmontel, and La Harpe, securely pensioned and parroting safely watered-down versions of the ideas of their great predecessors; on the other, a group of frustrated and ambitious Grub Street writers, the likes of Carra, Gorsas, Mercier, and Brissot, earning a precarious living and venting their frustration by means of the ephemeral productions—pamphlets, *libelles*, chronicles—of the literary underground.[115] It was the latter, Darnton argued, who provided the scorching critiques of the old order that were to metamorphose into the radical ideologies of the Revolution.

In the years since Darnton brilliantly opened up the question of the social bases of the link between the Enlightenment and the Revolution, historians have pointed to other groups that were influential in articulat-

---

114. Jacobson, "Criminal Law Reform," chap. 9. For a fuller account, see Marcel Marion, *Le Garde des sceaux Lamoignon et la réforme judiciaire de 1788* (Paris: Hachette, 1950).

115. Robert Darnton, "The High Enlightenment and the Low-Life of Literature in Prerevolutionary France," *Past and Present* 51 (May 1971): 81–115; reprinted in Robert Darnton, *The Literary Underground of the Old Regime* (Cambridge, Mass.: Harvard University Press, 1982), pp. 1–40.

ing and disseminating protorevolutionary ideas, such as journalists, Jansenist magistrates, and lesser-known (but not "underground") writers.[116] This study, and this chapter especially, suggests that we might do well to pay closer attention to the legal milieu, which produced its own cohort of talented, articulate, and much-listened-to critics of the old order. The men whom we have encountered taking on sensational cases and articulating critical ideas from the Maupeou years onward were very much of a generation. Outside of a few elder statesmen, such as Malesherbes and Target, all of them were born within a single decade: Linguet in 1736, Servan in 1737, Lecauchois in 1741, Falconnet in 1742, Delacroix in 1743, Fournel in 1745, and Dupaty in 1746.

Most of these men were *avocats,* while others, like Servan and Dupaty, were magistrates whose personal experiences had alienated them from the complacently privileged world of the *parlementaires.* Like the Grub Street writers, they had come of age in the high noon of the Enlightenment, had been in their teens and twenties during the struggles over the *Encyclopédie* and the Calas case, had never known a world over which Voltaire did not preside. They nearly all boasted literary connections and achievements and had read in Rousseau about the centrality of laws and legislators to a free, contractual polity. Through the publication of *mémoires judiciaires,* they married legal ability to literary skill and had an impact on readers at least as great as that of the Grub Street down-and-outers.

The causes célèbres of the mid-1780s brought this generation decisively to the fore, as they took on the roles of crusaders against an iniquitous criminal justice system. One of the remarkable features of the mémoires examined in this chapter is the way in which their authors began to cast themselves as central protagonists in the cases. Lecauchois depicted himself poring over the records of the Salmon case, agonizing over the decision to take it on; Dupaty's readers followed him as he visited the three men in prison and then stood up to the judges who had condemned them. Not only did the authors of mémoires invent

---

116. See, for instance, Jeremy Popkin, *News and Politics in the Age of Revolution: Jean Luzac's "Gazette de Leyde"* (Ithaca: Cornell University Press, 1989); Nina Gelbart, *Feminine and Opposition Journalism in Old Regime France: Le Journal des Dames* (Berkeley: University of California Press, 1987); Dale Van Kley, "The Jansenist Constitutional Legacy in the French Prerevolution," in Keith Baker, ed., *The Political Culture of the Old Regime* (Oxford: Pergamon Press, 1987), pp. 169–201; Keith Baker, *Inventing the French Revolution* (Cambridge: Cambridge University Press, 1990).

themselves in and through their fictions, they also brought into being a community of readers who shared their views. Just as the philosophes in their works had created rhetorically a "Republic of Letters," a world of like-minded readers that existed as an alternative to Old Regime society and polity, so did lawyers transform *their* readers into juries—institutions antithetical to the very principles of absolutism.[117]

As the public fame of the lawyers and their cases increased, so did the dangers of trivialization and the temptations of being co-opted into fashionable high society—as had happened to many a philosophe. The line between honest outrage and sentimental posturing was a fine one and easily crossed. When Condorcet finally did wed Dupaty's niece Sophie de Grouchy, he sent to Champagne for the young son of one of the Roués and had him dressed for his bride in the costume of an English jockey.[118] As for Victoire Salmon, her ordeals were far from over when she left the Palais de Justice a free woman. She and her defender Lecauchois were immediately paraded through the houses of the great, there to be plied with gifts; at the foundling hospital they jointly held a newborn as he was christened and named Pierre-Noël-Innocent.[119] There were engraved portraits sold all over the city showing Victoire in her country-girl's clothes and Lecauchois with the names of innocents he had saved, over lines of mediocre verse.[120] In the summer of 1786 the irrepressible Mme de Genlis once again exercised her talents as a stage manager by having Salmon wed a young man previously saved by Lecauchois. The elaborate ceremony was a repeat of countless rosière crownings, as the little daughter of the duc d'Orleans placed the wedding-wreath on Salmon's head and Genlis herself adorned her with a gold chain bearing a medallion of her lawyer.[121] Even as late as 1786, the theater of upper-class life was still threatening to take over the triumphs of the courtroom. Shortly before her wedding Salmon, still flanked by her lawyer, made her first visit to the Comédie-Française; they were ushered onto the balcony and applauded by the fashionable,

117. On the rhetorical creation of a "Republic of Letters," see Dena Goodman, "Story-Telling in the Republic of Letters: The Rhetorical Context of Diderot's *La Religieuse*," *Nouvelles de la République des Lettres* 1 (1986): 51–70.

118. B.N. Collection Joly de Fleury 2901, fos. 51, 54, 56.

119. B.N. Ms. Fr. 6685, 26 May 1786.

120. Le Corbeiller, *Victoire Salmon*, pp. 190–192; *Mémoires secrets* 33, 31 October 1786.

121. Le Corbeiller, *Victoire Salmon*, pp. 194–207.

L'INNOCENCE PRÉSUMÉE
Est Marie Françoise Victoire Salmon.
Non moriar sed vivam et narrabo opera Domini.

ANAGRAMME.
J'étais Forcée à mort sans vol ni crime.
Par M. le Gay Ingénieur de Riom en Auvergne.

7. Portrait of Victoire Salmon after she became a popular heroine. (Phot. Bibl. Nat. Paris)

8. Portrait of Pierre-Noël Lecauchois. The pages scattered under the portrait bear the names of his most famous clients with the dates of their cases. (Phot. Bibl. Nat. Paris)

9. The acquittal of Victoire Salmon by the Parlement of Paris. The print is dedicated to Mme de Genlis: note the rosière-like young girls in the lower right corner preparing to crown Salmon. (Phot. Bibl. Nat. Paris)

well-heeled audience, then received a second ovation when one of the actors onstage delivered a line about the triumph of truth.[122] The irony of such demonstrations could not be more profound in light of the criticisms of the social status quo that formed the core of Lecauchois's and Dupaty's writings.

Despite these attempts to turn them into sentimental theater for the upper classes, the "reforming" cases of the 1780s carried, through the

122. B.N. Ms. Fr. 6685, 8 June 1786; *Mémoires secrets* 33, 4 October 1786.

mémoires, messages more explicit and more subversive than any since the days of Voltaire's judicial crusades against *l'infâme*. English Showalter has noted in eighteenth-century French fiction an evolution in the portrayal of the individual's struggle against society. In the great novels of the 1750s and 1760s, *Manon Lescaut, La Nouvelle Héloïse, L'Ingénu, La Religieuse,* the status quo against which the protagonist rebels is incarnated in an individual—a father, an official, a priest, or a convent superior. In the following decades, Diderot in his tales and Laclos in *Les Liaisons dangereuses* moved toward a deeper understanding of evil as the expression of social structures and conventions—the libertines in Laclos's novel are shocking because they are *not* moral freaks but polished products of their class and time.[123] At a slightly later date, the *mémoire judiciaire* traveled a similar route.

Certainly Voltaire had addressed general problems in his cases of the 1760s, but these had to do with belief and prejudice rather than institutions; the antidote to the poison of *fanatisme* was not social change but vigilance, "enlightened reason," the power of the pen, and perhaps the silencing of benighted clerics and judges. In the 1770s, the problem addressed insistently in trial briefs was that of despotic authority in society and the state. The hallmark of the Maupeou-era mémoires was their conflating of social and political categories in the person of a single, usually male, oppressor. Morangiès, the lord of Salency, Richelieu, and Goezman embodied the abuse of authority by those in power, as did such fictional characters as Des Grieux's father in *Manon*, Julie's in *La Nouvelle Héloïse*, or the mother superiors in *La Religieuse* (in fiction, power was parental or surrogate-parental rather than sociopolitical). By the 1780s, however, mémoires began to address problems of social iniquity in impersonal, structural terms, denouncing the "vices and rigors" of the judicial system instead of dramatizing the malice of a defendant's antagonist, and pointing to the social bases of legal iniquity.

This change in approach reflected a change in political preoccupations from the 1770s to the 1780s. In the 1770s, the Maupeou crisis and its aftershocks had kept the spotlight in public affairs on the problem of "despotism" as the central threat to a monarchical state. In the 1780s, "despotism" continued to be a central issue in public life, especially, as we saw in connection with the Diamond Necklace Affair, when construed as the abuse of power by women. But in the last decade of

123. English Showalter, Jr., *The Evolution of the French Novel, 1641–1782* (Princeton: Princeton University Press, 1982), chap. 5.

the Old Regime, political concerns extended beyond the "despotic" abuse of power to a questioning of the laws that formed the basis of the sociopolitical system. In other words, the *mémoires judiciaires* appear to reflect a shift from a preoccupation with the *abuse* of social and political power to a critique of the very *bases* of that power—from a reaction against sociopolitical tyranny to a reflection on the nature of the social contract.

The Cléreaux, Salmon, and Trois Roués cases alerted the French reading public to the urgent necessity of a reform of the judicial system—and by implication, of the need to overhaul the realm's entire administrative system, as was eventually done in 1789–1791. The lawyers who wrote briefs in these cases appealed to their readers' emotions through melodramatic renditions of miscarriages of justice, and to their intellects by challenging them to weigh evidence and judge for themselves. Contemporary accounts suggest that readers were enthralled by the stories of innocents who narrowly escaped execution, and of the barristers who rescued them in extremis from ghastly fates; nonetheless, the experiences of provincial servants and laborers were bound to be remote from the lives of those who read about them. Such was not the case in a different spate of equally sensational judicial struggles, also unfolding in the mid to late eighties, which concerned the private lives of prosperous and educated Parisians. The two great "domestic" cases of the 1780s, the Sanois and Kornmann affairs, addressed fundamental questions about law and polity, but looked at these through the prism of marital discord. In doing so they illustrated for readers the manifold links between marriage contract and political covenant, between private misfortune and public concerns.

6

Domestic Drama
and the Social Contract

Marriage, parenthood, adultery, separation, loneliness—
these were the stuff of everyday joy and distress in the eighteenth century, as they are today. These were also the stuff of causes célèbres, and
especially of two major cases that unfolded in the years immediately preceding the French Revolution, the so-called Sanois (1786) and Kornmann (1787–89) affairs. The protagonists of both cases were men who
claimed to have been betrayed and victimized by their wives (in collusion with others). The count of Sanois said that his spouse, daughter,
and son-in-law had conspired to have him declared insane and locked
up in an asylum; the banker Guillaume Kornmann claimed that his attractive and wealthy young wife had abandoned him after being seduced
by an aristocratic rake, with the complicity of a group of illustrious and
powerful personages.

In both the Sanois and the Kornmann case, tales of marital betrayal
and breakdown became infused with political meaning. After the publication of the first important mémoire in the Sanois case, the *Mémoires
secrets* informed readers that the queen had had the brief read to her;
her husband, Louis XVI, was reported to exclaim that he wanted to read
it too because "they are having me give out lettres de cachet left and
right and I don't know the first thing about it."[1] As for the Kornmann
case, it took shape in the eye of a political storm, during the monarchy's
last-ditch effort to preempt financial disaster by convening an Assembly
of Notables; as we shall see, the Kornmann adultery scandal was per-

1. *Mémoires secrets* 32:238.

ceived as having both general and specific links to the crisis rocking the French state in 1787–88.

This chapter explores the analogy, widely perceived and commented on in these years, between the marriage contract and the social contract and explains the importance of this analogy at the ultimate point of transition from absolute monarchy to contractual government. On the basis of trial briefs relating to these affairs, of contemporary commentary, and of contemporary fiction, I argue that the archetypal narrative of a wife's infidelity and insubordination was laden, at this juncture, with connotations of political chaos and change, and that questions of style both in sexual conduct and in language were similarly charged with sociopolitical significance. This chapter traces the final and paradoxical evolution of the eighteenth-century *mémoire judiciaire* as it became simultaneously more personal and more explicitly political. I argue, in sum, that the Sanois and Kornmann cases offer vivid illustrations of the ways in which the public discussion of private life helped to shape the culture of the new public sphere.

The history of the institution of marriage in early modern France is that of a struggle between ecclesiastical and secular authorities, the latter having won the contest by the mid-eighteenth century. Although in the early Middle Ages marriage had been a purely secular legal contract, in the centuries after the year 1000 the French Church gradually took over the marriage act, redefining it as purely a sacrament, which, in theory at least, required the couple's consent. Although classical medieval canon law had allowed for the breaking of marriage vows in some cases (primarily in the case of nonconsummation), the post-Tridentine Catholic Church maintained that marriage was a sacrament and therefore could not be dissolved.[2] Beginning in the sixteenth century, however, the French state sought to assert its own view that marriage was in essence a secular juridical contract only subsequently sanctified by the Church.

---

2. James Traer, *Marriage and the Family in Eighteenth-Century France* (Ithaca: Cornell University Press, 1980), pp. 18–31; Sarah Hanley, "Family and State in Early Modern France: The Marriage Pact," in Marilyn Boxer and Jean Quataert, eds., *Connecting Spheres: Women in the Western World: 1500 to the Present* (Oxford: Oxford University Press, 1987), pp. 54–55, and "Engendering the State: Family Formation and State Building in Early Modern France," *French Historical Studies* 16 (Spring 1989): 4–27. For a history of a particular aspect of marriage law in France, see Pierre Darmon, *Damning the Innocent: A History of the Persecution of the Impotent in Pre-Revolutionary France,* trans. Paul Keegan (New York: Viking, 1985).

As Sarah Hanley has argued, this development accompanied the process of state building by the French monarchy, and it placed the business of defining and controlling marriage within the hands of royal officials, especially the legists of the parlements.[3]

By the eighteenth century, then, the French state had successfully laid claim to the definition of marriage as a "natural"—as opposed to religious—covenant. But while prominent jurists such as Pierre Le Ridant and Durand de Maillane propounded such ideas, they also firmly espoused the church's view that marriage was indissoluble; throughout the Old Regime, the only option for unhappy spouses was a legal separation, or *séparation de corps*, which in theory was granted only in the case of a wife's adultery or of danger to the life of one of the partners (a legal separation usually entailed the division of the assets each spouse had brought to the marriage; it did not, of course, allow either one to remarry).[4] Over the course of the eighteenth century, however, a number of writers began to articulate ideas about marriage that were at odds with both clerical *and* juridical orthodoxies. Most conspicuously, progressive writers argued for the legalization of divorce—an event some of them lived to see occur on 20 September 1792, the day before the proclamation of the first French Republic. The list of prerevolutionary authors who argued for divorce includes a sizable cohort of the canonical French Enlightenment—Montesquieu, Voltaire, Condorcet, Diderot, d'Argenson, d'Holbach, and Laclos all had their word to say on the subject; but there were also lesser-known men of letters, such as Cerfvol, who made a name (in this case, a pseudonym) for themselves by grinding out tract after tract on the subject of marriage and divorce.[5]

To the twentieth-century reader, eighteenth-century arguments in favor of divorce will seem almost comically naive. In the rosy dawn of physiocracy and of the pursuit of happiness, however, the freedom to terminate a marriage legally, on any grounds including incompatibility,

3. Hanley, "Family and State," pp. 54–57; Traer, *Marriage and the Family,* pp. 31–46.

4. Traer, *Marriage and the Family,* pp. 38–47; Roderick Phillips, *Putting Asunder: A History of Divorce in Western Society* (Cambridge: Cambridge University Press, 1988), chap. 5.

5. Francis Ronsin, *Le Contrat sentimental: Débats sur le mariage, l'amour, le divorce de l'Ancien Régime à le Restauration* (Paris: Aubier, 1990), chap. 2; Paul Hoffman, *La Femme dans la pensée des lumières* (Paris: Orphrys, 1977), pp. 281–286; Laurent Versini, *Laclos et la tradition* (Paris: Klincksieck, 1968), pp. 571–573; Roderick Phillips, *Family Breakdown in Late Eighteenth-Century France: Divorces in Rouen, 1792–1803* (Oxford: Clarendon Press, 1980), p. 11; Phillips, *Putting Asunder,* pp. 159–175.

appeared a panacea that would bring happiness to individuals and prosperity to the state. From the late 1760s right into the Revolution, philosophes and other polemicists argued that divorce would put an end to loveless marriages; that the mere possibility of voluntary dissolution would make all spouses more considerate of each other; that revocable marriages would boost morality by removing most of the rationale for adultery and unmarried cohabitation; that the resulting felicity within marriages would, by increasing fertility, spur population growth and hence increase the overall prosperity of the state.[6]

The meaning of the attention bestowed, in the second half of the eighteenth century, upon questions of marriage and divorce is of course revealed by the exact coincidence, in September of 1792, of the adoption of a permissive divorce law with the country's dramatic change in political regimes. While the analogy between family and polity has an ancient and quasi-universal history, in late-eighteenth-century France this took the form of an intense preoccupation with the making and breaking of contracts. There was undoubtedly a strong anticlerical component to enlightened writers' arguments against indissoluble marriage, a stance they had in turn inherited from generations of Gallican jurists arguing against their clerical rivals. One of the most outspokenly anticlerical works on the subject, Jacques Le Scène Desmaisons's *Contrat conjugal* (1781), energetically argued the case for marriage as a purely civil contract based on natural law, over which the state should have complete jurisdiction.[7] In his description of what would happen if the clergy gained complete control over marriage, Le Scène waxed apocalyptic: Would the clergy not be free, in that case, to marry people or not "according to whether or not they hold this or that doctrine, this or that belief, whether they accept or reject this or that formulary"? Was it not evident that the men in black could thus annihilate the population after laying their hands on its wealth? Would they not, at the very least, set up a destructively self-serving *regnum in regno*?[8]

Arguments that defined marriage as a secular and "natural" contract

6. Ronsin, *Le Contrat sentimental,* chap. 2; Traer, *Marriage and the Family,* chap. 2; Hoffman, *La Femme,* pp. 281–286. A good example of the classic eighteenth-century arguments in favor of divorce is Cerfvol [pseud.], *Législation du divorce,* 2d ed. (London, 1770).

7. Jacques Le Scène Desmaisons, *Le Contrat conjugal ou loix du mariage, de la répudiation, et du divorce* (n.p., 1781).

8. Ibid, p. 21.

were closely connected to the Enlightenment's struggle against confessional "fanaticism." In fact, the royal decree of October 1787 that finally granted French Protestants full civil rights was in part a direct response to just such arguments, as articulated by Jean-Baptiste Target in one of his most celebrated cases. In 1786, Target took on the defense of the marquise d'Anglure, a noblewoman born of the marriage of a Protestant man to a Catholic woman. Because the wedding had been performed clandestinely (*au désert*) by a Protestant pastor, members of the marquise's family challenged her inheritance rights on the grounds that the marriage was invalid and that she was therefore illegitimate. Target successfully countered such claims by arguing that the true essence of marriage was mutual consent, witnessed to and ratified by public opinion; since religious dissidents could not by definition comply with the terms of the ordinance of Blois, which required (Catholic) religious sanctification for all marriages, the civil contract between Protestant spouses should be considered legally binding. Target so effectively used the case to raise broader claims on behalf of France's Huguenot minority that he was entrusted with the preparation of the Edict of 1787.[9]

Target, Le Scène, and like-minded contemporaries argued that the state, not the clergy, should have complete control over marriage because the institution of marriage was the rock upon which society and the polity were built. In arguing this, eighteenth-century writers drew, explicitly and predictably, on the European natural law tradition, which stretches from Bodin to Locke. Citing Grotius, Pufendorf, Burlamaqui, and Locke, they argued that the marriage pact was the original social contract upon which all others rested and hence the foundation of civil society.[10] The future Girondin and mayor of revolutionary Paris Jérôme Pétion opened his *Essai sur le mariage* (1785) with the statement that "marriage is the first and most sacred of all bonds. Founded in nature, it forms the basis of all society."[11] Le Scène argued that marriage was, as he put it, *un système politique*—the first and most important of the private contracts, enforced by the state, which ensured the survival and

9. Paul Boulloche, *Un Avocat du XVIIIe siècle* (Paris: Calmann-Levy, 1893), pp. 34–35; S. Dumon, "Notice sur Target," in *Annales du barreau français: Barreau ancien* (Paris: Warée, 1826), pp. 6–7; Joseph Hudault, *Guy Jean Baptiste Target et sa contribution à la préparation de l'édit de novembre 1787 sur l'état-civil des Protestants* (Law thesis, University of Paris, 1866).

10. Hoffman, *La Femme,* pp. 256–274; Traer, *Marriage and the Family,* pp. 50–51.

11. Jérôme Pétion de Villeneuve, *Essai sur le mariage* (Geneva, 1785), p. 1.

perpetuation of mankind; marriage was also an expression of the natural urge toward appropriation, since spouses could in effect be considered each other's private property.[12]

Contractual theories of government usually carry egalitarian implications—at least as concerns the hypothetical state of nature, prior to the introduction of property rights. If the conjugal contract was considered the model and foundation of the contractual polity, a freely chosen and revokable mutual pact, did this not imply equality between the contracting spouses? Natural law thinkers, however, almost invariably accepted and justified the authority of husbands and fathers within the family.[13] Pétion, for instance, began with the assumption that men and women were equal within primitive families, although they instinctively adopted different roles. The need to regulate sexuality in society, however, led to matrimonial laws and customs that codified access to women and the division of labor within the family. Within the legally sanctioned household, the husband became the "revered chief of the family" enjoying "authority without limits"; this was inevitable, Pétion argued, because an association of two people needs a master and arbiter, and that role should logically be entrusted to the physically stronger of the two.[14]

It is tempting to dismiss such arguments as simply bad faith on the part of male writers whose commitment to principles of natural equality stopped dead at the thresholds of their homes. But, as Carole Pateman has argued, the inequality of partners within the "sexual contract" was not an aberration but an essential component of classical contractual theory.[15] The central myth of modern Western political thought is the story of the social contract—the free covenanting of equal men that gives birth to the state. This myth was given lasting form in John Locke's separation of paternal from political power, as the "fraternity" of covenanting men metaphorically killed the father and bonded to form civil society.

But, as Pateman points out, there are two parts to the story of the contract, one of which is usually glossed over or repressed; the social contract between fraternal men depends upon the relegation of paternal

---

12. Le Scène, *Contrat conjugal*, pp. 11–12, 14–15.
13. Traer, *Marriage and the Family*, p. 51.
14. Pétion, *Essai sur le mariage*, pp. 15–22.
15. Carole Pateman, *The Sexual Contract* (Stanford: Stanford University Press, 1988); in the summary that follows, I draw mostly on chaps. 1 and 4.

power to the private sphere, a sphere that is generally not seen as politically relevant. In classic accounts of the contract, such as those of Locke and Rousseau, women are judged to be "naturally" unfit for public civil life by virtue of their want of reason, strength, or control over their passions. Hence, the creation of civil society through the social contract is dependent upon the prior subjection of women within the private sphere—better still, the very definition of political manhood depends on its antithesis, "apolitical" or "private" womanhood: "To tell the story of the sexual contract is to show how sexual difference, what it is to be a 'man' or a 'woman,' and the construction of sexual difference as political difference, is central to civil society." [16]

The ideological climate of prerevolutionary France was receptive to contractual, or at least legal and constitutional, theories of government. Educated people with an interest in politics would be aware of the parlements' claim to "represent" the French people, and of their appeals to a French "constitution" and the rule of law (that awareness was much intensified, as we have seen, by the Maupeou crisis). They read texts that routinely used words like *citoyen* and *nation*. They were aware, whether they had read them or not, of Montesquieu's comparative analysis of types of government and of Rousseau's revival of classical republicanism. If they were intellectuals or men of law, they were conversant with sixteenth- and seventeenth-century natural law theory.

But the writer whose work most powerfully shaped and reflected the emerging culture of the prerevolutionary decades was Jean-Jacques Rousseau. Rousseau's works spoke to all aspects of his readers' lives, clarifying the connection between private experience and public ideals. His political works set up a model of healthy masculine republicanism as an antithesis to the over-civilized decay of monarchical France; his educational and fictional writings popularized new ideals of domestic life, of marital and parental happiness; his *Confessions* and other autobiographical works introduced readers to a man of courageous integrity, a self-proclaimed outcast who shunned the cultural and intellectual fashions of his day and dared to reveal in print his most shameful thoughts and actions.

Rousseau's influence pervades the two great "domestic" cases of the later 1780s, the Sanois and Kornmann affairs. In both cases, the most notable mémoires were confessional autobiographies of Rousseauesque men of virtue forced into confinement or exile; in both cases, the source

16. Ibid., p. 16.

of the hero's troubles was a wife who through infidelity or unnatural tyranny over her husband had broken the "sexual contract"; in both instances, the misconduct of a wife and the sufferings of a husband served as vehicles for an indictment of the sociopolitical status quo. The very recent Diamond Necklace Affair had warned the nation of the corruption and chaos that could follow from the untrammeled actions of "public women." The Sanois and Kornmann scandals brought that message home by applying it to the domestic intimacy of ordinary husbands and wives.

If contemporary writers and journalists are to be believed, the prerevolutionary French elites were unusually prone to wash their dirty linen in public. In his 1781 *Contrat conjugal,* Jacques Le Scène Desmaisons professed shock at the publicity surrounding separation cases: "Corrupt and brazen women . . . come and clamor their disgrace before the law courts; the secrets of the marriage bed are shamelessly revealed." Other writers like Pétion and the lawyer Jean-François Fournel similarly decried the exhibitionism and prurient curiosity around contemporary lawsuits between husbands and wives.[17] Indeed, browsing through chronicles like the *Mémoires secrets* and *Correspondance secrète* or a more specialized paper like the *Gazette des tribunaux,* one is easily convinced that a war of the sexes was raging in the capital throughout the 1770s and 1780s.

Women sued for separation from their husbands by recounting lurid tales of domestic violence; men dragged their wives' names through the mud for alleged adultery and had them locked up in convents and safehouses. Most of the cases considered notable involved members of the upper bourgeoisie or aristocracy—the struggle between the count of Mirabeau and his wife, Emilie de Marignane, was a soap opera played out over years in the 1780s—but occasionally a case involving protagonists of lesser social status made news if it was delectably scandalous.[18] In the 1770s, for instance, a Mme Guyot obtained a separation from

17. Le Scène, *Contrat conjugal,* p. 283; Pétion, *Essai sur le mariage,* pp. 35–36; Jean-François Fournel, *Traité de l'adultère considéré dans l'ordre judiciaire* (Paris, 1778), pp. xii-xiii.

18. For examples see the *Gazette des tribunaux* 1776, vol. 8. (Marquise de Gouy case); 1776, vol. 46 (M. and Mme. de B . . .); 1777, vol. 4 and vol. 11 (Guyot case); 1777, vol. 13 (Count and Countess de N . . .); 1786, vol. 2 (Carlier case). See also the *Mémoires secrets* 25:199–200; 29:250–251; 33:7, 12; and François Métra, *Correspondance secrète politique et littéraire,* 18 vols. (London, 1787–1790), 16:92–93; 18:79, 267, 393. On the Mirabeau case, see Pierre Dominique, *Mirabeau* (Paris: Flammarion, 1947), and Louis de Loménie, *Les Mirabeau,* 5 vols. (Paris: Dentu, 1889), vol. 3, chap. 9.

her abusive newlywed husband because the latter insisted that she was seven months' pregnant, accused her of sleeping with all of their acquaintances, and was overheard swearing that he would drag her to Paris to sell her to an Englishman.[19] High-society cases sure to make waves were eagerly taken up by famous or fame-seeking barristers—Jacques-Vincent Delacroix was notorious, it seems, for producing mémoires in prominent cases whether or not he had been hired to do so.[20] A sensational marital case was the ideal arena for two famous lawyers to cross rapiers. In 1785 those two old nemeses Gerbier and Target squared off once again on opposite sides of the Bellanger case. Mme Bellanger, a young and pretty Parisienne, was trying to get rid of her husband even though the latter, a wealthy American, was allegedly much in love with her and showered her with presents. The *Mémoires secrets* sided with the husband and concluded that one would be wrong to look upon this case as a *cause particulière*: "It is the lawsuit of one sex against the other."[21]

The case of the comte de Sanois, which provoked an intense flurry of interest among the Parisian public in 1786, also took on the aspect of a war between the sexes, although it involved neither allegations of adultery nor sensational descriptions of domestic violence.[22] In the spring of 1785, Jean-François de La Motte-Geffrard, count of Sanois, plagued by severe financial and domestic problems, abandoned his family and ran off to Switzerland. His wife, daughter, and son-in-law had him arrested there by the French authorities, brought back to France, and imprisoned in the insane asylum of Charenton by virtue of a "sealed letter," or *lettre de cachet*. While Sanois struggled for his release from Charenton, which he obtained after nine months of confinement, his wife sued for a separation on the grounds of her husband's cruelty, insanity, and fraudulent bankruptcy and demanded restitution of 400,000 livres of their joint assets with which she claimed he had absconded. In 1787 Mme de Sanois's case against her husband was dismissed; contemporary newspapers reported that the outcome of the case owed every-

19. *Gazette des tribunaux* 1777, vól. 4.

20. *Mémoires secrets* 33:7. According to this gossip-sheet, Delacroix had written an unsolicited brief for the marquise de Cabris; the latter was understandably furious, since she had engaged the prominent Bordelais barrister Raymond de Sèze (who later defended Louis XVI before the Constituent Assembly) as her only lawyer.

21. Métra, *Correspondance secrète* 18:79–80, 267.

22. The following account of the case is based on the synopsis in the *Mémoires secrets* 32:199–200, as well as on the judicial mémoires analyzed below.

thing to the acclaimed mémoires written for Sanois by the lawyer Pierre-Louis de Lacretelle.[23]

Lacretelle was thirty-five years old at the time of the case. He had arrived in Paris eight years earlier from his native Metz, having already made a name for himself there by publishing mémoires noted for their skill and literary merit. In the mid-1770s the *Gazette des tribunaux* gave warm reviews to the briefs he wrote in his early cases, offering the accurate prognosis that "this young orator has every reason to aspire to a solid reputation in the noble career of the bar."[24] In Paris, Lacretelle was immediately admitted to the ranks of the Order of Barristers. Although there is no reason to doubt the sincerity of his liberal and reformist convictions, it also seems clear that this scion of the legal profession (his father and brother were lawyers too) was a shrewd careerist, a man skilled at making the right moves and getting to know the right people.[25]

In his thirties Lacretelle became a member of the prestigious and well-connected group of intellectuals interested in judicial reform whom we encountered in the preceding chapter. (He was some fifteen years younger than the elder statesmen of the group, such as Servan and Target, the same age as Bergasse, a few years older than Brissot and Robespierre.) He dutifully turned out well-received essays analyzing the causes of crimes and denouncing the complexity of the legal system. In 1784 he won the first prize in an essay contest organized by the Academy of Metz for his *Discours sur le préjugé des peines infâmantes,* narrowly besting the runner-up, Maximilien de Robespierre. In the capital Lacretelle moved in high circles, as he pursued connections and a secondary career in the world of letters. His friends were young writers like Jean-Baptiste Suard and Dominique-Joseph Garat, and as his fame increased he rubbed shoulders with the likes of d'Alembert, Marmontel, Condorcet, and La Harpe and helped edit the literary journal *Le Mercure de France.* The late 1780s found Lacretelle churning out pamphlets about judicial and administrative reform. In 1789 he was chosen by La-

23. For a convenient summary of the newspaper reporting on the case, see the appendix to *Compte des recettes et dépenses de l'administration du comte de Sanois* (Geneva, 1787), pp. 93–115; see also Pierre-Louis de Lacretelle, *Oeuvres,* 6 vols. (Paris, 1823–24), 1:viii-ix.

24. *Gazette des tribunaux* 1775, vol. 5; see also 1776, vol. 8.

25. See the articles on Lacretelle in Louis Michaud, *Biographie universelle ancienne et moderne* (Paris, 1877), vol. 22; Ferdinand Hoefer, *Nouvelle biographie universelle* (Paris, 1852–1866), vol. 28.

fayette to serve on a committee charged with drafting a new system of political justice. Although Lacretelle was elected to the Legislative Assembly in 1791, his political beliefs as a member of the Feuillant group kept him to the right of the rising Girondin group; he was proscribed and went into hiding after the fall of the monarchy, not to return until after Thermidor.[26]

In Lacretelle, then, Sanois found a talented and ambitious champion who made his client into a martyr and the case into a political crusade. The single most important publication to come out of the case was the first brief written by Lacretelle, published in July of 1786.[27] The *Gazette de Leyde* gave it an enthusiastic review, praising its "order and method," its "warmth and energy," and predicting that readers would find it riveting from the very first pages; the review also stressed that the mémoire belonged among the most significant publications of its kind in that it transcended its specific purpose to raise issues of general importance (this being increasingly, as we have seen, the mark of an important mémoire).[28] Lacretelle's brief for Sanois captured the attention of readers and reviewers by playing to their interests and expectations in three respects. First, Lacretelle made full use of the literary potential of his story by combining strong melodrama with Rousseauean confessional autobiography. Second, Sanois's tale raised issues of gender and power, which, for the reasons described earlier in this chapter, had special resonance at this historical juncture. Finally, this two-hundred-page text connected the problems of a private family with a burning public issue, the use of lettres de cachet, which itself symbolized the excesses of arbitrary government. The success of Lacretelle's defense, in short, came from the unprecedentedly explicit and compelling way in which it linked a private affair to important public matters.

When Lacretelle sat down to write his first trial brief for Sanois in 1786, he was very much under the sway of Rousseau's *Confessions,* which had been published posthumously four years earlier. What he produced, however, was not the conventional first-person mémoire, but

26. Lacretelle's prerevolutionary writings include *De la Convocation prochaine des Etats-Généraux en France* (n.p., 1788) and *Projet de cahier pour le Tiers-Etat du bailliage et du vicomté de Paris* (n.p., 1789). For details on his career under the Revolution, see Barry Shapiro, "Revolutionary Justice in Paris, 1789–1790" (Ph.D. diss., University of California, Los Angeles, 1988).

27. Pierre-Louis de Lacretelle, *Mémoire pour le comte de Sanois ancien aide-major des gardes-françaises* (Paris, 1786).

28. *Gazette de Leyde,* 28 July 1776.

a more complex layering of voices: his own third-person narrative based, he claimed, on memoirs—in the other sense of the term—written by Sanois himself. Although the readers were not given direct access to the memoirs, they were repeatedly reminded, in tones reminiscent of Rousseau, that displaying one's life in writing was an automatic proof of virtue. The memoirs that Sanois had written to justify himself were, according to his lawyer, "an exact record of the misfortunes he suffers, of everything that occupies his mind and stirs his soul. Crime has not yet availed itself of this sort of defense, for every line would create impediments, and it could betray itself in a single page; but [such a defense] is perfectly suited to virtue, which has nothing to hide, wants to tell all, and opens up a whole life to illuminate a single fact."[29]

Rousseauean references occur throughout the text. It was convenient, of course, that Sanois had fled to Lausanne in search of "morals closer to those of his own heart," since thanks to Jean-Jacques the Swiss Alps came in useful for locating a person on the high moral ground.[30] There were sentences taken almost verbatim from Rousseau ("He tells the good and the bad about his enemies as about himself") and several dramatic encounters with the Supreme Being: "Then I will appear before the fearsome tribunal of the being who creates and avenges, and will address to him my justification in the sincerity of my heart."[31]

The *Mémoire pour le comte de Sanois* might not have created such a stir, however, had it simply sought to establish Sanois's innocence by lacing the account of his life with Rousseauean references. In a significant stylistic innovation, Lacretelle produced for his client not just a sentimental biography but a "framed" narrative whose "authenticity" was established by the lawyer as first-person narrator and as reader. In the first pages of the mémoire the reader is introduced not to Sanois but to Lacretelle himself, who, in the manner of a Sherlock Holmes or a Sam Spade, is sitting at his desk minding his own business when a haggard-looking stranger bursts in on him. While the lawyer-detective notes some telltale signs (a face drawn by distress and illness rather than old age, shabby but decent clothes, the ribbon of the order of Saint-Louis), the man at first refuses to disclose his name with the gloomy

29. Lacretelle, *Mémoire pour le comte de Sanois*, p. 11.
30. Ibid., p. 38.
31. Ibid., pp. 11, 73.

prognosis that "it would not be known to you, or if it were it would be through the calumnies of which I am a victim."[32]

There ensues a vivid dialogue between the lawyer and his future client, in the course of which an outline of Sanois's story emerges and Lacretelle's initial wariness turns to indignation. "Monsieur," exclaims the lawyer, "everything about your story amazes me; it is a continual reversal of natural feelings and of the rules of common behavior. How can the authorities, at last enlightened . . ." "The authorities, Sir," interrupts the stranger, "have the means for arresting citizens everywhere. They have no forms by which to judge them."[33] Sanois eventually leaves the lawyer two fat volumes of his autobiography, which Lacretelle proceeds to read and then to summarize for the benefit of his own readers.

At least one of those readers, Sanois's son-in-law the count of Courcy, accused of aiding in the conspiracy against his wife's father, scathingly dismissed the mémoire's opening gambit. "I am not speaking," he fumed, "of the dialogue that M. de Lacretelle places at the beginning of his work, in which he seems to suppose that the gradual impression that M. de Sanois makes upon him will be an argument or an object of interest to his readers. It seems to me that, in this respect, there is no lawyer who cannot in the same way substitute persuasion for reason; and if I were examining M. de Lacretelle's brief as a critic, I would add that this new form of dialoguing with one's client is merely insipid and bizarre."[34] But less-partisan reviewers, like the one in the *Gazette de Leyde,* praised the opening of the brief as artful and dramatic, worthy of engaging the attention of readers.[35]

In complaining that the lawyer had substituted "persuasion for reason," Courcy was, of course, going against the grain of his time. As we have seen in previous chapters, the recourse to drama for the purpose of persuading readers by playing upon their emotions was increasingly counted as the mark of a superior, successful mémoire. The premise behind this strategy was explicitly Lockean; even a conservative barrister like Pierre-Louis Gin could argue in his handbook on eloquence that sensations, classified, compared, and judged by mental faculties, formed

---

32. Ibid., pp. 4–5.
33. Ibid., p. 8.
34. De Courcy, *Réponse du comte de Courcy à M. le comte de Sanois et à M. de La Cretelle son défenseur* (Paris, n.d.), p. 10.
35. *Gazette de Leyde,* 28 July 1786.

the basis of all knowledge.[36] Lacretelle, however, took this strategy one step further. Casting himself in the role of impartial reader rather than writer, he heightened the effect of his account by anticipating and echoing his readers' reactions: "I cannot give a better idea of the case I am about to defend," he wrote, "prepare for the impression it must create, than by retracing the ideas, the impressions, which I received myself."[37] Never had sensationalism been better pressed into the service of forensic argument.

The story thus set up to arouse the emotions of readers was predictably one of clear moral dichotomies, of complete innocence hounded by utter evil in the persons of Sanois's "unnatural" wife, daughter, and son-in-law, and the officials they persuaded to carry out their wishes. The contrast between the count's probity and the miseries he endures is stressed throughout the text in tones of unrelenting hyperbole. Watching Sanois sucked into the vortex of betrayal and persecution set in motion by his evil relatives, "one is equally struck," wrote Lacretelle, "by the excess of innocence and the excess of calumny."[38] Indeed, the style of Lacretelle's brief is pervaded by the quintessential "mode of excess," melodrama. Under Sanois's pen, the count's life became one framed by "I know not what touching mixture of virtue and crime."[39]

The didactic and political uses of melodrama in the *mémoires judiciaires* of the prerevolutionary period have been discussed in previous chapters and need not detain us here. It is worth noting, however, that Lacretelle either was, or was soon to become, highly self-conscious about two sorts of connections, that between private woes and public issues, and that between the courtroom and the stage. In 1802, he published a melodramatic play—he called it a *roman théâtral*—for which he borrowed the title of Diderot's most famous *drame, Le Fils naturel.*[40] The play is set in 1776, at the time of Louis XVI's dismissal of his two "enlightened" ministers Malesherbes and Turgot, and it rather awkwardly combines this political backdrop with romantic and familial crises.

The play has not one but two heroes, Gourville and Malherbe, mod-

36. Pierre-Louis Gin, *De l'Eloquence du barreau* (Paris, 1767), p. 33.
37. Lacretelle, *Mémoire pour le comte de Sanois*, p. 3.
38. Ibid., p. 104.
39. Ibid., p. 101.
40. "Le Fils naturel," in Lacretelle, *Oeuvres* 1:6–225.

eled respectively on Beaumarchais and d'Alembert. Both face persecution at the hands of a thoroughly corrupt court grandee, the cardinal de Granville, for their opposition to the ministers' dismissal. At the core of the impossibly complex plot is the love between Malherbe and the countess de Lussan (modeled on Julie de Lespinasse), who is being coerced into a marriage with the marquis de Lusigny. Malherbe discovers in the course of the play that he is in fact the illegitimate older brother of the marquis, but renounces his claim to the family fortune in return for the hand of Mlle de Lussan. At different junctures both the two heroes and the young countess are threatened with lettres de cachet, but the courtier Granville's evil designs are foiled by Gourville's cleverness. The play ends with Malherbe's emotion on finding his biological mother (modeled on Mme de Tencin), while adopting as his parents the virtuous middle-class couple who raised him—all of this punctuated with such exclamations as "mon digne père!" "mon excellente mère!" "ô mère adorable!" "mon fils, mon bien-aimé!"

Lacretelle's later play drew on the themes and characters of the Old Regime to construct a plot that brought together, however clumsily, the administrative tyranny of the old monarchy with the romantic and familial ordeals of private persons. In his commentary on the play, the author pointed to lettres de cachet as the motor of the plot and as the central symbol of the dangerous confusion between familial and governmental authority characteristic of the Old Regime.[41] Equally important was the affinity he saw between courtroom and stage: "There are more relations than is usually supposed," he wrote, "between the famous events of the judicial realm and those which can inspire emotion on stage."[42] Lacretelle's friend the novelist Choderlos de Laclos presented the equation from the other side in his own comments on the play: "It is not only a theatrical event which the author puts before your eyes; it is a splendid judicial case which will be pleaded before you."[43] Many years after he made the Sanois case into narrative drama, Lacretelle produced a play that unfolded with all the complexity and bombast of an Old Regime *mémoire judiciaire*.

The women in Lacretelle's *Le Fils naturel* were conventionally goodhearted and virtuous. Such was not the case in the briefs the lawyer wrote for Sanois, which paint a picture of bitter marital conflict. At the

41. Ibid., 4:136.
42. Ibid., 4:iii.
43. Ibid., 4:22.

age of forty Sanois had agreed to a proper arranged marriage to a woman who, in Lacretelle's account at least, turned out to be an uneducated and shrewish social climber: "dissipated, prodigal, incapable of being happy in her own house or of being sought after in other people's, she was obliged to give herself over to an existence made up of the most senseless agitation." Mme de Sanois's frantic quest for social recognition forced her husband into the background of their lives to the point that guests who came to dinner had no idea that he was the master of the house.[44] Sanois's hopes for finding consolation in fatherhood were dashed when his only child, a daughter, grew up to be just as rude and snobbish as her mother, with whom she joined forces. (Naturally, Mme de Sanois's version of the story was very different, and Lacretelle underplayed the considerable financial reasons that prompted the count to hotfoot it to Switzerland.)[45]

Lacretelle summed up the chaos that reigned in the Sanois household as "despotism of the wife and servitude of the husband."[46] Against Mme de Sanois he invoked the laws of nature and society, which would have to be completely overturned, he wrote, "to grant to a wife those rights which only belong to a husband."[47] There was nothing particularly new, of course, to the suggestion that a "woman on top" was emblematic of social and cultural disorder.[48] But the Sanois case unfolded at a time when, as we saw in chapter 4, the conspicuousness of "public women" at court, and their alleged power over monarchs and ministers, had become a powerful symbol of political decay. In availing herself of a lettre de cachet to have her husband put away, Mme de Sanois had both violated the "sexual contract" that subordinated her to her husband and taken on the secret, arbitrary, coercive ways of absolutism; she had thus put herself in league with other dangerous "public women" such as Mme du Barry, Mme de La Motte, and Marie-Antoinette. When Lacretelle had Sanois declare, in a later mémoire, that his wife and daughter had used "credit, favors, and everything that human passion can dispense in order to silence the law and cause my ruin," readers would have recognized this as the familiar antithesis between the cor-

44. Lacretelle, *Mémoire pour le comte de Sanois,* pp. 30–31.

45. See Tronson du Coudray, *Mémoire pour la comtesse de Sanois, demanderesse en séparation de biens* (Paris: P. G. Simon, 1786).

46. Ibid., p. 31.

47. Ibid., p. 114.

48. See the classic essay by Natalie Davis, "Women on Top," in her *Society and Culture in Early Modern France* (Stanford: Stanford University Press, 1975), pp. 124–151.

rupt feminized behavior of the court and the healthy masculinity of the courtroom.[49]

The political message of Lacretelle's trial brief was thus inscribed in the sociosexual dynamics of the Sanois couple. The fact that a *woman* had availed herself of a lettre de cachet was not only a sign of disorder in the family and society but also a metaphor for political corruption. Within the usual categories of eighteenth-century liberal thought, archetypal feminine characteristics—subjectivity, unreason, passion, arbitrariness, devotion to private interests over the public good—were also, and not accidentally, traits characteristic of "despotic" or "tyrannical" governments. But Lacretelle also spelled out his political message explicitly in the last third of his mémoire, which is devoted to the history and uses of lettres de cachet, and which culminates in a profession of faith in legal and contractual government.

Lacretelle's preoccupation with arbitrary arrest and lettres de cachet certainly antedated his involvement in the Sanois case, for, as we have seen, he had been deeply involved long before 1786 in the campaign to reform France's judicial system. If the single most heinous aspects of the system in the eyes of reformers were arbitrariness and secrecy, lettres de cachet were the emblem of all of its vices. (As Roger Chartier has pointed out, lettres de cachet and mémoires represented, in late-eighteenth-century thought, two opposite poles of authority and justice: on the one hand, a secret and arbitrary procedure, on the other hand, an open, public appeal to reason and law.)[50] Whatever Lacretelle's convictions, there was surely some opportunism to his choice of the theme of arbitrary arrest and detention: Robert Darnton has discovered that the best-selling works of the 1780s included, near the top of every list, the count of Mirabeau's daring polemic, *Des Lettres de cachet et des prisons d'état* (1782), and the irrepressible Linguet's sensational account of his stay in the Bastille, *Mémoires sur la Bastille* (1783).[51] Both authors had recently experienced arbitrary imprisonment firsthand. Mirabeau's work was a lengthy denunciation of "tyrannical" government, based on the usual appeals to natural law (the author stressed particularly the nat-

49. Pierre-Louis de Lacretelle, *Supplément au mémoire du comte de Sanois* (Paris, 1786), p. 46.

50. Roger Chartier, *The Cultural Origins of the French Revolution,* trans. Lydia Cochrane (Durham: Duke University Press, 1991), p. 35.

51. Robert Darnton, *The Literary Underground of the Old Regime* (Cambridge, Mass.: Harvard University Press, 1982), p. 139, and *Edition et sédition: L'Univers de la littérature clandestine au XVIIIe siècle* (Paris: Gallimard, 1991), pp. 47, 54–55, 103, 146.

ural right to property of one's person). Linguet's exposé of the horrible conditions in which prisoners like himself were kept in the dark and insalubrious towers of the Bastille was shorter, more provocative, and equally successful.[52]

Given the success of these precedents, it is not surprising that Lacretelle seized upon the Sanois case in order to produce his own work on the model of those by Mirabeau and Linguet. Like those two works, the lawyer's brief included a horrific account of prison conditions, in a series of letters from Sanois to his family and to public officials describing illness, filth, sadistic jailers, and mental torment so unbearable as to drive the count to attempt suicide.[53] Like Mirabeau, Lacretelle moved from this account of prison conditions to a general discussion of the history and uses of lettres de cachet culminating in a profession of faith in lawful contractual government. While the use of arbitrary arrest originated in Louis XIV's forcible pacification of the realm, such a practice flew in the face of the "true principles" of civil society in general and of the French "constitution" in particular. Since society was based on the combination of wills whence emerged the law, every punishment of offenders "must be written into Law and inflicted by the Law." Any exception to this principle was an implicit attack on society. To those who might object on the grounds of monarchical prerogative, Lacretelle answered that, although monarchies might have their origins in usurpation, their survival (unlike that of despotic governments) was implicitly based on popular consent: "It is base flattery to have [monarchy] descend from heaven," he wrote; "it has a truer and equally noble sanction in the consent of the people."[54]

Lacretelle must surely have had Mirabeau's and Linguet's best-selling works in mind when he composed the latter half of his brief for Sanois. He also cited by name another source, Claude Mey and Nicolas Maultrot's *Maximes du droit public français* of 1772, which we have already

52. Gabriel-Honoré de Riquetti, count of Mirabeau, *Des Lettres de cachet et des prisons d'état* (1782), in Mirabeau, *Oeuvres,* 8 vols. (Paris, 1834–1835), vol. 7; Simon-Nicolas-Henri Linguet, *Mémoires sur la Bastille* (London, 1783); for an analysis of the latter, see Darline Gay Levy, *The Ideas and Careers of Simon-Nicolas-Henri Linguet: A Study in Eighteenth-Century French Politics* (Urbana: University of Illinois Press, 1980), pp. 207–209. For a general discussion of these and other contemporary texts on the Bastille, see Hans-Jürgen Lüsebrink and Rolf Reichardt, "La Bastille dans l'imaginaire social de la France à la fin du XVIIIe siècle, 1774–1789," *Revue d'histoire moderne et contemporaine* 30 (1983): 196–223.

53. Lacretelle, *Mémoire pour le comte de Sanois,* pp. 65–89.

54. Ibid., pp. 144f., 155, 164.

encountered as one of the most important and influential pieces of political writing to come out of the Maupeou crisis.[55] Basing their arguments on contractual theories, the authors, both *avocats au parlement,* argued not only for the parlements' immemorial right to represent the nation's wishes but also, and more radically, for the sovereignty of the nation itself over its monarchical rulers; the authors argued this while denouncing, in the strongest of terms, ministerial and royal "despotism."[56] Their treatise included a long section analyzing the use of lettres de cachet as one of the most egregious manifestations of "despotism." It concluded with the incendiary statement that "the Prince must therefore never forget that the Throne and the Law have the same source; that government has no other object, no other end, than to preserve for men the advantages which they sought to secure by making themselves subjects and citizens."[57] Lacretelle had thus reworked, at the end of his mémoire, a long and arid chunk of Mey and Maultrot's *Maximes*—one of the period's most famous manifestos of oppositional politics—into the conclusion of a private tale of marital breakdown and betrayal.

Published a mere three years before the Revolution, Lacretelle's *Mémoire pour le comte de Sanois* reflected, both in style and in content, the ultimate evolution of the cause célèbre brief into a vehicle for political instruction and persuasion. In its style, Lacretelle's mémoire made use of the melodramatic conventions of the genre, including sharp moral dichotomies, hyperbolic sentimentality, and lavish use of exclamation. These recently minted conventions were embedded, however, within the intimacy of a confessional first-person narrative, or rather two narratives—that of the lawyer and that of his client. As in the contemporary briefs for Victoire Salmon and the Trois Roués, the most famous of the Sanois briefs cast its barrister-author in a leading role, in a fashion considered by contemporaries both innovative and controversial.

Just as Dupaty took on the Trois Roués case in order to publicize the need for judicial reform, Lacretelle made no secret of the broader implications of his interest in Sanois's fate. Near the beginning of his

55. Lacretelle, *Mémoire pour le comte de Sanois,* p. 138.

56. For analyses of the *Maximes* and other similar works, see Dale Van Kley, "The Jansenist Constitutional Legacy in the French Prerevolution," in Baker, ed., *The Political Culture of the Old Regime,* pp. 169–201; Durand Echeverria, *The Maupeou Revolution: A Study in the History of Libertarianism* (Baton Rouge: Louisiana State University Press, 1985), chap. 2.

57. Claude Mey and Nicolas Maultrot, *Maximes du droit public français,* 2 vols. (Amsterdam, 1775), 1:210.

brief he wrote that "any particular affair that leads to general considerations, that is suited to becoming a great object of public attention, must be considered a great event"; he later stressed the point again: "This case is not an ordinary case; it must be made to serve the public interest; it uncovers a danger that threatens all citizens; it warns of the need to address it; it incriminates the established order of things, rather than the conduct of men."[58] In the 1770s, the impact of printed lawyers' briefs on contemporary public culture had been implicit in the form and function of such documents, but the link between a particular affair and the public life of the nation was rarely spelled out. The great mémoires of the 1780s, by contrast, made their points with vigorous explicitness, linking the fate of three paupers in prison to the iniquities of the judicial system, or the sufferings of a man imprisoned by lettre de cachet to the shocking survival of arbitrary arrest and imprisonment.

The Sanois case was unlike the Trois Roués and Salmon cases, however, in that it linked public issues to the private turmoil of a family whose social station was close to that of most readers of mémoires. Lettres de cachet were, after all, a form of justice employed by families against their own members, but whose use was ratified and enforced by a father-king.[59] In the Sanois case, the pernicious effects of private justice were highlighted by the fact that it was a wife, aided by a daughter and a son-in-law, who availed herself of a lettre de cachet against the head of the household. The Sanois case was transformed by Lacretelle into a parable about the evils of arbitrary authority, of a system that contradicted the laws of nature by allowing a wife to break the "sexual contract" that was the bedrock of family and society. But there were other, more banal forms of female misconduct that could endanger the family and the state. In the years immediately preceding the Revolution, readers of trial briefs in the Kornmann case were to learn of the ways in which socially sanctioned female infidelity could rend asunder a family while it exposed the corruption of high society and government.

Female adultery lies at the heart of many of the oldest and most powerful myths and fictions in Western culture. Male adultery, a banal and implicitly acceptable sin, has usually caused no great social tensions and

---

58. Lacretelle, *Mémoire pour le comte de Sanois,* pp. 15, 65.
59. See Arlette Farge and Michel Foucault, *Le Désordre des familles: Lettres de cachet des archives de la Bastille au XVIIIe siècle* (Paris: Gallimard, 1982).

therefore spawned no great myths. But as Tony Tanner observes, the most famous stories of female adultery draw their power from the link between sexual transgression and sociopolitical chaos. It is Helen's infidelity that precipitates the carnage of the Trojan wars, just as the love of Tristan and Isolde undermines the authority of King Mark, and the passion between Launcelot and Guenevere destroys the society of the Round Table.[60] The Kornmann case of 1787–1789, a tale of female infidelity, similarly connected the seduction of a married woman to the corruption of the political sphere.

In late-eighteenth-century France adultery was usually perceived as a problem relating to social class rather than to political stability. Habitual infidelity on the part of both spouses, whatever its actual incidence in society, was considered characteristic of the habits of the wealthy, mostly aristocratic elite (and not just in France, as William Hogarth's famous series of prints, *Marriage à la Mode,* shows). To critics writing at the end of the Old Regime, such as Jérôme Pétion in his *Essai sur le mariage* of 1785, the problem resided less in adulterous behavior per se than in the way it was considered a normal, almost necessary feature of the way of life of the libertine upper classes. Pétion brusquely dismisses the refinements of upper-class love-games, "gallant formulas, tender concern, elaborate attentions, languorous sighs, delicate and exaggerated expressions of feeling," as "a seductive jargon designed to embellish our vices and failings."[61] In Pétion's account, as in Hogarth's prints, fashionable spouses are torn apart, sucked into their separate pursuits of vapid gallantry and sexual conquest. Those who set the tone for this frantic pursuit of social and sexual pleasure are *les grands,* the high and mighty, whose vices are eagerly imitated by their inferiors.[62] Similar ideas are hammered out by Jacques Le Scène in his *Contrat conjugal* of 1781. Once again, the customs and manners indicted are those of the aristocracy. Young girls locked up in convents are only too eager to throw themselves into the first marriage their parents arrange, and the estranged spouses soon take their pleasure separately, outside of the conjugal bed: "The husband carries seduction and trouble into his neighbor's marriage, and his wife, freed by this desertion and encouraged by

60. Tony Tanner, *Adultery in the Novel: Contract and Transgression* (Baltimore: Johns Hopkins University Press, 1979), pp. 27–37.

61. Pétion, *Essai sur le mariage,* p. 32.

62. Ibid., p. 40.

the example of other women, gives her husband as many successors as her ambition, interest, and temperament dictate."[63] These are, of course, the fashionable vices of high society, Le Scène continues, but an inevitable process of social mimesis spreads them abroad like a plague that will infect the entire social order.[64] Le Scène's brutal summary of upper-class sexual ethics—"On se quitte sans regret comme on s'était pris sans amour"—echoes a phrase in that archetypal libertine tract, *La Nuit et le moment,* by Crébillon fils: "Comme on s'est pris sans s'aimer, on se sépare sans se haïr."[65]

Tony Tanner interprets the preoccupation with marriage and adultery in the fiction of the later eighteenth and the nineteenth century as quintessentially bourgeois. In the century or so between *La Nouvelle Héloïse* and *Madame Bovary* or *Anna Karenina,* the conspicuousness in fiction of the figure of the adulterous wife reflected, he argues, a preoccupation with marriage as "the means by which bourgeois society attempts to bring into harmonious alignment patterns of passion and patterns of property."[66] It is certainly the case that enlightened French writers of the late eighteenth century, barristers among them, wrote of marriage as a contract and of adultery as a form of theft. Lacretelle himself published in 1779 a short treatise, *The Elementary Principles of Covenants,* in which he characterized marriage as "a sort of sharing of oneself" whereby the spouses gave themselves to one another under conditions "that can be likened to a price."[67] But although marriage was commonly viewed as a reciprocal contract in texts of this sort, only female adultery was discussed as a violation of marital property.

The lawyer Jean-François Fournel, one of Victoire Salmon's defenders, disagreed with many of his contemporaries in arguing *against* divorce in his *Traité de l'adultère* of 1778. Nonetheless, his arguments for marital indissolubility were not religious but legal and contractual, as was his condemnation of adultery: "Adultery is a theft committed against the husband, an injury to the exclusive enjoyment solemnly sworn over to him, and for which he pays by acquitting himself of the duties attached to marital indissolubility." A husband's prerogatives included not only the possession of his wife's person, but also the

63. Le Scène, *Contrat conjugal,* pp. 47–48.
64. Ibid., pp. 48–49.
65. Ibid., p. 48; Claude-Prosper Jolyon de Crébillon, fils, *La Nuit et le moment* (Paris: Desjonquières, 1983), p. 25.
66. Tanner, *Adultery in the Novel,* p. 15.
67. Lacretelle, *Oeuvres* 1:347–427; quotes pp. 358–359.

right "to occupy her heart, to be the object of her attentions, of her fears . . . to direct her ideas, govern her mind, master her will"—all of these were the husband's possession (*jouissance*), of which adultery deprived him.[68]

Arguments against adultery can no doubt be termed bourgeois, first, in that the arguments against infidelity were usually couched in a discourse of property rather than honor, and second, in that they took the form of a repudiation of patterns of behavior perceived as characteristic of the libertine aristocracy. (It should be noted, however, that Enlightenment writers typically avoided using terms such as "nobility" or "aristocracy" in this context, preferring vaguer labels, such as *le grand monde* or *les grands*, which evoked wealth and power irrespective of lineage.) Tanner is no doubt correct in arguing that it is only when marriage "is felt to be the central contract upon which all others in some way depend that adultery becomes not an incidental deviance from the social structure, but a frontal attack on it."[69] But this leaves open the question as to whether contractual thought expressed a class interest (the bourgeoisie's investment in private property rather than lineage) or the most powerful ideological alternative to divine-right monarchy. It is interesting to note that the authors of the two treatises we have been discussing both went on to have active political careers in the Revolution: Pétion is familiar to students of the Revolution as the mayor of revolutionary Paris and a leading figure in the Girondin group; Le Scène served as district judge and commissioner to the provinces under the Constituent Assembly.

In the end, it is probably best to avoid drawing too sharp a line between the social and the political in prerevolutionary discourse—even, or especially, where matters of "private" life are concerned. Fashionable sexual dalliance of the sort denounced by Pétion and Le Scène was considered heinous, neither for strictly social nor for strictly political reasons, but because as a form of culture it cemented the fortress of a closed and powerful oligarchy. The case against adultery was not, after all, that it broke couples apart; as we have seen, the writers who denounced infidelity à la mode were the very same who argued passionately for divorce. The problem with adultery as practiced in high society was not that it ruined marriages, but that, on the contrary, it was al-

---

68. Jean-François Fournel, *Traité de l'adultère considéré dans l'ordre judiciaire* (Paris, 1778), p. 275–277.
69. Tanner, *Adultery in the Novel,* p. 17.

lowed to coexist with marriage, generating social and sexual situations ambiguous in the extreme.

As literary critics have long argued, the essence of eighteenth-century French libertinism was less moral depravity than linguistic hermeticism.[70] Anyone who has read *Les Liaisons dangereuses* will know that the name of the game for the true libertine was not only sexual conquest but also, and more important perhaps, the skillful manipulation of codes of language and behavior accessible only to insiders. Deceit, coded words, double and triple meanings—these were not signs of the "decay" of the French upper classes, but weapons crucial to their survival. Adultery—not of the passionate but of the cool and calculated variety—was singled out by critics as a powerful metaphor for the culture of the upper classes, a hermetic, elitist culture ruled by unspoken convention rather than explicit contractual agreement. Adultery was tolerable within a subculture in which marriages were entered into for the sake of fortune and family name and in which spouses were allowed to lead separate lives once they had fulfilled their procreative duties; in fact, casual promiscuity might even serve a constructive function in such a world, in that it reinforced the bonds between the members of a small ruling elite.

Marital infidelity, as practiced routinely by the upper classes, was much more than just a matter of personal morality. It was a matter of culture as translated into style—the social, sexual, and linguistic style that marked the ruling elites off from the rest of the nation; and style was, at this historical juncture, an important vehicle for ideology. The question of adultery is central to what were arguably the two most successful works of fiction of the later eighteenth century: Rousseau's *La Nouvelle Héloïse* (1761) and Beaumarchais's *Marriage of Figaro,* first performed in 1784. Since the warring sides in the Kornmann case were identified respectively with Rousseau and with Beaumarchais, an examination of the treatment of adultery in the novel and the play will help illuminate the moral and political issues at stake in the last great cause célèbre of the Old Regime.

Rousseau's *Julie ou la Nouvelle Héloïse,* an updated version of the story of Héloïse and Abélard set in the Swiss countryside, was the unri-

---

70. See, for instance, Peter Brooks, *The Novel of Worldliness: Crébillon, Marivaux, Laclos, Stendhal* (Princeton: Princeton University Press, 1969); Bernadette Fort, *Le Langage de l'ambiguïté dans l'oeuvre de Crébillon fils* (Paris: Klincksieck, 1978); Philip Stewart, *Le Masque et la parole: Le langage de l'amour au XVIIIe siècle* (Paris: J. Corti, 1973).

valed best-selling novel of prerevolutionary France. Not only was the response to the novel remarkable for its breadth—at least seventy editions were published before 1800—the work was also extraordinary for the reactions it provoked among readers, many of whom wrote to Rousseau describing the upheaval it created in their lives.[71] The story that struck so deep a chord among readers centered on the illicit passion between Julie d'Etange, the daughter of a country squire, and her penniless tutor, Saint-Preux. The subject of adultery comes up about halfway through the novel, as Julie, having been forced to give up her lover, is browbeaten into marrying the benign but cold-blooded M. de Wolmar, who once saved her father's life. While Julie awaits with dread her marriage to Wolmar, she continues to correspond with Saint-Preux, who has immersed himself in the social whirl of Paris in an attempt to forget his beloved.

The lengthy letter eighteen of part three, from Julie to Saint-Preux, is a turning point in the novel. In it, Julie evokes the history of their shared passion and explains why she felt it her duty to give in to her father's entreaties that she marry Wolmar; she describes her anguish as the marriage approaches, including desperate thoughts of betraying her new husband by continuing her relations with Saint-Preux. "My heart was so corrupted that my reason could not resist the language of your philosophes. Horrors, whose idea had never before defiled my mind, dared to approach it."[72] It is the marriage ceremony itself that reawakens the young woman's slumbering conscience. The solemnity of the occasion, the liturgy, and the very words of the Scripture deeply affect her: "An unknown power seemed suddenly to set aright the disorder of my feelings and to restore them in accord with the law of duty and of nature."[73] There follows an indignant rejection of adultery, which is also a response to the last letter she has received from Saint-Preux.

71. On the popularity of *La Nouvelle Héloïse,* see Daniel Mornet, *Les Origines intellectuelles de la révolution française* (Paris: Armand Colin, 1933), and the Introduction to Mornet's edition of *La Nouvelle Héloïse* (Paris, 1925). For a recent treatment of this subject, see "Readers Respond to Rousseau: The Fabrication of Romantic Sensitivity," in his *The Great Cat Massacre and Other Episodes in French Cultural History* (New York: Basic Books, 1984), pp. 215–256. The most recent synthesis on the subject of responses to Rousseau's work, Claude Labrosse, *Lire au XVIIIe siècle: La Nouvelle Héloïse et ses lecteurs* (Lyon: Presses Universitaires de Lyon, 1985), is disappointingly arcane.

72. Jean-Jacques Rousseau, *Julie ou la nouvelle Héloïse* (Paris: Garnier-Flammarion, 1967), p. 259. (The translations of Rousseau's novel are mine.)

73. Ibid., p. 260.

Saint-Preux's letter is written under the shock of the news of Julie's imminent marriage. His mind addled both by despair and by his recent exposure to Parisian society, he ventures to suggest that the scruples they share are merely naive and provincial: "What! shall we be better moralists than the crowds of wise men that people Paris and London, all of whom scoff at conjugal fidelity and look upon adultery as game?"[74] A secretly betrayed husband cannot suffer from that which he does not know, Saint-Preux continues, he may in fact live all the more happily as the beneficiary of the kindnesses bestowed on him by his guilty wife, "and this alleged crime, of which so much is made, is but one more link in society."[75] Julie's response to this train of thought is properly withering. This is no serious argument, she replies, but "an absurd and brutal joke which deserves only scorn and anger for an answer."[76] Her sharp retort focuses on Saint-Preux's suggestion that adultery can be considered "one more link in society." Saint-Preux's use of the term "society" is symptomatic of his temporary loss of moral standards, since by it he obviously means high society (and Julie's scornful references to *vos philosophes* are a reminder that the bulk of the novel was written just after Rousseau's break with the worldly coterie around the *Encyclopédie*).

Significantly, Julie answers his argument not only by describing her own moral reawakening to the beauty and truth of religion, but also with reference to her understanding of the broader social meaning of the marriage vow. The marriage pact concerns more than the spouses, she argues, it is a commitment that implicitly involves all of society through those who bear witness to it. Hence, adultery undermines the very foundations of society (in the general, nonelitist sense), for without marriage "nothing can survive of the legitimate order of human affairs."[77] As for the "reasoners" whose authority Saint-Preux invoked, Julie accuses them of wanting to destroy all of human society, which rests "on the faith placed in covenants"; and she concludes with a blistering denunciation of the corrupt social elite: "If any society results from this vile and contemptible commerce, it is similar to that of brigands, which must be destroyed and annihilated in order to ensure the

74. Ibid., p. 247.
75. Ibid., p. 248.
76. Ibid., p. 266.
77. Ibid., p. 265.

survival of legitimate societies."[78] In the exchange between Saint-Preux and Julie, then, we see the struggle (in this case, only momentary) between two different views of the effects of adultery, one of which sees it as conjunctive, the other as profoundly disjunctive.[79] Saint-Preux is speaking the language of the salon, Julie that of the social contract. By the 1780s, for most prominent intellectuals, the latter system of values had replaced—in theory, at least—the former.

Beaumarchais's problems in the 1780s came in some measure from his refusal to let go of precisely the language and culture evoked by Saint-Preux. No legend is more tenacious than that of Beaumarchais's radicalism, and of the prophetic subversiveness of his most famous play, *The Marriage of Figaro;* the evidence for this view comes from the play's popular success, from its barbs against censorship, the Bastille, and the privilege of noble birth, and from apocryphal comments, such as Louis XVI's alleged remark that if the play were performed, the Bastille would have to come down. As we saw in chapter 4, however, Beaumarchais's outlook was less that of the outcast rebel than that of the consummate social climber, and his apparent anger at the status quo was most often impatience with those obstacles that stood in the way of his own quest of fame and fortune.[80]

It is true, however, that Beaumarchais had the temperament of an adventurer ("Intrigue and money—you are in your element now!" says Suzanne to Figaro in the play);[81] in the years since the Goezman case he had worked as a secret agent for the French monarchy, negotiating with Grub Street pamphleteers in London to prevent the publication of libels against the French court and running guns for the American rebels. Before 1784, however, Beaumarchais's career as playwright had never gone as well as had his cloak-and-dagger ventures. His two *drames* of the 1760s, *Eugénie* and *Les Deux Amis,* were unsuccessful (it is telling that Beaumarchais never quite mastered the language of *sensibilité*), and his comedy *The Barber of Seville* only succeeded in

78. Ibid., p. 266.

79. Tanner, *Adultery in the Novel,* p. 166.

80. The events preceding and surrounding the first performance of the *Marriage of Figaro* are given pride of place in the many biographies of the writer; for titles of the best accounts of Beaumarchais's life, see chap. 3, supra, n. 58.

81. Pierre-Augustin Caron de Beaumarchais, *Théâtre* (Paris: Garnier, 1964), p. 182. The translation used here is by John Wood, *The Barber of Seville and the Marriage of Figaro* (London: Penguin Books, 1964), p. 109.

1775 after having been rewritten several times and having flopped at its first performance.

Beaumarchais's most famous play, *La Folle journée ou le mariage de Figaro* (its full title), was also by far his most successful. How Beaumarchais won his struggle with the censors, how the play came to be performed—thanks to the patronage of *gens en place*—in April of 1784, and how the opening night drew throngs of avid spectators, are stories too familiar to bear retelling here.[82] As to the play's success with the theatergoing public, there can be no doubt: it enjoyed sixty-eight consecutive performances to packed houses, far outdistancing any previous theatrical success. What traditional accounts of the play's history often fail to mention, however, is that *The Marriage of Figaro* was greeted with deep hostility on the part of most contemporary critics. Louis-Sébastien Mercier's comments in his *Tableau de Paris* are typical of the prevailing judgment of the play. After tagging it "an imbroglio seasoned with quips [*traits*] borrowed left and right," Mercier evaluates the play thus: "It is neither gay nor interesting; mostly, it was inappropriate for the national theater in that it gives off an odor of moral corruption, which is the reason for its success."[83] Criticism came from all quarters, but emanated with special force from writers on the left of the political spectrum: from Mercier himself, a maverick critic of most prevailing institutions, but also those writers whom Robert Darnton has identified as the "Grub Street radicals" of the 1780s—future revolutionaries like Jean-Louis Carra and Antoine Gorsas.[84] Grub Street had no love for the "radical" Beaumarchais.

82. Most biographies of Beaumarchais devote much attention to the night of the premiere, which is traditionally considered the apex of Beaumarchais's career and life. See, for instance, Félix Gaiffe, *Le Mariage de Figaro* (Paris: Malfère, 1928); Claude Petitfrère, *Le Scandale du "Mariage de Figaro": Prélude à la Révolution française* (Paris: Editions Complexe, 1989), is a recent account, which places the controversy around the play in a broader historical context; for a description within the context of the history of Parisian theatrical institutions and customs, see John Lough, *Paris Theatre Audiences in the Seventeenth and Eighteenth Centuries* (Oxford: Oxford University Press, 1957), pp. 222–223.

83. Louis-Sébastien Mercier, *Le Tableau de Paris*, 30 vols. (Amsterdam, 1788), 9:100.

84. To my knowledge the first scholar to draw attention in a systematic fashion to the critical hostility that greeted the play was Robert Darnton in his doctoral thesis, "Trends in Radical Propaganda on the Eve of the French Revolution" (Oxford University, 1964), chap. 8, especially pp. 353–355. Darnton's account of the hostility between Beaumarchais and the radical writers of the "Kornmann group" is discussed below. Thomas Crow draws on Darnton's material to mount a persuasive argument about the role of these same radi-

Why did the likes of Mercier believe that the play, which we read as a pleasing blend of irreverent satire and frothy farce, reeked of "moral corruption"? The plot of the comedy is familiar, if only from Mozart's opera, which follows it closely. Figaro and Suzanne, the servants of a Spanish grandee, Count Almaviva, are about to get married when they learn of their master's intention to avail himself of "a certain right"—the right to Suzanne's virginity, the mythical *droit du seigneur.* The mainspring of the plot consists in Figaro's thwarting of his master's designs with the help of his fiancée and their mistress, the long-suffering countess. Along the way, Figaro recognizes his mother in the acerbic spinster Marceline, just as she is about to succeed in blackmailing him into marrying her. Relationships between the main characters are further complicated by the presence of the adolescent page boy, Chérubin, whose nascent and unfocused sexuality—symbolized by his very name—draws him to his godmother the countess, to Suzanne, and to the gardener's daughter Fanchette.

What is most remarkable about the contemporary commentary on the play is the extent to which it *failed* to pick up on those passages in which posterity was to see premonitions of the Revolution, such as Figaro's famous monologue in act five ("What did you do to deserve such advantages? You gave yourself the trouble of being born, nothing more"). One of the few favorable reviews of the play, in the *Correspondance littéraire,* did note Beaumarchais's audacity with respect to the morals of the upper classes and the way he dared "to speak with gaiety of ministers, of the Bastille, of the freedom of the press, of the police, and even of censors"; but the reviewer saw this as mainly a commentary on the author's own experiences.[85] Another critic, this one hostile, had only this to say about the famous monologue: that it was out of character, came too late in the play, and slowed down the action.[86] What contemporaries judged to be controversial about the play was not its politics but its morals—or the lack thereof.

What was most obviously "immoral" about *The Marriage of Figaro* was the fact that it revolved around the possibility of two adulteries,

---

cal critics as art critics in the mid-1780s; see Thomas Crow, *Painters and Public Life in Eighteenth-Century France* (New Haven: Yale University Press, 1985), pp. 220–229.

85. Melchior Grimm, *Correspondance littéraire* 13:521. The review was probably written by Jakob Heinrich Meister, who was the editor of the *Correspondance* in 1784.

86. Pierre-Jean-Baptiste Nougaret, *Coup d'oeil d'un arabe sur la littérature française, ou le barbier de Bagdad faisant la barbe au barbier de Séville Figaro* (Paris, 1786), pp. 157–158.

each scandalous in its own right. One critic, in a preview almost a year before the premiere, put it this way: "The countess is rather tempted to have a hand in the little page boy's education, the count has a great desire to make use of an ancient right which offends both decency and the sanctity of the conjugal tie."[87] By the end of the play, these infidelities are unconsummated, but also unresolved. "Tout finit par des chansons": there is nothing at the end to stop the count from setting his sights on Suzanne again, and the curtain comes down on the uncomfortable suggestion of a self-perpetuating *ménage à quatre—à cinq*, indeed, if one counts the ubiquitous Chérubin. In this household adultery could very well be, in Saint-Preux's words, "one more link in society." The critic in *L'Année littéraire* protested that since infidelity had become a major problem in society, treating adultery as the running joke of a comedy was in the worst of taste.[88] "Judging from the brilliant gloss you lay upon them," wrote another reviewer, addressing Beaumarchais, "indecency, debauchery, adultery, and even incest are no more than jokes, light social quirks that can be laughed at."[89]

Beyond the obvious salaciousness of the plot, there were deeper reasons for the hostility evinced by most critics, and they can be summed up in one word: ambiguity. Reviewers objected to the characters of Figaro and Suzanne, who seemed like throwbacks to the ingratiating trickster-servants of old-fashioned comedy. Far from challenging their employers directly—Figaro, of course, delivers his famous monologue in the *absence* of the count—this household of disgusting *valetaille* duped them behind their backs but behaved as lowly flatterers (*bas complaisants*) to their faces.[90] Beyond the demeanor of Figaro and Suzanne, critics waxed indignant at the ways in which all of the characters violated sexual and social boundaries. They professed shock at the elaborate game of disguises in the last act, especially at the scene in which the count comes close to raping his own wife, whom he takes for Suzanne. Worse still was the incestuous subplot, which brings Figaro close to

87. Grimm, *Correspondance littéraire* 13:323.

88. Cited in Gunnar Von Proschwitz, *Introduction à l'étude du vocabulaire de Beaumarchais* (Stockholm: Almqvist and Wiksell, 1956), p. 52.

89. Nougaret, *Coup d'oeil,* p. 168.

90. *Mémoires secrets* 25:257; Nougaret, *Coup d'oeil,* pp. 87–88. On the ambiguous status of both real and fictional servants, see Sarah Maza, *Servants and Masters in Eighteenth-Century France: The Uses of Loyalty* (Princeton: Princeton University Press, 1983), chaps. 3 and 5.

marrying his own mother—indeed, some reviewers took the scene as suggesting that Figaro had already gone to bed with Marceline.[91]

The two characters singled out by critics as most objectionable were the countess and Chérubin, and it was the relationship between these two that drew the heaviest fire. It is true that in Chérubin Beaumarchais assembled the most elaborate combination of social and sexual ambiguities imaginable in a single character: as a page boy he occupies a liminal position between the world of the servants and that of the masters; as a sexually precocious adolescent he wavers between childhood and adulthood; he yearns for the countess, who, as his godmother, is his surrogate parent. (Chérubin is the incarnation of polymorphous desire—he always appears in the wrong place at the wrong time.)[92] The young page's obvious androgyny is emphasized both by the plot and by contemporary theatrical convention: the character was played by a girl dressed as a boy—as it still is in Mozart's opera—and the plot demands that this "boy" be cross–cross-dressed as a girl.

Many contemporaries found this intolerable and denounced the character as "a young libertine dying to throw himself into debauchery" or, even more inaccurately, as "the wife's procurer and the husband's lover-boy" ("Greluchon de la femme et mignon du mari").[93] The scenes between the countess and her page seem to have carried intimations of mother-child incest or, more explicitly, of the sort of elegantly decadent lesbianism later hinted at in the Diamond Necklace mémoires and explicitly portrayed in the literature against Marie-Antoinette. In short, Beaumarchais, once a writer of *drames* and author of a treatise on the new theatrical genre, had turned away from the clear dichotomies of good and evil, the relentless classifying and labeling of melodrama, to roam about in the gray areas of sexuality, gender, morality, and social status. *That* was the real scandal of the play, not the liberal pieties mouthed by Figaro.

Finally, the single most systematic criticism leveled at the play concerned its style, which critics unanimously judged to be detestable. Métra's *Correspondance* called it an *imbroglio*, a complicated *salmigondi*,

---

91. Grimm, *Correspondance*, 13:520–521; *Mémoires secrets* 25:267; Nougaret, *Coup d'oeil*, p. 168.

92. This insight was suggested to me by Professor Martin Mueller.

93. Grimm, *Correspondance*, 13:520; *Mémoires secrets* 25:280; Nougaret, *Coup d'oeil*, pp. 86, 105.

"a most refined literary monstrosity."[94] The four-hour play was too long, its plot too complicated, its language an unseemly mixture of high sentiment and low farce. In the same way that the plot and characters of *Le Mariage* were criticized for their studied ambiguities, so its style was reviled as *équivoque, bâtard, amphibie*.[95] Critics were particularly incensed at the play's puns, witticisms, and indecent allusions. The reviewer for the *Correspondance littéraire* complained that the dialogue was "a constant pursuit of witticism; the only motive for a question is its answer."[96] Beaumarchais was dubbed a *retourneur de phrases* for his relentless pursuit of clever repartee—as in the very first scene when Suzanne asks her fiancé when he will stop telling her of his love "from morning to night," and Figaro responds: "When I can prove it to you from night until morning."[97]

Since many of Beaumarchais's witticisms have stood the test of time, it is at first difficult to understand why contemporary critics found his jokes and mildly risqué allusions so objectionable. The answer to this puzzle takes us back once again to Beaumarchais's biography, to the social circles in which he moved and learned his craft as a playwright. Métra's *Correspondance* correctly identified one of the sources of Beaumarchais's style as the *parade*, the lewd, pseudopopular playlets that became fashionable among the French upper classes in the mid eighteenth century.[98] As we have seen, Beaumarchais's very first plays were *parades* he wrote for the wealthy Guillaume Le Normand's circle at Etiolles.[99] Characteristics of the *parade* included obscene allusions, puns, and mangled proverbs. While all are present in *Le Mariage*, only one character in the play, the peasant Grippe-Soleil, speaks something resembling the "country" French in which the *parades* were usually written.

The paradox, then, is that some of the elements of Beaumarchais's style that critics found obscene were associated, not with the working classes, but with parodies of popular speech aimed at the upper classes.

---

94. Métra, *Correspondance* 13:174; see also *Mémoires secrets* 25:266; Antoine-Joseph Gorsas, *L'Ane promeneur ou Critès promené par son âne* (n.p., 1786), pp. 23–24.

95. Von Proschwitz, *Vocabulaire*, pp. 2–10, 43–44; *Mémoires secrets* 25:267; Grimm, *Correspondance* 13:324; Nougaret, *Coup d'oeil*, pp. 100–101; Gorsas, *L'Ane promeneur*, pp. 11, 23–24.

96. Grimm, *Correspondance* 13:324.

97. Act I, scene 1; Wood translation, p. 110.

98. Métra, *Correspondance* 16:174. For background information on the *parade* and its influence on early-eighteenth-century high culture, see Crow, *Painters and Public Life*, pp. 53–55, 70–74.

99. Besides the standard biographies, see Pierre-Augustin Caron de Beaumarchais, *Parades*, ed. Pierre Larthomas (Paris: S.E.D.E.S., 1977), Introduction.

But then, as we have seen in the context of the Goezman case, Beaumarchais was fluent in the language of the upper classes. Here again, the criticisms aimed at Beaumarchais are revealing—he was denounced for studding his play with puns, witticisms, and epigrams. Such terms as *trait, persiflage,* and *épigramme* convey a distinct flavor of worldliness; and indeed, the pursuit of the witty repartee or trenchant epigram had characterized upper-class salons since the heyday of the seventeenth-century *précieuses.*[100] Nor was the style of worldliness extinct in the 1780s. The ever-observant Mercier reported that the *style à la mode* "injects wit at every occasion" and "always aims for the epigram," and that the style in vogue at the court conscientiously shunned any hint of passion. He noted that *les grands* spoke their "own language" with great facility as a result of their constant social intercourse and their innate self-confidence (*les grands* sounded impressive as long as they spoke, he added, but when they came to take up the pen their style "revolts nature itself"). To the styles of town and court Mercier opposed the "male, clear, firm, and simple" style of Rousseau and the abbé Raynal, which, he judged, "devours and crushes all inferior styles."[101]

Tony Tanner remarks astutely that puns and ambiguities are to ordinary language what adultery and other forms of sexual deviance are to conventional sexual behavior—both bring together things (meanings or people) that are normally kept apart.[102] Beaumarchais was reviled for making use of both linguistic and erotic ambiguity in *The Marriage of Figaro*; for making light of subjects such as adultery, which many contemporary writers insisted should be taken seriously; and for using, and adapting, the linguistic habits of high society to woo the crowds of spectators who flocked to his play night after night. That to his more radical contemporaries Beaumarchais represented the forces of stylistic, and hence political, conservatism would be further revealed by his role in the last cause célèbre of the Old Regime, the Kornmann affair.

Catherine Marie Faesch, a wealthy and attractive young Swiss girl, was married in 1772, at age fifteen, to a man seventeen years her senior, a

---

100. See Maurice Magendie, *La Politesse mondaine et les théories de l'honnêteté en France au XVIIe siècle de 1600 à 1660,* 2 vols. (Paris: Felix Alcan, 1925); Carolyn Lougee, *Le Paradis des femmes: Women, Salons, and Social Stratification in Seventeenth-Century France* (Princeton: Princeton University Press, 1976); Joan Landes, *Women and the Public Sphere in the Age of the French Revolution* (Ithaca: Cornell University Press, 1988), chap. 1.

101. Mercier, *Tableau de Paris* 8:71–77.

102. Tanner, *Adultery in the Novel,* p. 53.

banker from Strasbourg named Guillaume Kornmann.[103] She brought a considerable dowry of 360,000 livres to the marriage. By 1778 the couple had two children and were living in Paris, where one of the branches of Kornmann's family bank was located. The following year the Kornmanns were regularly receiving the man who was to touch off their marital problems, an elegant young nobleman named Daudet de Jossan. When the young man eventually seduced Mme Kornmann, her husband apparently found it convenient to look the other way. Daudet held the high municipal office of *syndic-adjoint* in Strasbourg; he was also a protégé of the prince de Nassau, and intimate with the then-powerful war minister, the prince de Montbarrey. A wife's indiscretions were a small price to pay for such interesting political connections.

By the early 1780s, however, this cozy arrangement was threatening to backfire against Kornmann. Daudet's political usefulness was compromised by the death of Montbarrey and the loss of his *syndic* position, and Catherine was planning to sue for a separation from her husband. Kornmann's reasons for opposing the separation probably had more to do with money than with love. The banker was in dire financial straits, having lost an investment of 300,000 livres in a scandal over the mismanagement of funds invested in the Quinze-Vingts hospital in Paris. Catherine's initiative no doubt reflected her fears for her own fortune and for her children's future, and indeed Kornmann was not about to let her walk off with her dowry.[104] In August of 1781 he had her imprisoned in a safe-house by lettre de cachet, his charge of adultery visibly confirmed by the fact that she was pregnant with her lover's child. Catherine was released, her husband sued to have her reincarcerated, and she in turn sued him for a pension; by 1787 several attempts at out-of-court settlement had failed amidst much rancor, and the sordid family business became a full-blown *affaire*.

Unlike the Sanois case, which seems genuinely to have concerned

103. The following account of the case is based on the following: *Mémoires secrets* 35:145–147, 159–166, 187–190, 218–232; Elaine Kruse, "Passion, Property, or Politics? The Implications of the Kornmann Affair," paper presented at the Western Society for French History meeting, November 1988, UCLA; Darnton, "Trends in Radical Propaganda," chap. 8. My interpretation of the case is indebted to Darnton's important and mostly unpublished work on the "Kornmann group."

104. The use of incarceration by husbands to prevent the withdrawal of their wives' assets from the marriage was common throughout the Old Regime: see Hanley, "Engendering the State," p. 24.

only the Sanois family, the Kornmann affair had ramifications aplenty into the intellectual and political life of the late 1780s—this much was obvious as soon as the mémoires on either side began to appear in the winter of 1787. The man who emerged as Kornmann's main defender was Nicolas Bergasse, a lawyer of radical leanings from Lyon, unattached to the Parisian Ordre des Avocats; born in 1750, Bergasse was one year older than Lacretelle, and like the latter he was a member of the group of lawyer-intellectuals pushing for the reform of the judicial system whom we encountered in the preceding chapter.[105] Before the Kornmann case made his name a household word, however, Bergasse was chiefly known as the leading French proponent of the "magnetic" theories of Franz Anton Mesmer. After Mesmer arrived in Paris in 1778 to found the Parisian Society of Harmony, Bergasse assisted him in offering titillating magnetic experiences to the capital's upper crust; but increasing factionalism within the not-so-harmonious Society led in the spring of 1785 to the expulsion of Bergasse along with a number of like-minded companions who made up the "radical" wing of the Mesmerist movement.[106] Bergasse's closest friend and collaborator among this splinter group was none other than Kornmann; it was only natural for Bergasse, a lawyer at least in name, to take up the pen in defense of his friend. As for Mme Kornmann, she found an equally controversial defender in a friend of Daudet and of the prince de Nassau, Beaumarchais himself. With Bergasse and Beaumarchais squaring off against each other, the case could not fail to cause a stir.

But there were larger interests still looming over the case, which broke out in a political climate no less electrically charged than Mesmer's tubs. The winter of 1787 had witnessed the collapse of the French monarchy's latest attempt at forcing fiscal reform down the throats of its wealthiest and most powerful subjects. The government's handpicked Assembly of Notables entered on a collision course with the king's finance minister, Calonne, and in April of 1787 the latter was dismissed by Louis XVI and fled the country. Throughout the winter and spring of 1787 many groups opposed Calonne for many different reasons. The Notables resented the controller-general's high-handed treatment of

105. See David Jacobson, "The Politics of Criminal Law Reform in Late Eighteenth-Century France" (Ph.D. diss., Brown University, 1976), pp. 101–104, 121–122.

106. Robert Darnton, *Mesmerism and the End of the Enlightenment in France* (New York: Schocken Books, 1968), chap. 2.

NICOLAS BERGASSE

Né en 1750.

Son zèle impétueux qu'inspire la droiture,
Sous l'aile du génie, offre un puissant renfort.
Trop heureux l'innocent trahi par l'imposture
Que verroit un Bergasse aux portes de la mort.

10. Nicolas Bergasse (1750–1832). (Phot. Bibl. Nat. Paris)

them and kept up a running campaign against him in the salons and clubs of the capital. The Parlement's Cour des Pairs joined in on the rebellion against Calonne's proposed encroachments on fiscal privilege; within the main body of the Parlement radical young magistrates, such as Jean-Jacques Duval d'Eprémesnil and Adrien Duport, sounded the familiar cries against ministerial "despotism."[107]

Fanning the flames of this anti-Calonne agitation were the partisans of the other great controller-general of the prerevolutionary decades, Jacques Necker. The Genevan "miracle worker," famous for his controversial *Compte-rendu,* headed French finances from 1777 to 1781, when he was brought down thanks to a cabal headed by Louis XVI's aging chief minister, Maurepas, and the king's archconservative brothers, the counts of Artois and Provence.[108] The "Neckerite" party at court kept up after 1781 a running campaign to get their man back into government, which met with success in 1788.[109] Necker was Swiss, Protestant, and open to progressive ideas—his wife ran the last great salon of the French Enlightenment—and his partisans tended to occupy the more liberal end of the political spectrum of the day; chief among them was the king's cousin Philippe d'Orléans, the future regicide Philippe-Egalité. The looming figure of Orléans provides us with a link back to the Kornmann case, for some of the Kornmann pamphlets were produced in a print-shop protected by Orléans, with premises in the duke's Palais-Royal.[110]

At the end of 1787 the critic La Harpe, commenting on the volatility of contemporary "opinion," noted that since the disbanding of the Assembly of Notables the public's interest had shifted back to Beaumarchais, "his court cases, his quarrels," and that "the controversies of M. de Calonne and M. Necker around the public debt have not caused more excitement than the mémoires of the banker Kornmann against Beaumarchais and those of Beaumarchais against Kornmann."[111] In fact it is tempting to see the Kornmann case as an *extension* of the Necker-

107. Jean Egret, *The French Prerevolution, 1787–1788,* trans. Wesley Camp (Chicago: University of Chicago Press, 1977), chap. 4; William Doyle, *Origins of the French Revolution* (Oxford: Oxford University Press, 1980), chap. 5.

108. Robert Harris, *Necker: Reform Statesman of the Ancien Régime* (Berkeley: University of California Press, 1979), chaps. 12 and 15.

109. Doyle, *Origins,* pp. 57–58; Harris, *Necker,* chap. 12.

110. Jeremy Popkin, "Pamphlet Journalism at the end of the Old Regime," *Eighteenth-Century Studies* 22 (Spring 1989): 362.

111. Jean-François de La Harpe, *Correspondance littéraire,* 6 vols. (Paris, 1804–1806), 5:188.

Calonne struggle, if only because Kornmann's partisans were so deeply involved in the onslaught upon Calonne, which became a pervasive motif in the case.

Bergasse and Kornmann formed the nucleus of the Mesmerist splinter-group that met at the banker's house and whose preoccupations soon reached far beyond discussions of animal magnetism.[112] What Darnton has termed the "Kornmann group" included, besides Bergasse and Kornmann, another banker, Etienne Clavière, and three writers with radical inclinations, Jacques-Pierre Brissot, Jean-Louis Carra, and Antoine Gorsas—with the exception of Kornmann all of these men were to play prominent roles in the Revolution as journalists and leaders of the Girondin faction. Somewhat less central to the group were other familiar names: the *parlementaire* firebrand Duval D'Eprémesnil, the count of Mirabeau, and the marquis de Lafayette. These men developed an ideological position, hammered out in pamphlet after pamphlet, whose overarching characteristic was hostility to established authority of every sort in the person of *les gens en place* or *les grands*—although their villain of choice was the authoritarian Calonne.

The Kornmann group's ideology derived from an odd conflation of Mesmer with Rousseau. They preached the simple values of nature and the family, arguing that true morality (*les moeurs*) was the expression of "natural" family bonds, themselves a form of magnetic "harmony" (Brissot wrote that a mother breast-feeding her child was in a state of "perpetual magnetism.")[113] They were especially attracted by the simple *moeurs* of America, as portrayed in Crevecoeur's *Letters of an American Farmer.* (The Kornmann group overlapped to a considerable extent Lafayette's contemporary Gallo-American society.) Mostly, they vilified Calonne, portraying him as a depraved autocrat whose aim was to ruin the country for his own profit.[114] Much of this denunciation centered on Calonne's private financial affairs and allegations that the minister was using inside information to help a group of speculators with whom he was involved. Pamphlets attacking Calonne's financial dealings appeared under Mirabeau's name—probably written by Clavière—and were circulated to the Notables, whom the Kornmann group was cultivating. Beneath the high-flying rhetoric about morals and freedoms, be-

112. The following description of the composition and ideology of the "Kornmann Group" is based on Darnton, "Trends in Radical Propaganda," passim, esp. chap. 2.

113. Ibid., p. 75.

114. Ibid., chap. 6.

yond the sad story of a family rent asunder, lurked some very prosaic financial interests. The Kornmann group, in the persons of Clavière and Mirabeau, speculated in the bear market; this placed them at logger-heads, even before the affair broke out, with Calonne and Beaumar-chais, who shared an interest in the bull market.[115] The type of specula-tion favored by either side seems nicely to reflect their prognosis as to the health of the ministry—or indeed of the Old Regime itself.

Many of these themes came together in the trial briefs written for Kornmann: Rousseauean aspirations to natural morality, idealizations of the family, and denunciations of the men in power and their agents—the ever slick and heartless Beaumarchais, Daudet de Jossan, Calonne, and Calonne's *créature*, the former Paris police chief Jean-Charles Le-noir (he had left the position in 1785). The Kornmann case represents both the ultimate evolution of the trial brief as a form of persuasion, and a decisive turning point. As in other great cases of the 1780s, the Kornmann briefs hammered out explicit political messages—on the level both of the personal attack and of the statement of ideological principle. We have seen the mémoires become increasingly personal and their authors emerge as characters within their own briefs; in this case the struggle between the Kornmann spouses was all but overshadowed by that between Bergasse and Beaumarchais, the real protagonists of the case. Finally, the Kornmann case was fought out between a writer, Beaumarchais, and Bergasse, the representative of a group of radical pamphleteers. What remained typical of the mémoire was the centrality of a private, domestic quarrel, which was used as a vehicle for the hammering-out of general ideas. In all other respects (concern with broad political issues, mudslinging, political partisanship, the champi-oning of certain political figures and the vilifying of others) the *mémoire judiciaire* on the eve of the Revolution had begun to metamorphose into its direct descendant—the revolutionary newspaper.[116]

Every cause célèbre of the eighteenth century seemed to produce a central, highly successful mémoire; in the Kornmann case, it was Nico-las Bergasse's *Mémoire sur une question d'adultère, de séduction, et de diffamation pour le Sr. Kornmann,* dated 20 February 1787, that shot the opening salvo and made the case an immediate sensation. Later that

115. Ibid., pp. 180–232.

116. See Jeremy Popkin, "The Prerevolutionary Origins of Political Journalism," in Keith Baker, ed., *The Political Culture of the Old Regime* (Oxford: Pergamon Press, 1987), pp. 203–223.

year, Bergasse claimed that his client had received six thousand letters from persons "of every estate" begging for copies of the brief, while the *Mémoires secrets* noted that four thousand people had signed up at Kornmann's house for copies. In June of 1788, Bergasse wrote that 100,000 copies of all of his briefs in the case, some of which had been reprinted, were in circulation.[117] Even if Bergasse was exaggerating, there must have been a kernel of truth to his claims, as well as to the hyperbolic description, by a supporter, of the reception of the first mémoire: "Everyone wanted it; it was devoured, learned by heart, it is still fought over. Since all persons guard their copies as carefully as their purses, anyone who agrees to lend one is sure to make a friend. The café waiters in the Palais-Royal have made a fortune renting theirs out to read; the copies returned to them are falling to pieces, and I have seen fifteen people at a doorstep, each avidly holding a sheet of the mémoire that had been distributed and was passed from hand to hand as each person scanned it. Concentration, pleasure, enthusiasm, or astonishment marked the faces of readers, depending on the page they were absorbed with, together with impatience in those who had finished their sheet and were waiting for the next one."[118] No doubt the mémoire's appeal was enhanced by the fact that the police tried ineffectively to suppress it by raiding print-shops, booksellers, and peddlers.[119]

The Kornmann affair reveals, as no other before it had done, the extent to which style, in the last years of the Old Regime, had become a vehicle for ideology. This was as true in the realm of visual art as in that of the written word. Thomas Crow has shown that in the mid-eighties, radical art critics, including Gorsas and Carra, understood and appreciated the deliberate awkwardness and austerity of David's great *Oath of the Horatii*, which baffled and displeased their conservative colleagues; Crow argues that the radical discourse of the prerevolution seized upon this "conflict between style and anti-style" as an organizing principle.[120] The same was true of the Kornmann group's articulation of their beliefs

---

117. *Mémoire du sieur Kornmann en réponse au mémoire du sieur de Beaumarchais* (Paris, 1787), p. 59; *Mémoires secrets* 35:179; *Mémoire pour le sieur Bergasse dans la cause du sieur Kornmann* (Paris, 1788), p. 18.

118. *Lettre à Milord *** au sujet de M. Bergasse et de ses observations dans l'affaire de M. Kornmann* (n.p., 1788), p. 3.

119. *Mémoires secrets* 35:145.

120. Crow, *Painters and Public Life*, chap. 7.

around the opposition between their own Rousseauean style and that incarnated in their chief opponent, Beaumarchais.

Two years after the beginning of the case, a hostile pamphleteer attacked Bergasse, calling him a cheap imitation of Jean-Jacques Rousseau and accusing him of aping the Genevan philosophe in his life and works: "Every time a man imitates, I say to myself: he is playing a role. The role you wish to play, monsieur, is that of Rousseau."[121] And indeed, throughout his pamphlets in the case, Bergasse did cast both himself and his client-friend Kornmann in the role of the Rousseauean antihero—virtuous, sensitive, solitary, and persecuted—exactly as Lacretelle had portrayed his client Sanois. Bergasse's initial mémoire in the case was a first-person narrative attributed to Kornmann. The story opened upon images of a happy couple, enthusiastically practicing Rousseauean (or perhaps "magnetic") domestic bliss. "Kornmann" wrote that his wife had chosen him of her own free will (which was not true) and that she had given birth to two children, whom she breast-fed herself under the eye of an attentive and loving husband.[122]

Once this domestic arcadia has been destroyed by Daudet and other "conspirators," Kornmann becomes a pathetically lonely figure, "the good man, always isolated when the wicked assemble to work at ruining him."[123] Just as Sanois fled to Lausanne after his family life turned sour, Kornmann dispatches himself to Spa, there to link up with an old friend (perhaps Bergasse). "We spent our days taking walks in the furthest and most solitary places," amidst "the imposing and peaceful scenes which nature deployed around us."[124] One originality of the Kornmann mémoires is not only that they place the author of the briefs, Bergasse, in the foreground, but that his identity increasingly fuses with that of his client-friend. Thus, while Kornmann is allowed to occupy center stage in the first brief, the figure of Bergasse as another distressed Man of Feeling looms increasingly larger in the later mémoires: "A hundred times I dragged myself, weak and suffering, from my bed to my desk, to finish the brief that many have read. I am told that this piece caused some tears to be shed; never as many as I myself shed while writing

121. *Lettre d'un magistrat de province à M. Bergasse* (n.p., 1789), pp. 6–7.

122. Nicolas Bergasse, *Mémoire sur une question d'adultère, de séduction, et de diffamation pour le sieur Kornmann contre la dame Kornmann son épouse* (Paris, 1787), pp. 8–9.

123. Ibid., p. 6.

124. Ibid., pp. 66–67.

it." [125] (Another Sensitive Man, Diderot, had similarly described himself weeping over the manuscript of *La Religieuse* as he wrote.)[126]

Much is made, in the pro-Kornmann briefs, of the banker's concern for his children. Tony Tanner has pointed out that disinclination to maternity, the lack or loss of a mother's interest in her children, appears as a standard theme in novels of adultery.[127] Bergasse's briefs followed this script. Initially presented as a devoted mother, Mme Kornmann after her transgression "pushed [her children] away from her bosom and shamelessly sacrificed them to the ambition of [her lover]." [128] This is contrasted with her husband's concern for his children's education, his only occupation once he has cut himself off from his fellow men—presumably he was raising them in accord with the principles laid out in Rousseau's *Emile*.[129] Here again, Bergasse, not to be outdone, also portrays himself as the Educator. He too loved children and felt especially drawn to Kornmann's because of the tragedy that had struck their family. He discussed their upbringing with their father, "and it is partly on the basis of my ideas that he drew up the plan for their education which he has them follow today." [130] The children's education is one of the ties binding together the two men in a *fraternité* occasioned by the woman's defection.

Unfortunately for Bergasse, there were elements of the story, impossible to deny, which contradicted the portrayal of Kornmann as the sensitive, moral, and devoted husband. Why, for instance, did he allow Catherine to see Daudet and carry on an affair with him? The author of a letter attributed to Daudet de Jossan—probably Beaumarchais himself—dwelt on this point with some relish. Assuring his readers that this "angelic household, this sweet and intimate union, was in truth a real inferno," he describes Kornmann pushing his wife into Daudet's arms and responding to her concern about appearances in vulgar, authoritarian tones: "I don't care two hoots about gossip. And am I not the master

---

125. Nicolas Bergasse, *Observations de MM. de Bergasse et de Kornmann sur un écrit de M. de Beaumarchais* (n.p., n.d.), p. 10.

126. Georges May, *Diderot et "La Religieuse"* (Paris: Presses Universitaires de France, 1954), p. 41. It is in the *Préface-annexe* of *La Religieuse* that Diderot reports that his friend d'Alainville found him in tears over the manuscript.

127. Tanner, *Adultery in the Novel*, p. 27.

128. Bergasse, *Mémoire sur une question d'adultère*, p. 39.

129. Ibid., pp. 85–86.

130. Bergasse, *Observations de MM. de Bergasse et de Kornmann*, pp. 7–8.

here? I like Daudet, I want you to treat him well."[131] Bergasse's explanation of the banker's attitude had predictably to be more convoluted; near the beginning of the first mémoire he has Kornmann tell his wife that if she fell victim to "the universal depravity of morals," he asked only that she keep up decent appearances, "so that while deploring in secret her faults I should not have to blush of them in public."[132] The other matter that required some fancy footwork on Bergasse's part was the fact that this allegedly sensitive husband had used a lettre de cachet against his wife. Since Bergasse could hardly deny that Kornmann had done this, he brazened it out by having the banker seized with a trembling fit and dissolving into tears as he clutches the sealed letter, knowing he will have to use it—for his wife's own good.[133]

The Kornmann story was the exact *opposite* of the Sanois tale: it was the husband, in this case, who had used the tools of "despotism" against his wife. Bergasse managed, however, to transform the sordid story of a couple's struggle over money and power into something quite different by having recourse to a certain style and imagery: the lachrymose first-person narrative, the emphasis on marriage and children, the hero's isolation and love of nature.

Images of domestic bliss destroyed were only half of the story told in the pro-Kornmann briefs. The other, no doubt more "scandalous" aspect of this literature was its denunciation of those responsible for this marital debacle—not just Daudet de Jossan, but also the other members of this "conspiracy": the sinister—and aptly named—police chief, Lenoir, the prince of Nassau, above all the archfiend Beaumarchais, and behind them all, Calonne. From the start "Kornmann" wrote of his wife as more a victim than a villain, "a guilty woman, but more worthy of pity than of blame."[134] She is portrayed as a naive and malleable woman, who after being ravished by her seducer and thrown in the midst of a "corrupt society" is made over in the image of those who have debauched her. In pamphlet after pamphlet, the world into which Catherine Kornmann was plunged after her "fall" is described in the heavily stereotyped terms used to evoke upper-class immorality: "the most cor-

---

131. *Lettre de M. Daudet de Jossan à M. Bergasse* (Kell, 1787), pp. 9–11; the supposition that the pamphlet was written by Beaumarchais is based both on its style and on the imprint "A Kell."

132. Bergasse, *Mémoire sur une question d'adultère,* p. 10.

133. Ibid., p. 26.

134. Ibid., p. 6.

rupt society," "the most depraved society in Paris," "the impure center
and germ of all vices," "a brilliant but depraved society where she heard
people speak with levity of the sacred duties of wife and mother."[135]
Sucked into the world of her ravishers, Mme Kornmann begins to
speak, write, and think like them, substituting "the tranquil tone of persiflage and irony to the troubled language of passion (*égarement*) and
distress."[136] The correspondence between her and Daudet, which her
husband discovers, reads more like *Les Liaisons dangereuses* than *La
Nouvelle Héloïse*—they are letters, wrote "Kornmann," "in which an
awful cynicism holds sway, in which the tone of the most vile libertinism
is alone apparent, in which one would seek in vain amidst obscene expressions the always touching language of passion."[137]

Among Mme Kornmann's ravishers, the one least conspicuous is
Daudet himself; he is never described in any detail, and having accomplished his initial seduction, he fades from the narrative. Bergasse and
Kornmann were more interested in getting at the men behind Daudet.
There was Lenoir, an ally of Daudet and Beaumarchais, initially portrayed as an unctuous hypocrite who, having helped to abduct the
young woman from the safe-house, adopts poses of studied compassion
and "sensibility" when her husband comes asking for help.[138] In April
of 1787, Bergasse devoted an entire mémoire to denouncing Lenoir as
one of the main culprits in the case—hinting, in passing, that Lenoir
got to share the young woman with Daudet as payment for his coopera-
tion.[139] Just before the piece appeared, the *Mémoires secrets* announced
it, adding that what made the affair so interesting was the public's
knowledge that Lenoir was Calonne's "right-hand man," and reporting
that Kornmann had the piece distributed to all of the Notables.[140] Since
other members of the Kornmann group had already published blistering denunciations of Calonne, there could be no doubt in people's
minds as to where the banker and his lawyer stood.[141]

The villain most explicitly and systematically targeted was of course

135. Bergasse, *Mémoire sur une question d'adultère*, p. 48; Bergasse, *Mémoire du sieur
Kornmann*, p. 7; Bergasse, *Observations de MM. de Bergasse et de Kornmann*, p. 5.

136. Bergasse, *Mémoire pour le sieur Bergasse*, p. 16.

137. Bergasse, *Mémoire sur une question d'adultère*, p. 24.

138. Ibid., pp. 42–44.

139. Nicolas Bergasse, *Observations du sieur Kornmann en réponse au mémoire de M.
Lenoir* (Paris, 1787).

140. *Mémoires secrets* 35:147.

141. Darnton, "Trends in Radical Propaganda," chap. 6.

Beaumarchais, who may have rued the day his dinner hosts, the prince and princess of Nassau, convinced him to take an interest in Catherine Kornmann's case. Right from the start, Beaumarchais is cast as the arch-villain of the affair. Even his accomplice, Lenoir, confides to Bergasse that he regards the playwright as a scoundrel, "but all the more danger-ous in that, being witty and knowing the art of amusing and seducing, he has the means of making allies everywhere, of arranging conspiracies if need be against anyone who has the bad fortune to displease him." [142] The accusations that should logically have been aimed at Daudet were in fact deflected onto Beaumarchais, whom Bergasse and Kornmann accused of having "prostituted" the young woman—an unfair charge, to say the least, given Kornmann's initial attitude toward his wife's affair.[143]

Beaumarchais naturally fought back by publishing a first mémoire (several others were to follow), which was eagerly awaited and upon its publication much reviled. Caron the jester, the darling of courts and salons, could not change his style even when his reputation was in grave danger. He produced "in four nights" a flippantly sarcastic piece in which he cast himself as a gallant man of the world coming to the rescue of a lady in distress; he tried to reconcile the Kornmann spouses, he assured his readers: "It is an article of faith with me that when an unfor-tunate woman has married a nasty man, it behooves her to be miserable by his side." [144] From the start, however, Beaumarchais's efforts were ill-received. La Harpe wrote that "the outcry against Beaumarchais has been universal"—he had been involved in too many intrigues, had too much credit at court, and was becoming insufferably self-important. The *Mémoires secrets* called Beaumarchais's brief "a mess" (*un gâchis*), a nasty piece well worthy of him, written only for profit.[145]

In the volley of pamphlets written against Beaumarchais in connec-tion with the case—some of them attributed to Mirabeau—the very same terms used to attack *The Marriage of Figaro* served once again as criticisms of his self-defense in the Kornmann case: *triviales expressions,*

142. Bergasse, *Mémoire sur une question d'adultère*, p. 33; see also Bergasse, *Observa-tions du sieur Kornmann*, p. 9.
143. Nicolas Bergasse, *Mémoire du sieur Kornmann en réponse au mémoire du sieur de Beaumarchais* (Paris, 1787), pp. 7–8.
144. Pierre-Augustin Caron de Beaumarchais, *Mémoire de Pierre-Augustin Caron de Beaumarchais en réponse au libelle diffamatoire signé Guillaume Kornmann* (Paris, 1787), p. 54.
145. La Harpe, *Correspondance* 5:188–189; *Mémoires secrets* 35:188.

plattes équivoques, jargon, pointes fades, calembours—the linguistic weapons of a bygone worldliness, now lambasted as the signs of moral corruption.[146] As Robert Darnton has argued, Beamarchais's problem was that he did not, and never could, speak the Rousseauean language of sincerity and passion, that he refused to believe that Voltairean wit could *not* be an effective weapon in a public dispute such as the Kornmann case.[147] According to Bergasse, Beaumarchais did try to create a different image for himself: he was having a large house built near the Porte Saint-Antoine and announced that he wished to live there "ignored, and as a true *philosophe*" in the sole company of his beloved wife—and of twenty friends. Bergasse sneered at this effort on Beaumarchais's part "to do through his architect what he could not do with his pen."[148]

Beyond serious lapses in style and taste, Beaumarchais's main problem (as his opponents perceived it, and as his most famous play demonstrated) was that he did not understand that adultery was a serious crime laden with political implications. Bergasse, on the other hand, was only too ready to expatiate upon the connections between morality, the law, and the political principles of governments, since this had always been for him a central concern. Earlier in his career, in his *Discours sur l'humanité des juges* (published in 1787, though written in 1774), Bergasse simply postulated that morals (*les moeurs*) resulted from the "political laws" of a society, which regulated relationships between people. But already in this early work, he articulated an antithesis to which he was often to return: that in the government of all, "men are free and morals are enslaved," whereas in the government of one, "men are enslaved but morals are free."[149] Bergasse's (profoundly secularist) assumption, in other words, is that individuals are most likely to impose a moral code on themselves when they follow laws that are the expression of their collective will, and least likely when they are furthest removed from the source of the law.

By the 1780s, Bergasse had added an important element to his scheme, namely the primacy of the family as the repository of the most

---

146. *Le Public à Pierre-Augustin Caron de Beaumarchais* (n.p., n.d.), pp. 3–4; *Lettre du Public parisien à Pierre-Augustin Caron de Beaumarchais* (n.p., n.d.), p. 10.

147. Darnton, "Trends in Radical Propaganda," pp. 83–89, 324–325, 339–344, 353–355.

148. Bergasse, *Mémoire pour le sieur Bergasse*, pp. 17–18.

149. Nicolas Bergasse, *Discours sur l'humanité des juges dans l'administration de la justice criminelle* (Paris, 1787), p. 12.

basic laws of nature. The emphasis on family bonds as a source of *moeurs* probably reflected Bergasse's Mesmerist beliefs: as we have seen, the members of the Kornmann group believed that family members were drawn to one another by the action of magnetic fluids, which could also be assimilated to natural morality.[150] These were the ideas that Bergasse built upon in the lengthy concluding section, entitled "Réflexions," of his highly successful first mémoire for Kornmann.

Bergasse proposed to develop his belief that adultery, which his own society regarded as no more than a peccadillo, was in fact "the crime whose consequences are most deadly and usually most irreparable."[151] Why? Because, Bergasse argued in classic contractual fashion, the bond between man and woman, and the family that resulted from that bond, were the expressions of the first laws of nature and the foundations of society. Since adultery was the crime that most threatened the family, it should therefore be considered the transgression most dangerous to society.[152] Where Bergasse had previously written of *les moeurs* as the expression of man-made laws, he now regarded morality as the code that ensured the integrity of the family unit: *moeurs* are good if they tend to the preservation of the family, bad if they threaten it.[153]

Logically, then, all societies should consider adultery the single most antisocial crime. If this was not the case—as it patently was not in France in the 1780s—this was because the crime of adultery varied both in frequency and in gravity, depending on a society's degree of removal from its natural state and on the political principles that governed it. In a primitive society, still close to nature, adultery would be both infrequent and a sign of great perversity. As society developed, human relationships became more shallow as they increased in complexity, hence the greater tolerance for marital infidelity.[154] Furthermore, adultery was generally acceptable in a society subjected to arbitrary power, since despotic rulers normally tolerated moral licence in order to placate their subjects and to distract them from their loss of political liberty. "Freedom," wrote Bergasse, "is a spring that cannot be compressed at all times in all places."[155] Despotic government could ultimately be held responsible for the proliferation of a crime that would eventually bring

---

150. Darnton, "Trends in Radical Propaganda," pp. 73–76.
151. Bergasse, *Mémoire sur une question d'adultère*, p. 95.
152. Ibid., pp. 95–102.
153. Ibid., p. 104.
154. Ibid., pp. 117–118.
155. Ibid., pp. 120–121.

about, to the ruler's advantage, the destruction of all social relationships.

Bergasse's discussion of adultery in the context of the Kornmann case was as explicitly and provocatively political as anything ever published in a mémoire. Bergasse did not just hint at the links between private morality and public values, he spelled them out. Some of the strategies adopted by Kornmann's defenders were part of the traditions that the genre of the trial brief had developed since the 1770s. Like many other cases, the Kornmann affair had its gallery of rogues—corrupt and manipulative villains, the embodiments or emissaries of "despotism" playing the system to perfection, unmasked by the courageous barrister. But Bergasse delved deeper than this, connecting issues of style (in speech, manner, and moral standards) to competing definitions of the polity. On one side were those willing to tolerate unfreedom for the sake of shallow pleasures, passing connections, and the empty display of wit; on the other, those who chose public freedom and were ready to pay the price in constraints on their personal life.

The Kornmann case was judged in April of 1789, on the very eve of the convening of the Estates-General. The Parlement's ruling went against Kornmann and Bergasse, who were condemned to pay one thousand livres in damages to Beaumarchais; over a year later, Catherine Kornmann was awarded the proceeds from the sale of her husband's house, and in 1793 she divorced him.[156] If Bergasse got any consolation from the outcome of the case, it would have been from the confirmation his defeat seemed to offer of the eloquent pages he had written denouncing the legal system of the monarchy, and the assumptions about power that underlay it. After all, Bergasse may have taken on the case of his friend Kornmann less in the hope of winning it than with an eye to exposing the flaws of the contemporary polity, as reflected in the development of the case.

In June of 1788, over a year into the case, Bergasse already seemed pessimistic about the likely outcome of his efforts. He warned his readers of what this meant: "If you reflect upon the manner in which arbitrary power has manifested itself in most of the circumstances I have laid before you . . . you will acquire one more proof, and a striking one at that, of the profound immorality of your political laws, of the laws that make up your administrative system."[157] Nicolas Bergasse, future deputy

156. Kruse, "Passion, Property, or Politics?" p. 7; Grendel, *Beaumarchais,* p. 240.
157. Bergasse, *Mémoire pour le sieur Bergasse,* p. 145.

to the National Assembly and member of the committee that overhauled France's judicial system, wrote this as the Parlement had been
exiled for the last time and the country in uproar heeded rumors, soon
to be confirmed, of the convening of the Estates-General of the realm.
Soon there would be no time for causes célèbres, no need to use the
problems of unhappy spouses as a vehicle for legal and moral education.
Within just over a year the nation would have changed in ways scarcely
imaginable even to the most farsighted reformer—the whole country
was soon to become a courtroom, its new governing institutions firmly
in the hands of men of law.

Conclusion

In the preceding chapters I have sought to describe and explain a major shift in French political (or more broadly, public) culture over the course of the last two decades of the Old Regime. In the seventeenth and eighteenth centuries, the effective and symbolic center of political life in France was the royal court, which was in essence a household writ large. In 1789, the court was displaced by that characteristically modern political entity, the all-male elective and representative assembly. Negotiating the transition over the course of the eighteenth century was an ancient institution competitive with the court, the parlement, which had its roots deep in the old order (it was a quintessentially corporate body, hierarchical, exclusive, and privileged) but which also paved the way for the new by articulating and publicizing, in opposition to monarchical absolutism, its claims to "represent" the French nation. This revolution in political culture is of great historical significance not only in itself, but also because it points to the more protracted cultural revolution, covering roughly the second half of the eighteenth century, which made possible so dramatic a change.

It has been my contention that the causes célèbres of the prerevolutionary decades not only reflected this transformation but contributed crucially to it, especially through the medium of the increasingly popular legal briefs, or *mémoires judiciaires,* thanks to which these cases were made public. The public impact of the great *affaires* of the seventies and eighties, the growing visibility and ambition of the barristers involved in them, the steadily increasing popularity of the printed matter relating to them, all point to the changing nature and to changing perceptions of the eighteenth-century French public sphere.

This period, I have argued, saw the transformation of the central metaphor for describing public life from that of the theater to that of the courtroom—a shift whose cultural implications were manifold. In the old system, power was acted out before a passive *audience;* in the new one, it justified itself by appealing—albeit most often rhetorically—to the judgment of a critical, active *public.* The Old Regime public sphere, that of the court and of high society, was symbolically feminized—it was a realm of display, of the visual, the iconic. The new public sphere was gendered male: it was the domain of the word, of textuality, of rationality. In the old symbolic order, the spotlight was on the stage, on the theatrical display of power at the core of which was the sacred body of the king; in the new, the focus was on the public, which was both the ultimate repository of power and that which needed to be taught, convinced, and controlled. As the preceding chapters have shown, the transition from theatrical to judicial metaphor was anything but neatly linear: from the 1760s to the 1780s, there was constant interchange between the two realms, as writers of mémoires borrowed the style and themes of the new theatrical *drame,* while high society sought again and again to make courtroom drama into sentimental theater. Once completed, however, the process was irreversible: for all of the glitter of Napoleon's court of nouveaux riches and nouveaux nobles, the emperor's enduring legacy to French political culture was a text of laws, the Code Civil.

The origins of this transformation are to be found in political, religious, and ideological struggles going back to the early decades of the eighteenth century. The appeals to "the public" and to "public opinion," which punctuate all of the great judicial mémoires of the prerevolutionary decades can be traced back to struggles over Jansenism in the 1720s and 1730s, when barristers closely connected to the Paris Parlement invoked such entities while defending dissenting priests against their ecclesiastical superiors. While the Parlement continued to claim the sanction of "the public" throughout mid-century struggles over religion, taxation, and the grain trade, appeals to public opinion also came from another quarter, the world of letters. Voltaire, to his contemporaries the embodiment of the Republic of Letters, made his readers and admirers into a "public," which he aroused in defense of victims of "fanaticism" like the Calas family or the chevalier de La Barre. Over the course of the long reign of Louis XV (1715–1774), then, the world of letters and the world of law collaborated in the creation of a "public" that was still mostly a rhetorical entity, but whose symbolic importance increased as the moral and political authority of the absolute monarchy began to falter.

The single most significant turning point in this period was the Maupeou crisis of 1771–1774, an event whose political and cultural repercussions continued to be felt until the end of the decade—and beyond. The "Maupeou years" were marked by unprecedented ideological effervescence and by an explosion of polemical printed matter chronicling and commenting on the crisis, from underground newsletters to political pamphlets to mudslinging libel. In the most general terms, it is this sudden opening up of the public sphere under the impact of political crisis that accounts for the appearance in those years of sensational causes célèbres and of the first bumper crop of prerevolutionary *mémoires judiciaires*. But there were specific institutional reasons for this development as well. Not only did the crisis force a high level of political awareness onto barristers in Paris (and elsewhere), many of whom went on strike in support of the magistrates exiled by Chancellor Maupeou; but the events of 1771 also disorganized the powerful and hierarchical Parisian Ordre des Avocats, thereby allowing for the sudden emergence of a younger generation of talented, ambitious, and fame-seeking barristers, free of traditional restraints and eager to promote themselves through news-making *affaires*.

Through the examination of both the subject matter and the literary techniques of the most successful mémoires of the seventies and eighties, I have traced the development of three literary-political themes: first, the great cases of the seventies brought together contemporary preoccupation with the twin evils of "despotism" and "aristocracy"; second, throughout the period but especially in the eighties prominent mémoires addressed issues of gender, and especially concerns about the public role of women that had been articulated most forcefully in the previous generation by Rousseau; and third, toward the end of the period *mémoires judiciaires* became both more personal (cast as intimate first-person narratives by the lawyer, his client, or both) and at the same time more explicitly political, openly linking the cases they discussed with such matters as the reform of the judicial system, the evils of arbitrary government, and the nature of the social contract. These themes and techniques did not actually follow one another in a neat sequence; they interlocked, overlapped, and accumulated. Thus, the last in the series of cases examined in this book, the Kornmann affair of 1787–1789, brought together a range of themes and techniques from the entire period: denunciations of administrative tyranny and aristocratic morgue, preoccupation with the role of women and the nature of the marriage contract, melodramatic narrative and sentimental autobiography, and explicit discussions of the link between moral norms and political systems. By the eve of the Revolution, such cases had become vehicles for explicit discussions of private morality in relation to the nature of the prevailing political system.

This examination of the causes célèbres of the 1770s and 1780s offers new ways of understanding some of the questions about French prerevolutionary and revolutionary culture that remain problematic in the current historiography of this period. It is now almost thirty years since waves of revisionism washing over the field began to chip away at, and ultimately toppled, the traditional view of the French Revolution as the inevitable outcome of deep and long-standing tensions between a rising middle class and a decaying noble elite. A first generation of revisionists, whose work appeared mostly in the 1970s, reacted against Marxian orthodoxy by taking the extreme position that the Revolution was in essence a political crisis that, owing to "accidental" factors such as hunger and fear at the bottom of society and political ineptitude and selfishness at the top, snowballed out of control: the French Revolution, George Taylor famously argued, was "a political revolution with social consequences" rather than the reverse.[1]

The 1980s witnessed a reaction against this extreme form of revisionism. Uncomfortable with the "ultra" revisionists' heavy reliance on contingency, but convinced that the key to the historical meaning of the French Revolution lay in the broad domain of the political, historians like François Furet, Lynn Hunt, Keith Baker, and William Doyle argued in different ways that between 1750 and 1800 France underwent a political revolution in the broadest sense of the term—a revolution in "political culture."[2] The Revolution itself brought to a culmination trends

1. George Taylor, "Noncapitalist Wealth and the Origins of the French Revolution," *American Historical Review* 72 (January 1967): 491. For a summary of the revisionist literature of the sixties and seventies, see William Doyle, *Origins of the French Revolution* (Oxford: Oxford University Press, 1980), pp. 7–40.

2. François Furet, *Interpreting the French Revolution,* trans. Elborg Forster (Cambridge: Cambridge University Press, 1980); Lynn Hunt, *Politics, Culture and Class in the French Revolution* (Berkeley: University of California Press, 1984); Keith Baker, *Inventing the French Revolution* (Cambridge: Cambridge University Press, 1990); Doyle, *Origins*.

that had begun at least as far back as the 1750s: the "desacralization" of the monarchy; the increasing factionalization of court politics, and the growing publicity surrounding these factional disputes; the rise of oppositional ideologies, especially as articulated within the parlements; growing public discussion of such concepts as constitutionalism, representation, citizenhood, and the national interest; and perhaps most important, the birth and increasing power of "public opinion" both as a rhetorical category and as a sociological reality. The Revolution brought such trends to their logical culmination—albeit in forms indelibly marked by the violence and suddenness of the political conflagration.

This is not the place to discuss whether or not, in the light of recent research in eighteenth-century French social and economic history, an exclusive emphasis on "the political," even in the broadest sense, remains valid at this stage.[3] But even within the terms of the revisionist argument, and within the realms of ideology and culture, recent work on the transformation of political culture at the end of the Old Regime leaves some important problems unsolved—problems arising, I would argue, from the emphasis in recent work on political ideologies construed narrowly as the explicit discussion of political theory and of public political issues. If French public life was transformed in the second half of the eighteenth century by new forms of political discourse, what becomes of the influence of the philosophes and Rousseau, much of whose writings has little to do with politics *stricto sensu?* If the Revolution was a political event, prepared for by a transformation of political life and political language, why was it to a large extent experienced and enacted as a *social* revolution, a crusade against both real and mythical *aristocrates?* Finally, if the development of oppositional ideas can no longer be explained as a matter of class interest, how did ordinary French men and women learn of such ideas, and how did they respond to them?

The answers suggested in the preceding chapters owe a lot in their formulation to the recent impact of feminist thought on current historical writing. Feminist scholarship has taught us both to rescue the apparently trivial and marginal from oblivion and to bring down the barriers

---

3. The case for a return to a social interpretation of the French Revolution has recently been made compellingly by Colin Jones, "Bourgeois Revolution Revivified: 1789 and Social Change," in Colin Lucas, ed., *Rewriting the French Revolution* (Oxford: Clarendon Press, 1991), pp. 69–118.

that conventionally mark the divide between certain realms of human experience.[4] Most obviously, feminist thought has challenged us to rethink the division between public and private life and to question our society's implicit privileging of the public realm as the arena in which the really *important* things happen. Similarly, the contents of the mémoires analyzed in this book, and the strong public responses they evinced, suggest that the categories into which twentieth-century historians divide eighteenth-century culture may not have existed for writers and readers at the time. Our own culture, for instance, separates the legal and political (the realm of reality and rationality) from the literary (the domain of imagination and emotion); the evidence in this book shows that the boundary between those areas was far more fluid in the late eighteenth century. We tend to make clear analytical distinctions between the political and the social; eighteenth-century writers, including the authors of *mémoires judiciaires,* postulated the existence of an intimate connection between political norms (*la loi*) and social values (*les moeurs*).

One of the questions the material in this book helps us to answer is that of the relationship between the literary achievements of the "High" Enlightenment and the political concerns of the Revolution. The young barristers who came of age and authored important mémoires in the 1770s and 1780s, constitute, as a group, an important link between the canonical philosophes, who had written their most significant works by the early sixties, and the political propagandists of the late eighties— Siéyès, Mirabeau, Condorcet, Desmoulins, and others. As we have seen, these lawyers self-consciously carried both the messages and the literary styles of the classical Enlightenment into the prerevolutionary decades: Voltaire's pioneering use of the legal brief as propaganda, Montesquieu's constitutionalism, Diderot's theory of drama, Rousseau's moralism and sentimentalism. Nearly all of them had literary ambitions and connections, and they made copious use, in their briefs, of the themes and techniques of contemporary fiction writing. Some of them (Target, Lacretelle, Bergasse) went on to play important roles in the Revolution. But while many others soon shied away from political

4. See, for instance, Joan Kelly, *Women, History and Theory: The Essays of Joan Kelly* (Chicago: University of Chicago Press, 1984); Joan Wallach Scott, *Gender and the Politics of History* (New York: Columbia University Press, 1988); Carole Pateman, *The Disorder of Women: Democracy, Feminism, and Political Theory* (Stanford: Stanford University Press, 1989), esp. chap. 6, "Feminist Critiques of the Public/Private Dichotomy," pp. 118–140.

involvement or turned against the Revolution altogether, they had as a group undoubtedly helped pave the way for the extraordinary predominance in Parisian revolutionary politics of men just like them: men of law who knew how to use literary talent and legal training in the service of political persuasion.

The *mémoires judiciaires* also help us to make some sense of the question left unanswered by recent revisionist writing: why does *social* rhetoric pervade this allegedly political upheaval? A reading of the most successful trial briefs of the prerevolution shows the extent to which political and social categories overlapped in these texts. Dale Van Kley has argued that the Maupeou years saw the emergence of two distinct themes in political propaganda: the "antidespotic" rhetoric of the proparlementary writers, and the "antiaristocratic" propaganda of the pro-Maupeou publicists. These themes, he argues, were to come together explosively in the pamphleteering of the early Revolution, most famously in the abbé Siéyès's *Qu'est-ce que le Tiers Etat?*[5] Here again, the literature of the *causes célèbres* provides a crucial missing link between the ideologies of the Maupeou era and those of the prerevolution. Many of the famous *mémoires* of the seventies and eighties chose as their target an aristocratic bully (Morangiès, Danré, Richelieu, Guines), the embodiment both of aristocratic privilege and of ministerial tyranny. The rhetorical creation of the sort of *aristocrate* who was to become the imaginary foe of the sansculottes would have been impossible, I have argued, without the convergence of a political trauma (the Maupeou crisis) and a powerful literary model (the *drame*).[6]

Finally and most obviously, the courtroom dramas of the seventies and eighties, and the publicity surrounding them, challenge our usual distinctions between the private and public spheres. In doing so, they validate, perhaps better than any other body of material from this period, the arguments set forth by Jürgen Habermas in *The Structural Transformation of the Public Sphere*. As we have seen, Habermas argues that the "authentic" or "bourgeois" public sphere grew out of the in-

5. Dale Van Kley, "New Wine in Old Wineskins: Continuity and Rupture in the Pamphlet Debate of the French Prerevolution, 1787–1789," *French Historical Studies* 17 (Fall 1991): 447–465.

6. For other accounts of the rhetorical creation of "aristocracy," see J. Q. C. Mackrell, *The Attack on "Feudalism" in Eighteenth-Century France* (Toronto: University of Toronto Press, 1973), and Patrice Higonnet, *Class, Ideology, and the Rights of Nobles during the French Revolution* (Oxford: Oxford University Press, 1981).

creasingly sharp separation between civil society and the state; it was in the zone of contact between state and society that a "critical" public was born, the precursor of a fully developed, modern public sphere.[7] For our purposes it is important to note, not only that this first authentic public sphere was "literary" (in France it coincided with the Republic of Letters), but also that its first preoccupations had to do, Habermas argues, with psychology and with individual experiences within the "intimate" sphere of the family.

The growing popularity of *mémoires judiciaires* in the later eighteenth century illustrates precisely Habermas's argument concerning the birth of the modern public sphere: that it grew out of the critical discussion of increasingly commodified cultural products (such as mémoires), and that concerns with individual psychology and the novel experience of privateness preceded, and laid the groundwork for, the explicit politicization of the new public sphere. In short, the evidence in this book confirms Habermas's insight that within the nascent oppositional public sphere of the eighteenth century, private and public experience were not sharply distinct categories, but were located along a continuum so that the one shaded off into the other. In one respect, though, the argument in this book complicates Habermas's thesis: rather than moving in linear fashion from private to public, the contents of the mémoires evolved in the late eighties into becoming at once more intimate *and* more explicitly political. This trend, as is made most clearly manifest in the Sanois and Kornmann cases, prefigures the revolutionary obsession with both public and private virtue: a truly moral polity could only exist as a reflection of the virtue of individual (male) citizens.

Our exploration of public opinion in prerevolutionary France as seen through the prism of famous court cases ultimately helps us to understand more clearly some crucial links between the culture of the waning Old Regime and that of the Revolution. Most obviously, it shows how a segment of the legal profession came out from under the shadow of

---

7. Jürgen Habermas, *The Structural Transformation of the Public Sphere: An Inquiry into a Category of Bourgeois Society,* trans. Thomas Burger and Frederick Lawrence (Cambridge, Mass.: MIT Press, 1989), pp. 27–31. See the very perceptive analysis of this aspect of Habermas's argument by Dena Goodman, "Public Sphere and Private Life: Toward a Synthesis of Current Historiographical Approaches to the Old Regime," *History and Theory* 31 (1992): 4–8.

the *parlementaire* magistracy and seized the leadership of public opinion by simultaneously appropriating the legacy of the philosophes and making the world of law (judges, barristers, and an active "public" of citizens) into the blueprint for a new polity. The dominance of men of law in all of the revolutionary governing assemblies was the direct consequence of this development. Nor did this trend come to an end after the Revolution. As Lucien Karpik has shown, lawyers remained a central force in French public life from the Restoration to the beginning of the Third Republic. In the first half of the nineteenth century especially, the legal profession followed a pattern of initial support of different regimes, which then turned into opposition and then active participation in revolutionary upheavals. As they had done at the end of the Old Regime, lawyers under the Restoration and July Monarchy used the courtroom as a "politico-judicial forum." Availing themselves of the contradiction between fundamental laws guaranteeing equality and personal liberties and the actual laws of repressive regimes that flouted such principles, lawyers were able to open a breach in successive governments, as they had done before the Revolution, by "playing off higher laws against ordinary laws." Thus, Karpik concludes, as long as the leadership of public opinion in France remained closely connected to the prestige of the law and the power of the word, and as long as the balance between the state and the social body remained unstable, lawyers continued to play a central political role as mediators between the state and civil society.[8]

One of the central themes in the preceding chapters is the metaphorical importance of gender in the culture of prerevolutionary France. The link between the demonization of women in some of the causes célèbres, and the ultimately violent misogyny of the radical Revolution has been discussed earlier; but the meaning of the Revolution's antifemale bias is further clarified by Lynn Hunt's recent foray into the psychosexual dimensions of the revolutionary upheaval. Hunt argues, following René Girard, that the Revolution can be likened to a "sacrificial crisis" that entails the search for a scapegoat and widespread fears of the loss of sexual differentiation—hence the scapegoating, under different guises but especially that of Marie-Antoinette, of the "Bad Mother," and the widespread concern about mannish women and the emascula-

---

8. Lucien Karpik, "Lawyers and Politics in France, 1814–1950: The State, the Market, and the Public," *Law and Social Inquiry* 13 (Fall 1988): 707–736, quote p. 714.

tion of men.[9] We have seen that the precocious articulation of such fears by Rousseau was later amplified by pamphlet literature concerning queens and royal mistresses, and by scandals like the Diamond Necklace Affair. The most important reason for this development was, I would argue, the rise of contractual thought, a process whose origins went back to the seventeenth century, and which culminated in the last decades of the eighteenth. If gender differentiation was no longer guaranteed by a divinely sanctioned chain of being that placed men above women, and if the polity was imagined as the collective expression of atomistic humans rather than a patriarchal household, how could sexual difference, the masculinity of men and the subjection of women, be ensured?[10] The Sanois and Kornmann cases reveal the extent to which in prerevolutionary culture the concern with women's "proper" place was linked to nascent contractual ideology. In the hothouse of Revolutionary politics, such concerns were carried to their logical, often violent, conclusion.

Finally, the unfolding of the prerevolutionary causes célèbres sheds light on the origins of the didactic impulse in revolutionary culture. Because of the Revolution's sudden and total break with the monarchical past, French revolutionary leaders set about remaking every aspect of the citizen's life, from schooling to costume, from festivals to speech. But historians like Lynn Hunt and Emmet Kennedy, who have analyzed the revolutionary obsession with the instructing and molding of citizens, fail to note the ways in which this was prefigured in certain aspects of prerevolutionary culture.[11] The prerevolutionary *mémoire judiciaire* and its theatrical analogue, the *drame*, I have argued, shared a concern with didactic demonstration, and through it, with the reform of the reader/spectator. Analyzing the common strategies of penal reform (the staging of the triumph of the law) and the new theatrical form (the *drame*), Scott Bryson writes that "these reforms conceive of representation, whether legal, theatrical, or pictorial, no longer as a static, idealized reflection or image of power, separate and aloof from the public,

9. Lynn Hunt, *The Family Romance of the French Revolution* (Berkeley: University of California Press, 1992), pp. 114–118.

10. See Carole Pateman, *The Sexual Contract* (Stanford: Stanford University Press, 1988). For a similar argument about biological definitions of gender, see Thomas Laqueur, *Making Sex: Body and Gender from the Greeks to Freud* (Harvard: Harvard University Press, 1990).

11. Hunt, *Politics, Culture and Class,* chap. 2; Emmet Kennedy, *A Cultural History of the French Revolution* (New Haven: Yale University Press, 1989), chaps. 6–11.

but as a dynamic strategy of manipulation and control that targets the spectator."[12]

In the seventies, the mémoires remained in form close to theatrical spectacle, staging "pathetic" tableaux for the benefit of the reader/spectator. By the eighties, the authors of trial briefs began to adopt techniques aimed at fostering the ideal of Rousseauean (and revolutionary) "transparency": by bringing to the fore the personality and reactions of the barrister-author and inviting their readers to share the intimacy of the *sensible* protagonist, the authors of mémoires sought to create an unmediated connection between the presumed virtue and sensibility of their client and that of their readers; this intimate connection between reader, lawyer, and client was then pressed into the service of the political argument spelled out in the mémoire. This rhetorical strategy points to the most ominous development of the Revolution, the Jacobin reign of Virtue and Terror. The politicization of the private (Habermas's "authentic" public sphere) was defined and limited, before the Revolution, by its opposition to the sociopolitical institutions of the Old Regime. But as Dena Goodman suggests, once the public sphere of the monarchy had been abolished, it became increasingly difficult to fix limits between the public and the private: "What had been a private realm with two faces [civil society and the intimate sphere] was now the whole of state and society."[13] By the early 1790s, the use of virtue and sensibility as didactic tools within forensic rhetoric (and other sorts of texts) culminated in the revolutionaries' attempts to control the hearts as well as the minds of citizens.

The Reign of Terror, however, was but the first and most catastrophic incarnation of what was to become an enduring French ideal—the belief in an egalitarian state rooted in a strong system of secular morality. The publicity around court cases in the prerevolutionary years helped bring about this ideal in several ways: by attacking the arrogance and exclusiveness of the social and political elites; by insisting that only openness in judicial and political institutions could guarantee the fair treatment of all; by demonstrating that the experiences of ordinary people were important enough to serve as a foundation for moral and legal norms. In the public culture of the early nineteenth century, the courtroom (as still chronicled in mémoires and in the hugely successful

12. Scott Bryson, *The Chastised Stage: Bourgeois Drama and the Exercise of Power* (Stanford: Anima Libri, 1991), p. 5.
13. Goodman, "Public Sphere and Private Life," p. 13.

Gazette des tribunaux) and the flourishing melodrama of "boulevard" theatre continued to strengthen in growing numbers of readers and spectators the belief in a democratic and secular morality. The French Revolution continues after two hundred years to rivet attention as a historical drama in which the subjects of one of Europe's oldest monarchies came to believe passionately in social equality and in the dignity of the middling sorts. The *memoires judiciaires* are part of that story.

Bibliography

Primary Sources

MANUSCRIPTS

ARCHIVES NATIONALES
Series X1B, Greffe du Parlement Civil
    8453   Salency Affair
Series X2B, Greffe du Parlement Criminel
    1382–1386   Tort-Guines Affair
    1417   Diamond Necklace Affair
    1422–1426   Richelieu–Saint-Vincent Affair

BIBLIOTHÈQUE NATIONALE
Manuscrits Français
    6680–6685   Journal of Siméon-Prosper Hardy
    9264   "La Rosière de Rosny: Comédie en 3 actes et en prose." 1783.
    9270   "La rosière à la mode." N.p., n.d.
Anisson Collection (Documents relating to the book trade)
    Volumes 22062, 22063, 22068, 22070, 22073, 22080, 22081, 22092, 22093, 22098, 22099, 22100, 22101, 22102, 22179.
Joly de Fleury Collection (Papers relating to the affairs of the Paris Parlement)
    Volumes 1682, 2067, 2082, 2084–2085, 2087, 2088–2089.

BIBLIOTHÈQUE HISTORIQUE DE LA VILLE DE PARIS
Manuscript Volumes 690 and 691 (Papers of Guy-Jean-Baptiste Target relating to the Diamond Necklace Affair).

PRINTED SOURCES

MÉMOIRES JUDICIAIRES

Rather than listing the titles of the *mémoires* that are the main source of this study, I refer the reader both to the footnotes to each chapter and to Augustin Corda's *Catalogue des factums et d'autres documents judiciaires antérieurs à 1790,* 7 vols. (Paris: Plon, 1890–1905), which lists lawyers' briefs and other pamphlet material relating to important cases under the names of the principal parties, with their Bibliothèque Nationale call numbers. I supplemented the Bibliothèque Nationale's collection with those of the Bibliothèque Historique de la Ville de Paris (on the Diamond Necklace Affair) and of the Newberry Library, Chicago (on the Kornmann Affair, Wing ZP 739 and 7391).

PERIODICAL PUBLICATIONS

Gazette de Leyde

Gazette d'Utrecht

Gazette des Tribunaux

Grimm, Melchior, et al. *Correspondance littéraire, philosophique et critique.* 16 vols. Paris: Garnier, 1877–1882.

[Petit de Bachaumont, Louis, et al.] *Mémoires secrets pour servir à l'histoire de la république des lettres en France.* 36 vols. London: John Adamson, 1777–1789.

[Pidansat de Mairobert, Mathieu.] *Journal historique de la révolution opérée dans la constitution de la monarchie françoise par M. de Maupeou, chancelier de France.* 7 vols. London: J. Adamson, 1776.

OTHER SOURCES

Anecdotes sur Mme la comtesse du Barri. Paris, 1776.

Beaumarchais, Pierre Augustin Caron de. *Oeuvres.* Paris: Gallimard, 1988.

———. *Oeuvres complètes.* 7 vols. Paris: Léopold Collin, 1809.

———. *Théâtre complet.* Paris: Gallimard, 1957.

Bergasse, Nicolas. *Discours sur l'humanité des juges dans l'administration de la justice criminelle.* Paris, 1787.

Berryer, Pierre Nicolas. *Souvenirs de M. Berryer, doyen des avocats de Paris de 1774 à 1838.* 2 vols. Paris: Ambroise Dupont, 1839.

Biarnoy de Merville, Pierre. *Règles pour former un avocat.* Paris: Durand, 1778.

Billardon de Sauvigny, Edmé-Louis. *La Rose ou la feste de Salency avec un supplément sur l'origine de cette fête.* Paris: Gauguery, 1770.

Blin de Sainmore. *Requête des filles de Salency à la reine.* Paris: Delalain, 1774.

Blondel, Jean. *Discussion des principaux objets de la législation criminelle.* Paris, 1789.

Bord*** R*** suivi d'un entretien secret entre la reine et le cardinal de Rohan après son entrée aux Etats-Généraux. N.p., n.d.

Brillon, Pierre Jacques. *Dictionnaire de jurisprudence et des arrêts.* 7 vols. Lyon, 1781–1788.

Brissot de Warville, Jacques-Pierre. *Le Sang innocent vengé ou discours sur les réparations dues aux accusés innocens.* Paris, 1781.

Camus, Armand Gaspard. *Lettres sur la profession d'avocat et sur les études néces-saires pour se rendre capable de l'exercer.* Paris: Hérissant, 1772.

Le Capitaine Tempête à Jeanne de La Motte. N.p., n.d.

Carmontelle, Louis Carrogis de. *Proverbes et comédies posthumes.* 2 vols. Paris: Ladvocat, 1825.

Cerfvol [pseud.]. *Législation du divorce.* London, 1770.

Chavray de Boissy, François René. *L'Avocat ou réflexions sur l'exercice du bar-reau.* Paris: Cellot, 1777.

Clair, M., and A. Clapier. *Le Barreau français: Collection des chefs d'oeuvre de l'éloquence judiciaire en France.* 16 vols. Paris: Panckoucke, 1823–1824.

Condorcet, Marie-Jean-Antoine, marquis de. *Réflexions d'un citoyen non gradué sur un procès très-connu.* Frankfurt, 1786.

Conférence entre Madame de Polignac et Madame de la Motte au parc Saint-James ou lettre de Monsieur de Vaudreuil à un abbé fort connu. N.p., n.d.

Delacroix, Jacques-Vincent. *Apologie de la constitution civile du clergé décrétée par l'Assemblée Nationale et acceptée par le roi.* Evreux, 1791.

———. *Combien le respect pour les moeurs contribue au bonheur des états.* Brus-sels, 1776.

———. *Discours et lettres sur différens sujets.* Amsterdam, 1777.

———. *Mémoire préliminaire sur le travail des Etats-Généraux.* N.p., n.d.

———. *Réflexions philosophiques sur l'origine de la civilisation et sur les moyens de remédier à quelques-uns des abus qu'elle entraîne.* Amsterdam, 1778.

———. *Réflexions sur les mémoires.* N.p., 1775.

Dernière pièce du fameux collier. N.p., n.d.

Diderot, Denis. *Entretiens sur le comédien précédé des Entretiens sur "Le fils na-turel."* Paris: Garnier-Flammarion, 1967.

Dupaty, Charles Marguerite. *Discours prononcé par M. Dupaty avocat-général le 13 Mars 1775 à la première audience de la Grand'Chambre après le rétablis-ment du Parlement.* N.p., 1775.

———. *Lettres sur l'Italie.* 2 vols. Rome, 1788.

———. *Justification de sept hommes condamnés par le Parlement de Metz en 1796 sur la seule déposition de Juifs plaignans.* N.p., 1787.

Essais historiques sur la vie de Marie-Antoinette d'Autriche, reine de France. London, 1789.

Falconnet, Ambroise. *Le Barreau français, partie moderne.* 2 vols. Paris: Guef-fier, 1806–1808.

———. *Essai sur le barreau grec, romain, et françois et sur les moyens de donner du lustre à ce dernier.* Paris: Grangé, 1773.

Les Fastes de Louis XV, ses ministres, maîtresses, généraux, et autres notables per-sonnages de son règne. N.p., 1782.

Fauchet, abbé Claude. *Discours sur les moeurs rurales.* Paris, 1788.

Favart, Charles. *La Rosière de Salenci.* Paris: Veuve Duchesne, 1770.

Ferrière, Claude. *Dictionnaire de droit et de pratique.* 2 vols. Paris: Brunet, 1749.

Fournel, Jean-François. *Histoire des avocats au Parlement et du Barreau de Paris.* Paris, 1813.

————. *Traité de l'adultère considéré dans l'ordre judiciaire.* Paris, 1778.

Genlis, Stéphanie-Félicité. *Mémoires.* 8 vols. Paris: Ladvocat, 1825.

————. *Théâtre d'éducation à l'usage de la jeunesse.* Paris: Didier, 1847.

Georgel, abbé Jean-François. *Mémoires pour servir à l'histoire des événemens de la fin du dix-huitieme siècle.* 6 vols. Paris, 1820.

Gin, Pierre-Louis-Claude. *De l'éloquence du barreau.* Paris: Herissant, 1767.

Gorsas, Antoine-Joseph. *L'Ane promeneur ou Critès promené par son âne.* N.p., 1786.

Grégoire, abbé Henri. *Histoire des sectes religieuses.* 6 vols. Paris: Baudoin, 1828.

Hennet, Albert Joseph. *Du divorce.* Paris: Desenne, 1789.

Histoire de la Rosière de Salancy, ou recueil de pièces tant en prose qu'en vers sur la Rosière. Paris: Mérigot, 1777.

Histoire véritable de Jeanne de Saint-Rémi ou les aventures de la comtesse de La Motte. N.p., 1786.

Isambert, François, et al. *Recueil général des anciennes lois françaises depuis 420 jusqu'à la Révolution.* 29 vols. Paris, 1821–1823.

[Kéralio, Louise de.] *Les Crimes des reines de France depuis le commencement de la monarchie jusqu'à Marie-Antoinette.* Paris, 1791.

Lacretelle, Pierre-Louis de. *De la convocation des prochains Etats-Généraux.* N.p., 1788.

————. *De l'éloquence judiciaire.* Paris, 1779.

————. *Oeuvres.* 6 vols. Paris: Bossange, 1823–1824.

Le Monnier, abbé. *Fêtes des bonnes gens de Canon et des rosières de Briquebec.* Paris: Prault, 1777.

Le Scène Desmaisons, Jacques. *Contrat conjugal ou lois du mariage, de la répudiation, et du divorce.* N.p., 1781.

Lettre à Milord M*** au sujet de M. Bergasse et de ses observations dans l'affaire de M. Kornmann. Paris, 1788.

Lettre d'un garde du roi pour faire suite aux mémoires sur Cagliostro. London, 1786.

Lettre du public parisien à Pierre-Augustin Caron de Beaumarchais. N.p., n.d.

Les Lettres de cachet presque ressucitées. N.p., n.d.

Malesherbes, Chrétien-Guillaume Lamoignon de. *Mémoires sur la librairie et sur la liberté de la presse.* Edited by Graham Rodnell. Chapel Hill: North Carolina Studies in the Romance Languages and Literatures, 1979.

Masson de Pezay. *La Rosière de Salenci.* Paris: Delalain, 1775.

Mémoires authentiques pour servir à l'histoire du comte de Cagliostro. Paris, 1786.

Mercier, Louis-Sébastien. *L'Indigent.* Paris: Le Jai, 1778.

————. *Le Juge.* Paris, 1774.

————. *Tableau de Paris.* 12 vols. Amsterdam, 1783–1788.

————. *Du théâtre ou nouvel essai sur l'art dramatique.* Amsterdam, 1773. Reprint. Geneva: Slatkine, 1970.

Mey, Claude, and Nicolas Maultrot. *Maximes du droit public françois.* 2 vols. Amsterdam: M. M. Rey, 1775.

Mirabeau, Gabriel-Honoré de Riquetti, comte de. *Oeuvres.* 8 vols. Paris, 1834–1835.

Moreau, Jacob-Nicolas. *Mes Souvenirs.* Edited by Camille Hermelein. Paris: Plon, 1898.

Nougaret, Pierre Jean Baptiste. *Coup d'oeil d'un Arabe sur la littérature française ou le barbier de Bagdad faisant la barbe au barbier de Séville.* London, 1786.

———. *Les Rosières.* Paris: Le Fuel, n.d.

Observations de P. Tranquille sur le premier mémoire de Madame de La Motte. N.p., 1786.

Pétion de Villeneuve, Jérôme. *Essai sur le mariage considéré sous des rapports naturels, moraux, et politiques.* Geneva, 1785.

Plan d'une conversation entre un avocat et M. le chancelier. N.p., 1771.

Recueil des fêtes et spectacles donnés devant sa majesté à Versailles à Choisy et à Fontainebleau. Paris, 1773.

La Reine dévoilée ou supplément au mémoire de Madame la comtesse de Valois de La Motte. London, 1789.

Servan, Michel de. *Discours sur l'administration de la justice criminelle.* Geneva, 1767.

Soulavie, Jean-Louis-Girard. *Memoirs of the Duke of Richelieu.* 3 vols. New York: Baker and Merrill, 1904.

Suite des observations de Motus sur le mémoire de Melle d'Oliva. N.p., 1786.

Target, Guy-Jean-Baptiste. *Discours prononcé en la Grand'Chambre par M. Target, avocat, le 28 novembre 1774 à la rentrée du Parlement.* Paris, 1774.

———. *Lettre d'un homme à un autre homme sur l'extinction de l'ancien Parlement et la création du nouveau.* N.p., n.d.

Vermeil, François. *Essai sur les réformes à faire dans notre législation criminelle.* Paris: Demonville, 1781.

Voltaire, François Marie Arouet de. *L'Affaire Calas et autres affaires.* Edited by Jacques Van den Heuvel. Paris: Gallimard, 1975.

———. *Oeuvres complètes.* 52 vols. Paris: Garnier, 1877–1885.

Secondary Sources

WORKS ON LAWYERS, COURT CASES, AND THE LEGAL PROFESSION

Adams, Christine. "Defining *Etat* in Eighteenth-Century France: The Lamothe Family of Bordeaux." *Journal of Family History* 17 (1992): 25–45.

Bien, David. *The Calas Affair: Persecution, Toleration and Heresy in Eighteenth-Century Toulouse.* Princeton: Princeton University Press, 1960.

Bell, David. "Lawyers and Politics in Eighteenth-Century Paris (1700–1790)." Ph.D. diss., Princeton University, 1991.

———. "Lawyers into Demagogues: Chancellor Maupeou and the Transformation of Legal Practice in France, 1771–1789." *Past and Present* 130 (1991): 107–141.

———. "Des stratégies d'opposition sous Louis XV: L'Affaire des avocats, 1730–1731." *Histoire, économie et société* 9 (1990): 567–590.

Bennett, W. Lance. "Rhetorical Transformation of Evidence in Criminal Trials: Creating Grounds for Legal Judgment." *Quarterly Journal of Speech* 65 (1979): 311–323.

———. "Storytelling in Criminal Trials: A Model of Social Judgment." *Quarterly Journal of Speech* 64 (1978): 1–22.

Bennett, W. Lance, and Martha Feldman. *Reconstructing Reality in the Courtroom: Justice and Judgment in American Culture.* New Brunswick: Rutgers University Press, 1981.

Berlanstein, Lenard. *The Barristers of Toulouse in the Eighteenth Century (1740–1793).* Baltimore: Johns Hopkins University Press, 1975.

———. "Lawyers in Pre-Revolutionary France." In *Lawyers in Early Modern Europe and America,* edited by Wilfred Priest. New York: Holmes and Meier, 1981.

Boulloche, Paul. *Un Avocat du XVIIIe siècle.* Paris: Calmann-Levy, 1893.

Cailleau de Courcelles, Henri-François. *Notes sur Gerbier, ancien bâtonnier de l'Ordre des Avocats au Parlement de Paris.* Paris: Balitout, 1881.

Carey, John. *Judicial Reform in France before the Revolution of 1789.* Cambridge, Mass.: Harvard University Press, 1981.

Carré, Henri. *Le Barreau de Paris et la radiation de Linguet.* Poitiers: Millet et Pain, 1892.

Damien, André. *Les Avocats du temps passé.* Paris: Henri Lefebvre, 1973.

Davis, Natalie Zemon. *Fiction in the Archives: Pardon Tales and Their Tellers in Sixteenth-Century France.* Stanford: Stanford University Press, 1987.

Delbeke, Francis. *L'Action politique et sociale des avocats au XVIIIe siècle: Leur part dans la préparation de la Révolution française.* Paris: Sirey, 1927.

Doyle, William. "Dupaty (1746–1788): A Career in the Late Enlightenment." *Studies on Voltaire and the Eighteenth Century* 230 (1985): 1–125.

———. *The Parlement of Bordeaux and the End of the Old Regime 1771–1790.* London: Ernest Benn, 1974.

Dumon, S. "Notice sur Target." In *Annales du barreau français* 3 (1826): 3–13.

Esmein, Albert. *Histoire de la procédure criminelle en France.* Paris: Larose et Forcel, 1882.

Everdell, William. "The *Rosières* Movement, 1766–1789: A Clerical Precursor of the Revolutionary Cults." *French Historical Studies* 9 (Spring 1975): 23–36.

Fitzsimmons, Michael. *The Parisian Order of Barristers and the French Revolution.* Cambridge, Mass.: Harvard University Press, 1987.

Funck-Brentano, Frantz. *L'Affaire du collier.* Paris: Hachette, 1901.

Gaudry, Joachim Antoine Joseph. *Histoire du Barreau de Paris.* Paris: Auguste Durand, 1864. Reprint. Geneva: Slatkine, 1977.

Girault de Coursac, P. *Marie-Antoinette et le scandale de Guines*. Paris: Galli-mard, 1962.

Gresset, Maurice. *Gens de justice à Besançon*. 2 vols. Paris: Bibliothèque Natio-nale, 1978.

Guilhermoz, Paul. "De la persistance du caractère oral dans la plaidoirie civile française." *Nouvelle Revue historique de droit français et étranger*, 1889, pp. 21–65.

Hay, Douglas, et al. *Albion's Fatal Tree: Crime and Society in Eighteenth-Century England*. New York: Pantheon, 1975.

Hudault, Joseph. "Guy-Jean-Baptiste Target et sa contribution à la prépara-tion de l'Edit de novembre 1787 sur l'état-civil des protestants." Law the-sis, University of Paris, 1866.

Imbert, Jean. *Quelques procès criminels des XVIIe et XVIIIe siècles*. Paris: Presses Universitaires de France, 1964.

Jacobson, David. "The Politics of Criminal Law Reform in Late Eighteenth-Century France." Ph.D. diss., Brown University, 1976.

———. "The Trois Roués Case and the Debate Over Criminal Law Reform in Late Eighteenth-Century France." In *Proceedings of the Fourth Annual Meeting of the Western Society for French Historical Studies*, 1977, pp. 168–173.

Kagan, Richard. "Law Students and Legal Careers in Eighteenth-Century France." *Past and Present* 68 (1975): 38–72.

Karpik, Lucien. "Lawyers and Politics in France, 1814–1950: The State, the Market, and the Public." *Law and Social Inquiry* 13 (Fall 1988): 707–736.

Laingui, André, and Arlette Lebigre. *Histoire du droit pénal*. 2 vols. Paris: Cu-jas, 1979.

Le Corbeiller, Armand. *Le Long Martyre de Françoise Salmon*. Paris: Perrin, 1927.

Levy, Darline Gay. *The Ideas and Careers of Simon-Nicolas-Henri Linguet: A Study in Eighteenth-Century French Politics*. Urbana: University of Illinois Press, 1980.

Lüsebrink, Hans-Jürgen. "L'Affaire Cléreaux (Rouen 1785–1790): Affronte-ments idéologiques et tensions institutionnelles sur la scène judiciaire de la fin du XVIIIe siècle." *Studies on Voltaire and the Eighteenth Century* 191 (1980): 892–900.

———. "Mémoire pour la fille Cléreaux (Rouen 1785)." *Studies on Voltaire and the Eighteenth Century* 208 (1982): 322–372.

Marion, Marcel. *Le Garde des sceaux Lamoignon et la réforme judiciaire de 1788*. Paris: Hachette, 1950.

Mary-Lafon, J. B. *Le Maréchal de Richelieu et Madame de Saint-Vincent*. Paris: Didot, 1863.

Maza, Sarah. "The Diamond Necklace Affair Revisited (1785–1786): The Case of the Missing Queen." In *Eroticism and the Body Politic*, edited by Lynn Hunt, pp. 63–89. Baltimore: The Johns Hopkins University Press, 1991.

————. "Domestic Melodrama as Political Ideology: The Case of the Comte de Sanois." *American Historical Review* 94 (1989): 1249–1264.

————. "The Rose-Girl of Salency: Representations of Virtue in Pre-Revolutionary France." *Eighteenth-Century Studies* 22 (1989): 395–412.

————. "Le Tribunal de la nation: Les mémoires judiciaires et l'opinion publique à la fin de l'ancien régime." *Annales: Economies, sociétés, civilisations* 42 (1987): 73–90.

Mossiker, Frances. *The Queen's Necklace.* New York: Simon and Schuster, 1961.

Nixon, Edna. *Voltaire and the Calas Case.* New York: Vanguard Press, 1961.

Poirot, Albert. "Le Milieu socio-professionnel des avocats du Parlement de Paris à la veille de la Révolution." Thesis of the Ecole des Chartes, 1977.

Prud'homme, Charles. *Michel de Servan (1737–1807): Un magistrat réformateur.* Paris: Larose et Tenin, 1905.

Renwick, John. "Voltaire et Morangiès 1772–1773 ou les lumières l'ont échappé belle." *Studies on Voltaire and the Eighteenth Century* 202 (1982): 9–149.

Seligman, Edmond. "L'Affaire des Trois Roués." *Revue de Paris,* 15 March 1901, pp. 413–425.

————. *La Justice en France pendant la Révolution.* 2 vols. Paris: Plon, 1901–1913.

Stone, Bailey. *The Parlement of Paris, 1774–1789.* Chapel Hill: University of North Carolina Press, 1981.

Wattine, Adolphe. *L'Affaire des Trois Roués.* Macon: Protat Frères, 1921.

OTHER WORKS

Abray, Jane. "Feminism in the French Revolution." *American Historical Review* 80 (1975): 43–62.

Agulhon, Maurice. *Marianne into Battle: Republican Imagery and Symbolism in France.* Translated by Janet Lloyd. Cambridge: Cambridge University Press, 1981.

Alméras, Henri d'. *Marie-Antoinette et les pamphlets royalistes et révolutionnaires.* Paris: Albin Michel, n.d.

Aubertin, Charles. *L'Esprit public au XVIIIe siècle.* Paris: Perrin, 1889.

Baczko, Bronislaw. *Les Imaginaires sociaux.* Paris: Payot, 1984.

Badinter, Elizabeth. *Les "Remontrances" de Malesherbes.* Paris: Union générale d'éditions, 1978.

Baker, Keith. *Inventing the French Revolution.* Cambridge: Cambridge University Press, 1990.

————, ed. *The Political Culture of the Old Regime.* Oxford: Pergamon Press, 1987.

Besterman, Theodore. *Voltaire.* Oxford: Basil Blackwell, 1976.

Bickart, Roger. *Les Parlements et la notion de souveraineté nationale au XVIIIe siècle.* Paris: Félix Alcan, 1932.

Booth, Wayne. *The Company We Keep: An Ethics of Fiction.* Berkeley: University of California Press, 1988.

Brooks, Peter. *The Melodramatic Imagination: Balzac, Henry James, Melodrama, and the Mode of Excess.* New York: Columbia University Press, 1985.

———. *The Novel of Wordliness: Crébillon, Marivaux, Laclos, Stendhal.* Princeton: Princeton University Press, 1969.

———. *Reading for the Plot: Design and Intention in Narrative.* New York: Knopf, 1984.

Bryson, Scott. *The Chastised Stage: Bourgeois Drama and the Exercise of Power.* Stanford: Anima Libri, 1991.

Carcassonne, Elie. *Montesquieu et le problème de la constitution française au XVIIIe siècle.* Paris, 1927. Reprint. Geneva: Slatkine, 1970.

Carré, Henri. *La Noblesse de France et l'opinion publique au XVIIIe siècle.* Paris: Champion, 1920.

Censer, Jack, and Jeremy Popkin. *Press and Politics in Pre-Revolutionary France.* Berkeley: University of California Press, 1987.

Chartier, Roger. *The Cultural Origins of the French Revolution.* Translated by Lydia Cochrane. Durham: Duke University Press, 1991.

———. *The Cultural Uses of Print in Early Modern France.* Translated by Lydia Cochrane. Princeton: Princeton University Press, 1987.

Chaussinand-Nogaret, Guy. *La Noblesse au XVIIIe siècle: De la féodalité aux lumières.* Paris: Hachette, 1976.

Crow, Thomas. "The Oath of the Horatii in 1785: Painting and Pre-Revolutionary Radicalism in France." *Art History* 1 (1978): 424–471.

———. *Painters and Public Life in Eighteenth-Century Paris.* New Haven: Yale University Press, 1985.

Darnton, Robert. *The Great Cat Massacre and Other Episodes in French Cultural History.* New York: Basic Books, 1984.

———. *The Literary Underground of the Old Regime.* Cambridge, Mass.: Harvard University Press, 1982.

———. "Trends in Radical Propaganda on the Eve of the French Revolution (1782–1788)." Ph.D. diss., Oxford University, 1964.

Davis, Lennard. *Factual Fictions: The Origins of the English Novel.* New York: Columbia University Press, 1983.

Davis, Natalie Zemon. *Society and Culture in Early Modern France.* Stanford: Stanford University Press, 1975.

Dommanget, Maurice. *Sylvain Maréchal l'égalitaire: "L'homme sans dieu."* Paris: Spartacus, 1950.

Donaldson, Ian. *The Rapes of Lucretia: A Myth and Its Transformation.* Oxford: Clarendon Press, 1979.

Doyle, William. *Origins of the French Revolution.* Oxford: Oxford University Press, 1980.

———. "The Parlements of France and the Breakdown of the Old Regime." *French Historical Studies* 6 (1970): 415–458.

Echeverria, Durand. *The Maupeou Revolution: A Study in the History of Liber-*

tarianism, France 1770–1774. Baton Rouge: Louisiana State University Press, 1985.

———. "The Pre-Revolutionary Influence of Rousseau's *Contrat Social.*" *Journal of the History of Ideas* 33 (1972): 543–560.

Egret, Jean. *Louis XV et l'opposition parlementaire.* Paris: Armand Colin, 1970.

Eisenstein, Elizabeth. *Print Culture and Enlightenment Thought.* Chapel Hill: Hanes Foundation, University of North Carolina, 1986.

Ellrich, Robert. "The Rhetoric of *La Religieuse* and Eighteenth-Century Forensic Rhetoric." *Diderot Studies* 3. Geneva: Droz, 1961.

Estivals, Roger. *La Statistique bibliographique de la France sous la monarchie absolue.* Paris: Mouton, 1965.

Ettema, James, and Theodore Glasser. "Narrative Form and Moral Force: The Realization of Innocence and Guilt through Investigative Journalism." *Journal of Communication* 38 (1988): 8–26.

Fairchilds, Cissie. *Domestic Enemies: Servants and Their Masters in Old Regime France.* Baltimore: Johns Hopkins University Press, 1984.

Faure, Edgar. *La Disgrâce de Turgot.* Paris: Gallimard, 1961.

Flammermont, Jules. *Le Chancelier Maupeou et les parlements.* Paris: Picard, 1883.

Fleischmann, Hector. *Les Pamphlets libertins contre Marie-Antoinette.* Paris, 1908. Reprint. Geneva: Slatkine, 1976.

Fort, Bernadette. *Le Langage de l'ambiguïté dans l'oeuvre de Crébillon fils.* Paris: Klincksieck, 1978.

Foucault, Michel. *Discipline and Punish.* Translated by Alan Sheridan. New York: Random House, 1979.

France, Peter. *Rhetoric and Truth in France: Descartes to Diderot.* Oxford: Clarendon Press, 1972.

Furet, François, et al. *Livre et société dans la France du XVIIIe siècle.* 2 vols. Paris: Mouton, 1965 and 1970.

Gaiffe, Félix. *Le Mariage de Figaro.* Amiens: Edgar Malfère, 1928.

———. *Le Drame en France au XVIIIe siècle.* Paris: Armand Colin, 1910.

Gelbart, Nina Rattner. *Feminine and Opposition Journalism in Old Regime France: Le Journal des Dames.* Berkeley: University of California Press, 1987.

———. "Frondeur Journalism in the 1770s." *Eighteenth-Century Studies* 17 (1984): 493–514.

Goodman, Dena. "Governing the Republic of Letters: The Politics of Culture in the French Enlightenment." *History of European Ideas* 13 (1991): 183–199.

———. "Public Sphere and Private Life: Toward a Synthesis of Current Historiographical Approaches to the Old Regime." *History and Theory* 31 (1992): 1–20.

———. "Story-Telling in the Republic of Letters: The Rhetorical Context of Diderot's *La Religieuse.*" *Nouvelles de la République des Lettres* 1 (1986): 51–70.

Green, F. C. *La Peinture des moeurs de la bonne société dans le roman français de 1715 à 1761.* Paris: Presses Universitaires de France, 1924.

Grendel, Frédéric. *Beaumarchais*. Translated by Roger Greaves. New York: Thomas Y. Crowell, 1977.

Guillot, Michel. "La Rosière de Suresnes et le mouvement des rosières en Ile-de-France." Manuscript.

Habermas, Jürgen. *The Structural Transformation of the Public Sphere: An Inquiry into a Category of Bourgeois Society*. Translated by Thomas Burger and Frederick Lawrence. Cambridge, Mass.: MIT Press, 1989.

Hampton, John. "The Literary Technique of the First Two *Mémoires* against Goezman." *Studies on Voltaire and the Eighteenth Century* 47 (1966): 177–205.

Hanley, Sarah. "Engendering the State: Family Formation and State Building in Early Modern France." *French Historical Studies* 16 (1989): 4–27.

———. "Family and State in Early Modern France: The Marriage Pact." In *Connecting Spheres: Women in the Western World, 1500 to the Present*, edited by Marilyn Boxer and Jean Quataert, pp. 53–63. Oxford: Oxford University Press, 1987.

Higonnet, Patrice. *Class, Ideology, and the Rights of Nobles During the French Revolution*. Oxford: Clarendon Press, 1981.

Hoffman, Paul. *La Femme dans la pensée des lumières*. Paris: Orphrys, 1977.

Howarth, W. D. "Tragedy into Melodrama: The Fortunes of the Calas Affair on the Stage." *Studies on Voltaire and the Eighteenth Century* 174 (1978): 121–150.

———. "The Playwright as Preacher: Didacticism and Melodrama in the French Theatre of the Enlightenment." *Forum for Modern Language Studies* 14 (April 1978): 97–115.

Hudson, David. "In Defense of Reform: French Government Propaganda during the Maupeou Crisis." *French Historical Studies* 8 (1973): 51–76.

Huet, Marie-Hélène. *Rehearsing the Revolution: The Staging of Marat's Death, 1793–1797*. Translated by Robert Hurley. Berkeley: University of California Press, 1982.

Hunt, Lynn. *The Family Romance of the French Revolution*. Berkeley: University of California Press, 1992.

———. *Politics, Culture and Class in the French Revolution*. Berkeley: University of California Press, 1984.

Jones, Colin. "The Bourgeois Revolution Revivified: 1789 and Social Change." In *Rewriting the French Revolution*, edited by Colin Lucas, pp. 69–118. Oxford: Clarendon Press, 1991.

Jouhaud, Christian. *Mazarinades: La Fronde des mots*. Paris: Aubier, 1985.

Jullien, Adolphe. *La Comédie à la cour: Les Théâtres de société royale pendant le siècle dernier*. Paris: Firmin Didot, 1885. Reprint. Geneva: Slatkine, 1971.

Landes, Joan. *Women and the Public Sphere in the Age of the French Revolution*. Ithaca: Cornell University Press, 1988.

Langbein, John. "*Albion's* Fatal Flaws." *Past and Present* 98 (February 1983): 96–120.

Leitch, Thomas. *What Stories Are: Narrative Theory and Narrative Interpretation*. University Park: Pennsylvania State University Press, 1986.

Loménie, Louis de. *Beaumarchais et son temps: Etudes sur la société en France au XVIIIe siècle.* 2 vols. Paris: Michel Levy, 1856.

Lüsebrink, Hans-Jürgen. "Les Représentations sociales de la criminalité en France au XVIIIe siècle." Ph.D. diss., University of Paris-I, 1983.

Lüsebrink, Hans-Jürgen, and Rolf Reichardt. "La Bastille dans l'imaginaire social de la France à la fin du XVIIIe siècle, 1774–1789." *Revue d'histoire moderne et contemporaine* 30 (1983): 196–223.

Mackrell, J. Q. C. *The Attack on "Feudalism" in Eighteenth-Century France.* Toronto: University of Toronto Press, 1973.

Marion, Marcel. *Dictionnaire des institutions de la France aux XVIIe et XVIIIe siècles.* Paris, 1923. Reprint. Paris: Picard, 1984.

Martin, Henri-Jean, and Roger Chartier, eds. *Histoire de l'édition française.* Vol. 2, *Le Livre triomphant, 1660–1830.* Paris: Fayard, 1990.

Maza, Sarah. *Servants and Masters in Eighteenth-Century France: The Uses of Loyalty.* Princeton: Princeton University Press, 1983.

Mornet, Daniel. *Les Origines intellectuelles de la Révolution française.* Paris: Armand Colin, 1933.

Mylne, Vivienne. *The Eighteenth-Century French Novel: Techniques of Illusion.* Manchester: Manchester University Press, 1965.

Nathans, Benjamin. "Habermas's 'Public Sphere' in the Era of the French Revolution." *French Historical Studies* 16 (1990): 620–647.

Ortner, Sherry. "The Virgin and the State." *Feminist Studies* 4 (1978): 19–35.

Ozouf, Mona. *La Fête révolutionnaire.* Paris: Gallimard, 1976.

———. "'Public Opinion' at the End of the Old Regime." *Journal of Modern History* 60 (Supplement, September 1988): S1–S21.

Pateman, Carole. *The Disorder of Women: Democracy, Feminism, and Political Theory.* Stanford: Stanford University Press, 1989.

———. *The Sexual Contract.* Stanford: Stanford University Press, 1988.

Phillips, Roderick. *Family Breakdown in Eighteenth-Century France: Divorces in Rouen, 1792–1803.* Oxford, Clarendon Press, 1980.

———. *Putting Asunder: A History of Divorce in Western Society.* Cambridge: Cambridge University Press, 1988.

Popkin, Jeremy. *News and Politics in the Age of Revolution: Jean Luzac's "Gazette de Leyde."* Ithaca: Cornell University Press, 1989.

———. "Pamphlet Journalism at the End of the Old Regime." *Eighteenth-Century Studies* 22 (1989): 351–367.

Price, Munro. "The 'Ministry of a Hundred Hours': A Reappraisal." *French History* 4 (September 1990): 317–339.

Przybos, Julia. *L'Entreprise mélodramatique.* Paris: José Corti, 1987.

Revel, Jacques. "Marie-Antoinette in Her Fictions: The Staging of Hatred." In *Fictions of the French Revolution,* edited by Bernadette Fort. Evanston, Ill.: Northwestern University Press, 1991.

Rocquain, Félix. *L'Esprit révolutionnaire avant la Révolution.* Paris: Plon, 1878.

Ronsin, Francis. *Le Contrat sentimental: Débats sur le mariage, l'amour, le divorce de l'Ancien Régime à la Restauration.* Paris: Aubier, 1990.

Root, Hilton. *Peasants and King in Burgundy: Agrarian Foundations of French Absolutism.* Berkeley: University of California Press, 1987.

Royer, Clément de. *Etude sur les Mémoires de Beaumarchais.* Paris: J. Claye, 1872.

Sarbin, Theodore. *Narrative Psychology: The Storied Nature of Human Conduct.* New York: Praeger, 1986.

Schwartz, Joel. *The Sexual Politics of Jean-Jacques Rousseau.* Chicago: University of Chicago Press, 1984.

Scott, Joan Wallach. *Gender and the Politics of History.* New York: Columbia University Press, 1988.

Segalen, Martine, and Josselyne Chamarat. "La Rosière et La 'Miss': Les 'Reines' des fêtes populaires." *L'Histoire* 53 (February 1983): 44–54.

Showalter, English, Jr. *The Evolution of the French Novel, 1641–1782.* Princeton: Princeton University Press, 1972.

Singham, Shanti. "'A Conspiracy of Twenty Million Frenchmen': Public Opinion, Patriotism, and the Assault on Absolutism during the Maupeou Years." Ph.D. diss., Princeton University, 1991.

Stone, Bailey. "Robe against Sword: The Parlement of Paris and the French Aristocracy, 1774–1789." *French Historical Studies* 9 (Fall 1975): 278–303.

Tanner, Tony. *Adultery in the Novel: Contract and Transgression.* Baltimore: Johns Hopkins University Press, 1979.

Thomas, Chantal. *La Reine scélérate: Marie-Antoinette dans les pamphlets.* Paris: Seuil, 1989.

Traer, James. *Marriage and the Family in Eighteenth-Century France.* Ithaca: Cornell University Press, 1980.

Udanck, Jack. "Beaumarchais's Transformations." *Modern Language Notes* 100 (September 1985): 829–870.

Van Kley, Dale. *The Damiens Affair and the Unraveling of the Ancien Régime, 1750–1770.* Princeton: Princeton University Press, 1984.

———. "The Jansenist Constitutional Legacy in the French Prerevolution." In *The Political Culture of the Old Regime,* edited by Keith Baker, pp. 169–201. Oxford: Pergamon Press, 1987.

———. *The Jansenists and the Expulsion of the Jesuits from France, 1757–1765.* New Haven: Yale University Press, 1975.

———. "New Wine in Old Wineskins: Continuity and Rupture in the Pamphlet Debate of the French Prerevolution." *French Historical Studies* 17 (Fall 1991): 448–465.

Versini, Laurent. *Laclos et la tradition: Essai sur les sources et la technique des "Liaisons dangereuses."* Paris: Klincksieck, 1968.

Von Proschwitz, Gunnar. *Introduction à l'étude du vocabulaire de Beaumarchais.* Stockholm: Almqvist and Wiksell, 1956.

Walter, Eric. "L'Affaire La Barre et le concept d'opinion publique." In *Le Journalisme d'ancien régime,* edited by Pierre Rétat, pp. 360–392. Lyon: Presses Universitaires de Lyon, 1982.

Warner, Marina. *Alone of All Her Sex: The Myth and the Cult of the Virgin Mary.* London: Weidenfeld and Nicolson, 1976.

———. *Joan of Arc: The Image of Female Heroism.* New York: Knopf, 1981.

———. *Monuments and Maidens: The Allegory of the Female Form.* New York: Atheneum, 1985.

Index

Absolutism: challenges to, 11; effects of *mémoires judiciaires* on, 140, 257; of judicial systems, 234, 238; monarchical, 12, 107, 170–71, 264; Rousseau on, 170–71; and violation of sexual contract, 278. *See also* Despotism

Academies, provincial, 5

Academy of Metz, 237, 272

Adultery, 263–64; among aristocracy, 283–86; as basis for separation, 265; Bergasse on, 308–10; danger to society, 309–10; effect of divorce on, 266; female, 282–84; in French fiction, 284, 286, 304; in Kornmann case, 296, 305–6, 308–10; male, 282; in *Marriage of Figaro,* 291–92, 295; Rousseau on, 286–89; scandals of, 263–64; sociopolitical implications of, 264, 270, 283

L'Affaire du cardinal. See Diamond Necklace Affair

Aguesseau, Henri François d', chancellor, 213, 250

Aiguillon, Armand du Plessis, duc d', 26–27; court faction of, 159, 162; departure from office, 112, 158; depiction by Choiseulists, 179; Linguet's defense of, 46; trial of, 52

Alembert, Jean le Rond d': Lacretelle's depiction of, 247, 272, 277. See also *Encyclopédie* (Diderot and d'Alembert)

Amar, André, 172

L'Ami des lois (Mariveaux), 113

L'An 2440 (Mercier), 64

L'Année littéraire (anti-philosophe journal), 83; on *Marriage of Figaro,* 292

Annette et Lubin (Favart), 80

Archetypes, in *mémoires judiciaires,* 14–16, 251

Argenson, René Louis, marquis d', 213; on divorce, 265

Aristocracy: adultery among, 283–86; Beaumarchais on, 139–40; cultivation of virtue among, 76; dissension among, 147, 148, 149, 150, 151–52, 166, 212; importance of rosière festivals to, 76, 79; language of, 295; in Maupeou crisis, 56; ministerial attacks on, 60; patronage of theatre, 73, 74, 82; portrayal in *mémoires judiciaires,* 103, 315, 319; of Provence, 148; sentiment against, 15n32, 21–23, 318; in Véron-Morangiès case, 21–22

Arrest, arbitrary, 213, 239, 282; in Sanois case, 279, 280

Artois, Charles, count of, 79; in rosières movement, 83

Assembly of Notables, 263, 297–98, 300; disbanding of, 299

Augustinians, 95

Authority: male, 111, 210; monarchical, 105, 121, 281; in Richelieu–Saint-

seau on, 170–71; transition to contractual government, 264. *See also* Absolutism

Montesquieu, Charles-Louis de, 8; constitutionalism of, 55, 318; on divorce, 265; on the law, 234, 236, 250

Morangiès, Jean-François de Molette, count of, 2, 19–21; published accounts of, 40–44, 59, 67. *See also* Véron-Morangiès case

Moreau, Jacob Nicolas, 8

Moreau Le Jeune, engraving of rosière festival, 74

Mornet, Daniel, 7

Moyens de droit pour Bradier, Simare, Lardoise (Dupaty), 250–51

Nantes (France), rosière festivals at, 79

Narrative, sentimental, Voltaire's use of, 47

Nassau, Charles, prince of, 305, 307

Nathans, Benjamin, 13

National Convention, condemnation of women by, 171

Natural law, 107, 234; and adultery, 309; marriage in, 267–69

Necker, Jacques, 178, 213; struggle with Calonne, 299–300

Neufchâteau, François, 154

Newspapers, 36; censorship of, 175; foreign-based, 5; Parisian, 119; revolutionary, 301

Nicolai, Judge, 139, 140

Nobles of the robe, 147, 149, 166. *See also* Aristocracy

Nobles of the sword, 147, 149, 150, 166. *See also* Aristocracy

La Nouvelle Héloïse (Rousseau), 14, 167, 261, 286–89, 306

Nouvelles à la main (newssheets), 119

Oath of the Horatii (David), 302

Old Regime: authority of women in, 110, 181, 208, 314; challenges to status quo, 4–5; cultural history of, 11; judicial practices of, 9, 16, 33–36, 213–14, 233, 238; literary culture of, 7n15, 8; marriage during, 265; penology of, 235; public culture of, 111, 168, 313–14, 320; reading practices in, 127–28; scandals of, 1, 147; social

stereotypes of, 14–16, 42, 251; sociopolitical institutions of, 6, 149, 317, 323

Opéra-comique, 79–80, 110

Ordinance of Blois, 267

Ordonnance Criminelle (1670), 34, 222; attacks on, 233, 238; Dupaty's critique of, 250, 251

Ordre des Avocats (Paris): admission to, 88; in Diamond Necklace Affair, 194; Jansenists among, 93; during Maupeou crisis, 54, 58, 315; political leanings of, 92; in Trois Roués case, 245

Orléans, Louis Philippe Joseph, duc d' (Philippe-Egalité): and rosières movement, 83; support of Necker, 299

Ozouf, Mona, 11, 120

Paisant de Beaulieu, M. and Mme, 223

Pamela (Richardson), 218, 219

Pamphleteers, 4–6; of court factions, 178; on disbanding of *parlements,* 53; Jansenist, 26; in Maupeou crisis, 60, 109; rabble-rousing, 8; sponsorship by establishment, 6

Pamphlet literature, 4–5, 15, 255–56, 256; against Calonne, 300; censorship of, 5; in Diamond Necklace Affair, 188–90, 196; of early Revolution, 318; muckraking, 203, 206; popularity of, 36; on public women, 178–83, 196; in reign of Louis XV, 182; in reign of Louis XVI, 179

Parades (farces), 78, 136, 294

Parc aux Cerfs (brothel), 178, 180, 210

Pâris-Duverney, Joseph, 132

Parlement of Aix, 38

Parlement of Bescançon, 96

Parlement of Bordeaux, 150; dispute with Dupaty, 247–48

Parlement of Brittany, trial of duc d'Aiguillon by, 27

Parlement of Paris: Choiseulists in, 157–58; in Diamond Necklace Affair, 183, 186–87; in Goezman affair, 134; Grand'Chambre of, 186–87; and Jansenist cases, 37; Jansenists in, 51–52; in Kornmann case, 310; in La Blache case, 132; during Maupeou years, 54–55; political theorists of, 8; recall

Compositor:	Graphic Composition, Inc.
Text:	10/13 Galliard
Display:	Galliard
Printer:	BookCrafters
Binder:	BookCrafters